JN496673

The Twentieth Century
English-American

SHORT STORIES

Annotated with Editor's Note
by
Yang, Byung-Taek

Shinasa

CONTENTS

EDITOR'S NOTE

20세기 영미 단편문학의 세계

단편소설이 하나의 문학유형으로 정립된 것은 19세기 이후지만, 20세기에 들어오면서부터 더욱 크게 발전하여 「단편 소설의 시대」를 이룩하였다. 이것은 단편소설이라는 간결하고도 명료한 문학 장르가 다른 어떤 문학양식보다 20세기 현대인의 감각과 일치하고, 또 문학에 대한 현대인의 경험과 욕망을 가장 쉽게 그리고 가장 효과적으로 표현할 수 있는 수단이기 때문이었다. 다시 말하면 복잡다단한 현대 사회의 끊임없이 변화해 가는 가치표준과 이념은 단편소설이라는 압축된 소설형식을 요구하게 되었으며, 눈부시게 빨라진 현대생활의 템포는 읽기에 알맞은 단편소설을 더욱 요구하게 되었기 때문이라 하겠다.

그리하여 20세기의 거의 모든 작가들은 이 새롭고도 매혹적인 문학형식에 관심을 갖게 되어, 영국에서는 Somerset Maugham, James Joyce, D. H. Lawrence, Aldous Huxley, Virginia Woolf, Katherine Mansfield, Kingsley Aims 같은 작가들, 그리고 미국에서는 Sherwood Anderson, Earnest Hemingway, William Faulkner, F. Scott Fitzgerald, John Steinbeck, Katherine Anne Porter, J. D. Salinger 같은 쟁쟁한 작가들을 비롯하여 수많은 단편작가들이 우수한 단편 작품을 수없이 발표하여, 그 양에 있어서나 질에 있어서나 20세기를 가리켜 「단편소설의 시대」라고까지 부르게 된 것이다. 따라서 현대 작가들이 다루는 단편문학의 세계는 무한히 확대되고 있으며, 그 주제면에서나 기교면에서 큰 변화와 발전을 가져왔다.

이처럼 현대 문학의 총아로 등장하게 된 단편문학은 그 기원을 인간의 역사와 때를 같이 하고 있으니, 그 기원은 고대인들의 짧은 서사문학에서 찾을 수 있다. 그리고 단편소설의 원시형태는 <구약성서>에 나오는 <룻기>나 <요나서>의 이야기, 혹은 <신약성서>의 <탕아의 비유> 같은 이야기에서 찾을 수 있다. 그리고 중세기와 르네상스 시대에 접어

들면서 단편소설의 형태를 갖춘 작품이 나오기 시작했는데 그 중에서도 Giovanni Boccaccio의 *Decameron*과 Geoffrey Chaucer의 *Canterbury Tales*가 가장 대표적인 것으로 손꼽히고 있다. 그러나 단편소설이 근대적인 형태를 갖추게 된 것은 19세기에 들어오면서였다.

소설은 다른 문학형식보다 뒤늦게 18세기에 들어와서야 발달했는데 사실 고대로부터 중세, 17세기에 이르기까지는, 시·로망·희곡·수필·평론과 같은 문학양식이 압도적이었다. 그러다가 산업혁명을 거친 사회는 과학과 기계문명의 발달 그리고 합리주의적인 사고를 더 존중하게 되었으며, 이러한 시대정신이 문학면에서는 새로운 형식의 산문문학, 즉 소설문학을 찾게 되었다. 그리하여 Daniel Defoe의 *Robinson Crusoe* (1719)나 Jonathan Swift의 *Gulliver's Travels* (1726), 그리고 Samuel Richardson의 *Pamela: or Virtue Rewarded* (1740), Henry Fielding의 *Tom Jones* (1749)와 같은 근대소설이 나오기 시작하였다.

그러나 낭만주의의 문학시대를 맞이하자 소설문학은 시문학에 압도되어 빛을 보지 못하고 지내오다가 19세기에 이르러서야 더욱 복잡해지고 다양해진 인간생활은 인간의 경험을 보다 단순하고 간결하게 표현할 수 있는 문학양식을 요구하게 되었다. 그리하여 미국을 비롯하여 독일, 러시아, 프랑스 등 여러 나라에서 거의 동시에 일련의 단편소설이 쏟아져 나오기 시작했다. 미국의 경우 Washington Irving의 *The Sketch Book*을 비롯하여 Edgar Allan Poe, Nathaniel Hawthorne 그리고 Herman Melville, 그들 뒤를 이은 Mark Twain, Henry James, Stephen Crane 같은 작가들이 우수한 단편을 발표했으며, 영국에서는 19세기 후반기에 가서야 Charles Dickens, Thomas Hardy, R. L. Stevenson을 비롯하여 Rudyard Kipling, John Galsworthy, H. G. Wells 등이 단편을 발표하여 단편문학의 시대를 열어 놓았다.

이 중에서도 Edgar Allan Poe는 독일의 Tieck과 Hoffmann 같은 미스터리 작가의 영향을 받아 그의 독특한 단편소설의 형식을 정립 하였다. 1832년 Philadelphia Saturday Courier지에 *Metzengerstein*이라는 단편을 발표하고 1835년에는 *Berenice*를 발표하여 단일효과를 나타낼 수 있는 기교를 사용하였으며, Nathaniel Hawthorne의 *The Ambitious Guest* (1835)와 더불어 영문학상 근대단편소설의 시초를 이룩했다. 뿐만 아니라 Poe는 단편문학의 이론적 체계를 마련하고 이 이론에 따라 창작하고 또 비평했으므로 그는 「단편소설의 할아버지」라고 불리고 있다.

Poe는 단편소설이 하나의 예술형태로 그 형식을 갖추기 위해서는 「간결성」「단일 효과」 및 「집중된 인상」「생의 단면」「통일성」「강도」「확고한 구성」 및 「정연한 형식미」가 필요하다고 주장했다. 즉 단편소설은 한 자리에서 중단 없이 읽을 수 있는 정도로 짧고(brevity), 번잡하게 옆으로 자꾸 가지를 펴지 않고 시종일관하여 통일된 완결체를 이루고(unity), 독자의 감정을 사로잡는 박력(intensity)를 갖추어야 한다는 것이었다. 이런 간결함에서 장편소설에서는 불가능한 단일 효과를 얻을 수 있다고 주장했으며, 이와 같은 이론은 1842년, Nathaniel Hawthorne의 *Twice Told Tales*를 평하는 글에서 요약하고 있으며, 일관성이나 통일성을 단편의 가장 기본적인 요소로 규정하고 있다.

> . . . We allude to the short prose narrative, requiring from a half-hour to one or two hours in its perusal. The ordinary novel is objectionable, from its length,. . . As it cannot be read at one sitting, it deprives itself, of course, of the immense force derivable from totality. . . During the hour of perusal the soul of the reader is at the writer's control. . . If wise, he has not fashioned his thoughts to accommodate his incidents; but having conceived, with deliberate care, a certain unique or single *effect* to be wrought out, he then invents such incidents—he then combines such events as may best aid him in establishing this preconceived effect. If his very initial sentence tend not to the outbringing of this effect, then he has failed in his first step. In the whole composition there should be no word written, of which the tendency, direct or indirect, is not to the one preconceived design. . ."
>
> (Poe: *Hawthorne's Twice Told Tales*)

즉 장편소설은 앉은 자리에서 끝까지 읽을 수 없기 때문에 전체가 주는 박력에 김이 빠지기 마련이고, 그 대신 반 시간에서 한두 시간 정도로 읽을 만한 것이면 독자의 마음을 전적으로 휘어잡을 수 있다. . . . 사건을 찾아내어 거기서 착상하는 것이 아니라 먼저 독자에게 이러

이러한 감명을 주기 위해 하나의 뚜렷한 효과를 착상하고 그 효과가 우러나오도록 사건을 꾸며, 독자가 그 한 가지 효과를 받도록 그것을 잘 배열해 놓는다. 첫머리부터 이 효과가 우러나지 않는 작품은 졸작이다. 그러므로 전체 창작 과정에서 직접 간접으로 그 효과를 자아내지 못할 말은 한 마디도 써서는 안된다고 말하고 있는데 이 말은 단편소설의 본질을 규정한 말로 유명하다.

Poe의 이러한 단편소설 이론은 그후 Guy de Mauppassant (1850~93)과 Anton Chekhov (1860~1904) 그리고 Henry James 등과 같은 19세기 후기 작가들을 통해, 미국 · 프랑스 · 러시아 등지에서 찬란하게 발전해 나갔다. 즉 Mauppassant은 명확한 관찰과 생생한 세부묘사 그리고 정확한 표현 등을 강조한 이른 바 「객관성의 전통」을 완성하여 인간의 경험을 보다 극적으로, 보다 객관적으로 표현하는 기교를 창안했다. 다시 말하면 치밀하고 질서정연한 구성을 통해 표현했으며, 주제를 close-up 하기 위해 대담하게 가지를 쳐버리는 간결 · 대담한 구성의 묘를 보여주었다. 그 다음 Chekhov은 Mauppassant의 「객관성의 전통」과는 달리 작중 인물의 단순한 내부 행동보다는 평범한 일상생활의 단면을 담담하게 그려내는 사실주의적인 작품을 썼다. 그리하여 그는 함축적이고 암시적인 테크닉을 통해 단편소설의 공간적 한계를 극복하야 인생의 한 단면에서 받는 인상을 추려서 그려내는 인상주의(Impressionism)의 방향을 세웠다. 게다가 미국의 작가 Henry James는 모든 소설을 살아 있는 하나의 유기체라고 보는 「유기체 이론」을 내세워 현대작가들에게 지대한 영향을 미치게 되었다.

이처럼 Plot 중심의 Poe와 Mauppassant 전통 그리고 성격묘사 중심의 Chekhov 전통은 Henry James의 「유기체이론」의 영향을 받고 20세기에 들어오면서부터 새로운 국면을 맞이하게 되었다. 그해까지의 단편소설은 대체로 전통적인 작품세계를 크게 벗어나지 못했으나 20세기의 현대작가들의 작품세계는 새롭고 혁신적이었다. 이들의 단편소설은 물론 전기한 Poe, Mauppassant, Chekhov의 전통을 이어 받았으나, 한 걸음 더 나아가 그들의 전통을 융합시켜, 현대인의 경험을 보다 정직하게 담을 수 있는 새로운 기법을 개척하여 인생의 단면을 보다 충실하게 실제적으로 옮겨 놓으려 했다. 이와 더불어 현대작가들은 시대적 변화의 영향을 받아 작가들의 의식과 태도 및 기법 등에 커다란 변화를 가져왔던 것이다.

특히 제 1차대전 이후 문학은 미술, 음악, 건축과 같은 다른 예술형태와 마찬가지로 혁명적인 변화를 가져왔다. 이는 흔히 「모더니즘」이라는 말로 요약되고 있는데, 주로 형식이나 기교상의 혁명이었다. 즉 이 모더니즘은 제 1차대전 이전에 팽배했던 전통이나 가치관과의 결별을 뜻하는 것이었다. 그리하여 첫째, 현대작가들은 대중적이고 집단적인 가치보다는 개인의 감각과 직관에 의존하는 가치를 소중히 여기게 되었으며, 인생과 진지하게 대면하면서 인생에서 직접 받는 인상(direct impression of life)을 깊이 다루었다. 그리고 개인의 본질적인 고독문제와 단절된 상태에서 탈피하려는 노력을 다루었다. 따라서 인간의 외부적 행동보다 내면적 의식을 강조했다. 그리하여 주제면에서는 집단보다 개인을, 이성이냐 윤리보다 개인의 직관이나 감정을 더 중시하고 현대인이 처해 있는 여러 문제를 즐겨 다루게 되었다. 그리고 개인과 사회와의 갈등이나 거기서 생기는 소외의식의 문제 따위를 또한 즐겨 다루게 되었다.

둘째로, 현대작가들은 시간에 대하여 새로운 관념을 갖게 되었는데 이것은 시간을 연대순으로 간주해 온 종래의 작가들과는 달리 시간을 개인의 의식 속에 흐르는 하나의 흐름이라고 본 것이다. 그러므로 현대작가들은 과거와 현재 그리고 미래가 모두 하나가 되어 끊임없이 흐르는 흐름이라고 보고, 현재는 과거의 총화이며, 따라서 인간의 의식은 복합적인 것이라고 본 것이다. 물론 이 새로운 시간관은 Freud와 Jung의 심리학에서 영향 받은 바 큰 것이지만 현대작가들은 이 이론에 입각하여 이른바 「의식의 흐름」이라는 새로운 수법을 창안하여 이를 단편소설에서도 사용하였다. James Joyce, William Faulkner를 비롯하여 많은 작가들이 이 수법을 성공적으로 사용하여 단편문학의 세계를 보다 확대 심화시키고 있다.

셋째로 현대작가들은 인생의 한 단면을 묘사하되 그 단면이 인생 전체에 의의를 부여하도록 하고 있다. 그러면서도 단편은 간결성과 압축성이 요구되므로 언어를 극도로 정제하여 최대의 효과를 올리기 위해 기교면에서 실험적인 요소를 많이 나타내고 있다. 특히 제 2차대전 이후

소위 전위작가들은 단편소설이라는 형식을 극한점에까지 밀고 나가 현대시에 못지않게 복잡하고 난해해 가는 경향을 보이고 있다. 이러한 추이는 현대생활 자체가 복잡하기 때문에, 또 그와 같은 복잡하고 다양한 인생경험을 표현하려는 데서 생기는 필연적인 결과라고 볼 수 있겠다.

그런데 단편소설은 형식면에서나 내용면에서 다른 문학양식 보다 많은 제약을 갖고 있으면서도 그것에 구애되지 않고 무한한 가능성을 시도하고 있다. 다시 말하면, 현대 작가들은 단편소설이라는 장르를 하나의 고정된 양식에 국한시키지 않고 이를 발전시켰다. 즉 항상 새로운 수법을 모색하거나 개발하여 그 문체나 분위기에서 새로운 다양성을 보이고 있다.

그 중에서도 두드러진 것은 첫째, 서정시에서 흔히 사용하는 기교를 도입하여 시적인 정서나 분위기를 자아내는 이른바 서정시적인 수법으로 묘사하기도 한다. 예를 들면 James Joyce의 *Araby*에서는 어느 사춘기 소년이 겪는 낭만과 환멸 그리고 절망이 시적인 수법으로 묘사되고 있다. 그 다음은 연극적인 수법으로서, 묘사나 설명은 최소한도로 줄이고 그 대신 작중 인물들의 주고 받는 대화와 구체적인 행동에 초점을 맞춤으로써 마치 연극을 보는 듯한 효과를 올리는 수법이다. 이 수법은 Hemingway의 *The Killers*에서 가장 잘 나타나고 있는데, 제한된 장면 안에서 생기에 넘치는 작중 인물의 대화와 몇 가지 구체적인 외부행동만으로 이야기를 이끌고 있다. 이밖에도 주위에서 일어나는 사건을 신변잡기 식으로 기록하거나 이야기하듯이 전달하는 소묘적인 수법으로 이야기를 끌어가기도 하고, 혹은 어느 특정한 사회의 일면을 객관적이고 사실 기록적으로 서술하는 수법을 쓰기도 한다.

사실 기교란 새로운 진실을 탐구하거나 또는 새로운 의미를 발견하는 수단에 지나지 않는다. 그러나 현대사회의 다변성과 여기에 따라 생기는 온갖 인생문제와 복잡하기 이를 데 없는 인간성, 그리고 현대 기계문명의 위험과 공포 등을 예술적인 형식 속에 표현하기 위해 여러 가지 기교를 실험적으로 시도하고 있음을 본다. 이처럼 20세기의 단편문학은 그 문체나 기교면에서도 주제면에 못지않게 다양성을 보이고 있다.

영국의 단편문학은 다른 나라보다 그 발전이 늦었다. 영국의 단편은 19세기 후반기의 위대한 사실주의 작가인 Charles Dickens에서 부터 시작하여 Hardy, Stevenson, H.G. Wells를 거쳐 20세기 초기에 장편과 함께 꽃을 피우기 시작했다. James Joyce와 D.H. Lawrence 같은 작가들은 위대한 장편을 발표함과 동시에 Katherine Mansfield와 더불어 훌륭한 단편소설을 많이 빌표하여 단편소실의 붐을 이룩했다. 그들은 단편의 옛 형식에서 벗어나, 종전의 단편소설의 전통을 융합하여, 인간의 경험을 보다 정직하게 담을 수 있는 새로운 면을 개척했다. 일부 비평가들이 말하듯이 영국의 단편소설은 미국이나 러시아의 그것만큼 뛰어나지 못할지 모르지만, 대체로 영국 작가들은 이야기를 지극히 자연스럽게 전개시키되 인위적인 구성을 노출시키지 않는 경향이 있다. 즉 작중인물의 극적인 전개보다 「인생의 단면」을 보다 충실하게 실제적으로 옮겨 놓고 있다.

1900년 전에 이미 성년이 되었지만 20세기에 속하는 중요한 단편작가로는 Saki(H.H. Munro)와 Somerset Maugham을 들 수 있다. Saki는 버마에서 영국 식민지 관리의 아들로 태어나 제 1차대전시 프랑스 전선에서 전사했지만, 수많은 단편을 썼고 참신한 풍자가로서 이름을 날렸다. 그의 작품은 차가운 도시적 감각과 우아한 매력을 지니고 있으나, 어린이의 눈을 통해 성인들의 비행과 약점을 예리하게 꿰뚫어 보고 이를 풍자했다. Maugham 역시 여러 가지 미묘한 인간성을 희극적인 냉소로 파헤쳐 풍자하기도 했다. 그의 작품은 이국적이고 감상적인 색채가 없지 않으나 이것을 상징적으로 격조 높게 승화시켰다. 그리고 원시와 문명을 대비시키면서 인간성을 파고드는 우수한 단편을 많이 남겼다.

이들의 작품은 전통적인 작품세계를 크게 벗어나지 못했으나 그들 뒤를 이은 Joyce, Lawrence, Mansfield 등의 작품세계는 지극히 새롭고 혁신적이었다. 대체로 20세기의 단편작가들은 Chekhov의 영향도 받았지만 그것보다 현대소설을 가능하게 했던 시대적인 변화의 영향을 더 크게 받았다.

James Joyce의 단편집 *Dubliners* (1914)는 Dublin 시민의 생태를 이모저모로 그린 것이나, 어린이의 눈에 비친 성인의 세계, 사춘기의 정열,

암담한 현실에서 헤어나지 못하는 남녀의 군상 그리고 Ireland의 정치적 · 종교적 현실의 어느 단면 등을 자연 주의적 기조로 다룬 것이다. 그는 각종인물의 내면적인 심리상태와 순간순간에 일어나는 상념과 감정의 변화에 관심을 가졌으며, 죽음과 사랑과 성의 문제를 주제로 삼았다.

D.H. Lawrence는 *The Prussian Officer* (1914)에서부터 *The Man Who Died* (1928)에 이르기까지 47편의 단편과 7편의 중편을 남겼다. Lawrence는 현대의 물질문명이 근원적인 생명의 바탕을 황폐하게 만든다고 믿어, 참된 이상적인 양성 관계를 탐구하여 사랑의 여러 가지 자태를 인식하고 분석해 가는 한편, 자기의 이상을 추구했다. Lawrence는 단편에서도 항상 본능의 편에 서서 원시적인 생명력의 참된 가치를 더 높이 외치며, 문명사회에 널리 산재해 있는 여러 가지 현상을 신랄하게 공격하기도 했다.

Katherine Mansfield는 *The Garden Party* (1922)를 발표하여 단편 작가로서의 지위를 확립했는데, Mansfield는 살육과 파괴와 혼돈 속에서 허덕이는 기계문명에 절망을 느껴, 천진스러운 유년 · 소녀시절을 동경하는 일련의 단편에서 작품의 구성과 서정적인 묘사로 원숙한 기교를 나타냈다. 그리고 평범한 사건을 다루되 작품인물의 마음가짐과 마음이 움직이는 분위기를 섬세하게 진지한 태도로 그렸다. Mansfield의 단편소설은 서정시의 수법으로 쓰고 있어 서정적인 특질을 지니고 있으며, 그 이야기는 동일성이 있고 형식이 간결하고 아름다우며 정감이 넘쳐흐르고 있다. 그리고 깊은 지성의 눈으로 인생을 관찰하여 인간 심리의 미묘한 움직임을 포착하고, 이를 예술적인 감각과 섬세하고 인상적인 필치로 그린 주옥과 같은 작품으로 20세기 단편문학을 빛냈다.

그 다음 주지주의(主知主義) 작가 Aldous Huxley는 단편보다 장편소설에서, 혹은 그 기발하고 예리한 평론수필에서 빛나고 있다. 그러나 그의 단편은 정교한 기교와 내용에 있어 단편소설의 하나의 샘플을 이루고 있다. 그는 현대의 부조리하고 추악한 현실을 냉소적인 시니시즘으로 묘사했다. 제 1차대전 이후의 혼란 속에 만연한 회의와 비판의 공기를 민감하게 반영하였다. 그리고 인생과 인간을 냉소적인 눈으로 응시하는 냉혹한 이지를 엿보게 했다.

그리고 John Collier는 환상적인 장편인 *His Monkey Wife*를 1929년에

발표하여 소설가로서 일약 유명해졌지만 그 후엔 환상적이고도 기괴한 단편을 많이 발표하여 사계의 귀재라는 평을 받았다. 그 다음은 미적이며 기상(奇想)에 넘친 단편작가인 A.E. Coppard와 아일랜드의 Chekhov이라 불리워지는 Frank O'Connor를 꼽을 수 있다. O'Connor의 단편은 그 주제에 있어, 그 인물에 있어, 그리고 색채 풍부한 언어에 있어 참신한 기쁨을 주고 있다. 역시 아일랜드 소설가로 Sean O'Faolain은 1932년부터 문필에 전념하여 *Midsummer Night Madness* (1932)라는 단편집을 비롯하여 *The Man Who Invented Sin and Other Stories* (1948) 등 많은 단편집을 내 놓았다. 그리고 여류작가로 Elizabeth Taylor는 영국 소설의 전통을 이어받은 단편에서 아름답고도 정확한 산문을 구사함으로써 높이 평가받고 있다.

1950년대 후반 「성난 젊은이들」의 문학그룹을 이끌어 온 Kingsley Aims 역시 날카롭고 냉소적인 언어와 유머로써 기성세대의 복잡성과 괴벽성을 풍자하는 단편을 발표했다. 그는 인간의 순수성을 갈망하고 위선과 허위에서 벗어난 참되고 자연스런 사회에 대한 향수를 풍기는 작품을 썼다.

이밖에도 *The Man of the House*라는 훌륭한 단편을 발표한 Ethel Colburn Mayne, 시인이면서도 *The Magic Shop, The Shout* 등 공포적인 단편을 쓴 Robert Graves, 영국 중산계급의 지방도시의 분위기를 즐겨 다룬 V.S. Pritchett 등을 들 수 있다.

미국의 단편문학은 Poe와 Hawthorne이 남겼던 전통을 이어 받아 이를 더욱 풍부히 확대 강화해 나갔다. 또 미국의 다양성과 미국 저널리즘의 본질로 인해 단편소설에 있어서의 성취도는 다른 어느 나라에서보다 높았다. 그리하여 세계문학에 뒤늦게 참여한 미국이 단편소설이라는 새로운 문학형식을 창조함과 동시에 이를 더욱 발전시켜 세계문학에 기여한 바 지대하였다.

20세기에 들어서자 미국의 장편문학이 괄목할만한 발전을 한 것과 마찬가지로 단편문학 역시 그 절정에 도달한 감이 있다. 이것은 이 시기에 Ernest Hemingway, William Faulkner와 같은 위대한 단편작가를 비롯하여 Sherwood Anderson, F. Scott Fitzgerald, Katherine Anne Porter, John Steinbeck, Erskin Caldwell, James T. Farrel 그리고 Irwin Shaw,

Eudora Welty, J.D. Salinger 등에 이르는 동안 미국은 단편의 기술을 어느 나라보다 잘 발달하여 단편문학의 양에 있어서나 질에 있어 당연히 단편문학의 왕국을 이루게 되었다.

Sherwood Anderson은 단편집 *Winesburg, Ohio* (1919)와 *The Triumph of the Egg* (1921)에서, 미국 사회의 내면생활의 심리와 의식을 추구하였으며 실의와 불만에 겨워하는 소시민의 억눌리고 비뚤어진 의식과 심리를 리얼하게 표현했다. Anderson은 동경을 추구하는 신비가이며 영혼의 탐구자이며, 온정 있는 해학과 예리한 관찰 그리고 풍부한 상상은 그의 독자성을 이루고 있으며, 단편작가로서의 우수성은 모파상이나, 체홉과 비견한다.

F. Scott Fitzgerald는 1920년대의 재즈시대를 대표하는 작가로서*This Side of Paradise, The Great Gatsby* 등 명작을 남겼으나 한편 *All the Sad Young Men* (1926)과 *Taps at Reveille* (1935) 등의 단편집에서 그 당시의 풍속이나 국외 거주자의 고단한 생활을 화려한 문체 속에 담아 단편문학의 새 국면을 열어 놓았다. *Rich Boy, Winter Dreams*는 그의 걸작으로 꼽히고 있다.

「잃어버린 세대」를 최고로 대표하는 Ernest Hemingway는 단편의 명수로서 *In Our Time* (1925), *Men Without Women* (1927), *Winner Take Nothing* (1927) 등 단편집에서 수많은 명단편을 발표했다. 그의 단편은 주제와 문체가 혼연일치되어 있으며, 특히 그의 비정의 문체는 허무와 죽음과 폭력의 비정세계를 리얼하게 나타내고 있다. 그 중에 서도 *The Killers, The Snow of Kilimanjaro, The Short Happy Life of Francis Macomber* 등의 단편은 금세기의 가장 우수한 단편으로 손꼽히고 있다.

William Faulkner는 복잡하고 난해한 문체와 뛰어난 독특한 기교로 미국 남부사회의 복잡기괴한 생활을 묘사하여, 하나의 상징적이며 신화적인 세계를 만들어낸 일련의 걸작을 발표하여 현대문학의 거성이 되고 있다. 그리고 단편에서도 장편에 못지않게 변질적인 악덕과 공포, 육욕, 타락, 그리고 애욕 등 죄악의 문제가 다루어지고 있는데, *A Rose for Emily*라는 유명한 단편을 수록한 *These 13* (1931), 탐정 소설적인 요소가 가미된 *Knight*'s *Gambit* (1949) 그리고 *Big Woods* (1955) 등의 단편집을 내놓아 단편문학의 세계를 확대 심화시켰다.

Hemingway와 Faulkner의 단편소설은 현대 단편문학의 전통을 확고히 다졌다고 할 수 있다. 즉 Poe가 주장하고 실천한 예술형태로서 의 단편을 Hawthorne과 Henry James의 뒤를 이어 높은 자리로 끌어 올렸으며, 따라서 그들의 단편은 그들 이후에 등장하는 단편들의 모델이 되었기 때문이다. 그리하여 그들 뒤를 이은 훌륭한 단편작가들이 특히 남부에서 많이 배출되어 단편소설의 전성기를 이루었다. 이를테면 Katherine Anne Porter, Robert Penn Warren, Eudora Welty 등이 남부사회를 소재로 하여 참신한 상징적 기교를 구사하여 예술적 작품을 만들어내는 데 성공했다.

Katherine Anne Porter의 첫 단편집 *Flowering Judas* (1935)와 *Pale Horse, Pale Rider* (1939) 그리고 *The Learning Tower* (1944)에 수록된 단편들은 예술적 향기가 높으며 상징성이 풍부하다. 즉 상징과 암시와 심리묘사가 풍부하고, 섬세한 시적 표현은 높이 평가되고 있다. 그리고 Porter처럼 환상과 현실의 교착된 세계를 교묘하게 그리는 Eudora Welty의 단편집 *A Curtain of Green* (1936)에서는 고독한 인간의 정신분석에 흥미를 보였으며, *The Wide Net* (1943)에서는 이상 심리의 그로테스크한 이야기를 교묘하게 다루고 있다. 이 두 여류의 단편들은 미국 단편문학의 최고수준에 도달하고 있다.

지방주의 문학의 대표자로서 손꼽히고 있는 John Steinbeck은 캘리포니아를 무대로 한 수많은 장편 이외에도 *Red Pony, The Long Valley* (1938)에서 능숙한 수법을 구사하여 걸작을 남기고 있다. 그는 예리한 관찰과 간결하고 정확한 표현으로 신비적인 분위기를 자아내면서, 시골의 순진한 인간들의 소박하고 따뜻한 휴머니즘을 부각시키고 있다. 이밖에도 조지아 출신의 Erskin Caldwell, 시카고 출신의 James T. Farrel, 캘리포니아 출신의 William Saroyan 등의 지방주의 작가들은 지방색이 짙은 훌륭한 단편집을 남기고 있다.

그 다음, 미국의 과거에 관심을 기울이는 Stephen Vincent Benét은 *Twenty-Five Short Stories* (1943)에서, 뉴욕의 지식·상류사회를 다루는 John O'hara는 *Sermons and Soda-Water* (1960), *Assembly* (1961), *Hat on the Bed* (1963)에서, 그리고 사회의식이 강한 작품을 쓴 Irwin Shaw는 *Act of Faith* (1946), *Mixed Company* (1950)에서 제각기 특색 있는 단편

을 발표했다. 그리고 풍자적 리얼리즘으로 이름을 날린 Ring Lardner와 James Grover Thurber의 여러 단편을 들 수 있다.

이처럼 제 1차대전 후 미국 단편작가의 수효는 참으로 많으며 따라서 작품수도 엄청나게 많다. 미국의 단편문학은 전술한 바와 같이 Poe로부터 Shaw에 이르는 동안, 그 기술은 어느 나라보다도 잘 발달해 그야말로 단편문학의 왕국을 이룩했다. 특히 잡지와 문학계간지의 보급, 시대요구 그리고 독자의 취향에 따라 온갖 종류의 단편이 생산되었다.

제 2차대전 이후 미국이 세계 최강대국으로 등장함에 따라 이러한 경향은 더 두드러졌다. 그 거대한 사회의 복잡성과 그것에 따라 생기는 온갖 문제, 과학문명의 발전이 가져오는 인간소외와 순응의 문제, 그리고 원자력과 핵전쟁에 의한 인류멸망의 위험과 공포 등은 오늘의 작가들에게 무궁무진한 창작의 재료를 제공하고 있다. 오늘의 단편작가들은 20세기가 안고 있는 여러 가지 문제뿐만 아니라, 현대 문명의 단편이나 이미지를 단편소설이라는 틀 속에서 다루고 있는데, 그 중에서도 중요한 단편작가들로서 Walter Van Tilburg Clark, John Cheever, James Baldwin, Hortense Calisher, Bernard Malamud, Jean Stafford, Carson McCullers, J.D. Salinger, Peter Taylor, Truman Capote, John Updike, Philip Roth 등을 들 수 있다.

이 중에서도 주목을 끄는 작가는 John Cheever인데, 그는 뉴욕 교외에 사는 사람들의 생활을 냉정한 유머로 그려 훌륭한 기교를 보안 *The Enormous Radio* (1954), *The Wapshot Chronicle* (1957)을 위시하여 많은 단편집을 내고 있다. *The Catcher in the Rye* (1951)로 일대 센세이션을 일으킨 J.D. Salinger는 첫 단편집 *Nine Stories* (1953)와 *Franny and Zooey* (1961)에서 어른들의 타락한 세계와 그 세계에서 순진한 젊은이가 겪는 고뇌를 정묘하게 다루고 있다. 그리고 Carson McCullers의 *The Ballad of the Sad Café* (1951), John Updike의 *The Same Door* (1959), *Pigeon Feathers* (1962) 등에서 성숙된 단편문학의 세계를 엿볼 수 있다.

20세기의 미국 단편문학은 마침내 성숙기에 들어서고 있는 것 같이 보인다. 미국인의 생활과 예술가들의 상상을 거의 완전하게 표현하도록 하는 하나의 특별한 형식으로서의 단편소설을 접할 수 있는 날이 멀지 않다고 본다.

후 기

현대 영미 단편문학의 정수, 현대의 고전을 뽑아 수록한 이 단편집은 Robert Penn Warren과 Albert Erskine이 공동 편집한 *Short Story Masterpieces*를 주로 하고, Milton Crane이 편집한 *50 Great Short Stories*와, Wallace와 Mary Stegner가 편집한 *Great American Short Stories,* 그리고 Christopher Isherwood의 *Great English Short Stories*를 참고하여 엮은 것이다.

작가와 작품을 선정한다는 것은 하나의 한계를 정하는 과정이기도 하므로 여기서는 29명의 작가를 골라 동수의 작품을 수록하기로 하였다. 그것도 대부분의 작가와 단편을 전기한 *Short Story Masterpieces* 에서 뽑았는데, 그것은 편자들이 책 이름 그대로 걸작만을 골라 수록했기 때문이다. 그리고 수록된 작가들 중에 Anderson, Maugham, Saki 등은 1900년 전에 이미 성인이 된 작가들이기는 하나 그들의 작품은 20세기에 속하는 중대한 작가들이기 때문에 여기에 포함시켰다. 그 다음 작품 선택의 기준은 작가 본위라기보다 작품 본위로 하였으며, 「한 작가 한 작품」 위주로 하였다. 그러므로 Faulkner나 Hemingway 같은 대작가의 단편도 하나씩만 택하기로 하였다. 그리고 대학의 교양영어 교과서에서 널리 알려진 작품은 중복을 피하는 뜻에서 다른 작품으로 대치했다. 이와 더불어 강의실에서 쉽고 재미있게 읽을 수 있는 비교적 짧은 단편을 택하였으며, 중편에 가까운 긴 단편은 －Huxley의 The Gioconda Smile을 제외하고는－ 택하지 않았다. 그리고 수록작가와 작품 중에 최근의 신예 작가를 다루지 않은 것은 가장 정평있는 작가와 작품만을 선정하여 결정판을 구성하려는 의도에서였다.

여기 수록된 작품들은 대부분 즐거움과 쾌감, 그리고 만족을 주는 동시 인생에 대한 하나의 「의의」를 느끼게 하며, 인생과 밀접히 접촉하여 인간가능성에 대한 우리의 감각능력을 확대시키는 그런 작품들이다. 한편 “That was exciting!” 혹은 “That was funny!” 혹은 “I certainly never expected that ending!”라고 감탄의 소리를 내게 될 그런 작품이면서도, 문체나 분위기나 구성에 있어 특색있는 작품이기도 하다. 그러면서도 비교적 쉽게 그리고 재미있게 읽을 수 있는 작품들이라고 하겠다.

The Twentieth Century
English-American

SHORT STORIES

Impulse

by Conrad Aiken

Conrad Aiken(1889~1973) was born in Saramah, Ga, of old New England stock, the eldest of three sons and his attractive mother's favorite. He wrote his first poem at nine.

Steeped from his college days in Freud, Aiken in his remarkable but comparatively rare short stories and novels as well as in his poetry utilizes the resources of psychoanalytical theory as foundations for intensely subjective and subtle character revelations.

MICHAEL LOWES hummed as he shaved, amused by the face he saw — the pallid, asymmetrical face, with the right eye so much higher than the left, and its eyebrow so peculiarly arched, like a "v" turned upside down. Perhaps this day wouldn't be as bad as the last. In fact, he knew it wouldn't be, and that was why he hummed. This was the bi-weekly day of escape,[1)] when he would stay out for the evening, and play bridge[2)] with Hurwitz, Bryant, and Smith. Should he tell Dora at the breakfast table? No, better not. Particularly in view of last night's row[3)] about unpaid bills. And there would be more of them, probably, beside his plate. The rent. The coal. The doctor who had attended to the children. Jeez, what a life. Maybe it was time to do a new jump. And Dora was beginning to get restless again —

But he hummed, thinking of the bridge game. Not that he liked Hurwitz or Bryant or Smith — cheap fellows, really — mere pick-up

1) the bi-weekly day of escape: 2주일에 한 번씩 도피하는 날.
2) bridge: a card game for four players resembling whist, in which the dealer or his partner declares the trump, and the dealer plays both his own and his partner's hand.
3) row: a noisy quarrel, disturbance; (Colloq.) squabble.

acquaintances.[1] But what could you do about making friends, when you were always hopping about from one place to another, looking for a living, and fate always against you! They were all right enough. Good enough for a little escape, a little party — and Hurwitz always provided good alcohol. Dinner at the Greek's, and then to Smith's room — yes. He would wait till late in the afternoon, and then telephone to Dora as if it had all come up suddenly. Hello, Dora-is that you, old girl? Yes, this is Michael — Smith has asked me to drop in for a hand of bridge — you know — so I'll just have a little snack[2] in town. Home by the last car as usual. Yes. . . . Good-bye! . . .

And it all went off perfectly, too. Dora was quiet, at breakfast, but not hostile. The pile of bills was there, to be sure, but nothing was said about them. And while Dora was busy getting the kids ready for school, he managed to slip out, pretending that he thought it was later than it really was. Pretty neat, that! He hummed again, as he waited for the train. Telooralooraloo. Let the bills wait, damn them! A man couldn't do everything at once, could he, when bad luck hounded him everywhere? And if he could just get a little night off, now and then, a rest and change, a little diversion,[3] what was the harm in that?

At half-past four he rang up Dora and broke the news to her. He wouldn't be home till late.

"Are you sure you'll be home at all?" she said, coolly.

That was Dora's idea of a joke. But if he could have foreseen — !

He met the others at the Greek restaurant, began with a couple of *araks,*[4] which warmed him, then went on to red wine, bad olives, *pilaf,*[5] and other obscure foods; and considerably later they all walked along Boylston Street to Smith's room. It was a cold night, the temperature below twenty, with a fine dry snow sifting the streets.

---

1) pick-up acquaintances: (Colloq.) acquaintances made without an introduction.

2) snack: a light meal.

3) diversion: amusement; entertainment; pastime.

4) *araks*: 술 이름.

5) *pilaf*: an Oriental dish consisting of rice boiled with mutton, fowl, or the like, and flavored with spices, raisins, etc.

But Smith's room was comfortably warm, he trotted out[1] some 'gin and the Porto Rican[2] cigars, showed them a new snapshot of Squiggles (his Revere Beach sweetheart), and then they settled down to a nice long cozy game of bridge.

It was during an intermission, when they all got up to stretch their legs and renew their drinks, that the talk started — Michael never could remember which one of them it was who had put in the first oar[3] — about impulse. It might have been Hurwitz, who was in many ways the only intellectual one of the three, though hardly what you might call a highbrow.[4] He had his queer curiosities, however, and the idea was just such as might occur to him. At any rate, it was he who developed the idea, and with gusto.[5]

"Sure," he said, "anybody might do it. Have you got impulses? Of course, you got impulses. How many times you think — suppose I do that? And you don't do it, because you know damn well if you do it you'll get arrested. You meet a man you despise — you want to spit in his eye. You see a girl you'd like to kiss — you want to kiss her. Or maybe just to squeeze her arm when she stands beside you in the street car. You know what I mean."

"Do I know what you mean!" sighed Smith. "I'll tell the world. I'll tell the cock-eyed[6] world! . . ."

"You would," said Bryant. "And so would I."

"It would be easy," said Hurwitz, "to give in to[7] it. You know what I mean? So simple. Temptation is too close. That girl you see is too damn good-looking — she stands too near you — you just put out your hand it touches her arm — maybe her leg — why worry? And you think, maybe if she don't like it I can make believe I didn't mean it. . . ."

---

1) trot out: (Colloq.) bring out for others to see.
2) Porto Rican: former name of Puerto Ricoan.
3) put in the first oar: put one's oar in; meddle; interfere.
4) highbrow: person who claims to care a great deal about knowledge and culture. *cf.* lowbrow
5) gusto: keen relish; hearty enjoyment; liking or taste.
6) cock-eyed: (Slang) foolish; silly.
7) give in to: ~에 굴복하다, 양보하다.

"Like these fellows that slash fur coats with razor blades," said Michael. "Just impulse, in the beginning, and only later a habit."

"Sure. . . . And like these fellows that cut off braids of hair with scissors. They just feel like it and do it. . . . Or stealing."

"Stealing?" said Bryant.

"Sure. Why, I often feel like it. . . . I see a nice little thing right in front of me on a counter — you know, a nice little knife, or necktie, or a box of candy — quick, you put it in your pocket, and then go to the other counter, or the soda fountain for a drink. What would be more human? We all want things. Why not take them? Why not do them? And civilization is only skin-deep. . . ."

"That's right. Skin-deep," said Bryant.

"But if you were caught, by God!" said Smith, opening his eyes wide.

"*Who's* talking about getting caught? . . . *Who's* talking about doing it? It isn't that we do it, it's only that we *want* to do it. Why, Christ, there's been times when I thought to hell with[1] everything, I'll kiss that woman if it's the last thing I do."

"It might be," said Bryant.

Michael was astonished at this turn of the talk. He had often felt both these impulses. To know that this was a kind of universal human inclination came over him with something like relief.

"Of *course,* everybody has those feelings," he said smiling. "I have them myself. . . . But suppose you *did* yield to them?"

"Well, we don't," said Hurwitz.

"I know — but suppose you did?"

Hurwitz shrugged his fat shoulders, indifferently.

"Oh, well," he said, "it would be bad business."

"Jesus, yes," said Smith, shuffling the cards.

"Oy," said Bryant.

The game was resumed, the glasses were refilled, pipes were lit, watches were looked at. Michael had to think of the last car from Sullivan Square, at eleven-fifty. But also he could not stop thinking

---

1) to hell with: ~을 타도하다, 매장하다.

of this strange idea. It was amusing. It was fascinating. Here was everyone wanting to steal — toothbrushes, or books — or to caress some fascinating stranger of a female in a subway train — the impulse everywhere — why not be a Columbus of the moral world and really do it? . . . He remembered stealing a conch shell[1] from the drawing room of a neighbor when he was ten — it had been one of the thrills of his life. He had popped it into his sailor blouse and borne it away with perfect aplomb.[2] When, later, suspicion had been cast upon him, he had smashed the shell in his back yard. And often, when he had been looking at Parker's collection of stamps — the early Americans —

The game interrupted his recollections, and presently it was time for the usual night-cap. Bryant drove them to Park Street. Michael was a trifle tight, but not enough to be unsteady on his feet. He waved a cheery hand at Bryant and Hurwitz and began to trudge through the snow to the subway entrance. The lights on the snow were very beautiful. The Park Street Church was ringing, with its queer, soft quarter-bells,[3] the half-hour. Plenty of time. Plenty of time. Time enough for a visit to the drugstore, and a hot chocolate — he could see the warm lights of the windows falling on the snowed sidewalk. He zigzagged across the street and entered.

And at once he was seized with a conviction that his real reason for entering the drugstore was not to get a hot chocolate — not at all! He was going to steal something. He was going to put the impulse to the test, and see whether *(one)* he could manage it with sufficient skill, and *(two)* whether theft gave him any real satisfaction. The drugstore was crowded with people who had just come from the theatre next door. They pushed three deep round the soda fountain, and the cashier's cage. At the back of the store, in the toilet and prescription department, there were not so many, but nevertheless enough to give him a fair chance. All the clerks were busy. His hands were in the side pockets of his overcoat — they were deep wide pockets and would

1) conch shell: a large, spiral sea shell.
2) aplomb: self-possession; poise.
3) quarter-bells: 15분마다 치는 괘종.

serve admirably. A quick gesture over a table or counter, the object dropped in —

Oddly enough, he was not in the least excited: perhaps that was because of the gin. On the contrary, he was intensely amused; not to say delighted. He was smiling, as he walked slowly along the right-hand side of the store toward the back; edging his way amongst the people, with first one shoulder forward and then the other, while with a critical and appraising eye he examined the wares piled on the counters and on the stands in the middle of the floor. There were some extremely attractive scent-sprays or atomizers[1)] — but the dangling bulbs might be troublesome. There were stacks of boxed letter-paper. A basket full of clothes-brushes. Green hot-water bottles. Percolators[2)] — too large, and out of the question. A tray of multicolored toothbrushes, bottles of cologne, fountain pens — and then he experienced love at first sight. There could be no question that he had found his chosen victim. He gazed, fascinated, at the delicious object — a *de luxe*[3)] safety-razor set, of heavy gold, in a snakeskin box which was lined with red plush. . . .

It wouldn't do, however, to stare at it too long — one of the clerks might notice. He observed quickly the exact position of the box — which was close to the edge of the glass counter — and prefigured with a quite precise mental picture the gesture with which he would simultaneously close it and remove it. Forefinger at the back — thumb in front — the box drawn forward and then slipped down toward the pocket — as he thought it out, the muscles in his forearm pleasurably contracted. He continued his slow progress round the store, past the prescription counter, past the candy counter; examined with some show of attention the display of cigarette lighters and blade sharpeners; and then, with a quick turn, went leisurely back to his victim. Everything was propitious. The whole section of counter was clear for the moment — there were neither customers nor clerks. He approached the counter,

1) atomizer: sprayer.

2) percolator: kind of coffee pot in which boiling water drains through ground coffee.

3) *de luxe:* of exceptionally good quality; elegant.

leaned over it as if to examine some little filigreed "compacts" at the back of the showcase,[1] picking up one of them with his left hand, as he did so. He was thus leaning directly over the box; and it was the simplest thing in the world to clasp it as planned between thumb and forefinger of his other hand, to shut it softly, and to slide it downward to his pocket. It was over in an instant. He continued then for a moment to turn the compact case this way and that in the light, as if to see it sparkle. It sparkled very nicely. Then he put it back on the little pile of cases, turned, and approached the soda fountain — just as Hurwitz had suggested.

He was in the act of pressing forward in the crowd to ask for his hot chocolate when he felt a firm hand close round his elbow. He turned, and looked at a man in a slouch hat and dirty raincoat, with the collar turned up. The man was smiling in a very offensive way.

"I guess you thought that was pretty slick,[2]" he said in a low voice which nevertheless managed to convey the very essence of venom and hostility. "You come along with me, mister!"

Michael returned the smile amiably, but was a little frightened. His heart began to beat.

"I don't know what you're talking about," he said, still smiling.

"No, of course not!"

The man was walking toward the rear of the store, and was pulling Michael along with him, keeping a paralyzingly tight grip on his elbow.[3] Michael was beginning to be angry, but also to be horrified. He thought of wrenching his arm free, but feared it would make a scene.[4] Better not. He permitted himself to be urged ignominiously along the shop, through a gate in the rear counter, and into a small room at the back, where a clerk was measuring a yellow liquid into a bottle.

"Will you be so kind as to explain to me what this is all about?"

---

1) as if to examine some little filigreed "compacts" at the back of the showcase: 진열장 뒤에 있는 어떤 조그마한 투시 세공을 한 콤팩트 같은 것을 자세히 살피기 위한 것처럼. filigree=(금은 따위의) 가는 줄세공(을 하다).

2) slick: (Colloq.) clever, ingenious, sly, tricky.

3) keeping a paralyzingly tight grip on his elbow: 그의 팔을 마비시킬 만큼 꽉 쥔 채.

4) make a scene: display, exhibit. scene=show of strong feelings in front of others.

he then said, with what frigidity of manner he could muster.[1] But his voice shook a little. The man in the slouch hat paid no attention. He addressed the clerk instead, giving his head a quick backward jerk as he spoke.

"Get the manager in here," he said.

He smiled at Michael, with narrowed eyes, and Michael, hating bim, but panic-stricken, smiled foolishly back at him.

"Now, look here — " he said.

But the manager had appeared, and the clerk; and events then happened with revolting and nauseating speed. Michael's hand was yanked violently from his pocket, the fatal snakeskin box was pulled out by the detective, and identified by the manager and the clerk. They both looked at Michael with a queer expression, in which astonishment, shame, and contempt were mixed with vague curiosity.

"Sure that's ours," said the manager, looking slowly at Michael.

"I saw him pinch[2] it," said the detective. "What about it?" He again smiled offensively at Michael. "Anything to say?"

"It was all a joke," said Michael, his face feeling very hot and flushed. "I made a kind of bet with some friends. . . . I can prove it. I can call them up for you."

The three men looked at him in silence, all three of them just faintly smiling, as if incredulously.

"Sure you can," said the detective, urbanely. "You can prove it in court. . . . Now come along with me, mister."

Michael was astounded at this appalling turn of events, but his brain still worked. Perhaps if he were to put it to this fellow as man to man, when they got outside? As he was thinking this, he was firmly conducted through a back door into a dark alley at the rear of the store. It had stopped snowing. A cold wind was blowing.

But the world, which had looked so beautiful fifteen minutes before, had now lost its charm. They walked together down the alley in six inches of powdery snow, the detective holding Michael's arm with

---

1) with what frigidity of manner he could muster: 될 수 있는 대로 냉정한 태도를 지니면서.

2) pinch: (Slang) steal.

affectionate firmness.

"No use calling the wagon," he said. "We'll walk. It ain't far."

They walked along Tremont Street. And Michael couldn't help, even then, thinking what an extraordinary thing this was! Here were all these good people passing them, and little knowing that he, Michael Lowes, was a thief, a thief by accident, on his way to jail. It seemed so absurd as hardly to be worth speaking of! And suppose they shouldn't believe him? This notion made him shiver. But it wasn't possible — no, it wasn't possible. As soon as he had told his story, and called up Hurwitz and Bryant and Smith, it would all be laughed off.[1] Yes, laughed off.

He began telling the detective about it: how they had discussed such impulses over a game of bridge. Just a friendly game, and they had joked about it and then, just to see what would happen, he had done it. What was it that made his voice sound so insincere, so hollow? The detective neither slackened his pace nor turned his head. His business-like grimness was alarming. Michael felt that he was paying no attention at all; and, moreover, it occurred to him that this kind of lowbrow official might not even understand such a thing. . . . He decided to try the sentimental.

"And good Lord, man, there's my wife waiting for me — !"

"Oh, sure, and the kids too."

"Yes, and the kids!"

The detective gave a quick leer[2] over the collar of his dirty raincoat.

"And no Santa Claus *this* year," he said.

Michael saw that it was hopeless. He was wasting his time.

"I can see it's no use talking to you," he said stiffly. "You're so used to dealing with criminals that you think all mankind is criminal, *ex post facto.*[3]"

"Sure."

Arrived at the station, and presented without decorum to the

---

1) laugh off: 일소에 부치다.

2) leer: a sly sidelong look; evil glance.

3) *ex post facto*: made or done after something but applying to it. 과거로 소급해서까지.

lieutenant at the desk, Michael tried again. Something in the faces of the lieutenant and the sergeant, as he told his story, made it at once apparent that there was going to be trouble. They obviously didn't believe him — not for a moment. But after consultation, they agreed to call up Bryant and Hurwitz and Smith, and to make inquiries. The sergeant went off to do this, while Michael sat on a wooden bench. Fifteen minutes passed, during which the clock ticked and the lieutenant wrote slowly in a book, using a blotter very frequently. A clerk had been dispatched, also, to look up Michael's record, if any. This gentleman came back first, and reported that there was nothing. The lieutenant scarcely looked up from his book, and went on writing. The first serious blow then fell. The sergeant, reporting, said that he hadn't been able to get Smith (of course — Michael thought — he's off somewhere with Squiggles) but had got Hurwitz and Bryant. Both of them denied that there had been any bet. They both seemed nervous, as far as he could make out over the phone. They said they didn't know Lowes well, were acquintances of his, and made it clear that they didn't want to be mixed up[1] in anything. Hurwitz had added that he knew Lowes was hard up.[2]

At this, Michael jumped to his feet, feeling as if the blood would burst out of his face.

"The damned liars!" he shouted. "The bloody liars! By God — !"

"Take him away," said the lieutenant, lifting his eyebrows, and making a motion with his pen.

Michael lay awake all night in his cell, after talking for five minutes with Dora on the telephone. Something in Dora's cool voice had frightened him more than anything else.

And when Dora came to talk to him the next morning at nine o'clock, his alarm proved to be well-founded. Dora was cold, detached, deliberate. She was not at all what he had hoped she might be — sympathetic and helpful. She didn't volunteer to get a lawyer, or in fact to do anything — and when she listened quietly to his story, it

1) mix up: involve, concern.

2) hard up: (Colloq.) needing money or anything very badly. 궁색하다.

seemed to him that she had the appearance of a person listening to a very improbable lie. Again, as he narrated the perfectly simple episode — the discussion of "impulse" at the bridge game, the drinks, and the absurd tipsy[1] desire to try a harmless little experiment — again, as when he talked to the store detective, he heard his own voice becoming hollow and insincere. It was exactly as if he knew himself to be guilty. His throat grew dry, he began to falter, to lose his thread, to use the wrong words. When he stopped speaking finally, Dora was silent.

"Well, say something!" he said angrily, after a moment. "Don't just stare at me. I'm not a criminal!"

"I'll get a lawyer for you," she answered, "but that's all I can do."

"Look here, Dora — you don't mean you — "

He looked at her incredulously. It wasn't possible that she really thought him a thief? And suddenly, as he looked at her, he realized how long it was since he had really known this woman. They had drifted apart. She was embittered, that was it — embittered by his non-success.[2] All this time she had slowly been laying up a reserve of resentment.[3] She had resented his inability to make money for the children, the little dishonesties they had had to commit in the matter of unpaid bills, the humiliations of duns,[4] the too-frequent removals from town to town — she had more than once said to him, it was true, that because of all this she had never had any friends — and she had resented, he knew, his gay little parties with Hurwitz and Bryant and Smith, implying a little that they were an extravagance which was to say the least inconsiderate.[5] Perhaps they *had* been. But was a man to have no indulgences? . .

"Perhaps we had better not go into that," she said.

"Good Lord — you don't believe me!"

"I'll get the lawyer — though I don't know where the fees are to

1) tipsy: somewhat intoxicated but not thoroughly drunk.

2) was it — embittered by his non-success: 그가 성공을 이루지 못한 데에 염증을 느끼고 있었다.

3) lay up a reserve of resentment: 원한의 도를 쌓아올리다.

4) the humiliations of duns: 채권자들로부터의 굴욕.

5) they were an extravagance which was to say the least inconsiderate: 그들은 전혀 지각없는 사람들이라고 말하기 마땅한 난봉꾼들이었다.

come from. Our bank account is down to seventy-seven dollars. The rent is due a week from today. You've got some salary coming, of course, but I don't want to touch my own savings, naturally, because the children and I may need them."

To be sure. Perfectly just. Women and children first. Michael thought these things bitterly, but refrained from saying them. He gazed at this queer cold little female with intense curiosity. It was simply extraordinary — simply astonishing. Here she was, seven years his wife, he thought he knew her inside and out, every quirk of her handwriting, inflection of voice; her passion for strawberries, her ridiculous way of singing; the brown moles on her shoulder, the extreme smallness of her feet and toes, her dislike of silk underwear. Her special voice at the telephone, too — that rather chilly abruptness, which had always surprised him, as if she might be a much harder woman than he thought her to be. And the queer sinuous cat-like rhythm with which she always combed her hair before the mirror at night, before going to bed — with her head tossing to one side, and one knee advanced to touch the chest of drawers. He knew all these things, which nobody else knew, and nevertheless, now, they amounted to nothing. The woman herself stood before him as opaque as a wall.1)

"Of course," he said, "you'd better keep your own savings."

His voice was dull. "And you'll, of course, look up Hurwitz and the others? They'll appear, I'm sure, and it will be the most important evidence. In fact, *the* evidence."

"I'll ring them up, Michael," was all she said, and with that she turned quickly on her heel and went away. . . .

Michael felt doom closing in upon him; his wits went round in circles; he was in a constant sweat. It wasn't possible that he was going to be betrayed? It wasn't possible! He assured himself of this. He walked back and forth, rubbing his hands together, he kept pulling out his watch to see what time it was. Five minutes gone. Another five minutes gone. Damnation, if this lasted too long, this confounded business, he'd lose his job. If it got into the papers, he might lose

1) as opaque as a wall: 담벽인 것처럼 불투명하게. opaque=not transparent, dark.

it anyway. And suppose it was true that Hurwitz and Bryant had said what they said — maybe they were afraid of losing their jobs too. Maybe that was it! Good God. . . .

This suspicion was confirmed, when, hours later, the lawyer came to see him. He reported that Hurwitz, Bryant and Smith had all three refused flatly to be mixed up in the business. They were all afraid of the effects of the publicity. If subpenaed,[1)] they said, they would state that they had known Lowes only a short time, had thought him a little eccentric, and knew him to be hard up. Obviously — and the little lawyer picked his teeth with the point of his pencil — they could not be summoned. It would be fatal.

The Judge, not unnaturally perhaps, decided that there was a perfectly clear case. There couldn't be the shadow of a doubt that this man had deliberately stolen an article from the counter of So-and-so's drugstore. The prisoner had stubbornly maintained that it was the result of a kind of bet with some friends, but these friends had refused to give testimony in his behalf. Even his wife's testimony — that he had never done such a thing before — had seemed rather half-hearted; and she had admitted, moreover, that Lowes was unsteady, and that they were always living in a state of something like poverty. Prisoner, further, had once or twice jumped his rent and had left behind him in Somerville unpaid debts of considerable size. He was a college man, a man of exceptional education and origin, and ought to have known better. His general character might be good enough, but as against all this, here was a perfectly clear case of theft, and a perfectly clear motive. The prisoner was sentenced to three months in the house of correction.

By this time, Michael was in a state of complete stupor. He sat in the box and stared blankly at Dora who sat very quietly in the second row, as if she were a stranger. She was looking back at him, with her white face turned a little to one side, as if she too had never seen him before, and were wondering what sort of people criminals

---

1) subpena: (*v.*) subpenaed, subpenaing. summon with an official written order commanding a person to appear in law court.

might be. Human? Sub-human? She lowered her eyes after a moment, and before she had looked up again, Michael had been touched on the arm and led stumbling out of the courtroom. He thought she would of course come to say goodbye to him, but even in this he was mistaken; she left without a word.

And when he did finally hear from her, after a week, it was in a very brief note.

"Michael," it said, "I'm sorry, but I can't bring up the children with a criminal for a father, so I'm taking proceedings for a divorce. This is the last straw. It was bad enough to have you always out of work and to have to slave night and day to keep bread in the children's mouths. But this is too much, to have disgrace into the bargain. As it is, we'll have to move right away, for the schoolchildren have sent Dolly and Mary home crying three times already. I'm sorry, and you know how fond I was of you at the beginning, but you've had your chance. You won't hear from me again. You've always been a good sport, and generous, and I hope you'll make this occasion no exception, and refrain from contesting the divorce. Goodbye — Dora."

Michael held the letter in his hands, unseeing, and tears came into his eyes. He dropped his face against the sheet of notepaper, and rubbed his forehead to and fro across it. . . Little Dolly!. . . Little Mary!. . . Of course. This was what life was. It was just as meaningless and ridiculous as this; a monstrous joke; a huge injustice. You couldn't trust anybody, not even your wife, not even your best friends. You went on a little lark,[1)] and they sent you to prison for it, and your friends lied about you, and your wife left you. . . .

Contest it? Should he contest the divorce? What was the use? There was the plain fact: that he had been convicted for stealing. No one had believed his story of doing it in fun, after a few drinks; the divorce court would be no exception. He dropped the letter to the floor and turned his heel on it, slowly and bitterly. Good riddance[2)] — good riddance! Let them all go to hell. He would show them. He would

1) go on a little lark: have fun; play pranks. lark=(Colloq.) a merry adventure; frolic.
2) Good riddance: 잘 떼어버렸다, 홀가분하다. riddance=a clearing away or out; removal.

go west, when he came out — get rich, clear his name somehow. . . But how?

He sat down on the edge of his bed and thought of Chicago. He thought of his childhood there, the Lake Shore Drive, Winnetka, the trip to Niagara Falls with his mother. He could hear the Falls now. He remembered the Fourth of July on the boat; the crowded examination room at college; the time he had broken his leg in baseball, when he was fourteen; and the stamp collection which he had lost at school. He remembered his mother always saying, "Michael, you *must* learn to be orderly"; and the little boy who had died of scarlet fever next door; and the pink conch-shell smashed in the back yard. His whole life seemed to be composed of such trivial and infinitely charming little episodes as these; and as he thought of them, affectionately and with wonder, he assured himself once more that he had really been a good man. And now, had it all come to an end? It had all come foolishly to an end.

The Egg

by Sherwood Anderson

Sherwood Anderson (1876-1941) was born in Camden, Ohio, and much of his boyhood was spent in Clyde, another small Ohio town. The poverty of his family was perhaps the chief reason why he quit school at the age of fourteen and got a job. Thereafter, for a good many years, he worked at a great variety of jobs (all requiring manual labor), first in Clyde and then in Chicago. In 1898 he joined the National Guard, and his company was sent to Cuba for patrol duty after the defeat of the Spanish forces. Upon his return from Cuba in 1899, he enrolled <somewhat belatedly — he was twenty-three) in Wittenberg Academy, a preparatory school in Springfield, Ohio, and was graduated the following year. Soon thereafter, he became a writer of advertising copy. He was so successful in this line that he organized, in 1907, in Elyria, Ohio, the Anderson Manufacturing Company, which specialized in roof paint. In 1912 Anderson — though married and the father of three children, and eminently successful in the manufacture and sale of roof paint — left his factory and did not return. Anderson went at once to Chicago, where he soon became a member of the circle of writers who were making the "Chicago Renaissance."

Though the Midwest was his rightful milieu, and Chicago his proper cosmopolitan center, Anderson moved restlessly to this place and that, always seeking a fulfillment which he could never achieve; to New York, which he mistakenly regarded as a better place for him than Chicago, and where he sought the guidance of Waldo Frank and Van Wyck Brooks; to Paris, where he met Ernest Hemingway and Gertrude Stein; to New Orleans, where his association with William Faulkner probably contributed little to his literary career. After 1927 he lived (with his fourth wife) on a farm near Marion, Virginia, and, having bought the two newspapers in the town, gave much of his time to journalism. Even here, he was unhappy, presumably because of the failure of his creative powers and the decline of his literary reputation.

In *Winesburg, Ohio* and in the two collections (*The Triumph of the Egg and Horses and Men*) which followed it, Anderson created stories which, because of their intensity and unconventionality, are his special contributions to American literature.

My Father was, I am sure, intended by nature to be a cheerful, kindly man. Until he was thirty-four years old he worked as a farm hand[1] for a man named Thomas Butterworth whose place lay near the town of Bidwell, Ohio. He had then a horse of his own and on

1) a farm hand: a farm laborer.

Saturday evenings drove into town to spend a few hours in social intercourse with other farmhands. In town he drank several glasses of beer and stood about[1] in Ben Head's saloon[2] — crowded on Saturday evenings with visiting farmhands. Songs were sung and glasses thumped on the bar. At ten o'clock father drove home along a lonely country road, made his horse comfortable for the night and himself went to bed, quite happy in his position in life. He had at that time no notion of trying to rise in the world.[3]

It was in the spring of his thirty-fifth year that father married my mother, then a country school teacher, and in the following spring I came wriggling and crying into the world. Something happened to the two people. They became ambitious. The American passion for getting up in the world took possession of[4] them.

It may have been that mother was responsible. Being a schoolteacher she had no doubt read books and magazines. She had, I presume, read of how Garfield,[5] Lincoln,[6] and other Americans rose from poverty to fame and greatness and as I lay beside her — in the days of her lying-in[7] she may have dreamed that I would someday rule men and cities. At any rate she induced father to give up his place as a farm hand, sell his horse and embark on[8] an independent enterprise of his own. She was a tall silent woman with a long nose and troubled gray eyes.[9] For herself she wanted nothing. For father and myself she was incurably ambitious.

The first venture into which the two people went turned out[10] badly. They rented ten acres of poor stony land on Griggs's Road, eight miles from Bidwell, and launched into[11] chicken raising. I grew into boyhood

1) stood about: stood here and there (in front of the bar).
2) saloon: public house.
3) to rise in the world: to succeed; to get up in the world.
4) took possession of: possessed; took hold of.
5) Garfield: James Abram(1831-81), the 20th President of the United States.
6) Lincoln: Abraham Lincoln(1809-1865), the 16th President of the United States.
7) lying-in: confinement in childbirth; childbirth.
8) embark on: start, set out.
9) troubled gray eyes: 수심에 찬 회색빛 두 눈.
10) turned out: resulted; became.
11) launched into: start, begin.

on the place and got my first impressions of life there. From the beginning they were impressions of disaster and if, in my turn, I am a gloomy man inclined to see the darker side of life, I attribute it to the fact that what should have been for me the happy joyous days of childhood were spent on a chicken farm.

One unversed in such matters[1] can have no notion of the many and tragic things that can happen to a chicken. It is born out of an egg, lives for a few weeks as a tiny fluffy thing such as you will see pictured on Easter[2] cards, then becomes hideously naked, eats quantities of corn and meal bought by the sweat of your father's brow, gets diseases called pip,[3] cholera, and other names, stands looking with stupid eyes at the sun, becomes sick and dies. A few hens and now and then a rooster, intended to serve God's mysterious ends, struggle through to maturity.[4] The hens lay eggs out of which come other chickens and the dreadful cycle is thus made complete. It is all unbelievably complex. Most philosophers must have been raised on chicken farms. One hopes for so much from a chicken and is so dreadfully disillusioned. Small chickens, just setting out[5] on the journey of life, look so bright and alert and they are in fact so dreadfully stupid. They are so much like people[6] they mix one up in one's judgments of life. If disease does not kill them they wait until your expectations are thoroughly aroused and then walk under the wheels of a wagon —to go squashed and dead back to their maker.[7] Vermin infest their youth, and fortunes must be spent for curative powders. In later life I have seen how a literature[8] has been built up on the subject of

1) one unversed in such matters: one who is unexperienced [unpracticed, unskilled] in such things.
2) Easter: day for celebrating Christ's rising from the dead, observed on the first Sunday after the first full moon after March 21.
3) pip: a contagious disease of birds, characterized by the secretion of thick mucus in the mouth and throat.
4) struggle through to maturity: 가까스로 성숙기에 이르다.
5) set out: start to go.
6) They are so much like people: 다음에 that를 보충하여 so~that의 구문으로 생각한다.
7) their maker: their creator(=God).
8) literature: (Colloq.) printed matter of any kind; the writings(dealing with a

fortunes to be made out of the raising of chickens. It is intended to be read by the gods who have just eaten of the tree of the knowledge of good and evil. It is a hopeful literature and declares that much may be done by simple ambitious people who own a few hens. Do not be led astray by it. It was not written for you. Go hunt for gold on the frozen hills of Alaska, put your faith in the honesty of a politician, believe if you will that the world is daily growing better and that good will triumph over evil, but do not read and believe the literature that is written concerning the hen. It was not written for you.

I, however, digress. My tale does not primarily concern itself with the hen. If correctly told it will center on the egg. For ten years my father and mother struggled to make our chicken farm pay[1] and then they gave up that struggle and began another. They moved into the town of Bidwell, Ohio and embarked in the restaurant business. After ten years of worry with incubators that did not hatch, and with tiny — and in their own way lovely — balls of fluff that passed on into semi-naked pullerhood[2] and from that into dead henhood, we threw all aside and packing our belongings on a wagon drove down Griggs's Road toward Bidwell, a tiny caravan of hope looking for a new place from which to start on our upward journey through life.

We must have been a sad looking lot,[3] not, I fancy, unlike refugees fleeing from a battlefield. Mother and I walked in the road. The wagon that contained our goods had been borrowed for the day from Mr. Albert Griggs, a neighbor. Out of its sides stuck the legs of cheap chairs and at the back of the pile of beds, tables, and boxes filled with kitchen utensils was a crate[4] of live chickens, and on top of that the baby carriage in which I had been wheeled about in my infancy. Why we stuck to[5] the baby carriage I don't know. It was unlikely other children would be born and the wheels were broken. People

---

particular subject).

1) pay: be profitable 수지가 맞다.

2) pullerhood: state of being a young hen, usually less than a year old.

3) lot: group.

4) crate: a large box used to pack furniture.

5) stuck to: kept close.

who have few possessions cling tightly to those they have. That is one of the facts that make life so discouraging.

Father rode on top of the wagon. He was then a baldheaded man of forty-five, a little fat and from long association with mother and the chickens he had become habitually silent and discouraged. All during our ten years on the chicken farm he had worked as a laborer on neighboring farms and most of the money he had earned had been spent for remedies to cure chicken diseases, on Wilmer's White Wonder Cholera Cure or Professor Bidlow's Egg Producer or some other preparations that mother found advertised in the poultry papers. There were two little patches of hair on father's head just above his ears. I remember that as a child I used to sit looking at him when he had gone to sleep in a chair before the stove on Sunday afternoons in the winter. I had at that rime already begun to read books and have notions of my own and the bald path that led over the top of his head was, I fancied, something like a broad road, such a road as Caesar might have made on which to lead his legions out of Rome and into the wonders of an unknown world. The tufts of hair that grew above father's ears were, I thought, like forests. I fell into a half-sleeping, half-waking state and dreamed I was a tiny thing going along the road into a far beautiful place where there were no chicken farms and where life was a happy eggless affair.

One might write a book concerning our flight from the chicken farm into town. Mother and I walked the entire eight miles — she to be sure that nothing fell from the wagon and I to see the wonders of the world. On the seat of the wagon beside father was his greatest treasure. I will tell you of that.

On a chicken farm where hundreds and even thousands of chickens come out of eggs, surprising things sometimes happen. Grotesques are born out of eggs as out of people. The accident does not often occur — perhaps once in a thousand births. A chicken is, you see, born that has four legs, two pairs of wings, two heads or what not.[1] The things do not live. They go quickiy back to the hand of their maker

1) or what not: all kinds of other things.

that has for a moment trembled. The fact that the poor little things could not live was one of the tragedies of life to father. He had some sort of notion that if he could but bring into henhood or roosterhood a five-legged hen or a two-headed rooster his fortune would be made. He dreamed of taking the wonder about to county fairs and of growing rich by exhibiting it to other farmhands.

At any rate he saved all the little monstrous things that had been born on our chicken farm. They were preserved in alcohol and put each in its own glass bottle. These he had carefully put into a box and on our journey into town it was carried on the wagon seat beside him. He drove the horses with one hand and with the other clung to the box. When we got to our destination the box was taken down at once and the bottles removed. All during our days as keepers of a restaurant in the town of Bidwell, Ohio, the grotesques in their little glass bottles sat on a shelf back of the counter. Mother sometimes protested but father was a rock on the subject of his treasure. The grotesques were, he declared, valuable. People, he said, liked to look at strange and wonderful things.

Did I say that we embarked in the restaurant business in the town of Bidwell, Ohio? I exaggerated a little. The town itself lay at the foot of a low hill and on the shore of a small river. The railroad did not run through the town and the station was a mile away to the north at a place called Pickleville. There had been a cider mill[1] and pickle factory at the station, but before the time of our coming they had both gone out of business.[2] In the morning and in the evening busses came down to the station along a road called Turner's Pike[3] from the hotel on the main street of Bidwell. Our going to the out-of-the-way place to embark in the restaurant business was mother's idea. She talked of it for a year and then one day went off and rented an empty store building opposite the railroad station. It was her idea that the restaurant would be profitable. Travelling men, she said, would be always waiting around to take trains out of town and town people

1) cider mill: 사과주 공장.
2) go out of business: 파업하다.
3) Turner's Pike: pike는 turnpike road. 통행료를 받는 highway.

would come to the station to await incoming trains. They would come to the restaurant to buy pieces of pie and drink coffee. Now that I am older I know that she had another motive in going. She was ambitious for me. She wanted me to rise in the world, to get into a town school and become a man of the towns.

At Pickleville father and mother worked hard as they always had done. At first there was the necessity of putting our place into shape[1)] to be a restaurant. That took a month. Father built a shelf on which he put tins of vegetables. He painted a sign on which he put his name in large red letters. Below his name was the sharp command — "EAT HERE" — that was so seldom obeyed. A showcase was bought and filled with cigars and tobacco. Mother scrubbed the floor and the walls of the room. I went to school in the town and was glad to be away from the farm and from the presence of the discouraged, sad-looking chickens. Still I was not very joyous. In the evening I walked home from school along Turner's Pike and remembered the children I had seen playing in the town school yard. A troop of little girls had gone hopping about and singing. I tried that. Down along the frozen road I went hopping solemnly on one leg. "Hippity Hop To The Barber Shop,"[2)] I sang shrilly. Then I stopped and looked doubtfully about. I was afraid of being seen in my gay mood. It must have seemed to me that I was doing a thing that should not be done by one who, like myself, had been raised on a chicken farm where death was a daily visitor.

Mother decided that our restaurant should remain open at night. At ten in the evening a passenger train went north past our door followed by a local freight. The freight crew had switching[3)] to do in Pickleville and when the work was done they came to our restaurant for hot coffee and food. Sometimes one of them ordered a fried egg. In the morning at four they returned north-bound[4)] and again visited us. A

1) putting ~ into shape: arranging 꾸미다.
2) Hippity hop to the barber shop: 동요의 일종. Hippity에는 별다른 뜻이 없고 가락을 맞추기 위한 것임.
3) switching: shifting a train from one track to another.
4) north-bound: bound for north; ready or intending to go for north.

little trade began to grow up. Mother slept at night and during the day tended the restaurant and fed our boarders while father slept. He slept in the same bed mother had occupied during the night and I went off to the town of Bidwell and to school. During the long nights, while mother and I slept, father cooked meats that were to go into sandwiches for the lunch baskets of our boarders. Then an idea in regard to getting up in the world came into his head. The American spirit took hold of him. He also became ambitious.

In the long nights when there was little to do father had time to think. That was his undoing.[1] He decided that he had in the past been an unsuccessful man because he had not been cheerful enough and that in the future he would adopt a cheerful outlook on life.[2] In the early morning he came upstairs and got into bed with mother. She woke and the two talked. From my bed in the corner I listened.

It was father's idea that both he and mother should try to entertain the people who came to eat at our restaurant. I cannot now remember his words, but he gave the impression of one about to become in some obscure way a kind of public entertainer. When people, particularly young people from the town of Bidwell, came into our place, as on very rare occasions they did, bright entertaining conversation was to be made. From father's words I gathered that something of the jolly innkeeper effect was to be sought. Mother must have been doubtful from the first, but she said nothing discouraging. It was father's notion that a passion for the company of himself and mother would spring up in the breasts of the younger people of the town of Bidwell. In the evening bright happy groups would come singing down Turner's Pike. They would troop shouting with joy and laughter into our place. There would be song and festivity. I do not mean to give the impression that father spoke so elaborately of the matter. He was as I have said an uncommunicative man. "They want some place to go. I tell you they want some place to go," he said over and over. That was as far as he got. My own imagination has filled in the blanks.

For two or three weeks this notion of father's invaded our house.

---

1) undoing: case of destruction or ruin.

2) a cheerful outlook on life: a cheerful way of thinking about life.

We did not talk much but in our daily lives tried earnestly to make smiles take the place of glum looks. Mother smiled at the boarders and I, catching the infection,[1)] smiled at our cat. Father became a little feverish in his anxiety to please. There was no doubt lurking somewhere in him a touch of the spirit of the showman. He did not waste much of his ammunition[2)] on the railroad men he served at night but seemed to be waiting for a young man or woman from Bidwell to come in to show what he could do. On the counter in the restaurant there was a wire basket kept always filled with eggs, and it must have been before his eyes when the idea of being entertaining was born in his brain. There was something pre-natal[3)] about the way eggs kept themselves connected with the development of his idea. At any rate an egg ruined his new impulse in life. Late one night I was awakened by a roar of anger coming from father's throat. Both mother and I sat upright in our beds. With trembling hands she lighted a lamp that stood on a table by her head. Downstairs the front door of our restaurant went shut with a bang and in a few minutes father tramped up the stairs. He held an egg in his hand and his hand trembled as though he were having a chill. There was a half insane light in his eyes. As he stood glaring at us I was sure he intended throwing the egg at either mother or me. Then he laid it gently on the table beside the lamp and dropped on his knees beside mother's bed. He began to cry like a boy and I, carried away by his grief,[4)] cried with him. The two of us filled the little upstairs room with our wailing voices. It is ridiculous, but of the picture we made I can remember only the fact that mother's hand continually stroked the bald path that ran across the top of his head. I have forgotten what mother said to him and how she induced him to tell her of what had happened downstairs. His explanation also has gone out of my mind. I remember only my own grief and fright and the shiny path over father's head glowing in the lamplight as he knelt by the bed.

---

1) catching the infection: infecting.
2) his ammunition: 그의 실력(재간).
3) pre-natal: previous to birth.
4) carried away by his grief: inspired by his grief 아버지의 슬픔에 감염되어.

As to what happened downstairs. For some unexplainable reason I know the story as well as though I had been a witness to my father's discomfiture.[1] One in time[2] gets to know many unexplainable things. On that evening young Joe Kane, son of a merchant of Bidwell, came to Pickleville to meet his father, who was expected on the ten o'clock evening train from the south. The train was three hours late and Joe came into our place to loaf about[3] and to wait for its arrival. The local freight train came in and the freight crew were fed. Joe was left alone in the restaurant with father.

From the moment he came into our place the Bidwell young man must have been puzzled by my father's actions. It was his notion that father was angry at him for hanging around.[4] He noticed that the restaurant keeper was apparently disturbed by his presence and he thought of going out. However, it began to rain and he did not fancy the long walk to town and back. He bought a five-cent cigar and ordered a cup of coffee. He had a newspaper in his pocket and took it out and began to read. "I'm waiting for the evening train. It's late," he said apologetically.

For a long time father, whom Joe Kane had never seen before, remained silently gazing at his visitor. He was no doubt suffering from an attack of stage fright. As so often happens in life he had thought so much and so often of the situation that now confronted him that he was somewhat nervous in its presence.

For one thing, he did not know what to do with his hands. He thrust one of them nervously over the counter and shook hands with Joe Kane. "How-de-do,"[5] he said. Joe Kane put his newspaper down and stared at him. Father's eye lighted on the basket of eggs that sat on the counter and he began to talk. "Well," he began hesitatingly, "well, you have heard of Christopher Columbus, eh?" He seemed to

1) discomfiture: defeat of plans or hopes.
2) in time: sooner or later.
3) loaf about: idle away; hang around.
4) hang around: to pass time or stay near without any real purpose or aim; loaf near or in.
5) How-de-do: Howdy(=How do you do?).

be angry. "That Christopher Columbus was a cheat,"[1] he declared emphatically. "He talked of making an egg stand on its end. He talked, he did, and then he went and broke the end of the egg."

My father seemed to his visitor to be beside himself[2] at the duplicity of Christopher Columbus. He muttered and swore. He declared it was wrong to teach children that Christopher Columbus was a great man when, after all, he cheated at the critical moment. He had declared he would make an egg stand on end and then when his bluff had been called[3] he had done a trick. Still grumbling at Columbus, father took an egg from the basket on the counter and began to walk up and down. He rolled the egg between the palms of his hands. He smiled genially. He began to mumble words regarding the effect to be produced on an egg by the electricity that comes out of the human body. He declared that without breaking its shell and by virtue of rolling it back and forth in his hands he could stand the egg on its end. He explained that the warmth of his hands and the gentle rolling movement he gave the egg created a new center of gravity, and Joe Kane was mildly interested. "I have handled thousands of eggs," father said. "No one knows more about eggs than I do."

He stood the egg on the counter and it fell on its side. He tried the trick again and again, each time rolling the egg between the palms of his hands and saying the words regarding the wonders of electricity and the laws of gravity. When after a half hour's effort he did succeed in making the egg stand for a moment, he looked up to find that his visitor was no longer watching. By the time he had succeeded in calling Joe Kane's attention to the success of his effort, the egg had again rolled over and lay on its side.

Afire with[4] the showman's passion and at the same time a good deal disconcerted[5] by the failure of his first effort, father now took the bottles containing the poultry monstrosities down from their place

---

1) cheat: 사기꾼.
2) be beside himself: be very much excited; be somewhat crazy.
3) when his bluff had been called: 그 장담을 실천해 보도록 요청을 받자.
4) afire with: enthused by.
5) disconcerted: disturbed; confused.

on the shelf and began to show them to his visitor. "How would you like to have seven legs and two heads like this fellow?" he asked, exhibiting the most remarkable of his treasures. A cheerful smile played over his face. He reached over the counter and tried to slap Joe Kane on the shoulder as he had seen men do in Ben Head's saloon when he was a young farmhand and drove to town on Saturday evenings. His visitor was made a little ill by the sight of the body of the terribly deformed bird floating in the alcohol in the bottle and got up to go. Coming from behind the counter, father took hold of the young man's arm and led him back to his seat. He grew a little angry and for a moment had to turn his face away and force himself to smile. Then he put the bottles back on the shelf. In an outburst of generosity he fairly compelled Joe Kane to have a fresh cup of coffee and another cigar at his expense. Then he took a pan and filling it with vinegar, taken from a jug that sat beneath the counter, he declared himself about to do a new trick. "I will heat this egg in this pan of vinegar," he said. "Then I will put it through the neck of a bottle without breaking the shell. When the egg is inside the bottle it will resume its normal shape and the shell will become hard again. Then I will give the bottle with the egg in it to you. You can take it about with you wherever you go. People will want to know how you got the egg in the bottle. Don't tell them. Keep them guessing. That is the way to have fun with this trick."

Father grinned and winked at his visitor. Joe Kane decided that the man who confronted him was mildly insane but harmless. He drank the cup of coffee that had been given him and began to read his paper again. When the egg had been heated in vinegar, father carried it on a spoon to the counter and going into a back room got an empty bottle. He was angry because his visitor did not watch him as he began to do his trick, but nevertheless went cheerfully to work. For a long time he struggled, trying to get the egg to go through the neck of the bottle. He put the pan of vinegar back on the stove, intending to reheat the egg, then picked it up and burned his fingers. After a second bath in the hot vinegar, the shell of the egg had been softened a little but not enough for his purpose. He worked and worked and a spirit of desperate determination took possession of him. When he thought that at last the trick was about to be consummated, the delayed train came in at the station and Joe Kane started to go nonchalantly out at the door. Father made a last desperate effort to conquer the egg and make it do the thing that would establish his reputation as one who knew how to entertain guests who came into his restaurant. He worried the egg. He attempted to be somewhat rough with it. He swore and the sweat stood out on his forehead. The egg broke under his hand. When the contents spurted over his clothes, Joe Kane, who had stopped at the door, turned and laughed.

A roar of anger rose from my father's throat. He danced and shouted a string of inarticulate words. Grabbing another egg from the basket on the counter, he threw it, just missing the head of the young man as he dodged[1] through the door and escaped.

Father came upstairs to mother and me with an egg in his hand. I do not know what he intended to do. I imagine he had some idea of destroying it, of destroying all eggs, and that he intended to let mother and me see him begin. When, however, he got into the presence of mother something happened to him. He laid the egg gently on the table and dropped on his knees by the bed as I have already explained. He later decided to close the restaurant for the night and to come upstairs and get into bed. When he did so he blew out the light and after much muttered conversation both he and mother went to sleep. I suppose I went to sleep also, but my sleep was troubled. I awoke at dawn and for a long time looked at the egg that lay on the table. I wondered why eggs had to be and why from the egg came the hen who again laid the egg. The question got into my blood. It has stayed there, I imagine, because I am the son of my father. At any rate, the problem remains unsolved in my mind. And that, I conclude, is but another evidence of the complete and final triumph of the egg — at least as far as my family is concerned.

---

1) dodge: move quickly to one side.

In Greenwich There Are Many Gravelled Walks

by Hortense Calisher

Hortense Calisher (19ll-) was born in New York City and educated at Barnard College, New York.

One quality is common to her stories whether they treat of school, loneliness or the supernatural-love of the English language. She uses words carefully, thoughtfully, and in fresh ways, as a graphic artist might use unexpected shapes and colors.

ON AN afternoon in early August, Peter Birge, just returned from driving his mother to the Greenwich sanitarium she had to frequent at intervals,[1] sat down heavily on a furbelowed sofa in the small apartment he and she had shared ever since his return from the Army a year ago. He was thinking that his usually competent solitude had become more than he could bear. He was a tall, well-built young man of about twenty-three, with a pleasant face whose even, standardized look was the effect of proper food, a good dentist, the best schools, and a brush haircut.[2] The heat, which bored steadily into the room through a Venetian blind[3] lowered over a half-open window, made his white T shirt cling to his chest and arms, which were still brown from a week's sailing in July at a cousin's place on the Sound. The family of cousins, one cut[4] according to the pattern of a two-car-and-country club suburbia,[5] had always looked with distaste on his

---

1) at intervals: now and then.

2) brush haircut: brush cut (=a mode of hair cut in which all the hair (front top, and sides) is cut to the same short length, usu. less than an inch).

3) Venetian blind: a window blind made of many horizontal wooden slats that can be opened or closed to regulate the light, air, etc.

4) one cut: one style or fashion.

5) a two-car-and-country club suburbia: 차 두 대를 갖고 컨트리 클럽에 출입하는 교외 거주자.

precocious[1] childhood with his mother in the Village[2] and, the few times he had been farmed out[3] to them during those early years, had received his healthy normality with ill-concealed surprise, as if they had clearly expected to have to fatten up[4] what they undoubtedly referred to in private as "poor Anne's boy." He had only gone there at all, this time, when it became certain that the money saved up for a summer abroad,[5] where his Army stint[6] had not sent him, would have to be spent on one of his mother's trips to Greenwich, leaving barely enough, as it was, for his next, and final, year at the School of Journalism. Half out of disheartenment over his collapsed summer,[7] half to provide himself with a credible "out"[8] for the too jovially pressing cousins at Rye, he had registered for some courses at the Columbia summer session. Now these were almost over, too, leaving a gap before the fall semester began. He had cut[9] this morning's classes in order to drive his mother up to the place in Connecticut.

He stepped to the window and looked through the blind at the convertible[10] parked below, on West Tenth Street. He ought to call the garage for the pickup man, or else, until he thought of someplace to go, he ought to hop down and put up the top. Otherwise, baking there in the hot sun, the car would be like a griddle when he went to use it, and the leather seats were cracking badly anyway.

It had been cool when he and his mother started, just after dawn that morning, and the air of the well-ordered countryside had had that almost speaking freshness of early day.[11] With her head bound

---

1) precocious: developed earlier than usual.
2) the Village: Greenwich Village (=section of New York City, famous as a district where artists and writers live).
3) farmed out: assigned. 원래는 baseball에서 assign to a minor league team을 말함.
4) fatten up: make fat.
5) for a summer abroad: 여름철의 외국여행을 위해.
6) stint: task assigned; limit; limitation.
7) his collapsed summer: 여름에 외국여행 하겠다는 꿈이 깨어진 것을 말함.
8) a credible "out": 수긍이 갈 만한 구실 "out"=excuse; a way out.
9) cut: be absent from a class.
10) convertible: automobile with a folding top.
11) had that almost speaking freshness of early day: 이른 아침의 신선함을 말해주는 듯했다.

in a silk scarf and her chubby little chin tucked into the cardigan[1)] which he had buttoned on her without forcing her arms into the sleeves, his mother, peering up at him with the near-gaiety born of relief,[2)] had had the exhausted charm of a child who has just been promised the thing for which it has nagged. Anyone looking at the shingled[3)] hair, the feet in small brogues[4)] — anyone not close enough to see how drawn and beakish her nose looked in the middle of her little round face, which never reddened much with drink but at the worst times took on a sagging, quilted whiteness — might have thought the two of them were a couple, any couple, just off for a day in the country. No one would have thought that only a few hours before, some time after two, he had been awakened, pounded straight up on his feet, by the sharp, familiar cry and then the agonized susurrus of prattling[5)] that went on and on and on, that was different from her everyday, artlessly confidential prattle only in that now she could not stop, she could not stop, *she could not stop,* and above the small, working mouth with its eliding, spinning voice, the glazed button eyes opened wider and wider, as if she were trying to breathe through them. Later, after the triple bromide,[6)] the warm bath, and the crooning, practiced soothing he administered so well,[7)] she had hiccuped into crying,[8)] then into stillness at last, and had fallen asleep on his breast. Later still, she had awakened him, for he must have fallen asleep there in the big chair with her, and with the weak, humiliated goodness which always followed these times she had even tried to help him with the preparations for the journey — preparations which, without a word between them, they had set about at once. There'd been no doubt, of course, that

---

1) cardigan: a knitted woolen jacket(named for the Earl of Cardigan(1797-1866)).

2) with the near-gaiety born of relief: 안심하듯 기쁜 표정으로.

3) shingled: cut(the hair) short.

4) brogue: a coarse, strong shoe.

5) prattle: *(v.)* talk as a child does; *(n.)* simple artless talk; baby talk.

6) after the triple bromide: 진정제를 세 알 먹은 다음. bromide=a drug used to calm nervousness, cause sleep, etc.

7) the crooning, practiced soothing he administered so well: 그가 나지막한 목소리로 아주 잘 달래면서 위로하자. croon=murmur in a low tone.

8) hiccuped into crying: 딸국질하며 울었다. hiccup=hie-cough.

she would have to go. There never was.

He left the window and sat down again in the big chair, and smoked one cigarette after another. Actually, for a drunkard — or an alcoholic, as people preferred to say these days — his mother was the least troublesome of any. He had thought of it while he packed the pairs of daintily kept shoes, the sweet-smelling blouses and frou-frou[1] underwear, the tiny, perfect dresses — of what comfort it was that[2] she had never grown raddled[3] or blowsy.[4] Years ago, she had perfected the routine within which she could feel safe for months at a time. It had gone on for longer than he could remember: from before the death of his father, a Swedish engineer, on the income of whose patents they had always been able to live fairly comfortably; probably even during her life with that other long-dead man, the painter whose model and mistress she had been in the years before she married his father. There would be the long, drugged sleep[5] of the morning, then the unsteady hours when she manicured herself back into cleanliness and reality. Then, at about four or five in the afternoon, she and the dog (for there was always a dog) would make their short pilgrimage to the clubby, cozy little hangout where she would be a fixture until far into the morning, where she had been a fixture for the last twenty years.

Once, while he was at boarding school, she had made a supreme effort to get herself out of the routine — for his sake, no doubt — and he had returned at Easter to a new apartment, uptown,[6] on Central Park West. All that this had resulted in was inordinate taxi fares and the repetitious nightmare evenings when she had gotten lost and he had found her, a small, untidy heap, in front of their old place. After a few months, they had moved back to the Village, to those few important blocks where she felt safe and known and loved. For they all knew

1) frou-frou: rustling.

2) (had thought) of what comfort it was that…: …라는 것이 얼마나 다행인가 하고 생각했다.

3) raddle: (얼굴을) 연지로 발라대다.

4) blowsy: blowzy; untidy; red-faced and coarse-looking.

5) There would be the long, drugged sleep: (아침에는) 약의 힘으로 오래도록 잠을 자곤 했다.

6) uptown: the fashionable or residential area of a city.

her there, or got to know her — the aging painters, the newcomer poets, the omniscient news hacks,[1] the military spinsters[2] who bred dogs, the anomalous, sandalled young men. And they accepted her, this dainty hanger-on who neither painted nor wrote but hung their paintings on her walls, faithfully read their parti-colored[3] magazines, and knew them all — their shibboleths,[4] their feuds, the whole vocabulary of their disintegration, and, in a mild, occasional manner, their beds.

Even this, he could not remember not knowing. At ten, he had been an expert compounder of remedies for hang-over,[5] and of an evening, standing sleepily in his pajamas to be admired by the friends his mother sometimes brought home, he could have predicted accurately whether the party would end in a brawl[6] or in a murmurous coupling in the dark.

It was curious, he supposed now, stubbing out a final cigarette, that he had never judged resentfully either his mother or her world. By the accepted standards, his mother had done her best; he had been well housed, well schooled, even better loved than some of the familied boys he had known. Wisely, too, she had kept out of his other life,[7] so that he had never had to be embarrassed there except once, and this when he was grown, when she had visited his Army camp. Watching her at a post party for visitors, poised there, so chic,[8] so distinctive, he had suddenly seen it begin: the fear, the scare, then the compulsive talking, which always started so innocently that only he would have noticed at first — that warm, excited, buttery flow of harmless little lies[9] and pretensions which gathered its dreadful speed and content

---

1) the omniscient news hacks: 모르는 것이 없는 뉴스기자들. hack=person hired to do routine literary work.
2) the military spinsters: (개를 키우는) 사내 같은 노처녀들. spinster=unmarried woman.
3) parti-colored: colored differently in different parts.
4) shibboleth: criterion, test, or watchword; a party cry or pet phrase.
5) an expert compounder of remedies for hang-over: 숙취를 푸는 약을 조제하는 전문가.
6) brawl: noisy quarrel.
7) kept out of his other life: 그의 사회생활에는 참견하지 않았다.
8) chic: (Colloq.) clever; neat.
9) buttery flow of harmless little lies: 거침없이 흐르는 해롭지 않은 거짓말.

and ended then, after he had whipped her away, just as it had ended this morning.

On the way up this morning, he had been too clever to subject her to a restaurant, but at a drive-in place[1)] he was able to get her to take some coffee. How grateful they had both been for the coffee, she looking up at him, tremulous, her lips pecking at the cup, he blessing the coffee as it went down her! And afterward, as they flew onward, he could feel her straining like a homing pigeon toward their destination, toward the place where she felt safest of all, where she would gladly have stayed forever if she had just had enough money for it, if they would only let her stay. For there the pretty little woman and her dog — a poodle[2)] this time — would be received like the honored guest that she was, so trusted and docile a guest, who asked only to hide there during the season of her discomfort, who was surely the least troublesome of them all.

He had no complaints, then, he assured himself[3)] as he sat on the burning front seat of the convertible trying to think of somewhere to go. It was just that while others of his age still shared a communal wonder at what life might hold,[4)] he had long since been solitary in his knowledge of what life was.

Up in a sky as honestly blue as a flag, an airplane droned smartly toward Jersey. Out at Rye, the younger crowd at the club would be commandeering[5)] the hot blue day, the sand, and the water, as if these were all extensions of themselves. They would use the evening this way, too, disappearing from the veranda after a dance, exploring each other's rhythm-and-whiskey-whetted appetites[6)] in the backs of cars.

---

1) drive-in place: place where customers may make purchases, eat, attend movies, etc., while seated in their cars.

2) poodle: one of an intelligent breed of pet dogs with thick hair.

3) He had no complaints, then, he assured himself: 그러자 그는 아무런 불평도 없다고 자신에게 다짐했다.

4) a communal wonder at what life might hold: 앞으로의 생활이 어떻게 될 것인가에 대한 사회 일반의 호기심.

5) commandeer: (Colloq.) take by force.

6) rhythm-and-whisky-whetted appetite: 율동과 위스키로 흥분된 욕구. whetted= stimulated; made keen or eager.

They all thought themselves a pretty sophisticated bunch,[1] the young men who had graduated not into a war but into its hung-over peace, the young girls attending junior colleges so modern that the deans had to spend all their time declaring that their girls were being trained for the family and the community. But when Peter looked close and saw how academic their sophistication was, how their undamaged eyes were still starry with expectancy,[2] their lips still avidly open for what life would surely bring, then he became envious and awkward with them, like a guest at a party to whose members he carried bad news he had no right to know) no right to tell.

He turned on the ignition[3] and let the humming motor prod him into a decision. He would drop in at Robert Vielum's, where he had dropped in quite often until recently, for the same reason that others stopped by at Vielum's — because there was always likely to be somebody there. The door of Robert's old-fashioned apartment, on Claremont Avenue, almost always opened on a heartening jangle of conversation[4] and music, which meant that others had gathered there, too, to help themselves over the pauses so endemic to university life[5] — the life of the mind — and there were usually several members of Robert's large acquaintance among the sub-literary,[6] quasi-artistic,[7] who had strayed in, ostensibly en route somewhere,[8] and who lingered on hopefully on the chance that in each other's company they might find out what that somewhere was.

Robert was a perennial taker of courses[9] — one of those nonmatri-

---

1) sophisticated bunch: 세련된 집단. bunch=(Colloq.) a group of people.
2) how their undamaged eyes were still starry with expectancy: 그들의 상처 입지 않은 눈이 얼마나 반짝이고 있는가.
3) turn on the ignition: 엔진을 걸다.
4) a heartening jangle of conversation: 마음놓고 떠들며 하는 이야기. jangle=quarrel, dispute.
5) to help themselves over the pauses so endemic to university life: 대학생활에 특유한 휴식시간을 (그들 스스로) 보내기 위해.
6) sub-literary: 얼치기 문인.
7) quasi-artistic: 엉터리 예술인.
8) ostensibly en route somewhere: 분명히 어디로 가는 도중.
9) a perennial taker of conrses: 청강생.

culated students[1] of indefinable age and income, some of whom pursued, with monkish zeal and no apparent regard for time, this or that freakishly peripheral research project of their own conception,[2] and others of whom, like Robert, seemed to derive a Ponce de Léon sustenance from the young.[3] Robert himself, a large man of between forty and fifty, whose small features were somewhat cramped together in a wide face, never seemed bothered by his own lack of direction, implying rather that this was really the catholic approach of the "whole man,"[4] alongside of which the serious pursuit of a degree was somehow foolish, possibly vulgar. Rumor connected him with a rich Boston family that had remittanced him at least as far as New York, but he never spoke about himself, although he was extraordinarily alert to gossip. What ever income he had he supplemented by renting his extra room to a series of young men students. The one opulence among his dun-colored, perhaps consciously Spartan effects[5] was a really fine record-player, which he kept going at all hours with selections from his massive collection. Occasionally he annotated the music, or the advance-copy novel[6] that lay on his table. with foreign-language tags[7] drawn from the wide, if obscure, latitudes of his travels, and it was his magic talent for assuming that his young friends, too, had known, had experienced, that, more than anything, kept them enthralled.[8]

"*Fabelhaft!*[9] Isn't it?" he would say of the Mozart "Remember how they did it that last time at Salzburg!" and they would all sit there. included, belonging, headily remembering the Salzburg to which they had never been. Or he would pick up the novel and lay it down again.

1) non-matriculated students: non-enrolled students 무적학생.
2) this or that freakishly peripheral research project of their own conception: 이것저것 자기 멋대로의 기분적이고 말초적인 연구과제.
3) to derive a Ponce de Léon sustenance from the young: (탐험가) 폰세 데레온과 같은 힘을 젊은이들에게서 끌어내다.
4) the catholic approach of the "whole man": '전인' 형성의 보편적인 방법.
5) effects: personal property; belongings.
6) advance-copy novel: 신간 작품(의 견본).
7) tags: the last line or lines of a song, play, actor's speech, etc.
8) enthralled: fascinated.
9) *Fabelhaft!* : Good!

"*La plume de mon oncle,*[1] I'm afraid. *La plume de mon oncle Gide. Eheu,* poor Gide!" — and they would each make note of the fact that one need not read that particular book, that even, possibly, it was no longer necessary to read Gide.

Peter parked the car and walked into the entrance of Robert's apartment house, smiling to himself, lightened by the prospect of company. After all, he had been weaned on[2] the salon talk of such circles; these self-fancying little bohemias at least made him feel at home. And Robert was cleverer than most — it was amusing to watch him. For just as soon as his satellites[3] thought themselves secure on the promontory of some "trend" he had pointed out to them, they would find that he had deserted them, had gone on to another trend, another eminence, from which he beckoned, cocksure and just faintly concealed some skeleton of a weakness, some closeted Difference with the Authorities, he kept it decently interred.

As Peter stood in the dark, soiled hallway and rang the bell of Robert's apartment, he found himself as suddenly depressed again, unaccountably reminded of his mother. There were so many of them, and they affected you so, these charmers who, if they could not offer you the large strength, could still atone for the lack with so many small decencie s.[4] It was admirable, surely, the way they managed this. And surely, after all, they harmed no one.

Robert opened the door. "Why, hello, Peter!" He seemed surprised, almost relieved. "Greetings!" he added, in a voice whose boom was more in the manner than the substance.[5] "Come in, Pietro, come in!" He wore white linen shorts, a zebra-striped beach shirt, and huaraches, in which he moved easily, leading the way down the dark hall of the apartment, past the two bedrooms, into the living room.

---

1) *La plume de mon oncle:* The book of my uncle.
2) wean on: accustom to.
3) satellites: follower or attendant upon a person of importance.
4) could still atone for the lack with so many small decencies: 여러 가지 조그만 친절을 베풂으로써 부족한 것을 보충할 수 있었다. atone=make up; make amends (for).
5) in a voice whose boom was more in the manner than the substance: 좀 의례적인 목소리로. boom=a deep hollow sound.

All of the apartment was on a court, but on the top floor, so it received a medium, dingy light from above. The living room, long and pleasant, with an old white mantel, a gas log,[1] and many books, always came as a surprise after the rest of the place, and at any time of day Robert kept a few lamps lit, which rouged the room with an evening excitement.

As they entered, Robert reached over in passing and turned on the record-player. Music filled the room, muted but insistent, as if he wanted it to patch up some lull he had left behind. Two young men sat in front of the dead gas log. Between them was a table littered with maps, an open atlas, travel folders, glass beer steins. Vince, the current roomer, had his head on his clenched fists. The other man, a stranger, indolently raised a dark, handsome head as they entered.

"Vince!" Robert spoke sharply. "You know Peter Birge. And this is Mario Osti. Peter Birge."

The dark young man nodded and smiled, lounging in his chair.

Vince nodded. His red-rimmed eyes looked beyond Peter into some distance he seemed to prefer.

"God, isn't it but hot!" Robert said. "I'll get you a beer." He bent over Mario with an inquiring look, a caressing hand on the empty glass in front of him.

Mario stretched back on the chair, smiled upward at Robert, and shook his head sleepily. "Only makes me hotter." He yawned, spread his arms languorously, and let them fall. He had the animal self-possession of the very handsome; it was almost a shock to hear him speak.

Robert bustled off to the kitchen.

"Robert!" Vince called, in his light, pouting voice.

"Get me a drink. Not a beer. A drink." He scratched at the blond stubble on his cheek with a nervous, pointed nail. On his round head and retrousse face,[2] the stubble produced the illusion of a desiccated[3] baby, until, looking closer, one imagined that he might never have

---

1) gas log: 가스 난로(의 둥근 열판).

2) retrousse face: turned up face.

3) desiccated: dried thoroughly.

been one, but might have been spawned[1] at the age he was,[2] to mummify perhaps but not to grow. He wore white shorts exactly like Robert's, and his blue-and-white striped shirt was a smaller version of Robert's brown-and-white, so that the two of them made an ensemble, like the twin outfits the children wore on the beach at Rye.

"You know I don't keep whiskey here." Robert held three steins deftly balanced, his heavy hips neatly avoiding the small tables which scattered the room. "You've had enough, wherever you got it." It was true, Peter remembered, that Robert was fonder of drinks with a flutter of ceremony about *them-cafe brulé,*[3] perhaps, or, in the spring, a *Maibowle,*[4] over which he could chant the triumphant details of his pursuit of the necessary woodruff.[5] But actually one tippled[6] here on the exhilarating effect of wearing one's newest facade,[7] in the fit company of others similarly attired.

Peter picked up his stein. "You and Vince all set for Morocco, I gather."

"Morocco?" Robert took a long pull at his beer. "No. No, that's been changed. I forgot you hadn't been around. Mario's been brushing up[8] my Italian. He and I are off for Rome the day after tomorrow."

The last record on the changer ended in an archaic battery of horns.[9] In the silence while Robert slid on a new batch of records, Peter heard Vince's nail scrape, scrape along his cheek. Still leaning back, Mario shaped smoke with his lips. Large and facilely drawn, they looked, more than anything, accessible — to a stream of smoke, of food, to another mouth, to any plum that might drop.

---

1) spawn: give birth to.
2) might have been spawned at the age he was: 날 때부터 지금 있는 그대로 태어났을지도 모른다.
3) *cafe brulé:* 바싹 태운 커피.
4) *Maibowle:* 독일 칵텔의 일종.
5) the triumphant details of his pursuit of the necessary woodruff: 필요한 선갈퀴(화채용)를 요구하는데 대해 의기양양한 듯 자세하게(떠벌일 수 있었다).
6) tipple: drink (alcoholic liquor) often.
7) on the exhilarating effect of wearing one's newest facade: 새 옷 입는 것을 자랑하며 즐겁게.
8) brush up: refresh one's knowledge.
9) an archaic battery of horns: 옛날풍의 피리 합주(로 끝났다).

"You going to study over there?" Peter said to him.

"Paint." Mario shaped and let drift another corolla of smoke.

"No," Robert said, clicking on the record arm. "I'm afraid Africa's démodé." A harpsichord began to play, its dwarf notes hollow and perfect. Robert raised his voice a shade above the music. "Full of fashion photographers. And little come-lately writers.[1]" He sucked in his cheeks and made a face. "Trying out their passions under the beeg, bad sun."

"*Eheu,* poor Africa?" said Peter.

Robert laughed. Vince stared at him out of wizened eyes. Not drink, so much, after all, Peter decided, looking professionally at the mottled cherub face[2] before he realized that he was comparing it with another face, but lately left. He looked away.

"Weren't you going over, Peter?" Robert leaned against the machine.[3]

"Not this year." Carefully Peter kept out of his voice the knell the words made in his mind. In Greenwich, there were many gravel-led walks, unshrubbed except for the nurses who dotted them, silent and attitudinized as trees. "Isn't that Landowska playing?"

"Hmm. Nice and cooling on a hot day. Or a fevered brow."[4] Robert fiddled with the volume control. The music became louder, then lowered. "Vince wrote a poem about that once. About the Mozart, really, wasn't it, Vince? 'A lovely clock between ourselves and time.'" He enunciated daintily, pushing the words away from him with his tongue.[5]

"Turn it off!" Vince stood up, his small fists clenched, hanging at his sides.

"No, let her finish." Robert turned deliberately and closed the lid of the machine, so that the faint hiss of the needle vanished from the frail, metronomic notes. He smiled. "What a time-obsessed crowd writers are. Now Mario doesn't have to bother with that dimension."

---

1) And little come-lately writers.: 그리고 신진작가들은 적었다.

2) the mottled cherub face: 허물을 벗은 듯한 토실토실한 얼굴.

3) the machine: the record player를 말함.

4) Or a a fevered brow.: Nice and Cooling on a fevered brow. 열이 있는 이마[친구]에게 좋겠다.

5) pushing the words away from him with his tongue: 말을 혀끝으로 굴리면서.

"Not unless I paint portraits." Mario said. His parted lips exposed his teeth, like some white, unexpected flint of intelligence.

"*Dolce far niente,*"[1] Robert said softly. He repeated the phrase dreamily, so that half-known Italian words-"*loggia,*"[2] — the "Ponte Vecchio,"[3] the "Lungarno"[4] — imprinted themselves one by one on Peter's mind, and he saw the two of them, Mario and Roberto now, already in the frayed-gold light of Florence, in the umber dusk of half-imagined towns.

A word, muffled, came out of Vince's throat. He lunged for the record-player. Robert seized his wrist and held it down on the lid. They were locked that way, staring at each other, when the doorbell rang.

"That must be Susan," Robert said. He released Vince and looked down, watching the blood return to his fingers, flexing his palm.

With a second choked sound, Vince flung out his fist in an awkward attempt at a punch.[5] It grazed Robert's cheek, clawing downward. A thin line of red appeared on Robert's cheek. Fist to mouth, Vince stood a moment; then he rushed from the room. They heard the nearer bedroom door slam and the lock click. The bell rang again, a short, hesitant burr.

Robert clapped his hand to his cheek, shrugged, and left the room. Mario got up out of his chair for the first time. "Aren't you going to ask who Susan is?"

"Should I?" Peter leaned away from the face bent confidentially near, curly with glee.

"His daughter," Mario whispered. "He said he was expecting his *daughter.* Can you imagine? *Robert!*"

Peter moved farther away from the mobile, pressing face and, standing at the window, studied the gritty details of the courtyard. A vertical

---

1) *Dolce far niente:* (It.) 무위(無爲)의 즐거움, 안일.
2) *loggia:* (It.) (로지아) 한쪽에 벽이 없는 복도 모양의 양.
3) Ponte Vecchio: 오래된 다리.
4) Lungarno: 아르노강변의 길.
5) flung out his fist in an awkward attempt at a punch: 한 대 치려고 주먹을 서투르게 휘둘렀다.

line of lighted windows, each with a glimpse of stair, marked the hallways on each of the five floors. Most of the other windows were dim and closed, or opened just a few inches above their white ledges, and the yard was quiet. People would be away or out in the sun, or in their brighter front rooms dressing for dinner, all of them avoiding this dark shaft that connected the backs of their lives. Or, here and there, was there someone sitting in the fading light, someone lying on a bed with his face pressed to a pillow? The window a few feet to the right, around the corner of the court, must be the window of the room into which Vince had gone. There was no light in it.

Robert returned, a Kleenex[1)] held against his cheek. With him was a pretty, ruffle-headed girl in a navy-blue dress with a red arrow at each shoulder. He switched on another lamp. For the next arrival, Peter thought, surely he will tug back a velvet curtain or break out with a heraldic flourish of drums,[2)] recorded by Red Seal. Or perhaps the musty wardrobe was opening at last and this was the skeleton —this girl who had just shaken hands with Mario, and now extended her hand toward Peter, tentatively, timidly, as if she did hot habitually shake hands but today would observe every custom she could.

"How do you do?"

"How do you do?" Peter said. The hand he held for a moment was small and childish, the nails unpainted, but the rest of her was very correct for the eye of the beholder, like the young models one sees in magazines, sitting or standing against a column, always in three-quarter view, so that the picture the ensemble, will not be marred by the human glance. Mario took from her a red dressing case that she held in her free hand, bent to pick up a pair of white gloves that she had dropped, and returned them with an avid interest which over-balanced, like a waiter's gallantry. She sat down, brushing at the gloves.

"The train was awfully dusty—and crowded." She smiled tightly at Robert, looked hastily and obliquely at each of the other two, and

---

1) Kleenex: 부드러운 인조직물의 손수건 (상표명).

2) break ont with a heraldic flourish of drums: 요란한 북소리로 시작하다. break out=begin; start.

bent over the gloves, brushing earnestly, stopping as if someone had said something, and, when no one did, brushing again.

"Well, well, well" Robert said. His manners, always good, were never so to the point of clichés,[1] which would be for him what nervous *gaffes*[2] were for other people. He coughed, rubbed his cheek with the back of his hand, looked at the hand, and stuffed the Kleenex into the pocket of his shorts. "How was camp?"

Mario's eyebrows went up. The girl was twenty, surely, Peter thought.

"All right," she said. She gave Robert the stiff smile again and looked down into her lap. "I like helping children. They can use it." Her hands folded on top of the gloves, then inched under and hid beneath them.

"Susan's been counselling at a camp which broke up[3] early because of a polio scare," Robert said as he sat down. "She's going to use Vince's room while I'm away, until college opens."

"Oh — " She looked up at Peter. "Then you aren't Vince?" "No. I just dropped in. I'm Peter Birge?"

She gave him a neat nod of acknowledgement. "I'm glad, because I certainly wouldn't want to inconvenience — "

"Did you get hold of your mother in Reno?" Robert asked quickly.

"Not yet. But she couldn't break up her residence term anyway. And Arthur must have closed up the house here. The phone was disconnected."

"Arthur's Susan's stepfather," Robert explained with a little laugh. "Number three, I think. Or is it *jour,* Sue?"

Without moving, she seemed to retreat, so that again there was nothing left for the observer except the girl against the column, anyone of a dozen with the short, anonymous nose, the capped hair, the foot arched in the trim shoe, and half an iris glossed with an expertly aimed photoflood.[4] "Three," she said. Then one of the hidden hands stole

1) were never so to the point of clichés: 몹시 상투적인 진부한 태도였었다.
2) *gaffes:* blunder. 실수, 과실, 실언.
3) break up: put an end to; stop.
4) half an iris glossed with an expertly aimed photoflood: 능숙하게 비쳐진 사진 플래시를 받아 반짝이는 눈동자의 반.

out from under the gloves, and she began to munch evenly on a fingernail.

"Heavens, you haven't still got that *habit!*" Robert said. "What a heavy papa you make, Roberto," Mario said.

She flushed, and put the hand back in her lap, tucking the fingers under. She looked from Peter to Mario and back again. "Then you're not Vince," she said. "I didn't think you were."

The darkness increased around the lamps. Behind Peter, the court had become brisk with lights, windows sliding up, and the taps running.

"Guess Vince fell asleep. I'd better get him up and send him on his way." Robert shrugged, and rose.

"Oh, don't! I wouldn't want to be an inconvenience," the girl said, with a polite terror which suggested she might often have been on.

"On the contrary." Robert spread his palms, with a smile, and walked down the hall. They heard him knocking on a door, then his indistinct voice.

In the triangular silence, Mario stepped past Peter and slid the window up softly. He leaned out to listen, peering sidewise at the window to the right. As he was pulling himself back in, he looked down. His hands stiffened on the ledge. Very slowly he pulled himself all the way in and stood up. Behind him a tin ventilator clattered inward and fell to the floor. In the shadowy lamplight his too classic face was like marble which moved numbly. He swayed a little, as if with vertigo.[1)]

"I'd better get out of here!"

They heard his heavy breath as he dashed from the room. The slam of the outer door blended with Robert's battering, louder now, on the door down the hall.

"What's down there?" She was beside Peter, otherwise he could not have heard her. They took hands, like strangers met on a narrow footbridge or on one of those steep places where people cling together more for anchorage against their own impulse than for balance. Carefully they leaned out over the sill. Yes—it was down there, the shirt, zebra-

---

1) as if with vertigo: 현기증이 난 것처럼. vertigo=dizziness; giddiness.

striped, just decipherable on the merged shadow of the courtyard below.

Carefully, as if they were made of eggshell, as if by some guarded movement they could still rescue themselves from disaster, they drew back and straightened up. Robert, his face askew with the impossible question, was behind them.

After this, there was the hubbub[1] — the ambulance from St. Luke's,[2] the prowl car, the two detectives from the precinct station house, and finally the "super,"[3] a vague man with the grub pallor and shamble of those who live in basements. He pawed over the keys on the thong around his wrist and, after several tries, opened the bedroom door. It was quiet, unviolent room with a tossed bed and an open window, with a stagy significance acquired only momentarily in the minds of those who gathered in a group at its door.

Much later, after midnight, Peter and Susan sat in the bald glare of an all-night restaurant. With hysterical eagerness, Robert had gone on to the station house with the two detectives to register the salient facts, to help ferret out[4] the relatives in Ohio, to arrange, in fact, anything that might still be arrangeable about Vince. Almost without noticing, he had acquiesced in[5] Peter's proposal to look after Susan. Susan herself, after silently watching the gratuitous burbling of her father, as if it were a phenomenon she could neither believe nor leave, had followed Peter without comment. At his suggestion, they had stopped off at the restaurant on their way to her stepfather's house, for which she had a key.

"Thanks. I was starved." She leaned back and pushed at the short bang of hair on her forehead.

"Hadn't you eaten at all?"

"Just those pasty sandwiches they sell on the train. There wasn't any diner."

"Smoke?"

---

1) hubbub: a noisy tumult; uproar.
2) St. Lukes: 성 누가 병원.
3) "super": 감독.
4) ferret out: 찾아내다, 수색하다.
5) acquiesce in: (계획, 제안)을 잠자코 받아들이다.

"I do, but I'm just too tired. I can get into a hotel all right, don't you think? If I can't get in at Arthur's?"

"I know the manager of a small one near us," Peter said. "But if you don't mind coming to my place, you can use my mother's room for tonight. Or for as long as you need, probably."

"What about your mother?"

"She's away. She'll be away for quite a while."

"Not in Reno, by any chance?" There was a roughness, almost a coarseness, in her tone, like that in the overdone camaraderie of the shy.[1)]

"No. My father died when I was eight. Why?"

"Oh, something in the way you spoke. And then you're so competent. Does she work?"

"No. My father left something. Does yours?"

She stood up and picked up her bedraggled gloves. "No," she said, and her voice was suddenly distant and delicate again. "She marries." She turned and walked out ahead of him.

He paid, rushed out of the restaurant, and caught up with her.

"Thought maybe you'd run out on me," he said.

She got in the car without answering.

They drove through the Park, toward the address in the East Seventies that she had given him. A weak smell of grass underlay the gas-blended air, but the Park seemed limp and worn, as if the strain of the day's effluvia had been too much for it. At the Seventy-second Street stop signal, the blank light of a street lamp invaded the car.

"Thought you might be feeling Mrs. Grundyish[2)] at my suggesting the apartment,"[3)] Peter said.

"Mrs. Grundy wasn't around much when I grew up."[4)] The signal

1) in the overdone camaraderie of the shy: 수줍어하는 사람의 지나친 우정에서의. camaraderie=comradeship.

2) Mrs. Grundyish: Mrs. Grundy 세상평판. Thomas Morton의 희극 중의 인물로부터 생긴 말.

3) Thought you might be feeling Mrs. Grundyish at my suggesting the apartment: 제가 방을 쓰셔도 좋다고 했을 때 사람들이 뭐랄까 염려했다.

4) Mrs. Grundy wasn't around much when I grew up.: 평판 따위는 별로 개의치 않고 자랐다.

changed and they moved ahead.

They stopped in a street which had almost no lights along its smartly converted house fronts. This was one of the streets, still sequestered by money, whose houses came alive only under the accelerated, febrile glitter of winter and would dream through the gross summer days, their interiors deadened with muslin or stirred faintly with the subterranean clinkings of caretakers.[1] No.4 wasdark.

"I would rather stay over at your place, if I have to," the girl said. Her voice was offhand and prim. "I hate hotels. We always stopped at them in between."

"Let's get out and see."

They stepped down into the areaway in front of the entrance, the car door banging hollowly behind them. She fumbled in her purse and took out a key, although it was already obvious that it would not be usable. In his childhood, he had often hung around in the areaways of old brownstones such as this had been.[2] In the corners there had always been a soft, decaying smell, and the ironwork, bent and smeared, always hung loose and brokentoothed. The areaway of this house had been repaved with slippery flag; even in the humid night there was no smell. Black-tongued grillwork, with an oily shine and padlocked, secured the windows and the smooth door. Fastened on the grillwork in front of the door was the neat, square proclamation of a protection agency.[3]

"You don't have a key for the padlocks, do you?"

"No." She stood on the curb, looking up at the house. "It was a nice room I had there. Nicest one I ever did have, really." She crossed to the car and got in.

He followed her over to the car and got in beside her. She had her head in her hands.

---

1) stirred faintly with the subterranean clinkings of caretakers: 집지기의 딸그락거리는 소리가 지하실에서 희미하게 들려 왔다. subterranean=underground. caretaker =person who takes care of a place.

2) hung around in the areaways of old brownstons such as this had been: 이와 비슷한 갈색 사암(砂岩)으로 지은 지하출입구 주위를 배회했다.

3) the neat, square proclamation of a protection agency: 보호하는 힘이 있다는 것을 간단명료하게 선언하는 것(이었다).

"I don't. I don't care about any of it, really." She sat up, her face averted. "My parents, or any of the people they tangle with." She wound the lever on the door slowly, then reversed it. "Robert, or my mother, or Arthur," she said, "although he was always pleasant enough. Even Vince — even if I'd known him."

"He was just a screwed-up kid.[1] It could have been anybody's window."

"No." Suddenly she turned and faced him. "I should think it would be the best privilege there is, though. To care, I mean."

When he did not immediately reply, she gave him a little pat on the arm and sat back. "Excuse it, please. I guess I'm groggy."[2] She turned around and put her head on the crook of her arm. Her words came faintly through it. "Wake me when we get there."

She was asleep by the time they reached his street. He parked the car as quietly as possible beneath his own windows. He himself had never felt more awake in his life. He could have sat there until morning with her sleep-secured beside him. He sat thinking of how different it would be at Rye, or anywhere, with her along, with someone along who was the same age. For they were the same age, whatever that was, whatever the age was of people like them. There was nothing he would be unable to tell her.

To the north, above the rooftops, the electric mauve of midtown blanked out any auguries in the sky,[3] but he wasn't looking for anything like that. Tomorrow he would take her for a drive — whatever the weather. There were a lot of good roads around Greenwich.

---

1) a screwed-up kid: a spolied [ruined, confused) kid. 비뚤어진 놈.

2) groggy: drunk; intoxicated.

3) the electric mauve of midtown blanked out any auguries in the sky: 도심지의 자주빛 전깃불이 불타올라 하늘마저 물들게 하여 아무런 징조도 점칠 수 없었다. augury=indication; sign; omen.

Torch Song

by John Cheever

John Cheever(1912-), born in Quiney, Massachusetts, left home at the age of seventeen after his expulsion from the Thayer Academy at South Braintree, Massachusetts. Since then, except for service in the army and teaching in the English Department of Barnard, his career has been devoted to his writing. A large number of his short stories have appeared in *The New Yorker.*

Cheever defends middle-class suburbia as the setting for many of his short stories by saying, "Life can be as good and rich there as anyplace else." Although set in Italy, even *Some People, Places, and Things That Will Not Appear in My Next Novel.* according to one critic, has as characters "the same bewildered suburbanites" that appear in his other works.

AFTER JACK Lorey had known Joan Harris in New York for a few years, he began to think of her as The Widow. She always wore black, and he was always given the feeling, by a cunous disorder in her apartment, that the undertakers had just left. This impression did not stem from malice on his part, for he was fond of Joan. They came from the same city in Ohio and had reached New York at about the same time in the middle thirties. They were the same age, and during their first summer in the city they used to meet after work and drink Martinis[1] in places like the Brevoort and Charles', and have dinner and play checkers[2] at the Lafayette.

Joan went to a school for models when she settled in the city, but it turned out that she photographed badly, so after spending six weeks learning how to walk with a book on her head she got a job as a hostess in a Longchamps. For the rest of the summer she stood by the hatrack, bathed in an intense pink light and the string music of

1) Martini(s): a cocktail containing gin and dry vermouth.

2) checkers: game played on a checkerboard by two people. Each player has 12 round, flat pieces to move.

heartbreak, swinging her mane of dark hair and her black skirt as she moved forward to greet the customers. She was then a big, handsome girl with a wonderful voice, and her face, her whole presence, always seemed infused with a gentle and healthy pleasure at her surroundings, whatever they were. She was innocently and incorrigibly convivial,[1] and would get out of bed and dress at three in the morning if someone called her and asked her to come out for a drink, as Jack often did. In the fall, she got some kind of freshman executive job in a department store. They saw less and less of each other and then for quite a while stopped seeing each other altogether. Jack was living with a girl he had met at a party, and it never occurred to him to wonder what had become of Joan.

Jack's girl had some friends in Pennsylvania, and in the spring and summer of his second year in town he often went there with her for weekends. All of this — the shared apartment in the Village, the illicit relationship,[2] the Friday-night train to a country house — were what he had imagined life in New York to be, and he was intensely happy. He was returning to New York with his girl one Sunday night on the Lehigh line. It was one of those trains that move slowly across the face of New Jersey, bringing back to the city hundreds of people, like the victims of an immense and strenuous picnic,[3] whose faces are blazing and whose muscles are lame.[4] Jack and his girl, like most of the other passengers, were overburdened with vegetables and flowers. When the train stopped in Pennsylvania Station, they moved with the crowd along the platform, toward the escalator. As they were passing the wide, lighted windows of the diner,[5] Jack turned his head and saw Joan. It was the first time he had seen her since Thanksgiving, or since Christmas. He couldn't remember.

Joan was with a man who had obviously passed out.[6] His head

---

1) convivial: fond of eating and drinking with friends.
2) the illicit relationship: forbidden, improper relation 위법적인 관계.
3) like the victims of an immense and strenuous picnic: 굉장히 고된 피크닉에 지쳐 버린 사람들처럼.
4) lame: stiff and sore.
5) diner: a railroad car in which meals are served.
6) pass out: (Colloq.) faint; lose consciousness.

was in his arms on the table, and an overturned highball[1] glass was near one of his elbows. Joan was shaking his shoulders gently and speaking to him. She seemed to be vaguely troubled, vaguely amused. The waiters had cleared off all the other tables and were standing around Joan, waiting for her to resurrect her escort.[2]

It troubled Jack to see in these straits a girl who reminded him of the trees and the lawns of his home town, but there was nothing he could do to help. Joan continued to shake the man's shoulders, and the crowd pressed Jack past one after another of the diner's windows, past the malodorous kitchen, and up the escalator.

He saw Joan again, later that summer, when he was having dinner in a Village restaurant. He was with a new girl, a Southerner. There were many Southern girls in the city that year. Jack and his belle[3] had wandered into the restaurant because it was convenient, but the food was terrible and the place was lighted with candles. Halfway through dinner, Jack noticed Joan on the other side of the room, and when he had finished eating, he crossed the room and spoke to her. She was with a tall man who was wearing a monocle. He stood, bowed stiffly from the waist, and said to Jack, "We are very pleased to meet you." Then he excused himself and headed for[4] the toilet. "He's a count, he'sa Swedish count," Joan said. "He's on the radio, Friday afternoons at four-fifteen. Isn't it exciting?" She seemed to be delighted with the count and the terrible restaurant.

Sometime the next winter, Jack moved from the Village to an apartment in the East Thirties. He was crossing Park A venue one cold morning on his way to the office when he noticed, in the crowd, a woman he had met a few times at Joan's apartment. He spoke to her and asked about his friend. "Haven't you heard?" she said. She pulled a long face. "Perhaps I'd better tell you. Perhaps you can help." She and Jack had breakfast in a drugstore on Madison Avenue and

1) highball: whiskey, brandy, etc., mixed with soda water or ginger ale and served with ice in a tall glass.
2) to resurrect her escort: to bring her escort back to life.
3) belle: a beautiful woman or girl.
4) head for: move toward.

she unburdened herself of the story.[1]

The count had a program called "The Song of the Fiords," or something like that, and he sang Swedish folk songs. Everyone suspected him of being a fake, but that didn't bother Joan. He had met her at a party and, sensing a soft touch,[2] had moved in with her the following night. About a week later, he complained of pains in his back and said he must have some morphine. Then he needed morphine all the time. If he didn't get morphine, he was abusive and violent. Joan began to deal with those doctors and druggists who peddle dope,[3] and when they wouldn't supply her, she went down to the bottom of the city. Her friends were afraid she would be found some morning stuffed in a drain. She got pregnant. She had an abortion. The count left her and moved to a flea bag[4] near Times Square, but she was so impressed by then with his helplessness, so afraid that he would die without her, that she followed him there and shared his room and continued to buy his narcotics. He abandoned her again, and Joan waited a week for him to return before she went back to her place and her friends in the Village.

It shocked Jack to think of the innocent girl from Ohio having lived with a brutal dope addict[5] and traded with criminals, and when he got to his office that morning, he telephoned her and made a date for dinner that night. He met her at Charles'. When she came into the bar, she seemed as wholesome and calm as ever.

Her voice was sweet, and reminded him of elms, of lawns, of those glass arrangements that used to be hung from porch ceilings to tinkle in the summer wind. She told him about the count. She spoke of him charitably and with no trace of bitterness, as if her voice, her disposition, were incapable of registering anything beyond simple affection and pleasure. Her walk, when she moved ahead of him toward their table, was light and graceful. She ate a large dinner and talked

---

1) unburdened herself of the story: relieved her mind by talking the story.
2) sensing a soft touch: 부드러운 감촉을 느끼자.
3) dope: (Slang) a harmful, narcotic drug, such as opium, morphine, etc.
4) flea bag: 빈민굴.
5) dope addict: a person who is a slave to a dope; opium-eater.

enthusiastically about her job. They went to a movie and said goodbye in front of her apartment house.

That winter, Jack met a girl he decided to marry. Their engagement was announced in January and they planned to marry in July. In the spring, he received, in his office mail, an invitation to cocktails at Joan's. It was for a Saturday when his financee was going to Massachusetts to visit her parents, and when the time came and he had nothing better to do, he took a bus to the Village. Joan had the same apartment. It was a walk up.[1] You rang the bell above the mailbox in the vestibule[2] and were answered with a death rattle in the lock. Joan lived on the third floor. Her calling card was in a slot on the mailbox, and above her name was written the name Hugh Bascomb.

Jack climbed the two flights of carpeted stairs, and when he reached Joan's apartment, she was standing by the open door in a black dress. After she greeted Jack, she took his arm and guided him across the room. "I want you to meet. Hugh, Jack," she said.

Hugh was a big man with a red face and pale-blue eyes. His manner was courtly and his eyes were inflamed with drink. Jack talked with him for a little while and then went over to speak to someone he knew, who was standing by the mantelpiece. He noticed then, for the first time, the indescribable disorder of Joan's apartment. The books were in their shelves and the furniture was reasonably good, but the place was all wrong, somehow. It was as if things had been put in place without thought or real interest, and for the first time, too, he had the impressian that there had been a death there recently.

As Jack moved around the room, he felt that he had met the ten or twelve guests at other parties. There was a woman executive with a fancy hat, a man who could imitate Roosevelt, a grim couple whose play was in rehearsal, and a newspaperman who kept turning on the radio for news of the Spanish Civil War. Jack drank Martinis and talked with the woman in the fancy hat. He looked out of the window at the back yards and the ailanthus trees and heard, in the distance,

1) walk up: an apartment house or building having no elevator.

2) vestibule: passage or hall between the outer door and the inside of a building.

thunder exploding off the cliffs of the Hudson.

Hugh Bascomb got very drunk. He began to spill liquor, as if drinking, for him, were a kind of jolly slaughter and he enjoyed the bloodshed and the mess. He spilled whiskey from a bottle. He spilled a drink on his shirt and then tipped over someone else's drink. The party was not quiet, but Hugh's hoarse voice began to dominate the others. He attacked a photographer who was sitting in a corner explaining camera techniques to a homely woman. "What did you come to the party for if all you wanted to do was to sit there and stare at your shoes?" Hugh shouted. "What did you come for? Why don't you stay at home?"

The photographer didn't know what to say. He was not staring at his shoes. Joan moved lightly to Hugh's side. "Please don't get into a fight now, darling," she said. "Not this afternoon."

"Shut up," he said. "Let me alone. Mind your own business."

He lost his balance, and in struggling to steady himself he tipped over a lamp.

"Oh, your lovely lamp, Joan," a woman sighed.

"Lamps!" Hugh roared. He threw his arms into the air and worked them around his head as if he were bludgeoning[1] himself. "Lamps. Glasses. Cigarette boxes. Dishes. They're killing me. They're killing me, for Christ's sake. Let's all go up to the mountains, for Christ's sake. Let's all go up to the mountains and hunt and fish and live like men, for Christ's sake."

People were scattering as if a rain had begun to fall in the room.

It had, as a matter of fact, begun to rain outside. Someone offered Jack a ride uptown,[2] and he jumped at the chance. Joan stood at the door, saying goodbye to her routed friends. Her voice remained soft, and her manner, unlike that of those Christian women who in the face of disaster can summon new and formidable sources of composure,[3] seemed genuinely simple. She appeared to be oblivious

1) bludgeon: strike with a club; bully; threaten.

2) a ride uptown: a ride to the upper part of a town. uptown=the fashion-able or residential area of a city or town.

3) can summon new and formidable sources of composure: 무서운 침착성을 새로이 불러일으킬 수 있는.

of the raging drunk at her back, who was pacing up and down, grinding glass into the rug, and haranguing[1] one of the survivors of the party with a story of how he, Hugh, had once gone without food for three weeks.

In July, Jack was married in an orchard in Duxbury, and he and his wife went to West Chop for a few weeks. When they returned to town, their apartment was cluttered with presents, including a dozen after-dinner coffee cups from Joan. His wife sent her the required note,[2] but they did nothing else.

Later in the summer, Joan telephoned Jack at his office and asked if he wouldn't bring his wife to see her; she named an evening the following week. He felt guilty about not having called her, and accepted the invitation. This made his wife angry. She was an ambitious girl who liked a social life that offered rewards, and she went unwillingly to Joan's Village apartment with him.

Written above Joan's name on the mailbox was the name Franz Denzel. Jack and his wife climbed the stairs and were met by Joan at the open door. They went into her apartment and found themselves among a group of people for whom Jack, at least, was unable to find any bearings.[3]

Franz Denzel was a middle-aged German. His face was pinched with bitterness or illness. He greeted Jack and his wife with that elaborate and clever politeness that is intended to make guests feel that they have come too early or too late. He insisted sharply upon Jack's sitting in the chair in which he himself had been sitting, and then went and sat on a radiator. There were five other Germans sitting around the room, drinking coffee. In a corner was another American couple, who looked uncomfortable. Joan passed Jack and his wife small cups of coffee with whipped cream. "These cups belonged to Franz's mother," she said. "Aren't they lovely? They were the only things he took from Germany when he escaped from the Nazis."

---

1) harangue: *(n.)* a noisy speech; a long, pompous speech; *(v.)* deliver a harangue; address in a harangue.
2) the required note: 사랫장.
3) bearings: relation; reference.

Franz turned to Jack and said, "Perhaps you will give us your opinion on the American educational system. That is what we were discussing when you arrived."

Before Jack could speak, one of the German guests opened an attack on the American educational system. The other Germans joined in. and went on from there to describe every vulgarity that had impressed them in American life and to contrast German and American culture generally. Where, they asked one another passionately, could you find in America anything like the Mitropa dining cars,[1)] the Black Forest,[2)] the pictures in Munich,[3)] the music in Bayreuth? Franz and his friends began speaking in German. Neither Jack nor his wife nor Joan could understand German, and the other American couple had not opened their mouths since they were introduced. Joan went happily around the room, filling everyone's cup with coffee, as if the music of a foreign language were enough to make an evening for her.

Jack drank five cups of coffee. He was desperately uncomfortable. Joan went into the kitchen while the Germans were laughing at their German jokes, and he hoped she would return with some drinks, but when she came back, it was with a tray of ice cream and mulberries.

"Isn't this pleasant?" Franz asked, speaking in English again.

Joan collected the coffee cups, and as she was about to take them back to the kitchen, Franz stopped her.

"Isn't one of those cups chipped?"

"No, darling," Joan said. "I never let the maid touch them. I wash them myself."

"What's that?" he asked, pointing at the rim of one of the cups.

"That's the cup that's always been chipped, darling. It was chipped when you unpacked it. You noticed it then."

"These things were perfect when they arrived in this country," he said.

Joan went into the kitchen and he followed her.

Jack tried to make conversation with the Germans. From the kitchen

1) Mitropa dining cars: 미트로파 식당차.

2) Black Forest: mountains covered with forests in SW Germany.

3) Munich: city in SW Germany.

there was the sound of a blow and a cry. Franz returned and began to eat his mulberries greedily. Joan came back with her dish of ice cream. Her voice was gentle. Her tears, if she had been crying, had dried as quickly as the tears of a child. Jack and his wife finished their ice cream and made their escape. The wasted and unnerving evening enraged Jack's wife, and he supposed that he would never see Joan again.

Jack's wife got pregnant early in the fall, and she seized on all the prerogatives[1] of an expectant mother. She took long naps, ate canned peaches in the middle of the night, and talked about the rudimentary kidney. She chose to see only other couples who were expecting children, and the parties that she and Jack gave were temperate. The baby, a boy, was born in May, and Jack was very proud and happy. The first party he and his wife went to after her convalescence was the wedding of a girl whose family Jack had known in Ohio.

The wedding was at St. James', and afterward there was a big reception at the River Club. There was an orchestra dressed like Hungarians, and a lot of champagne and Scotch. Toward the end of the afternoon, Jack was walking down a dim corridor when he heard Joan's voice. "Please don't, darling," she was saying. "You'll break my arm. *Please* don't, darling." She was being pressed against the wall by a man who seemed to be twisting her arm. As soon as they saw Jack, the struggle stopped. All three of them were intensely embarrassed. Joan's face was wet and she made an effort to smile through her tears at Jack. He said hello and went on without stopping. When he returned, she and the man had disappeared.

When Jack's son was less than two years old, his wife flew with the baby to Nevada to get a divorce. Jack gave her the apartment and all its furnishings and took a room in a hotel near Grand Central. His wife got her decree in due course,[2] and the story was in the newspapers. Jack had a telephone call from Joan a few days later.

"I'm awfully sorry to hear about your divorce, Jack," she said. "She seemed like *such* a nice girl. But that wasn't what I called you about.

1) prerogative: right or priviledge that nobody else has.

2) got her decree in due course: 적당히 수속을 밟아 이혼 소송의 판결을 받았다.

I want your help, and I wonder? if you could come down to my place tonight around six. It's something I don't want to talk about over the phone."

He went obediently to the Village that night and climbed the stairs. Her apartment was a mess. The pictures and the curtains were down and the books were in boxes. "You moving, Joan?" he asked.

"That's what I wanted to see you about, Jack. First, I'll give you a drink." She made two Old-Fashioneds.1) "I'm being evicted, Jack," she said. "I'm being evicted2) because I'm an immoral woman. The couple who have the apartment downstairs — they're charming people, I've always thought — have told the real-estate agent that I'm a drunk and a prostitute and all kinds of things. Isn't that fantastic? This real-estate agent has always been so nice to me that I didn't think he'd believe them, but he's cancelled my lease, and if I make any trouble, he's threatened to take the matter up with the store, and I don't want to lose my job. This nice real-estate agent won't even talk with me any more. When I go over to the office, the receptionist leers at3) me as if I were some kind of dreadful woman. Of course, there have been a lot of men here and we sometimes are noisy, but I can't be expected to go to bed at ten every night. Can I? Well, the agent who manages this building has apparently told all the other agents in the neighborhood that I'm an immoral and drunken woman, and none of them will give me an apartment. I went in to talk with one man — he seemed to be such a nice old gentleman — and he made me an indecent proposal. Isn't it fantastic? I have to be out of here on Thursday and I'm literally being turned out into the street."

Joan seemed as serene and innocent as ever while she described this scourge of agents and neighbors. Jack listened carefully for some sign of indignation or bitterness or even urgency in her recital, but there was none. He was reminded of a torch song, of one of those forlorn and touching ballads4) that had been sung neither for him nor

1) Old Fashioneds: 술 이름.
2) evict: expel by a legal process from land, a building, etc.
3) leer at: give a sly sidelong look at; glance evilly at.
4) one of those forlorn and touching ballads: 쓸쓸하고도 심금을 울리는 민요의 한 가락.

for her but for their older brothers and sisters by Marion Harris. Joan seemed to be singing her wrongs.

"They've made my life miserable," she went on quietly. "If I keep the radio on after ten o'clock, they telephone the agent in the morning and tell him I had some kind of orgy[1] here. One night when Phillip — I don't think you've met Phillip; he's in the Royal Air Force; he's gone back to England — one night when Phillip and some other people were here, they called the police. The police came bursting in the door and talked to me as if I were I don't know what and then looked in the bedroom. If they think there's a man up here after midnight, they call me on the telephone and say all kinds of disgusting things. Of course, I can put my furniture into storage and go to a hotel, I guess. I guess a hotel will take a woman with my kind of reputation, but I thought perhaps you might know of an apartment. I thought —"

It angered Jack to think of this big, splendid girl's being persecuted by her neighbors, and he said he would do what he could. He asked her to have dinner with him, but she said she was busy.

Having nothing better to do, Jack decided to walk uptown to his hotel. It was a hot night. The sky was overcast.[2] On his way, he saw a parade in a dark side street off Broadway near Madison Square. All the buildings in the neighborhood were dark. It was so dark that he could not see the placards the marchers carried until he came to a street light. Their signs urged the entry of the United States into the war, and each platoon represented a nation that had been subjugated by the Axis powers.[3] They marched up Broadway, as he watched, to no music, to no sound but their own steps on the rough cobbles. It was for the most part an army of elderly men and women — Poles, Norwegians, Danes, Jews, Chinese. A few idle people like himself lined the sidewalks, and the marchers passed between them with all the self-consciousness of enemy prisoners. There were children among

---

1) orgy: a wild, drunken revel.
2) overcast: cloudy; dark; gloomy.
3) the Axis powers: Germany, Italy, Japan and their allies, before the end of World War II.

them dressed in the costumes in which they had, for the newsreels,[1] presented the Mayor with a package of tea, a petition, a protest, a constitution, a check, or a pair of tickets. They hobbled through the darkness of the loft neighborhood like a mortified and destroyed people, toward Greeley Square.

In the morning, Jack put the problem of finding an apartment for Joan up to his secretary. She started phoning real-estate agents, and by afternoon she had found a couple of available apartments in the West Twenties. Joan called Jack the next day to say that she had taken one of the apartments and to thank him.

Jack didn't see Joan again until the following summer. It was a Sunday evening; he had left a cocktail party in a Washington Square apartment and had decided to walk a few blocks up Fifth Avenue before he took a bus. As he was passing the Brevoort, Joan called to him. She was with a man at one of the tables on the sidewalk. She looked cool and fresh, and the man appeared to be respectable. His name, it turned out, was Pete Bristol. He invited Jack to sit down and join in a celebration. Germany had invaded Russia that weekend, and Joan and Pete were drinking champagne to celebrate Russia's changed position in the war. The three of them drank champagne until it got dark. They had dinner and drank champagne with their dinner. They drank more champagne afterward and then went over to the Lafayette and then to two or three other places. Joan had always been tireless in her gentle way. She hated to see the night end, and it was after three o'clock when Jack stumbled into his apartment. The following morning he woke up haggard and sick, and with no recollection of the last hour or so of the previous evening. His suit was soiled and he had lost his hat. He didn't get to his office until eleven. Joan had already called him twice, and she called him again soon after he got in. There was no hoarseness at all in her voice. She said that she had to see him, and he agreed to meet her for lunch in a sea-food restaurant in the Fifties.

He was standing at the bar when she breezed[2] in, looking as though

1) for the newsreels: to take a motion picture showing current event.

2) breeze: (Colloq.) proceed easily or briskly.

she had taken no part in that calamitous[1] night. The advice she wanted concerned selling her jewelry. Her grandmother had left her some jewelry, and she wanted to raise money on it but didn't know where to go. She took some rings and bracelets out of her purse and showed them to Jack. He said that he didn't know anything about jewelry but that he could lend her some money. "Oh, I couldn't brorrow money from you, Jack," she said. "You see I want to get the money for Pete. I want to help him. He wants to open an advertising agency, and he needs quite a lot to begin with." Jack didn't press her to accept his offer of a loan after that, and the project wasn't mentioned again during lunch.

He next heard about Joan from a young doctor who was a friend of theirs. "Have you seen Joan recently?" the doctor asked Jack one evening when they were having dinner together. He said no. "I gave her a checkup last week," the doctor said, "and while she's been through enough to kill the average mortal[2] — and you'll never know what she's been through — she still has the constitution of a virtuous and healthy woman. Did you hear about the last one? She sold her jewelry to put him into some kind of a business, and as soon as he got the money, he left her for another girl, who had a car — a convertible"[3]

Jack was drafted into the Army in the spring of 1942. He was kept at Fort Dix for nearly a month, and during this time he came to New York in the evening whenever he could get permission. Those nights had for him the intense keenness of a reprieve, a sensation that was heightened by the fact that on the train in from Trenton[4] women would often press upon him dog-eared copies[5] of *Life* and half-eaten boxes of candy, as though the brown clothes he wore were surely cerements.[6] He telephoned Joan from Pennsylvania Station one night. "Come right over, Jack," she said. "Come right over. I want you to

1) calamitous: disastrous.
2) while she's been through enough to kill the average mortal: 보통 사람 같으면 죽었을 그런 고비를 겪었는데도.
3) convertible: automobile with a folding top.
4) Trenton: capital of New Jersey, in the W part.
5) dog-eared copies: folded down the corner of a book.
6) cerements: cloth or garment.

meet Ralph."

She was living in that place in the West Twenties that Jack had found for her. The neighborhood was a slum. Ash cans stood in front of her house, and an old woman was there picking out bits of refuse[1) and garbage and stuffing them into a perambulator. The house in which Joan's apartment was located was shabby, but the apartment itself seemed familiar. The furniture was the same. Joan was the same big, easy-going girl. "I'm so glad you called me," she said. "It's so good to see you. I'll make you a drink. I was having one myself. Ralph ought to be here by now. He promised to take me to dinner." Jack offered to take her to Cavanagh's, but she said that Ralph might come while she was out. "If he doesn't come by nine, I'm going to make myself a sandwich. I'm not really hungry."

Jack talked about the Army. She talked about the store. She had been working in the same place for — how long was it? He didn't know. He had never seen her at her desk and he couldn't imagine what she did. "I'm terribly sorry Ralph isn't here," she said. "I'm sure you'd like him. He's not a young man. He's a heart specialist who loves to play the viola." She turned on some lights, for the summer sky had got dark. "He has this dreadful wife on Riverside Drive and four ungrateful children. He — "

The noise of an air-raid siren, lugubrious and seeming to spring from pain, as if all the misery and indecision in the city had been given a voice, cut her off.[2) Other sirens, in distant neighborhoods, sounded, until the dark air was full of their noise. "Let me fix you another drink before I have to turn out the lights," Joan said, and took his glass. She brought the drink back to him and snapped off the lights. They went to the windows, and, as children watch a thunderstorm, they watched the city darken. All the lights nearby went out but one. Air-raid wardens had begun to sound their whistles in the street. From a distant yard came a hoarse shriek of anger. "Put out your lights, you Fascists!" a woman screamed. "Put out your lights,

1) refuse: useless stuff; waste; rubbish.

2) The noise... cut her off. =She stopped suddenly by the noise of an air-raid siren, ...

you Nazi Fascist Germans. Turn out your lights. Turn out your lights." The last light went off. They went away from the window and sat in the lightless room.

In the darkness, Joan began to talk about her departed lovers, and from what she said Jack gathered that they had all had a hard time. Nils, the suspect count, was dead. Hugh Bascomb, the drunk, had joined the Merchant Marine and was missing in the North Atlantic. Franz, the German, had taken poison the night the Nazis bombed Warsaw. "We listened to the news on the radio," Joan said, "and then he went back to his hotel and took poison. The maid found him dead in the bathroom the next morning." When Jack asked her about the one who was going to open an advertising agency, she seemed at first to have forgotten him. "Oh, Pete," she said after a pause. "Well, he was always very sick, you know. He was supposed to go to Saranac, but he kept putting it off[1] and putting it off and — " She stopped talking when she heard steps on the stairs, hoping, he supposed, that it was Ralph, but whoever it was turned at the landing and continued to the top of the house. "I wish Ralph would come," she said, with a sigh. "I want you to meet him." Jack asked her again to go out, but she refused, and when the all-clear[2] sounded, he said goodbye.

Jack was shipped from Dix to an infantry training camp in the Carolinas and from there to an infantry division stationed in Georgia. He had been in Georgia three months when he married a girl from the Augusta boarding-house aristocracy. A year or so later. he crossed the continent in a day coach and thought sententiously that the last he might see of the country he loved was the desert towns like Barstow, that the last he might hear of it was the ringing of the trolleys on the Bay Bridge. He was sent into the Pacific and returned to the United States twenty months later, uninjured and apparently unchanged. As soon as he received his furlough,[3] he went to Augusta. He presented his wife with the souvenirs he had brought from the islands, quarrelled violently with her and all her family, and, after making arrangements

1) put off: postpone; lay aside.
2) all-clear: signal indicating the end of an air-raid.
3) furlough: leave of absence, esp. for a soldier.

for her to get an Arkansas[1)] divorce, left for New York.

Jack was discharged from the Army at a camp in the East a few months later. He took a vacation and then went back to the job he had left in 1942. He seemed to have picked up his life at approximately the moment when it had been interrupted by the war. In time, everything came to look and feel the same. He saw most of his old friends. Only two of the men he knew had been killed in the war. He didn't call Joan, but he met her one winter afternoon on a crosstown bus.

Her fresh face, her black clothes, and her soft voice instantly destroyed the sense — if he had ever had such a sense — that anything had changed or intervened since their last meeting, three or four years ago. She asked him up for cocktails and he went to her apartment the next Saturday afternoon. Her room and her guests reminded him of the parties she had given when she had first come to New York. There was a woman with a fancy hat, an elderly doctor, and a man who stayed close to the radio, listening for news from the Balkans. Jack wondered which of the men belonged to Joan and decided on an Englishman who kept coughing into a handkerchief that he pulled out of his sleeve. Jack was right. "Isn't Stephen brilliant?" Joan asked him a little later, when they were alone in a corner. "He knows more about the Polynesians[2)] than anyone else in the world."

Jack had returned not only to his old job but to his old salary. Since living costs had doubled and since he was paying alimony to two wives, he had to draw on his savings. He took another job, which promised more money, but it didn't last long and he found himself out of work. This didn't bother him at all. He still had money in the bank, and anyhow it was easy to borrow from friends. His indifference was the consequence not of lassitude or despair but rather of an excess of hope. He had the feeling that he had only recently come to New York from Ohio. The sense that he was very young and that the best years of his life still lay before him was an illusion that he could not seem to escape. There was all the time in the world.

---

1) Arkansas: a southern State of the United States.

2) Polynesians: members of the brown race inhabiting Polynesia (= group of many small islands in the Pacific, E of Australia and the Phillippines).

He was living in hotels then, moving from one to another every five days.

In the spring, Jack moved to a furnished room[1] in the badlands west of Central Park. He was running out of[2] money. Then, when he began to feel that a job was a desperate necessity, he got sick. At first, he seemed to have only a bad cold, but he was unable to shake it and he began to run a fever and to cough blood. The fever kept him drowsy most of the time, but he roused himself occasionally and went out to a cafeteria for a meal. He felt sure that none of his friends knew where he was, and he was glad of this. He hadn't counted on[3] Joan.

Late one morning, he heard her speaking in the hall with his landlady. A few moments later, she knocked on his door. He was lying on the bed in a pair of pants and a soiled pajama top, and he didn't answer. She knocked again and walked in. "I've been looking everywhere for you, Jack," she said. She spoke softly. "When I found out that you were in a place like this I thought you must be broke[4] or sick. I stopped at the bank and got some money, in case you're broke. I've brought you some Scotch. I thought a little drink wouldn't do you any harm. Want a little drink?"

Joan's dress was black. Her voice was low and serene. She sat in a chair beside his bed as if she had been coming there every day to nurse him. Her features had coarsened, he thought, but there were still very few lines[5] in her face. She was heavier. She was nearly fat. She was wearing black cotton gloves. She got two glasses and poured Scotch into them. He drank his whiskey greedily. "I didn't get to bed until three last night," she said. Her voice had once before reminded him of a gentle and despairing song, but now, perhaps because he was sick, her mildness, the mourning[6] she wore, her stealthy grace,

1) a furnished room: a room supplied with furniture, equipment, etc.
2) run out of: use up; have no more.
3) count on: depend on; rely on; trust.
4) broke: (Slang) without money.
5) lines: wrinkles.
6) the mourning: the wearing of black or some other color (white in the Orient), to show sorrow for a person's death.

made him uneasy. "It was one of those nights," she said. "We went to the theatre. Afterward, someone asked us up to his place. I don't know who he was. It was one of those places. They're so strange. There were some meat-eating plants and a collection of Chinese snuff bottles. Why do people collect Chinese snuff bottles? We all autographed a lampshade, as I remember, but can't remember much."

Jack tried to sit up in bed, as if there were some need to defend himself, and then fell back again, against the pillows. "How did you find me, Joan?" he asked.

"It was simple," she said. "I called that hotel. The one you were staying in. They gave me this address. My secretary got the telephone number. Have another little drink."

"You know you've never come to a place of mine before — never," he said. "Why did you come now?"

"Why did I come, darling?" she asked. "What a question! I've known you for thirty years. You're the oldest friend I have in New York. Remember that night in the Village when it snowed and we stayed up until morning and drank whiskey sours[1] for breakfast? That doesn't seem like twelve years ago. And that night — "

"I don't like to have you see me in a place like this," he said earnestly. He touched his face and felt his beard.

"And all the people who used to imitate Roosevelt," she said, as if she had not heard him, as if she were deaf. "And that place on Staten Island where we all used to go for dinner when Henry had a car. Poor Henry. He bought a place in Connecticut and went out there by himself, one weekend. He fell asleep with a lighted cigarette and the house, the barn, everything burned. Ethel took the children out to California." She poured more Scotch into his glass and handed it to him. She lighted a cigarette and put it between his lips. The intimacy of this gesture, which made it seem not only as if he were deathly ill but as if he were her lover, troubled him.

"As soon as I'm better," he said, "I'll take a room at a good hotel. I'll call you then. It was nice of you to come."

---

1) sours: an acid beverage containing alcohol.

"Oh, don't be ashamed of this room, Jack," she said. "Rooms never bother me. It doesn't seem to matter to me where I am. Stanley had a filthy room in Chelsea. At least, other people told me it was filthy. I never noticed it. Rats used to eat the food I brought him. He used to have to hang the food from the ceiling, from the light chain."

"I'll call you as soon as I'm better," Jack said. "I think I can sleep now if I'm left alone. I seem to need a lot of sleep."

"You really *are* sick, darling," she said. "You must have a fever." She sat on the edge of his bed and put a hand on his forehead.

"How is that Englishman, Joan?" he asked. "Do you still see him?"

"What Englishman?" she said.

"You know. I met him at your house. He kept a handkerchief up his sleeve. He coughed all the time. You know the one I mean."

"You must be thinking of someone else," she said. "I haven't had an Englishman at my place since the war. Of course, I can't remember everyone." She turned and, taking one of his hands, linked her fingers in his.

"He's dead, isn't he?" Jack said. "That Englishman's dead." He pushed her off the bed, and got up himself. "Get out," he said.

"You're sick, darling," she said. "I can't leave you alone here."

"Get out," he said again, and when she didn't move, he shouted, "What kind of an obscenity are you that you can smell sickness and death the way you do?"[1)]

"You poor darling."

"Does it make you feel young to watch the dying?" he shouted. "Is that the lewdness that keeps you young? Is that why you dress like a crow? Oh, I know there's nothing I can say that will hurt you. I know there's nothing filthy or corrupt or depraved or brutish or base that the others haven't tried, but this time you're wrong. I'm not ready. My life isn't ending. My life's beginning. There are wonderful years ahead of me. There are, there are wonderful, wonderful, wonderful years ahead of me, and when they're over, when it's time, then I'll

---

1) What kind of an obscenity are you that you can smell sickness and death the way you do?: 그렇게도 지독하게 병과 죽음을 냄새 맡을 수 있으니 너야말로 참 음탕한 여자가 아니고 뭐란 말이야?

call you. Then, as an old friend, I'll call you and give you whatever dirty pleasure you take in watching the dying, but until then, you and your ugly and misshapen forms will leave me alone."

She finished her drink and looked at her watch. "I guess I'd better show up[1] at the office," she said. "I'll see you later. I'll come back tonight. You'll feel better then, you poor darling." She closed the door after her, and he heard her light step on the stairs.

Jack emptied the whiskey bottle into the sink. He began to dress. He stuffed his dirty clothes into a bag. He was trembling and crying with sickness and fear. He could see the blue sky from his window, and in his fear it seemed miraculous that the sky would be blue, that the white clouds should remind him of snow, that from the side walk he could hear the shrill voices of children shrieking, "I'm the king of the mountain, I'm the king of the mountain, I'm the king of the mountain." He emptied the ashtray containing his nail parings and cigarette butts into the toilet, and swept the floor with a shirt, so that there would be no trace of his life, of his body, when that lewd[2] and searching shape of death came there to find him in the evening.

1) show up: come; appear; (Colloq.) put in an appearance.
2) lewd: indecent; obscene.

The Wind and the Snow of Winter

by Walter van Tilburg Clark

Walter Van Tilburg Clark (1909-) was born in East Oriand, Maine. He spent his early childhood in Weat Nyack, New York, and in 1917 moved with his family to Reno, Nevada, where his father was President of the University of Nevada. He was educated in the public schools of Reno and at the University of Nevada. Clark then returned to his native New England, where he studied for two years at the University of Vermont. In 1945, by then the author of two published novels and a number of short stories (one of these, "The Wind and the Snow of winter" won the O. Henry prize in 1945) he gave up teaching to devote full time to writing.

IT WAS near sunset when Mike Braneen came onto the last pitch[1] of the old wagon road which had led into Gold Rock from the east since the Comstock days.[2] The road was just two ruts in the hard earth, with sagebrush[3] growing between them, and was full of steep pitches and sharp turns. From the summit it descended even more steeply into Gold Rock, in a series of short switch-backs[4] down the slope of the canyon. There was a paved highway on the other side of the pass[5] now, but Mike never used that. Cars coming from behind made him uneasy, so that he couldn't follow his own thoughts long, but had to keep turning around every few minutes, to see that his burro, Annie, was staying out on the shoulder of the road,[6] where she would be safe. Mike didn't like cars anyway, and on the old road he could forget about them and feel more like himself. He could forget

1) pitch: slope.

2) the Comstock days : 캄스톡크 은광 시절. 미국 네바다주 서부에 있는 대규모의 은광으로 1850년대에 발견되어 70년대까지 호황기를 누렸음.

3) sagebrush: a grayish green shrub. common on the dry plains of tile West United States.

4) switch-back: a road dim bing a steep grade in a zigzag course.

5) pass: a narrow road; path; way.

6) the shoulder of the road: 길 옆 변두리.

about Annie too, except when the light, quick tapping of her hoofs behind him stopped. Even then he didn't really break his thoughts. It was more as if the tapping were another sound from his own inner machinery, and when it stopped he stopped too, and turned around to see what she was doing. When he began to walk ahead again at the same slow, unvarying pace, his arms scarcely swinging at all, his body bent a little forward from the waist, he would not be aware that there had been any interruption of the memory or the story that was going on in his head. Mike did not like to have his stories interrupted except by an idea of his own, something to do with his prospecting,[1] or the arrival of his story at an actual memory which warmed him to closer recollection or led into a new and more attractive story.

An intense, golden light, almost liquid, fanned out[2] from the peaks above him and reached eastward under the gray sky, and the snow which occasionally swarmed across this light was fine and dry. Such little squalls had been going on all day, and still there was nothing like real snow down, but only a fine powder which the wind swept along until it caught under the brush, leaving the ground bare. Yet Mike Braneen was not deceived. This was not just a flurrying day;[3] it was the beginning of winter. If not tonight, then tomorrow, or the next day, the snow would begin which shut off[4] the mountains, so that a man might as well be on a great plain for all he could see,[5] perhaps even the snow which blinded a man at once and blanketed[6] the desert in an hour. Fifty-two years in this country had made Mike Braneen sure about such things, although he didn't give much thought to them, but only to what he had to do because of them. Three nights before he had been awakened by a change in the wind, It was no

---

1) something to do with his prospecting: 그의 시굴(試掘)과 관련된 무슨 생각. prospect=search(for gold).

2) fan out: spread out like an open fan.

3) flurrying day: a snowfalling day.

4) shut off: close.

5) so that a man might as well be on a great plain for all he could see: 그래서 흡사 대평원에 서 있는 것 같아 아무 것도 볼 수 없게 된다. for all he could see (어떻게 되건) 그는 볼 수 없었다. *cf.* for all I care. (어떻게 되건) 내가 알 바 아니다.

6) blanketed: coverd.

longer a wind born in the near mountains, cold with night and altitude, but a wind from far places, full of a damp chill which got through his blankets and into his bones. The stars had still been clear and close above the dark humps of the mountains, and overhead the constellations had moved slowly in full panoply, unbroken by any invisible lower darkness; yet he had lain there half awake for a few minutes, hearing the new wind beat the brush around him, hearing Annie stirring restlessly and thumping in her hobble.[1] He had thought drowsily, "Smells like winter this time," and then, "It's held off a long time this year,[2] pretty near the end of December," Then he had gone back to sleep, mildly happy because the change meant he would be going back to Gold Rock. Gold Rock was the other half of Mike Braneen's life. When the smell of winter came he always started back for Gold Rock. From March or April until the smell of winter he wandered slowly about among the mountains, anywhere between the White Pines and the Virginias, with only his burro for company.[3] Then there would come the change, and they would head[4] back for Gold Rock.

Mike had traveled with a good many burros during that time, eighteen or twenty, he thought, although he was not sure. He could not remember them all, but only those he had had first, when he was a young man and always thought most about seeing women when he got back to Gold Rock, or those with something queer about them, like Baldy, who'd had a great pa e patch, like a bald spot, on one side of his belly, or those who'd had something queer happen to them, like Maria. He could remember just how it had been that night. He could remember it as if it were last night. It had been in Hamilton He had felt unhappy, because he could remember Hamilton when the whole hollow was full of people and buildings, and everything was new and active. He had gone to sleep in the hollow shell[5] of the Wells Fargo Building,

1) hobble: rope or strap used to tie the legs of a horse.

2) It's held off a long time this year: 올해도 (겨울이) 늦게 오고 있다. hold off=keep at a distance; keep from acting.

3) with only his burro for company: 나귀를 벗삼고.

4) head: move or face (toward).

5) shell: framework.

hearing an old iron shutter banging against the wall in the wind. In the morning Maria had been gone. He had followed the scuffing track she made on account of her loose hobble, and it had led far up the old snow gullied road to Treasure Hill, and then ended at one of the black shafts[1] that opened like mouths right at the edge of the road. A man remembered a thing like that. There weren't many burros that[2] foolish. But burros with nothing particular about them were hard to remember — especially those he'd had in the last twenty years or so, when he had gradually stopped feeling so personal about them and had begun to call all the jennies[3] Annie and all the burros Jack.

The clicking of the little hoofs behind him stopped, and Mike stopped too, and turned around. Annie was pulling at a line of yellow grass along the edge of the road.

"Come on, Maria," Mike said patiently. The burro at once stopped pulling at the dead grass and came on up toward him, her small black nose working, the ends of the grass standing out on each side of it like whiskers. Mike began to climb again, ahead of her.

It was a long time since he had been caught by a winter too. He could not remember how long. All the beginnings ran together in his mind, as if they were all the beginning of one winter so far back that he had almost forgotten it. He could still remember clearly, though, the winter he had stayed out on purpose, clear[4] into January. He had been a young man then, thirty-five or forty or forty-five, somewhere in there. He would have to stop and try to bring back a whole string of memories about what had happened just before, in order to remember just how old he had been, and it wasn't worth the trouble. Besides, sometimes even that system didn't work. It would lead him into an old camp where he had been a number of times, and the dates would get mixed up. It was impossible to remember any other way, because all his comings and goings had been so much alike. He had been young, anyhow, and not much afraid of anything except running out

1) shaft: a deep passage sunk in the earth. The entrance to a mine is called a shaft.
2) that: (*adv.*) to such an extent or degree; so. *Ex.* He cannot stay up that late.
3) jenny: female of certain animals.
4) clear: completely; entirely.

of[1] water in the wrong place; not even afraid of the winter. He had stayed out because he'd thought he had a good thing, and he had wanted to prove it. He could remember how it felt to be out in the clear winter weather on the mountains, the pinon trees and the junipers weighted down with feathery snow, and making sharp blue shadows on the white slopes. The hills had made blue shadows on one another too, and in the still air his pick had made the beginning of a sound like a bell's. He knew he had been young, because he could remember taking a day off now and then, just to go tramping around those hills, up and down the white and through the blue shadows, on a kind of holiday. He had pretended to his common sense that he was seriously prospecting, and had carried his hammer and even his drill along, but he had really just been gallivanting,[2] playing colt. Maybe he had been even younger than thirty-five, though he could still be stirred a little, for that matter, by the memory of the kind of weather which had sent him gallivanting. High-blue weather, he called it. There were two kinds of high-blue weather, besides the winter kind, which didn't set him off very often, spring and fall. In the spring it would have a soft, puffy wind and soft, puffy white clouds which made separate shadows that traveled silently across hills that looked soft too. In the fall it would be still, and there would be no clouds at all in the blue, but there would be something in the golden air and the soft, steady sunlight on the mountains that made a man as uneasy as the spring blowing, though in a different way, more sad and not so excited. In the spring high-blue a man had been likely to think about women he had slept with, or wanted to sleep with, or imaginary women made up with the help of newspaper pictures of actresses or young society matrons, or of the old oil paintings in the Lucky Boy Saloon, which showed pale, almost naked women against dark, sumptuous backgrounds — women with long hair or braided hair, calm, virtuous faces, small hands and feet, and ponderous limbs, breasts, and buttocks. In the fall high-blue, though it had been much longer since he had seen a woman, or heard a woman's voice, he was more likely to think

1) run out of: use up; have no more.
2) gallivant: go about seeking pleasure; gad about.

about old friends, men, or places he had heard about, or places he hadn't seen for a long time. He himself thought most often about Goldfield[1] the way he had last seen it in the summer in 1912. That was as far south as Mike had ever been in Nevada. Since then he had never been south of Tonopah.[2] When the high-blue weather was past, though, and the season worked toward winter, he began to think about Gold Rock. There were only three or four winters out of the fifty-two when he hadn't gone home to Gold Rock, to his old room at Mrs. Wright's, up on Fourth Street, and to his meals in the dining room at the International House, and to the Lucky Boy, where he could talk to Tom Connover and his other friends, and play cards, or have a drink to hold in his hand while he sat and remembered.

This journey had seemed a little different from most, though. It had started the same as usual, but as he had come across the two vast valleys, and through the pass in the low range between them, he hadn't felt quite the same. He'd felt younger and more awake, it seemed to him, and yet, in a way, older too, suddenly older. He had been sure that there was plenty of time, and yet he had been a little afraid of getting caught in the storm. He had kept looking ahead to see if the mountains on the horizon were still clearly outlined, or if they had been cut off by a lowering of the clouds. He had thought more than once how bad it would be to get caught out there when the real snow began, and he had been disturbed by the first flakes. It had seemed hard to him to have to walk so far too. He had kept thinking about distance. Also the snowy cold had searched out the regions of his body where old injuries had healed. He had taken off his left mitten[3] a good many times, to blow on the fingers which had been frosted the year he was sixty-three, so that now it didn't take much cold to turn them white and stiffen them.[4] The queer tingling,

---

1) Goldfield: 네바다주 서남부에 있는 소도시. 1902년 금광이 발견되어 경기를 누렸고 1910년을 절정으로 기울어졌음.

2) Tonopah: 네바다주의 도시. 은광으로 유명했음.

3) mitten: kind of winter glove covering the four fingers together and the thumb separately.

4) so that now it . . . stiffen them: 그래서 지금은 조금만 차가워도 손가락이 하얗게 뻣뻣해 지고 만다.

partly like an itch and partly like a pain, in the patch on his back that had been burned in that old powder blast was sharper than he could remember its ever having been before. The rheumatism in his joints, which was so old a companion that it usually made him feel no more than tight-knit and stiff, and the place where his leg had been broken and torn when that ladder broke in '97 ached, and had a pulse he could count. All this made him believe that he was walking more slowly than usual, although nothing, probably not even a deliberate attempt, could actually have changed his pace. Sometimes he even thought, with a moment of fear, that he was getting tired.

On the other hand, he felt unusually clear and strong in his mind. He remembered things with a clarity[1] which was like living them again — nearly all of them events from many years back, from the time when he had been really active and fearless and every burro had had its own name. Some of these events, like the night he had spent in Eureka with the little brown-haired whore, a night in the fall in 1888 or '89, somewhere in there, he had not once thought of for years. Now he could remember even her name. Armandy, she had called herself: a funny name. They all picked names for their business, of course, romantic names like Cecily or Rosamunde or Belle or Claire, or hard names like Diamond Gert or Horseshoe Sal, or names that were pinned on them, like Indian Kate or Roman Mary, but Armandy was different.

He could remember Armandy as if he were with her now, not the way she had behaved in bed; he couldn't remember anything particular about that. In fact he couldn't be sure that he remembered anything about that at all. There were others he could remember more clearly for the way they had behaved in bed, women he had been with more often. He had been with Armandy only that one night. He remembered little things about being with her, things that made it seem good to think of being with her again. Armandy had a room upstairs in a hotel. They could hear a piano playing in a club across the street. He could hear the tune, and it was one he knew, although he didn't

1) with a clarity: 생생하게.

know its name. It was a gay tune that went on and on the same, but still it sounded sad when you heard it through the hotel window, with the lights from the bars and hotels shining on the street, and the people coming and going through the lights, and then, beyond the lights, the darkness where the mountains were. Armandy wore a white silk dress with a high waist,[1] and a locket on a gold chain. The dress made her look very brown and like a young girl. She used a white powder on her face, that smelled like violets, but this could not hide her brownness. The locket was heart-shaped, and it opened to show a cameo[2] of a man's hand holding a woman's hand very gently, just their fingers laid out long together, and the thumbs holding, the way they were sometimes on tombstones. There were two little gold initials on each hand, but Armandy would never tell what they stood for,[3] or even if the locket was really her own. He stood in the window, looking down at the club from which the piano music was coming, and Armandy stood beside him, with her shoulder against his arm, and a glass of wine in her hand. He could see the toe of her white satin slipper showing from under the edge of her skirt. Her big hat, loaded with black and white plumes, lay on the dresser behind them. His own leather coat, with the sheep-skin lining, lay across the foot of the bed. It was a big bed, with a knobby brass foot and head. There was one oil lamp burning in the chandelier in the middle of the room. Armandy was soft-spoken, gentle, and a little fearful, always looking at him to see what he was thinking. He stood with his arms folded. His arms felt big and strong upon his heavily muscled chest. He stood there, pretending to be in no hurry, but really thinking eagerly about what he would do with Armandy, who had something about her which tempted him to be cruel. He stood there, with his chin down into his heavy, dark beard, and watched a man come riding down the middle of the street from the west. The horse was a fine black, which lifted its head and feet with pride. The man sat very

---

1) with a high waist: waistline을 (가슴에 까지) 치켜 올린.

2) cameo: a precious or semiprecious stone carved so that there is a raised part on a background.

3) stand for: mean; represent.

straight, with a high rein, and something about his clothes and hat made him appear to be in uniform, although it wasn't a uniform he was wearing. The man also saluted friends upon the sidewalks like an officer, bending his head just slightly, and touching his hat instead of lifting it. Mike Braneen asked Armandy who the man was, and then felt angry because she could tell him, and because he was an important man who owned a mine that was in bonanza.[1] He mocked the airs with which the man rode, and his princely greetings He mocked the man cleverly, and Armandy laughed and repeated what he said, and made him drink a little of her wine as a reward. Mike had been drinking whisky, and he did not like wine anyway, but this was not the moment in which to refuse such an invitation.

Old Mike remembered all this, which had been completely forgotten for years. He could not remember what he and Armandy had said, but he remembered everything else, and he felt very lonesome for Armandy, and for the room with the red, figured carpet and the brass chandelier with oil lamps in it, and the open window with the long tune coming up through it, and the young summer night outside on the mountains. This loneliness was so much more intense than his familiar loneliness that it made him feel very young. Memories like this had come up again and again during these three days. It was like beginning life over again. It had tricked him into thinking, more than once, "Next summer I'll make the strike, and this time I'll put it into something safe for the rest of my life, and stop this fool wandering around while I've still got some time left" — a way of thinking which he had really stopped a long time before.

It was getting darker rapidly in the pass. When a gust of wind brought the snow against Mike's face so hard that he noticed the flakes felt larger, he looked up. The light was still there, although the fire was dying out of it, and the snow swarmed across it more thickly. Mike remembered God. He did not think anything exact. He did not think about his own relationship to God. He merely felt the idea as a comforting presence. He'd always had a feeling about God whenever

---

1) in bonanza: 크게 횡재하여. bonanza=accidental discovery of a rich mass of ore in a mine 노다지.

he looked at a sunset, especially a sunset which came through under a stormy sky. It had been the strongest feeling left in him until these memories like the one about Armandy had begun. Even in this last pass his strange fear of the storm had come on him again a couple of times, but now that he had looked at the light and thought of God it was gone. In a few minutes he would come to the summit and look down into his lighted city. He felt happily hurried by this anticipation.

He would take the burro down and stable her in John Hammersmith's shed, where he always kept her. He would spread fresh straw for her, and see that the shed was tight against the wind and snow, and get a measure of grain for her from John. Then he would go up to Mrs. Wright's house at the top of Fourth Street, and leave his things in the same room he always had, the one in front, which looked down over the roofs and chimneys of his city, and across at the east wall of the canyon, from which the sun rose late. He would trim his beard with Mrs. Wright's shears, and shave the upper part of his cheeks. He would bathe out of the blue bowl and pitcher, and wipe himself with the towel with yellow flowers on it, and dress in the good dark suit and the good black shoes with the gleaming box toes, and the good black hat which he had left in the chest in his room. In this way he would perform the ceremony which ended the life of the desert and began the life of Gold Rock. Then he would go down to the International House, and greet Arthur Morris in the gleaming bar, and go into the dining room and eat the best supper they had, with fresh meat and vegetables, and new-made pie, and two cups of hot clear coffee. He would be served by the plump blond waitress who always joked with him, and gave him many little extra things with his first supper, including the drink which Arthur Morris always sent in from the bar.

At this point Mike Braneen stumbled in his mind, and his anticipation wavered. He could not be sure that the plump blond waitress would serve him. For a moment he saw her in a long skirt, and the dining room of the International House, behind her, had potted palms standing in the corners, and was full of the laughter and loud, manly talk of many customers who wore high vests and mustaches and beards. These men leaned back from tables covered with empty dishes. They patted their tight vests and lighted expensive cigars. He knew all their faces. If he were to walk down the aisle between the tables on his side they would all speak to him. But he also seemed to remember the dining room with only a few tables, with oilcloth on them instead of linen, and with moody young men sitting at them in their work clothes — strangers who worked for the highway department, or were just passing through, or talked mining in terms which he did not understand or which made him angry.

No, it would not be the plump blond waitress. He did not know who it would be. It didn't matter. After supper he would go up Canyon Street under the arcade to the Lucky Boy Saloon, and there it would be the same as ever. There would be the laurel wreaths on the frosted glass panels of the doors, and the old sign upon the window, the sign that was older than Tom Connover, almost as old as Mike Braneen himself. He would open the door and see the bottles and the white women in the paintings, and the card table in the back corner and the big stove and the chairs along the wall. Tom would look around from his place behind the bar.

"Well, now," he would roar, "look who's here, boys. Now will you believe it's winter?" he would roar at them.

Some of them would be the younger men, of course, and there might even be a few strangers, but this would only add to the dignity of his reception, and there would also be his friends. There would be Henry Bray with the gray walrus mustache, and Mark Wilton and Pat Gallagher. They would all welcome him loudly.

"Mike, how are you, anyway?" Tom would roar, leaning across the bar to shake hands with his big, heavy, soft hand with the diamond ring on it. "And what'll it be, Mike? The same?" he'd ask, as if Mike had been in there no longer ago than the night before.

Mike would play that game too. "The same," he would say. Then he would really be back in Gold Rock; never mind the plump blond waitress.

Mike came to the summit of the old road and stopped and looked down. For a moment he felt lost again, as he had when he'd thought about the plump blond waitress. He had expected Canyon Street to look much brighter. He had expected a lot of orange windows close together on the other side of the canyon. Instead there were only a few scattered lights across the darkness, and they were white. They made no communal glow upon the steep slope, but gave out only single white needles of light, which pierced the darkness secretly and lonesomely, as if nothing could ever pass from one house to another over there. Canyon Street was very dark too. There it went, the street he loved, steeply down into the bottom of the canyon, and down its length there were only the few street lights, more than a block apart, swinging in the wind and darting about that cold, small light. The snow whirled and swooped under the nearest street light below.

"You are getting to be an old fool," Mike Braneen said out loud to himself, and felt better. This was the way Gold Rock was now, of course, and he loved it all the better. It was a place that grew old with a man, that was going to die sometime too. There could be an understanding with it.

He worked his way slowly down into Canyon Street, with Annie slipping and checking behind him. Slowly, with the blown snow behind them, they came to the first built-up block and passed the first dim light showing through a smudged window under the arcade. They passed the dark places after it, and the second light. Then Mike Braneen stopped in the middle of the street, and Annie stopped beside him, pulling her rump in[1] and turning her head away from the snow. A highway truck, coming down from the head of the canyon, had to get way over onto the wrong side of the street to pass them. The driver leaned out as he went by, and yelled, "Pull over, Pop.[2] You're in town now."

Mike Braneen didn't hear him. He was staring at the Lucky Boy. The Lucky Boy was dark, and there were boards nailed across the big window that had shown the sign. At last Mike went over onto the boardwalk to look more closely. Annie followed him, but stopped at the edge of the walk and scratched her neck against a post of the

1) pulling her rump in: 궁둥이를 움츠리고.
2) Pop: father; any elderly man.

arcade. There was the other sign, hanging crossways under the arcade, and even in that gloom Mike could see that it said Lucky Boy and had a Jack of Diamonds painted on it. There was no mistake. The Lucky Boy sign, and others like it under the arcade, creaked and rattled in the wind.

There were footsteps coming along the boards. The boards sounded hollow, and sometimes one of them rattled. Mike Braneen looked down slowly from the sign and peered at the approaching figur. It was a man wearing a sheepskin coat with the collar turned up around his head. He was walking quickly, like a man who knew where he was going, and why, and where he had been.

Mike almost let him pass. Then he spoke.

"Say, fella — "

He even reached out a hand as if to catch hold of the man's sleeve, though he didn't touch it. The man stopped and asked, impatiently, "Yeah?" and Mike let the hand down again slowly.

"Well, what is it?" the man asked.

"I don't want anything," Mike said. "I got plenty." "Okay, okay," the man said. "What's the matter?"

Mike moved his hand toward the Lucky Boy. "It's closed," he said.

"I see it is, Dad," the man said. He laughed a little. He didn't seem to be in quite so much of a hurry now.

"How long has it been closed?" Mike asked.

"Since about June, I guess," the man said. "Old Tom Connover, the guy that ran it, died last June."

Mike waited for a moment. "Tom died?" he asked.

"Yup. I guess he'd just kept it open out of love of the place anyway. There hasn't been any real business for years. Nobody cared to keep it open after him."

The man started to move on, but then he waited, peering, trying to see Mike better.

"This June?" Mike asked finally. "Yup. This last June."

"Oh," Mike said. Then he just stood there. He wasn't thinking anything. There didn't seem to be anything to think.

"You knew him?" the man asked.

"Thirty years," Mike said. "No, more'n that," he said, and started to figure out how long he had known Tom Connover, but lost it, and said, as if it would do just as well, "He was a lot younger than I am, though."

"Hey," said the man, coming closer, and peering again. "You're Mike Braneen, aren't you?"

"Yes," Mike said.

"Gee, I didn't recognize you at first. I'm sorry."

"That's all right," Mike said. He didn't know who the man was, or what he was sorry about.

He turned his head slowly and looked out into the street. The snow was coming down heavily now. The street was all white. He saw Annie with her head and shoulders in under the arcade, but the snow settling on her rump.

"Well, I guess I'd better get Molly under cover," he said. He moved toward the burro a step, but then halted.

"Say, fella — "

The man had started on, but he turned back. He had to wait for Mike to speak.

"I guess this about Tom's mixed me up."[1)]

"Sure," the man said. "It's tough, an old friend like that." "Where do I turn up to get to Mrs. Wright's place?"

"Mrs. Wright?"

"Mrs. William Wright," Mike said. "Her husband used to be a foreman in the Aztec. Got killed in the fire."

"Oh," the man said. He didn't say anything more, but just stood there, looking at the shadowy bulk of old Mike.

"She's not dead too, is she?" Mike asked slowly.

"Yeah, I'm afraid she is, Mr. Braneen," the man said. "Look," he said more cheerfully. "It's Mrs. Branley's house you want right now, isn't it? Place where you stayed last winter?"

Finally Mike said, "Yeah. Yeah, I guess it is."

"I'm going up that way. I'll walk up with you," the man said. After

---

1) I guess this about Tom's mixed me up.: 톰의 소식을 듣고 내 정신이 나간 것 같구려.

they had started Mike thought that he ought to take the burro down to John Hammersmith's first, but he was afraid to ask about it. They walked on down Canyon Street, with Annie walking along beside them in the gutter. At the first side street they turned right and began to climb the steep hill toward another of the little street lights dancing over a crossing. There was no sidewalk here, and Annie followed right at their heels. That one street light was the only light showing up ahead.

When they were halfway up to the light Mike asked, "She die this summer too?"

The man turned his body half around, so that he could hear inside his collar.

"What?"

"Did she die this summer too?"

"Who?"

"Mrs. Wright," Mike said.

The man looked at him, trying to see his face as they came up toward the light. Then he turned back again, and his voice was muffled by the collar.

"No, she died quite a while ago, Mr. Braneen."

"Oh," Mike said finally.

They came up onto the crossing under the light, and the snowladen wind whirled around them again. They passed under the light, and their three lengthening shadows before them were obscured by the innumerable tiny shadows of the flakes.

The Chaser[1]

by John Collier

English by birth, John Collier(1901-) has spent his recent years in Los Angeles and is frequently published in American magazines. He has written poetry and novels, but is best known for his short stories, which often have an odd, ironic twist with a touch of the supernatural.

"The Chaser" is from *Fancies and Goodnights*(1951). Other collections of Collier's work include *A Touch of Nutmeg*(1945) and *The John Collier Reader*(1972).

ALAN AUSTEN, as nervous as a kitten,[2] went up certain dark and creaky stairs in the neighborhood of Pell Street,[3] and peered about[4] for a long time on the dime landing[5] before he found the name he wanted written obscurely on one of the doors.

He pushed open this door, as he had been told[6] to do, and found himself in a tiny room, which contained no furniture but a plain kitchen table,[7] a rocking-chair, and an ordinary chair. On one of the dirty buff-coloured[8] walls were a couple of shelves, containing in all perhaps a dozen bottles and jars. An old man sat in the rocking-chair, reading a newspaper. Alan, without a word, handed him the card he had been given.

"Sit down, Mr. Austen," said the old man very politely.

"I am glad to make your acquaintance."

"Is it true," asked Alan, "that you have a certain mixture that has — er — quite extraordinary effects?"

---

1) chaser: (Informal) a drink of water or beer taken after a drink of hard liquor.
2) kitten: a baby cat.
3) Pell Street: a rather poor street in New York's Chinatown.
4) peered about: looked around intently, unable to see well.
5) landing: the area at the top of a flight of stairs.
6) had been told: had been told (by the person who sent him).
7) no furniture but a plain kitchen table: only a plain kitchen table.
8) buff-coloured: a pale yellowish-brown.

"My dear sir," replied the old man, "my stock in trade[1] is not very large — I don't deal in laxatives[2] and teething mixtures[3] — but such as it is, it is varied. I think nothing I sell has effects which could be precisely described as ordinary."

"Well, the fact is — " began Alan.

"Here, for example," interrupted the old man, reaching for a bottle from the shelf. "Here is a liquid as colourless as water, almost tasteless, quite imperceptible[4] in coffee, wine, or any other beverage. It is also quite imperceptible to any known method of autopsy."[5]

"Do you mean it is a poison?" cried Alan, very much horrified.

"Call it a glove-cleaner if you like," said the old man indifferently.

"Maybe it will clean gloves. I have never tried. One might call it a life-cleaner. Lives need cleaning sometimes."

"I want nothing of that sort,"[6] said Alan.

"Probably it is just as well," said the old man. "Do you know the price of this? For one teaspoonful,[7] which is sufficient, I ask five thousand dollars. Never less. Not a penny less."

"I hope all your mixtures are not as expensive," said Alan apprehensively.[8]

"Oh dear, no," said the old man. "It would be no good charging that sort of price for a love potion,[9] for example. Young people who need a love potion very seldom have five thousand dollars. Otherwise they would not need a love potion."

"I am glad to hear that," said Alan.

"I look at it like this," said the old man. "Please[10] a customer with one article, and he will come back when he needs another. Even if

---

1) my stock in trade: 나의 재고품.
2) laxatives: a medicine or drug that causes a bowel movement. 설사약.
3) teething mixtures: a medicine to lessen the pain of a baby's teeth growing in
4) imperceptible: not able to be seen.
5) autopsy: the medical examination of a body to determine the casue of death. 검시.
6) I want nothing of that sort=I don't want anything of that sort.
7) teaspoonful: five liquid grams.
8) apprehensively: worriedly; fearfully.
9) love potion: a magic liquid, most often associated with love.
10) Please: satisfy.

it is more costly.[1] He will save up for it, if necessary."

"So," said Alan, "you really do sell love potions?"

"If I did not sell love potions," said the old man, reaching for another bottle, "I should not have mentioned the other matter to you. It is only when one is in a position to oblige that one can afford to be so confidential."

"And these potions," said Alan. "They are not just — just — er[2] — "

"Oh, no," said the old man. "Their effects are permanent, and extend far beyond the mere casual impulse. But they include it. Oh, yes they include it. Bountifully,[3] insistently. Everlastingly."

"Dear me!" said Alan, attempting a look of scientific detachment. "How very interesting!"

"But consider the spiritual side," said the old man.

"I do, indeed," said Alan.

"For indifference," said the old man, they substitute devotion.[4] For scorn, adoration.[5] Give one tiny measure of this to the young lady — its flavor is imperceptible in orange juice, soup, or cocktails — and however gay and giddy[6] she is, she will change altogether. She will want nothing but solitude and you."

"I can hardly believe it," said Alan. "She is so fond of parties."

"She will not like them any more," said the old man. "She will be afraid of the pretty girls you may meet."

"She will actually be jealous?" cried Alan in a rapture.[7] "Of me?"

"Yes, she will want to be everything to you."

"She is, already. Only she doesn't care about it."

"She will, when she has taken this. She will care intensely. You

---

1) costly: expensive.

2) er: Alan이 수줍어서 하지 못하는 말은 "arousing sexual passion"의 뜻인 aphrodisiac 라는 말.

3) bountifully: generously; in great quantity.

4) For indifference they substitute devotion.=They substitude devotion for indifference. substitute A for B=B 대신에 A를 대응하다.

5) For scorn, adoration.=For scorn, (they substitute) adoration.

6) giddy: silly, not serious toward life.

7) rapture: state of great happiness.

will be her sole[1)] interest in life."

"Wonderful!" cried Alan.

"She will want to know all you do," said the old man. "All that has happened to you during the day. Every word of it. She will want to know what you are thinking about, why you smile suddenly, why you are looking sad."

"That is love!" cried Alan.

"Yes," said the old man. "How carefully she will look after you! She will never allow you to be tired, to sit in a draught,[2)] to neglect your food. If you are an hour late, she will be terrified. She will think you are killed, or that some siren[3)] has caught you."

"I can hardly imagine Diana like that!" cried Alan, overwhelmed with joy.

"You will not have to use your imagination," said the old man. "And, by the way, since there are always sirens, if by any chance you *should*, later on, slip a little, you need not worry. She will forgive you, in the end. She will be terribly hurt, of course, but she will forgive you — in the end."

"That will not happen," said Alan fervently.[4)]

"Of course not," said the old man. "But, if it did, you need not worry. She would never divorce you. Oh, no! And, of course, she will never give you the least, the very least, grounds[5)] for — uneasiness."

"And how much," said Alan, "is this wonderful mixture?"

"It is not as dear,"[6)] said the old man, "as the glove-cleaner, or life-cleaner, as I sometimes call it. No. That is five thousand dollars, never a penny less. One has to be older than you are, to indulge in that sort of thing. One has to save up for it."

"But the love potion?" said Alan.

"Oh, that," said the old man, opening the drawer in the kitchen

---

1) sole: only.
2) draught: draft=a current of air.
3) siren: a seductive woman.
4) fervently: with great sincerity and passion.
5) grounds: basis, reason.
6) dear: expensive.

table, and taking out a tiny, rather dirty-looking phial.[1] "That is just a dollar."

"I can't tell you how grateful I am," said Alan, watching him fill it.

"I like to oblige," said the old man. "Then customers come back, later in life, when they are rather better off,[2] and want more expensive things. Here you are. You will find it very effective."

"Thank you again," said Alan. "Good-bye."

"*Au revoir,*"[3] said the man.

---

1) phial: a small glass tube.

2) rather better off: wealthier, richer.

3) *Au revoir*: (French) Good-bye until we meet again.

Wash

by William Faulkner

William Faulkner (1897-1962) was born in New Albany, Mississippi, and lived for most of his life in the neighboring county seat, Oxford, where the University of Mississippi is situated. The Faulkner (or Falkner) family has long been prominent in politics, railroad building, and planting; one great-grandfather of William's was the author of a popular antebellum romance, *The White Rose of Memphis*. The Sartoris family, prominent in a number of Faulkner's novels, appears to be in part a projection of his own clan.

Early in World War I, Faulkner, just out of high school, ran off to Canada to join the British air force. He was sent to England for training and was about one year of service in France before he was wounded in a crash. Back in Mississippi, he was for a time a student in the university; he then worked at such odd jobs as clerking in the college postal station and house-painting. Encouragement for his writing apparently came from various friends, among them Phil Stone, an Oxford lawyer; Stark Young, then teaching at Amherst; and Sherwood Anderson, with whom he lived in New Orleans in 1922.

In 1929 he married Estelle Oldham and by that time had already decided on writing as his career. After 1936 he occasionally went to Hollywood to write for various motion pictures, and made some visits abroad for the State Department. However, in spite of these trips and occasional visits to New York, Faulkner spent much of his time in Oxford, Mississippi. Even after he became a writer in residence at the University of Virgina, he continued to return to Oxford until 1959 when he announced his intention to settle in Charlottesville, Virgina. He held an honorary post at the University until his death in 1962. He received among other awards the Pulitzer Prize for both *A Fable* (1954) and *The Town* (1957) and, in 1950, the Nobel Prize for Literature.

SUTPEN STOOD above the pallet bed[1] on which the mother and child lay. Between the shrunken planking of the wall[2] the early sunlight fell in long pencil strokes,[3] breaking upon his straddled legs and upon the riding whip in his hand, and lay across the still[4] shape of the mother, who lay looking up at him from still, inscrutable, sullen eyes,

1) pallet bed: bed of straw; poor bed.
2) Between the shrunken planking of the wall: 쪼그라든 벽판자 사이로.
3) stroke: a mark traced by or as if by a pen, pencil, brush, or the like.
4) still: not moving; motionless.

the child[1] at her side wrapped in a piece of dingy though clean cloth.[2] Behind them an old Negro woman squatted beside the rough hearth where a meager fire smoldered.

"Well, Milly,"[3] Sutpen said, "too bad you're not a mare. Then I could give you a decent stall in the stable."

Still the girl on the pallet did not move. She merely continued to look up at him without expression, with a young, sullen, inscrutable face still pale from recent travail.[4] Sutpen moved, bringing into the splintered pencils of sunlight the face of a man of sixty. Pie said quietly to the squatting Negress,[5] "Griselda foaled this morning."

"Horse or mare?" the Negress said.

"A horse. A damned fine colt. . . . What's this?" He indicated the pallet with the hand which held the whip.

"That un's a mare, I reckon."[6]

"Hah," Sutpen said. "A damned fine colt. Going to be[7] the spit[8] and image of old Rob Roy when I rode him North in '61.[9] Do you remember?"

"Yes, Marster."

"Hah." He glanced back towards the pallet. None could have said if the girl still watched him or not. Again his whip hand indicated the pallet. "Do whatever they need with whatever we've got to do it with." He went out, passing out the crazy[10] doorway and stepping down into the rank[11] weeds (there yet leaned rusting against the corner of the porch the scythe[12] which Wash had borrowed from him three

1) the child: 앞의 with를 보충할 것.
2) a piece of dingy though clean cloth: 거무스름하지만 세탁된 헝겊 조각.
3) Milly: 이 단편의 주인공 Wash의 손녀딸.
4) travail: toil; labor.
5) Negress: a Negro woman. *cf.* nigger=a Negro man.
6) That un's a mare, I reckon.: That one is a mare, I suppose.
7) Going to be: It is going to be; It will be.
8) spit: (Colloq.) the image; likeness.
9) '61: 1861 남북전쟁이 시작된 해.
10) crazy: liable to break or fall to pieces.
11) rank: growing with excessive luxuriance.
12) there yet leaned rusting against the corner of the porch the scythe: 현관 구석에는 아직도 낫이 녹슬은 채로 비스듬히 세워져 있었다.

months ago to cut them with) where his horse waited, where Wash stood holding the reins.

When Colonel Sutpen rode away to fight the Yankees,[1] Wash did not go. "I'm looking after the Kernel's place[2] and niggers," he would tell all who asked him and some who had not asked — a gaunt, malaria-ridden[3] man with pale, questioning eyes, who looked about thirty-five, though it was known that he had not only a daughter but an eight-year-old granddaughter as well. This was a lie, as most of them — the few remaining men between eighteen and fifty — to whom he told it, knew, though there were some who believed that he himself really believed it, though even these believed that he had better sense than to put it to the test with Mrs. Sutpen or the Sutpen slaves. Knew better or was just too lazy and shiftless to try it, they said, knowing that his sole connection with the Sutpen plantation lay in the fact that for years now Colonel Sutpen had allowed him to squat[4] in a crazy shack[5] on a slough[6] in the river bottom on the Sutpen place, which Sutpen had built for a fishing lodge in his bachelor days and which had since fallen in dilapidation from disuse, so that now it looked like an aged or sick wild beast crawled terrifically there to drink in the act of dying.

The Sutpen slaves themselves heard of his statement. They laughed. It was not the first time they had laughed at him, calling him white trash behind his back.[7] They began to ask him themselves, in groups, meeting him in the faint road[8] which led up from the slough and the old fish camp, "Why ain't you at de war, white man?"[9]

Pausing, he would look about the ring of black faces and white

---

1) Yankees: native of any of the Northern States; a Northerner.
2) the Kernel's place: the Colonel's place.
3) malaria-ridden: 말라리아에 걸린. ridden=(Slang) harassed or tormented.
4) squat: settle on another's land without title or right.
5) shack: a roughly built hut or cabin.
6) slough: a marshy or ready pool, pond, inlet or the like.
7) calling him white trash behind his back: 그가 없는 데서 그를 가난한 백인이라고 불렀다. white trash=a poor white.
8) faint road: 거의 보이지 않게 지워진 길.
9) "Why ain't you at de war, white man?": "Why aren't you at the war, white man?"

eyes and teeth behind which derision lurked. "Because I got[1] a daughter and family to keep," he said. "Git[2] out of my road, niggers."

"Niggers?" they repeated; "niggers?" laughing now. "Who him, calling us niggers?"

"Yes," he said. "I ain't got no niggers[3] to look after my folks if I was gone."

"Nor nothing else but dat shack down yon dat Gunnel wouldn't *let* none of us live in."[4]

Now he cursed them; sometimes he rushed at them, snatching up a stick from the ground while they scattered before him, yet seeming to surround him still with that black laughing,[5] derisive,[6] evasive, inescapable, leaving him panting and impotent and raging. Once it happened in the very back yard of the big house itself. This was after bitter news[7] had come down from the Tennessee mountains and from Vicksburg, and Sherman[8] had passed through the plantation, and most of the Negroes had followed him. Almost everything else had gone with the Federal troops, and Mrs. Sutpen had sent word to Wash that he could have the scuppernongs[9] ripening in the arbor in the back yard. This time it was a house servant, one of the few Negroes who remained; this time the Negress had to retreat up the kitchen steps, where she turned. "Stop right dar, white man. Stop right whar you is.[10] You ain't never crossed dese steps whilst Gunnel here, and you ain't ghy' do hit now."[11]

---

1) got: have got=have.
2) Git: Get.
3) I ain't got no niggers: I haven't any niggers ain't=(Colloq.) am not, aren't, isn't, haven't, hasn't 등의 대용으로 쓰인다.
4) Nor nothing else but dat … live in: Nor anything else but that shack down yonder that Colonel wouldn't let any of us live in.
5) that black laughing: 그 흑인 특유의 웃음소리.
6) derisive: mocking.
7) bitter news: 비보. bitter=grievous; distressful.
8) Sherman: William Tecumseh Sherman(1820-1891), Great Union general in the American Civil War.
9) scuppernongs: 미국 남부산인 알이 큰 포도의 일종.
10) Stop right whar you is.: Stop right where you are.
11) You ain't never crossed … hit now: You have never crossed these steps while Colonel is here, and you aren't going to do it now.

This was true. But there was this of a kind of pride: he had never tried to enter the big house, even though he believed that if he had, Sutpen would have received him, permitted him. "But I ain't going to give no black nigger the chance to tell me I can't go nowhere," he said to himself. "I ain't even going to give Kernel the chance to have to cuss[1] a nigger on my account."[2] This, though he and Sutpen had spent more than one afternoon together on those rare Sundays when there would be no company in the house. Perhaps his mind knew that it was because Sutpen had nothing else to do, being a man who could not bear his own company. Yet the fact remained that the two of them would spend whole afternoons in the scuppernong arbor, Sutpen in the hammock and Wash squatting against a post, a pail of cistern water between them, taking drink for drink from the same demijohn.[3] Meanwhile on weekdays he would see the fine figure of the man — they were the same age almost to a day,[4] though neither of them (perhaps because Wash had a grandchild while Sutpen's son was a youth in school) ever thought of himself as being so — on the fine figure of the black stallion, galloping about the plantation. For that moment his heart would be quiet and proud. It would seem to him that that world in which Negroes, whom the Bible told him had been created and cursed by God to be brute and vassal[5] to all men of white skin, were better found and housed and even clothed than he and his; that world[6] in which he sensed always about him mocking echoes of black laughter was but a dream and an illusion, and that the actual world was this one across which his own lonely apotheosis seemed to gallop on the black thoroughbred,[7] thinking how the Book

---

1) cuss: curse.
2) on my account: 나 때문에.
3) a pail of cistern water between them, taking drink for drink from the same demijohn: 저수지 물 한 통을 그들 사이에 두고 목이 가는 큰 술병에서 한 모금씩 마시면서. cistern=reservoir or tank for storing waterdemijohn=a large bottle of earthenware enclosed in wicker.
4) to a day: 생일 날짜까지도 같은 (동갑이다).
5) vassal: characteristic of a vassal(=a servant or slave).
6) that world: 앞에 나오는 It would seem to him에 걸린다.
7) that the actual world was … on the black thoroughbred: 역시 앞에 나오는 It would seem to him에 걸린다. 실제의 세계는 자신의 외롭고 신격화된 모습이 까만

said also that all men were created in the image of God and hence all men made the same image in God's eyes at least; so that he could say, as though speaking of himself, "A fine proud man. If God Himself was to come down and ride the natural earth, that's what He would aim to look like."

Sutpen returned in 1865, on the black stallion. He seemed to have aged ten years. His son had been killed in action the same winter in which his wife had died. He returned with his citation for gallantry[1] from the hand of General Lee[2] to a ruined plantation, where for a year now his daughter had subsisted partially on the meager bounty of the man to whom fifteen years ago he had granted permission to live in that tumbledown fishing camp whose very existence he had at the time forgotten. Wash was there to meet him, unchanged: still gaunt, still ageless, with his pale, questioning gaze, his air diffident, a little servile, a little familiar. "Well, Kernel," Wash said, "they kilt us but they ain't whupped us yit, air they?"[3]

That was the tenor[4] of their conversation for the next five years. It was inferior whisky which they drank now together from a stoneware jug, and it was not in the scuppernong arbor. It was in the rear of the little store which Sutpen managed to set up on the highroad: a frame shelved room where, with Wash for clerk and porter, he dispense d[5] kerosene and staple[6] foodstuffs and stale[7] gaudy candy and cheap beads and ribbons to Negroes or poor whites of Wash's own kind, who came afoot or on gaunt mules to haggle tediously for dimes and quarters with a man who at one time could gallop (the black stallion

순종말을 타고 달려가는 것같이 보이는 세계였던 것이다. apotheosis=raising of a human being to the rank of a god. this one=this world. thoroughbred=a thoroghbred horse.

1) citation for gallantry: 용맹에 대해서 주어진 표창.

2) General Lee: Robert Edward Lee(1807-1870), the most famous Confederate general in the Civil War.

3) "they kilt us but they ain't whupped us yit, air they?": "they killed us but they haven't whipped us yet, have they?" whup=whip=(Colloq.) defeat. air=are

4) tenor: general purport.

5) dispense: give out; distribute; sell.

6) staple: chief.

7) stale: not fresh; dry or hardened.

was still alive; the stable in which his jealous get[1] lived was in better repair[2] than the house where the master himself lived) for ten miles across his own fertile land and who had led troops gallantly in battle; until Sutpen in fury would empty the store, close and lock the doors from the inside. Then he and Wash would repair[3] to the rear and the jug. But the talk would not be quiet now, as when Sutpen lay in the hammock, delivering an arrogant monologue while Wash squatted guffawing[4] against his post. They both sat now, though Sutpen had the single chair while Wash used whatever box or keg was handy, and even this for just a little while, because soon Sutpen would reach that stage of impotent and furious undefeat[5] in which he would rise, swaying and plunging, and declare again that he would take his pistol and the black stallion and ride single-handed[6] into Washington and kill Lincoln, dead now, and Sherman, now a private citizen. "Kill them!" he would shout. "Shoot them down like the dogs they are —"

"Sho, Kernel;[7] sho, Kernel," Wash would say, catching Sutpen as he fell. Then he would commandeer[8] the first passing wagon or, lacking that, he would walk the mile to the nearest neighbor and borrow one and return and carry Sutpen home. He entered the house now. He had been doing so for a long time, taking Sutpen home in whatever borrowed wagon might be, talking him into locomotion with cajoling murmurs as though he were a horse, a stallion himself.[9] The daughter would meet them and hold open the door without a word. He would carry his burden through the once white formal entrance, surmounted

1) get: offspring of an animal. 동물의 새끼.
2) repair: the state of being repaired, or fit for use.
3) repair; (v.) go (to a place).
4) guffaw: (v.) laugh loudly and coarsely.
5) that stage of impotent and furious undefeat: 그 무력하고도 격렬한 불패(정신을 갖는) 단계.
6) single-handed: acting alone or unaided.
7) Sho, Kernel: Sure, Colonel.
8) commandeer: (Colloq.) take by force.
9) talking him into locomotion ··· a stallion himself: 마치 그가 말이나 종마(種馬)이기나 한 것처럼 달콤한 말로 속삭여 그를 움직이도록 했다. locomotion=moving. cajole=persudade by flattery or promise.

by a fanlight imported piece by piece from Europe and with a board now nailed over a missing pane, across a velvet carpet from which all nap was now gone, and up a formal stairs, now but a fading ghost of bare boards between two strips of fading paint, and into the bedroom. It would be dusk by now, and he would let his burden sprawl[1] onto the bed and undress it and then he would sit quietly in a chair beside. After a time the daughter would come to the door. "We're all right now," he would tell her. "Don't you worry none,[2] Miss Judith."

Then it would become dark, and after a while he would lie down on the floor beside the bed, though not to sleep, because after a time — sometimes before midnight — the man on the bed would stir and groan and then speak. "Wash?"

"Hyer I am, Kernel.[3] You go back to sleep. We ain't whupped yit, air we? Me and you kin do hit."[4]

Even then he had already seen the ribbon about his grand- daughter's waist. She was now fifteen, already mature, after the early way of her kind.[5] He knew where the ribbon came from; he had been seeing it. and its kind daily for three years, even if she had lied about where she got it, which she did not, at once[6] bold, sullen, and fearful. "Sho now,"[7] he said. "Ef Kernel wants to give hit to you,[8] I hope you minded to thank him."

His heart was quiet, even when he saw the dress, watching her secret, defiant, frightened face when she told him that Miss Judith, the daughter, had helped her to make it. But he was quite grave when he approached Sutpen after they closed the store that afternoon, following the other to the rear.

"Get the jug," Sutpen directed.

---

1) sprawl: lie or sit with the limbs spread out esp. ungracefully.
2) Don't you worry none: =Don't worry.
3) Hyer I am, Kernel.: Here I am, Colonel.
4) Me and you kin do hit.: I and you can do it.
5) after the early way of her kind: 그녀의 종족이 일찍 성숙해지는 것을 본떠서. kind=race.
6) at once: at one and the same time.
7) Sho now: Sure now.
8) Ef Kernel wants to give hit to you: If Colonel wants to give it to you.

"Wait," Wash said. "Not yit for a minute."

Neither did Sutpen deny the dress. "What about it?" he said.

But Wash met his arrogant stare; he spoke quietly. "I've knowed[1] you for going on twenty years. I ain't never yit denied to do what you told me to do. And I'm a man nigh[2] sixty. And she ain't nothing but a fifteen-year-old gal."[3]

"Meaning that I'd harm a girl? I, a man as old as you are?" "If you was ara other man,[4] I'd say you was as old as me. And old or no old, I wouldn't let her keep that dress nor nothing else that come from your hand. But you are different."

"How different?" But Wash merely looked at him with his pale, questioning, sober eyes. "So that's why you are afraid of me?"

Now Wash's gaze no longer questioned. It was tranquil, serene. "I ain't afraid. Because you air brave. It ain't that you were a brave man at one minute or day of your life and got a paper to show hit from General Lee. But you air brave, the same as you air alive and breathing. That's where hit's different. Hit don't need no ticket from nobody to tell me that. And I know that whatever you handle or tech,[5] whether hit's a regiment of men or a ignorant gal or just a hound dog, that you will make hit right."

Now it was Sutpen who looked away, turning suddenly, brusquely. "Get the jug," he said sharply.

"Sho, Kernel," Wash said.

So on that Sunday dawn two years later, having watched the Negro midwife, which he had walked three miles to fetch, enter the crazy door beyond which his granddaughter lay wailing, his heart was still quiet though concerned. He knew what they had been saying — the Negroes in cabins about the land, the white men who loafed all day

1) knowed: known.
2) nigh: near.
3) And she ain't nothing but a fifteen-year-old gal.: And she is only a fifteen-year-old girl.
4) If you was ara other man: If you were any other man.
5) tech: touch.

long about the store, watching quietly the three of them: Sutpen, himself, his granddaughter with her air of brazen and shrinking defiance as her condition became daily more and more obvious,[1] like three actors that came and went upon a stage. "I know what they say to one another," he thought. "I can almost hyear[2] them: *Wash Jones has fixed[3] old Sutpen at last. Hit taken him[4] twenty years, but he has done hit at last.*"

It would be dawn after a while, though not yet. From the house, where the lamp shone dim beyond the warped doorframe, his granddaughter's voice came steadily as though run by a clock, while thinking went slowly and terrifically, fumbling, involved somehow with a sound of galloping hooves, until there broke suddenly free in mid-gallop the fine proud figure of the man on the fine proud stallion, galloping; and then that at which thinking fumbled, broke free too and quite clear, not in justification nor even explanation, but as the apotheosis, lonely, explicable, beyond all fouling by human touch: "He is bigger than all them Yankees that kilt his son and his wife and taken his niggers and ruined his land, bigger than this hyer durn country that he fit for[5] and that has denied him into keeping a little country store; bigger than the denial which hit helt to his lips like the bitter cup in the Book.[6] And how could I have lived this nigh to him for twenty years without being teched and changed by him? Maybe I ain't as big as him and maybe I ain't done none of the galloping. But at least I done been drug along.[7] Me and him kin do hit, if so be[8] he will show me what he aims for me to do."

Then it was dawn. Suddenly he could see the house, and the old

---

1) as her condition became daily more and more obvious: 그녀의 상태가 나날이 분명해졌을 때. 즉 배가 나오게 되었을 때를 말함.

2) hyear: hear.

3) *fixed*: (Colloq.) put in a condition or position favorable to oneself or unfavorable to one's opponents; arrange; prepare.

4) *Hit taken him*: It took him.

5) this hyer durn country that he fit for: this here darn country that he fought for. darn=(Colloq.) damn; cursed.

6) bigger than the denial which … like the bitter cup in the Book: 그 사람은 성경에 나오는 고배의 잔처럼 그의 입술에 들이댄 거부에 끄떡도 안했다.

7) I done been drug along: I have been dragged along.

8) if so be: if.

Negress in the door looking at him. Then he realized that his granddaughter's voice had ceased. "It's a girl," the Negress said. "You can go tell him if you want to." She re-entered the house.

"A girl," he repeated; "a girl"; in astonishment, hearing the galloping hooves, seeing the proud galloping figure emerge again. He seemed to watch it pass, galloping through avatars which marked the accumulation of years, time,[1] to the climax where it galloped beneath a brandished saber[2] and a shot-torn flag rushing down a sky in color like thunderous sulphur,[3] thinking for the first time in his life that perhaps Sutpen was an old man like himself. "Gittin a gal,"[4] he thought in that astonishment; then he thought with the pleased surprise of a child: "Yes, sir. Be dawg if I ain't lived[5] to be a great-grandpaw[6] after all."

He entered the house. He moved clumsily, on tiptoe, as if he no longer lived there, as if the infant which had just drawn breath and cried in light had dispossessed him,[7] be it of his own blood too though it might.[8] But even above the pallet he could see little save the blur of his granddaughter's exhausted face. Then the Negress squatting at the hearth spoke, "You better gawn tell him if you going to. Hit's daylight now."

But this was not necessary. He had no more than turned the corner of the porch where the scythe leaned which he had borrowed three months ago to clear away the weeds through which he walked, when Sutpen himself rode up on the old stallion. He did not wonder how

---

1) avatars which marked the accumulation of years, time: 세월과 시간의 축적을 나타내고 있는 신의 화신(化身)들. avatars=the descent of a deity to the earth in an incarnate form or some manifest shape; the incarnation of a god.

2) a brandished saber: a waved sword.

3) sulphur: sulfur; a greenish yellow.

4) Gittin a gal; Getting a girl.

5) Be dawg if I ain't lived…: 제기랄 나도 그래 오래 살았구나라는 뜻. dog=used in mild profane inprecations.

6) grandpaw=grandpa(=grand father).

7) as if the infant … had dispossessed him: 마치 방금 숨을 쉬고 빛을 보고 운 갓난아기가 그를 (집에서) 내쫓은 것처럼. dispossess=force to give up the possession of a house, land, etc.

8) be it of his own blood too though it might: though it might be of his own blood too.

Sutpen had got the word. He took it for granted that this was what had brought the other out at this hour on Sunday morning, and he stood while the other dismounted, and he took the reins from Sutpen's hand, an expression on his gaunt face almost imbecile[1] with a kind of weary triumph, saying, "Hit's a gal, Kernel. I be dawg if you ain't as old as I am — " until Sutpen passed him and entered the house. He stood there with the reins in his hand and heard Sutpen cross the floor to the pallet. He heard what Sutpen said, and something seemed to stop dead[2] in him before going on.

The sun was now up, the swift sun of Mississippi latitudes, and it seemed to him that he stood beneath a strange sky, in a strange scene, familiar only as things are familiar in dreams, like the dreams of falling to one who has never climbed. "I kain't have heard what I thought I heard," he thought quietly. "I know I kain't." Yet the voice, the familiar voice which had said the words was still speaking, talking now to the old Negress about a colt foaled[3] that morning. "That's why he was up so early," he thought. "That was hit. Hit ain't me and mine. Hit ain't even hisn that got him outen bed."[4]

Sutpen emerged. He descended into the weeds, moving with that heavy deliberation[5] which would have been haste when he was younger. He had not yet looked full at Wash. He said, "Dicey will stay and tend to her. You better — " Then he seemed to see Wash facing him and paused. "What?" he said.

"You said — " To his own ears Wash's voice sounded flat and ducklike, like a deaf man's. "You said if she was a mare, you could give her a good stall in the stable."

"Well?" Sutpen said. His eyes widened and narrowed, almost like a man's fists flexing and shutting,[6] as Wash began to advance towards

---

1) imbecile: silly: absurd.
2) stop dead: stop very quickly or with great force.
3) foaled: gave birth to.
4) Hit ain't even hisn that got him outen bed: It isn't even his that got him out of bed.
5) with that heavy deliberation: with that they heavy and slaw action.
6) like a man's fists flexing and shutting: 굽혔다 닫혔다 하는 사람 주먹처럼. 앞에 나오는 His eyes …에 걸린다.

him, stooping a little. Very astonishment kept Sutpen still for the moment, watching that man whom in twenty years he had no more known to make any motion save at command than he had the horse which he rode. Again his eyes narrowed and widened; without moving he seemed to rear[1] suddenly upright. "Stand back," he said suddenly and sharply. "Don't you touch me."

"I'm going to tech you, Kernel," Wash said in that flat, quiet, almost soft voice, advancing.

Sutpen raised the hand which held the riding whip; the old Negress peered around the crazy door with her black gargoyle face[2] of a worn gnome.[3] "Stand back, Wash," Sutpen said. Then he struck. The old Negress leaped down into the weeds with the agility of a goat and fled. Sutpen slashed Wash again across the face with the whip, striking him to his knees.[4] When Wash rose and advanced once more he held in his hands the scythe which he had borrowed from Sutpen three months ago and which Surpen would never need again.

When he re-entered the house his granddaughter stirred on the pallet bed and called his name fretfully. "What was that?" she said.

"What was what, honey?"

"That ere racket out there."[5]

"Twarn't nothing,"[6] he said gently. He knelt and touched her hot forehead clumsily. "Do you want ara thing?"

"I want a sup[7] of water," she said querulously. "I been laying here wanting a sup of water a long time, but don't nobody care enough to pay me no mind."[8]

"Sho now," he said soothingly. He rose stiffly and fetched the dipper of water and raised her head to drink and laid her back and watched

---

1) rear: raise; lift up.
2) gargoyle face: 괴물같이 흉한 얼굴.
3) gnome[noum]: dwarf supposed to live in the earth and guard precious treasures.
4) striking him to his knees: 그를 때려서 무릎 꿇게 했다.
5) That ere racket out there.: That (there) racker out there.
6) 'Twarn't nothing: It wasn't anything; It was nothing.
7) sup: sip.
8) don't nobody care enough to pay me no mind: anybody doesn't care enough to pay me and mind.

her turn to the child with an absolutely stonelike face. But a moment later he saw that she was crying quietly. "Now, now," he said, "I wouldn't do that. Old Dicey says hit's a right fine gal. Hit's all right now. Hit's all over now. Hit ain't no need to cry now."

But she continued to cry quietly, almost sullenly, and he rose again and stood uncomfortably above the pallet for a time, thinking as he had thought when his own wife lay so and then his daughter in turn: "Women. Hit's a mystry[1] to me. They seem to want em, and yit when they git em they cry about hit. Hit's a mystry to me. To ara man." Then he moved away and drew a chair up to the window and sat down.

Through all that long, bright, sunny forenoon he sat at the window, waiting. Now and then he rose and tiptoed to the pallet. But his granddaughter slept now, her face sullen and calm and weary, the child in the crook of her arm. Then he returned to the chair and sat again, waiting, wondering why it took them so long, until he remembered that it was Sunday. He was sitting there at mid-afternoon when a half-grown white boy came around the corner of the house upon the body and gave a choked cry and looked up and glared for a mesmerized instant at Wash in the window before he turned and fled. Then Wash rose and tiptoed again to the pallet.

The granddaughter was awake now, wakened perhaps by the boy's cry without hearing it. "Milly," he said, "air you hungry?" She didn't answer, turning her face away. He built up the fire on the hearth and cooked the food which he had brought home the day before: fatback[2] it was, and cold corn pone;[3] he poured water into the stale coffee pot and heated it. But she would not eat when he carried the plate to her, so he ate himself, quietly, alone, and left the dishes as they were and returned to the window.

Now he seemed to sense, feel, the men who would be gathering with horses and guns and dogs — the curious, and the vengeful: men

1) mystry: mystery.
2) fatback: the fat and fat meat from the upper part of a side of pork, usually cured by salt.
3) corn pone: bread made of corn meal.

of Sutpen's own kind, who had made the company about Sutpen's table in the time when Wash himself had yet to approach nearer to the house than the scuppernong arbor — men who had also shown the lesser ones how to fight in battle,[1] who maybe also had signed papers from the generals saying that they were among the first of the brave; who had also galloped in the old days arrogant and proud on the fine horses across the fine plantations — symbols also of admiration and hope; instruments too of despair and grief.

That was whom they would expect him to run from.[2] It seemed to him that he had no more to run from than he had to run to. If he ran, he would merely be fleeing one set of bragging and evil shadows for another just like them,[3] since they were all of a kind[4] throughout all the earth which he knew, and he was old, too old to flee far even if he were to flee. He could never escape them, no matter how much or how far he ran: a man going on sixty could not run that far. Not far enough to escape beyond the boundaries of earth where such men lived, set the order and the rule of living. It seemed to him that he now saw for the first time, after five years, how it was that Yankees or any other living armies had managed to whip them: the gallant, the proud, the brave; the acknowledged and chosen best among them all to carry courage and honor and pride. Maybe if he had gone to the war with them he would have discovered them sooner. But if he had discovered them sooner, what would he have done with his life since? How could he have borne to remember for five years what his life had been before?

Now it was getting toward sunset. The child had been crying; when he went to the pallet he saw his granddaughter nursing it, her face

1) men who had also shown the lesser ones how to fight in battle: 신분이 보다 낮은 사람들에게 전투하는 방법을 가르쳐 주었던 사람들.

2) That was whom they would expect him to run from.: That was the people whom they would expect him to run from. That는 앞에 묘사된 납부의 지주들. they는 일반 사람들을 가리킨다.

3) If he ran … evil shadows for another just like them: 설사 그가 도망치더라도 그는 한 무리의 사악하고 거만한 사람들로부터 그들과 똑같은 다른 무리에게로 도망치는 것이 될 것이다.

4) of a kind: of the same kind; same.

still bemused, sullen, inscrutable. "Air you hungry yit?" he said.

"I don't want nothing."

"You ought to eat."

This time she did not answer at all, looking down at the child. He returned to his chair and found that the sun had set. "Hit kain't be much longer," he thought. He could feel them quite near now, the curious and the vengeful.[1] He could even seem to hear what they were saying about him, the undercurrent of believing beyond the immediate fury: *Old Wash Jones he come a tumble at last. He thought he had Sutpen, but Sutpen fooled him. He thought he had Kernel where he would have to marry the gal or pay up. And Kernel refused.* "But I never expected that, Kernel!" he cried aloud, catching himself at the sound of his own voice, glancing quickly back to find his granddaughter watching him.

"Who you talking to now?" she said.

"Hit ain't nothing. I was just thinking and talked out before I knowed hit."

Her face was becoming indistinct again, again a sullen blur in the twilight. "I reckon so. I reckon you'll have to holler[2] louder than that before he'll hear you, up yonder at that house. And I reckon you'll need to do more than holler before you get him down here too."

"Sho now," he said. "Don't you worry none." But already thinking was going smoothly on: "You know I never. You know how I ain't never expected or asked nothing from ara living man but what I expected from you. And I never asked that. I didn't think hit would need. I said, *I don't need to. What need has a fellow like Wash Jones to question or doubt the man that General Lee himsetf says in a handwrote*[3] *ticket that he was brave*? Brave," he thought. "Better if nara one of them had never rid back home in '65"[4]; thinking *Better if his kind and mine*

1) the curious and the vengeful: the curious people and the vengeful people.

2) holler: to inform to the police or to a superior; to squeal.

3) *handwrote*: handwritten.

4) Better if nara one of them had never rid back home in '65: Better if not any one of them had ever ridden back home in 1865.

too had never drawn the breath of life on this earth. Better that all who remain of us be blasted from the face of earth than that another Wash Jones should see his whole life shredded from him and shrivel away like a dried shuck[1] thrown onto the fire.

He ceased, became still. He heard the horses, suddenly and plainly; presently he saw the lantern and the movement of men, the glint of gun barrels, in its moving light. Yet he did not stir. It was quite dark now, and he listened to the voices and the sounds of underbrush[2] as they surrounded the house. The lantern itself came on; its light fell upon the quiet body in the weeds and stopped, the horses tall and shadowy. A man descended and stooped in the lantern light, above the body. He held a pistol; he rose and faced the house. "Jones," he said.

"I'm here," Wash said quietly from the window. "That you, Major?"

"Come out."

"Sho," he said quietly. "I just want to see to[3] my granddaughter."

"We'll see to her. Come on out."

"Sho, Major. Just a minute."

"Show a light. Light your lamp."

"Sho. In just a minute." They could hear his voice retreat into the house, though they could not see him as he went swiftly to the crack in the chimney where he kept the butcher knife: the one thing in his slovenly life and house in which he took pride, since it was razor sharp.[4] He approached the pallet, his granddaughter's voice:

"Who is it? Light the lamp, grandpaw."

"Hit won't need no light, honey. Hit won't take but a minute," he said, kneeling, fumbling toward her voice, whispering now.

"Where air you?"

"Right here," she said fretfully. "Where would I be? What is. . ." His hand touched her face. "What is. . . Grandpaw! Grand. . . ."

"Jones!" the sheriff said. "Come out of there!"

---

1) *shuck*: husk; pod.
2) underbrush: undergrowth; shrubs.
3) see to: attend to; take care of.
4) razor sharp: sharp as a razor.

"In just a minute, Major," he said. Now he rose and moved swiftly. He knew where in the dark the can of kerosene was, just as he knew that it was full, since it was not two days ago that he had filled it at the store and held it there until he got a ride home with it, since the five gallons were heavy. There were still coals on the hearth; besides, the crazy building itself was like tinder: the coals, the hearth, the walls exploding in a single blue glare. Against it the waiting men saw him in a wild instant springing toward them with the lifted scythe before the horses reared and whirled. They checked the horses and turned them back toward the glare, yet still in wild relief against it[1)] the gaunt figure ran toward them with the lifted scythe.

"Jones!" the sheriff shouted; "stop! Stop, or I'll shoot. Jones! *Jones*!" Yet still the gaunt, furious figure came on against the glare and roar of the flames. With the scythe lifted, it bore down upon them,[2)] upon the wild glaring eyes of the horses and the swinging glints of gun barrels, without any cry, any sound.

---

1) in wild relief against it: 그것을 배경으로 뚜렷하게. in relief=standing out from a surface.

2) it bore down upon them: 그것은 그들을 향해 달려오고 있었다. it는 the gaunt, furious figure를 말함.

Winter Dreams

by F. Scott Fitzgerald

F. Scott Fitzgerald (1896-1940) was bern in St. Paul, Minnesota, and educated in the public schools of St. Paul at the Newman School of Hackensack, New Jersey, and at Princeton University. In college he formed a friendship with Edmund Wilson and contributed poems and stories to the *Nassau Literary Magazine*. He left Princeton in 1917 to join the army, soon after the United States entered World War I. He was commissioned a lieutenant in the infantry but was not sent overseas. In 1920 he married Zelda Sayre of Montgomery, Alabama. That same year he published *This Side of Paradise*, a novel about the flaming youth of the postwar era, which made him famous. Thereafter, Fitzgerald devoted himself to the writing of prose fiction. He often lived abroad — in Paris, in Italy, and on the French Riviera. His last years were spent in Hollywood, where he died of a heart attack.

Fitzgerald is admired particularly for capturing the spirit of the 1920's — both the recklessness and the fear and cynicism that colored its gaiety. During the late 1940's and early 1950's there was a notable Fitzgerald revival to which many distinguished writers and critics contributed, and Fitzgerald achieved, suddenly, a critical importance. Most students are now inclined to agree with Arthur Mizner's judgment that "Fitzgerald's reputation as a serious novelist is secure."

I

Some Of the caddies[1] were poor as sin and lived in oneroom houses with a neurasthenic cow in the front yard, but Dexter Green's father owned the second best grocery-store in Black Bear — the best one was "The Hub," patronized by the wealthy people from Sherry Island — and Dexter caddied only for pocket-money.

In the fall when the days became crisp and gray, and the long Minnesota[2] winter shut down like the white lid of a box, Dexter's skis moved over the snow that hid the fairways[3] of the golf course.

---

1) caddy: person who carries a golf player's clubs and finds the ball, etc.

2) Minnesota: middle western state of the United States.

3) fairway: (Golf) the mowed and tended area between the tee and putting green.

At these times the country gave him a feeling of profound melancholy — it offended him that the links[1] should lie in enforced fallowness, haunted by ragged sparrows for the long season. It was dreary, too, that on the tees[2] where the gay colors fluttered in summer there were now only the desolate sand-boxes knee-deep in crusted ice.[3] When he crossed the hills the wind blew cold as misery, and if the sun was out he tramped with his eyes squinted up against the hard dimensionless glare.[4]

In April the winter ceased abruptly. The snow ran down into Black Bear Lake scarcely tarrying for[5] the early golfers to brave[6] the season with red and black balls. Without elation, without an interval of moist glory, the cold was gone.

Dexter knew that there was something dismal about this Northern spring, just as he knew there was something gorgeous about the fall. Fall made him clinch his hands and tremble and repeat idiotic sentences to himself, and make brisk abrupt gestures of command to imaginary audiences and armies. October filled him with hope which November raised to a sort of ecstatic triumph, and in this mood the fleeting brilliant impressions of the summer at Sherry Island were ready grist to his mill.[7] He became a golf champion and defeated Mr. T. A. Hedrick in a marvellous match played a hundred times over the fairways of his imagination, a match each detail of which he changed about untiringly — sometimes he won with almost laughable ease, sometimes he came up magnificently from behind. Again, stepping from a

---

1) links: golf course.

2) tee: a little mound of sand on which a golf ball is placed when a player drives.

3) there were now only the desolate sand-boxes knee-deep in crusted ice: 지금은 무릎까지 빠지는 엉겨 굳어진 얼음판에 파묻혀 있는 모래 상자만이 보일 뿐 쓸쓸한 광경이었다.

4) he tramped with his eyes squinted up against the hard dimensionless glare: 그는 그 강력하고도 형태도 없는 (길이도, 너비도, 높이도 없는) 햇빛에 눈을 가느다랗게 뜨면서 무거운 발걸음을 옮겼다.

5) scarcely tarrying for: ~을 기다리지 못하고. tarry=wait for.

6) brave: meet without fear; defy; dare.

7) ready grist to his mill: 그의 (꿈의) 제분공장에서 가공되는 제분용 곡물(이었다).라는 것은 그에게 알맞는 꿈을 제공했다라는 뜻. grist=grain to be ground
cf. All is grist that comes to his mill. (속담) 그는 무엇이든지 이용한다. bring grist to the mill 벌이가 되다.

Pierce-Arrow automobile,[1] like Mr. Mortimer Jones, he strolled frigidly into the lounge of the Sherry Island Golf Club — or perhaps, surrounded by an admiring crowd, he gave an exhibition of fancy diving from the spring-board[2] of the club raft.[3] . . . Among those who watched him in open-mouthed wonder was Mr. Mortimer Jones.

And one day it came to pass[4] that Mr. Jones — himself and not his ghost — came up to Dexter with tears in his eyes and said that Dexter was the — best caddy in the club, and wouldn't he decide not to quit if Mr. Jones made it worth his while,[5] because every other caddy in the club lost one ball a hole[6] for him — regularly —

"No, sir," said Dexter decisively, "I don't want to caddy any more." Then, after a pause: "I'm too old."

"You're not more than fourteen. Why the devil did you decide just this morning that you wanted to quit? You promised that next week you'd go over to the State tournament[7] with me."

"I decided I was too old."

Dexter handed in[8] his "A Class" badge, collected what money was due him[9] from the caddy master, and walked home to Black Bear Village.

"The best — caddy I ever saw," shouted Mr. Mortimer Jones over a drink[10] that afternoon. "Never lost a ball! Willing! Intelligent! Quiet! Honest! Grateful!"

The little girl who had done this was eleven — beautifully ugly as

---

1) Pierce-Arrow automobile: 자동차 이름. 이 회사는 Buick과 같이 1901년에 설립되었음.
2) spring-board: a projecting board from which persons dive.
3) raft: logs or boards fastened together to make a floating platform.
4) came to pass: happened.
5) wouldn't he decide not to quit if Mr. Jones made it worth his while: 보수를 넉넉히 줄 것이니 캐디를 그만 두지 않겠다고 결심하지 않겠는가. and he asked, "Will you not decide to stay if I pay you a good sum of money?"라고 직접화법으로 고쳐볼 수 있다.
6) lost one ball a hole: 홀마다 공을 잃었다.
7) state tournament: 주(州) 선수권 대회.
8) hand in: turn in; to give to someone; deliver to someone.
9) what money was due him: amount of money to be paid to him.
10) over a drink: 한 잔 마시면서.

little girls are apt to be who are destined after a few years to be inexpressibly lovely and bring no end of misery[1] to a great number of men. The spark, however, was perceptible. There was a general ungodliness in the way her lips twisted down at the corners when she smiled, and in the — Heaven help us! — in the almost passionate quality of her eyes. Vitality is born early in such women. It was utterly in evidence now, shining through her thin frame in a sort of glow.

She had come eagerly out on to the course at nine o'clock with a white linen nurse and five small new golf-clubs in a white canvas bag which the nurse was carrying. When Dexter first saw her she was standing by the caddy house, rather ill at ease[2] and trying to conceal the fact[3] by engaging her nurse in an obviously unnatural conversation graced by startling and irrelevant grimaces from herself.[4]

"Well, it's certainly a nice day, Hilda," Dexter heard her say. She drew down the corners of her mouth, smiled, and glanced furtively around, her eyes in transit falling for an instant on Dexter.

Then to the nurse:

"Well, I guess there aren't very many people out here this morning, are there?"

The smile again — radiant, blatantly artificial[5] — convincing.

"I don't know what we're supposed to do now," said the nurse, looking nowhere in particular.

"Oh, that's all right. I'll fix it up.[6]"

Dexter stood perfectly still, his mouth slightly ajar. He knew that if he moved forward a step his stare would be in her line of vision — if he moved backward he would lose his full view of her face. For a moment he had not realized how young she was. Now he

---

1) bring no end of misery: bring endless misery.

2) ill at ease: uncomfortable.

3) the fact: to be ill at ease라는 사실.

4) by engaging her nurse … irrelevant grimaces from herself: (사람의 눈을) 놀라게 하며, 소녀에겐 어울리지도 않는 찌푸린 얼굴로 분명히 부자연한 이야기를 유모와 주고 받음으로써 (그 사실을 얼버무리려 하고 있었다). grimace=twisting of the face

5) blatantly artificial: 아주 부자연스러운.

6) fix it up: arrange it; settle it.

remembered having seen her several times the year before in bloomers.[1)]

Suddenly, involuntarily, he laughed, a short abrupt laugh — then, startled by himself, he turned and began to walk quickly away.

"Boy!"

Dexter stopped.

"Boy — "

Beyond question he was addressed.[2)] Not only that, but he was treated to that absurd smile, that preposterous smile[3)] — the memory of which at least a dozen men were to carry into middle age.[4)]

"Boy, do you know where the golf teacher is?"

"He's giving a lesson."

"Well, do you know where the caddy-master is?"

"He isn't here yet this morning."

"Oh." For a moment this baffled her. She stood alternately on her right and left foot.

"We'd like to get a caddy," said the nurse. "Mrs. Mortimer Jones sent us out to play golf, and we don't know how without we get a caddy."

Here she was stopped by an ominous glance from Miss Jones, followed immediately by the smile.

"There aren't any caddies here except me," said Dexter to the nurse, "and I got to stay here in charge[5)] until the caddy-master gets here."

"Oh."

Miss Jones and her retinue now withdrew, and at a proper distance from Dexter became involved in a heated conversation, which was concluded by Miss Jones taking one of the clubs and hitting it on the ground with violence. For further emphasis she raised it again and was about to bring it down smartly[6)] upon the nurse's bosom, when the

---

1) bloomers: loose trousers, gathered at the knee, worn by women and girls for physical training.
2) was addressed: was spoken to.
3) that preposterous smile: that absurd smile.
4) the memory of which … into middle age: 그것은 적어도 뭇 남자들이 중년에 이르기까지 잊어버릴 수 없이 가슴 속 깊이 간직하는 추억.
5) in charge: trusted to take care of.
6) smartly: sharply.

nurse seized the club and twisted it from her hands.

"You damn little mean old *thing*!"[1] cried Miss Jones wildly.

Another argument ensued. Realizing that the elements of the comedy were implied in the scene, Dexter several times began to laugh, but each time restrained the laugh before it reached audibility. He could not resist the monstrous conviction that the little girl was justified in beatin g[2] the nurse.

The situation was resolved by the fortuitous appearance[3] of the caddy-master, who was appealed to immediately by the nurse.

"Miss Jones is to have a little caddy, and this one[4] says he can't go."

"Mr. McKenna said I was to wait here till you came," said Dexter quickly.

"Well, he's here now." Miss Jones smiled cheerfully at the caddy-master. Then she dropped her bag and set off[5] at a haughty mince[6] toward the first tee.

"Well?" The caddy-master turned to Dexter. "What you standing there like a dummy[7] for? Go pick up[8] the young lady's clubs."

"I don't think I'll go out to-day," said Dexter.

"You don't — "

"I think I'll quit."

The enormity of his decision frightened him. He was a favorite caddy, and the thirty dollars a month he earned through the summer were not to be made elsewhere around the lake. But he had received a strong emotional shock, and his perturbation[9] required a violent and immediate outlet.

It is not so simple as that, either. As so frequently would be the

---

1) mean old *thing*: nasty, old thing 놈; 년.
2) was justified in beating: 때리는 것도 당연하였다.
3) by the fortuitous appearance: 뜻밖에 나타남으로써. fortuitous=accidental; happening by chance.
4) this one: this caddy.
5) set off: started; went.
6) at a haughty mince: with short little steps in an effected manner.
7) dummy: a stupid person.
8) Go pick up: Go and pick up.
9) perturbation: mental agitation.

case in the future, Dexter was unconsciously dictated to by his winter dreams.

II

Now, of course, the quality and the seasonability[1)] of these winter dreams varied, but the stuff of them remained. They persuaded Dexter several years later to pass up[2)] a business course at the State university — his father, prospering now, would have paid his way — for the precarious advantage of attending an older and more famous university in the East, where he was bothered by his scanty funds. But do not get the impression, because his winter dreams happened to be concerned at first with musings on the rich, that there was anything merely snobbish in the boy. He wanted not association with glittering things and glittering people — he wanted the glittering things themselves. Often he reached out for[3)] the best without knowing why he wanted it — and sometimes he ran up against[4)] the mysterious denials and prohibitions in which life indulges.[5)] It is with one of those denials and not with his career as a whole that this story deals.

He made money. It was rather amazing. After college he went to the city from which Black Bear Lake draws its wealthy patrons. When he was only twenty-three and had been there not quite two years, there were already people who liked to say: "Now there's a boy — " All about him rich men's sons were peddling[6)] bonds precariously, or investing patrimonies precariously, or plodding through the two dozen volumes of the "George Washington Commercial Course," but Dexter borrowed a thousand dollars on his college degree and his confident mouth, and bought a partnership in a laundry.

---

1) seasonability: seasonableness.
2) pass up: give up.
3) reached out for: ~에 손을 뻗쳤다.
4) ran up against: ~에 부딪쳤다.
5) the mysterious denials and prohibitions in which life indulges: 생활이 빠지는 불가사의한 절제와 금제. 즉 인생에 있어서 마음대로 되지 않는 운명을 뜻함.
6) peddle: sell.

It was a small laundry when he went into it but Dexter made a specialty of learning how the English washed fine woollen golf-stockings without shrinking them, and within a year he was catering to the trade[1] that wore knickerbockers.[2] Men were insisting that their Shetland hose[3] and sweaters go to his laundry just as they had insisted on a caddy who could find golf-balls. A little later he was doing their wives' lingerie[4] as well — and running five branches in different parts of the city. Before he was twenty-seven he owned the largest string of laundries in his section of the country. It was then that he sold out and went to New York. But the part of his story that concerns us goes back to the days when he was making his first big success.

When he was twenty-three Mr. Hart — one of the gray-haired men who like to say "Now there's a boy"— gave him a guest card[5] to the Sherry Island Golf Club for a week-end. So he signed his name one day on the register, and that afternoon played golf in a foursome[6] with Mr. Hart and Mr. Sandwood and Mr. T. A. Hedrick. He did not consider it necessary to remark that he had once carried Mr. Hart's bag over this same links, and that he knew every trap and gully[7] with his eyes shut — but he found himself glancing at the four caddies who trailed them,[8] trying to catch a gleam[9] or gesture that would remind him of himself, that would lessen the gap which lay between his present and his past.

It was a curious day, slashed abruptly with fleeting, familiar impressions.[10] One minute he had the sense of being a trespasser — in the

1) was catering to the trade: 고객의 요구를 충족시키고 있었다. cater=provide or supply.
2) knickerbockers: short loose-fitting trousers gathered in at or just below the knee.
3) Shetland hose: 영국 쉐트랜드 산 스타킹. Shetland=British islands NE of Scotland. hose=stockings.
4) lingerie: women's underwear.
5) guest card: invitation card.
6) foursome: in golf a game played by four people, two on each side.
7) trap and gully: pit fall and ditch.
8) trailed them: followed them.
9) gleam: gleam of eyes.
10) slashed abruptly with fleeting, familiar impressions: 지나간 그리운 인상으로 갑자기 새겨진 (기묘한 날이었다). slash abruptly with~=cut suddenly with.

next[1] he was impressed by the tremendous superiority he felt toward Mr. T. A. Hedrick, who was a bore[2] and not even a good golfer any more.

Then, because of a ball Mr. Hart lost near the fifteenth green,[3] an enormous thing happened. While they were searching the stiff grasses of the rough[4] there was a clear call of "Fore!"[5] from behind a hill in their rear. And as they all turned abruptly from their search a bright new ball sliced abruptly over the hill and caught Mr. T. A. Hedrick in the abdomen.

"By Gad!"[6] cried Mr. T. A. Hedrick, "they ought to put some of these crazy women off[7] the course.[8] It's getting to be outrageous."

A head and a voice came up together over the hill:

"Do you mind if we go through?"

"You hit me in the stomach!" declared Mr. Hedrick wildly.

"Did I?" The girl approached the group of men. "I'm sorry. I yelled 'Fore!'"

Her glance fell casually on each of the men — then scanned the fairway for her ball.

"Did I bounce into the rough?"

It was impossible to determine whether this question was ingenuous or malicious. In a moment, however, she left no doubt, for as her partner came up over the hill she called cheerfully:

"Here I am! I'd have gone on the green except that I hit something."

As she took her stance[9] for a short mashie[10] shot, Dexter looked at her closely. She wore a blue gingham[11] dress, rimmed at throat

1) in the next: in the next minute.
2) a bore: a dull, tiresome person.
3) green: putting green 경타구역(輕打區域). 즉 hole의 주위 20야드 이내의 곳.
4) the rough: any portion of a golf course on which grass, weeds, etc., are untrimmed.
5) Fore: Take care, it's dangerous in front as the ball goes!.
6) By Gad: By God!.
7) put ~ off: take ~ away.
8) course: golf course.
9) took her stance: 자세를 취했다. stance=the position of a player whn striking.
10) mashie: club with a short sloping face made of steel.
11) gingham: a cotton cloth made from colored threads, usually in stripes, plaids, or checks.

and shoulders with a white edging that accentuated her tan.[1] The quality of exaggeration, of thinness, which had made her passionate eyes and down-turning mouth absurd at eleven, was gone now. She was arrestingly beautiful. The color in her cheeks was centred[2] like the color in a picture — it was not a "high" color,[3] but a sort of fluctuating and feverish warmth,[4] so shaded that it seemed at any moment it would recede and disappear. This color and the mobility of her mouth gave a continual impression of flux,[5] of intense life, of passionate vitality — balanced only partially by the sad luxury of her eyes.

She swung her mashie impatiently and without interest, pitching the ball into a sand-pit on the other side of the green. With a quick, insincere smile and a careless "Thank you!" she went on after it.

"That Judy Jones!" remarked Mr. Hedrick on the next tee, as they waited — some moments — for her to play on ahead. "All she needs is to be turned up and spanked[6] for six months and then to be married off to an old-fashioned cavalry captain."

"My God, she's good-looking!" said Mr. Sandwood, who was just over thirty.

"Good-looking!" cried Mr. Hedrick contemptuously, "she always looks as if she wanted to be kissed! Turning those big cow-eyes on every calf[7] in town!"

It was doubtful if Mr. Hedrick intended a reference to the maternal instinct.

"She'd play pretty good golf if she'd try," said Mr. Sandwood.

"She has no form," said Mr. Hedrick solemnly.

"She has a nice figure," said Mr. Sandwood.

"Better thank the Lord she doesn't drive a swifter ball," said Mr.

---

1) accentuated her tan: 그녀의 햇볕에 탄 얼굴을 더욱 뚜렷이 하였다. tan=the brown color of a person's skin resulting from being in the sun mand air.
2) centred: collected at a center.
3) "high" color: 강한 빛깔; 홍조를 띤 안색.
4) a sort of fluctuating and feverish warmth: 일종의 파동치는 열띤 따스함(을 지니고 있었다).
5) flux: flow; state of flowing.
6) spanked: strike with the open hand on the buttocks.
7) calf: (Colloq.) a silly boy.

Hart, winking at Dexter.

Later in the afternoon the sun went down with a riotous swirl of gold and varying blues and scarlets, and left the dry, rustling night of Western summer. Dexter watched from the veranda of the Golf Club, watched the even overlap of the waters[1] in the little wind, silver molasses under the harvest-moon. Then the moon held a finger to her lips[2] and the lake became a clear pool, pale and quiet. Dexter put on his bathing-suit and swam out to the farthest raft, where he stretched dripping on the wet canvas of the springboard.

There was a fish jumping and a star shining and the lights around the lake were gleaming. Over on a dark peninsula a piano was playing the songs of last summer and of summers before that — songs from "Chin-Chin"[3] and "The Count of Luxemburg"[4] and "The Chocolate Soldier"[5] — and because the sound of a piano over a stretch of water had always seemed beautiful to Dexter he lay perfectly quiet and listened.

The tune the piano was playing at that moment had been gay and new five years before when Dexter was a sophomore at college. They had played it at a prom[6] once when he could not afford the luxury of proms, and he had stood outside the gymnasium and listened. The sound of the tune precipitated[7] in him a sort of ecstasy and it was with that ecstasy he viewed what happened to him now. It was a mood of intense appreciation, a sense that, for once, he was magnificently attune to life and that everything about him was radiating a brightness and a glamour he might never know again.[8]

---

1) the even overlap of the waters: 거듭 겹치는 수면의 잔 물결.
2) held a finger to her lips: a signal to be silent.
3) Chin-Chin: 중국어로 축배할 때 하는 인사. 여기서는 Chin-Chin-China man 즉 Austrian actor, play wright and the theatrical manager였던 Oscar Asche(1872 -1936)가 작곡한 musical comedy, "Chin-Chin-Chow"(1916)일 것이다.
4) The Count of Luxemburg: 헝가리 오페레타 작곡가 Frant Lehai(1870-1948)가 1909년의 작곡한 operetta.
5) "The Chocolate Soldier": Oskar Straus가 Bernard Shaw의 극 *Arms and the Man*에서 1908년 작곡한 operetta.
6) prom: dance or ball given by a college.
7) precipitated: brought about suddenly.
8) a sense that, for once, he was magnificently attune to life … know again: 이번만은 인생에 멋들어지게 조화를 이루고 있으며, 자기를 둘러싼 온갖 것이 두 번 다시 알 수 없는 광휘와 매력을 발산하고 있다는 의식(이었다).

A low, pale oblong detached itself suddenly from the darkness of the Island, spitting forth the reverberate sound of a racing motor-boat. Two white streamers of cleft water rolled themselves out behind it and almost immediately the boat was beside him, drowning out the hot tinkle of the piano in the drone of its spray. Dexter raising himself on his arms was aware of a figure standing at the wheel, of two dark eyes regarding him over the lengthening space of water — then the boat had gone by and was sweeping in an immense and purposeless circle of spray round and round in the middle of the lake.[1] With equal eccentricity[2] one of the circles flattened out and headed back toward the raft.

"Who's that?" she called, shutting off her motor. She was so near now that Dexter could see her bathing-suit, which consisted apparently of pink rompers.[3]

The nose of the boat bumped the raft, and as the latter tilted rakishly he was precipitated toward her. With different degrees of interest they recognized each other.

"Aren't you one of those men we played through this afternoon?" she demanded.

He was.

"Well, do you know how to drive a motor-boat? Because if you do I wish you'd drive this one so I can ride on the surf-board[4] behind. My name is Judy Jones" — she favored him with an absurd smirk[5] — rather, what tried to be a smirk, for, twist her mouth as she might, it was not grotesque, it was merely beautiful — "and I live in a house over there on the Island, and in that house there is a man waiting for me. When he drove up at the door I drove out of the dock because he says I'm his ideal."

There was a fish jumping and a star shining and the lights around the lake were gleaming. Dexter sat beside Judy Jones and she explained

---

1) was sweeping in an immense and purposeless circle … in the middle of the lake: 호심(湖心) 근처에 커다란 비밀의 원(파문)이 까닭 없이 그려지고 있었다.

2) With equal eccentricity: 조금 전과 똑같이 괴상하게도. eccentricity=unusual manner.

3) rompers: a loose outer garment, worn by children at play.

4) surf-board: a long, narrow board for riding the surf.

5) smirk: a smile in an affected, silly, self-satisfied way.

how her boat was driven. Then she was in the water, swimming to the floating surfboard with a sinuous crawl.[1] Watching her was without effort to the eye, watching a branch waving or a sea-gull flying. Her arms, burned to butternut,[2] moved sinuously among the dull platinum ripples, elbow appearing first, casting the forearm back with a cadence of falling water,[3] then reaching out and down, stabbing a path ahead.[4]

They moved out into the lake; turning, Dexter saw that she was kneeling on the low rear of the now uptilted surfboard.

"Go faster," she called, "fast as it'll go."

Obediently he jammed the lever forward[5] and the white spray mounted at the bow. When he looked around again the girl was standing up on the rushing board, her arms spread wide, her eyes lifted toward the moon.

"It's awful cold," she shouted. "What's your name?"

He told her.

"Well, why don't you come to dinner tomorrow night?"

His heart turned over like the fly-wheel[6] of the boat, and, for the second time, her casual whim gave a new direction to his life.

III

Next evening while he waited for her to come downstairs, Dexter peopled[7] the soft deep summer room[8] and the sun-porch that opened from it with the men who had already loved Judy Jones. He knew the sort of men they were — the men who when he first went to college had entered from the great prep schools[9] with graceful clothes and

---

1) crawl: crawl stroke.
2) burned to butternut: 호두빛깔로 탄. butternut=dark brown.
3) casting the forearm back with a cadence of falling water: 앞팔을 떨어지는 물결소리와 더불어 되돌리면서.
4) stabbing a path ahead: 앞으로 앞으로 헤엄쳐 나아갔다.
5) jammed the lever forward: (속도를 조절하는) 레바[조종간]를 앞으로 밀었다.
6) fly-wheel: heavy wheel attached to machinery to keep the speed even.
7) peopled … with~: filled in imagination with~.
8) summer room: room with alrge windows, mostly for summer use.
9) prep schools: preparatory school.

the deep tan of healthy summers. He had seen that, in one sense, he was better than these men. He was newer and stronger. Yet in acknowledging to himself that he wished his children to be like them he was admitting that he was but the rough, strong stuff from which they eternally sprang. When the time had come for him to wear good clothes, he had known who were the best tailors in America, and the best tailors in America had made him the suit he wore this evening. He had acquired that particular reserve peculiar to his university, that set it off[1] from other universities. He recognized the value to him of such a mannerism and he had adopted it; he knew that to be careless in dress and manner required more confidence than to be careful. But carelessness was for his children. His mother's name had been Krimelich. She was a Bohemian[2] of the peasant class and she had talked broken English[3] to the end of her days. Her son must keep to the set patterns.[4]

At a little after seven Judy Jones came down-stairs. She wore a blue silk afternoon dress, and he was disappointed at first that she had not put on something more elaborate. This feeling was accentuated when, after a brief greeting, she went to the door of a butler's pantry and pushing it open called: "You can serve dinner, Martha." He had rather expected that a butler would announce dinner, that there would be a cocktail. Then he put these thoughts behind him as they sat down side by side on a lounge[5] and looked at each other.

"Father and mother won't be here," she said thoughtfully.

He remembered the last time he had seen her father, and he was glad the parents were not to be here tonight — they might wonder who he was. He had been born in Keeble, a Minnesota village fifty miles farther north, and he always gave Keeble as his home instead of Black Bear Village. Country towns were well enough to come from if they weren't inconveniently in sight and used as footstools by

---

1) set it off: 그 대학을 (타 대학과) 구별하다.
2) Bohemian: a native of Bohemia.
3) broken English: imperfectly spoken English.
4) Her son must keep to the set patterns: 그녀의 아들만은 올바른 모범적인 인간이 되지 않으면 안되었다.
5) lounge: couych; sofa.

fashionable lakes.[1])

They talked of his university, which she had visited frequently during the past two years, and of the near-by city which supplied Sherry Island with its patrons, and whither[2]) Dexter would return next day to his prospering laundries.

During dinner she slipped into a moody[3]) depression which gave Dexter a feeling of uneasiness. Whatever petulance she uttered in her throaty voice[4]) worried him. Whatever she smiled at — at him, at a chicken liver, at nothing — it disturbed him that her smile could have no root in mirth, or even in amusement. When the scarlet corners of her lips curved down, it was less a smile than an invitation to a kiss.

Then, after dinner, she led him out on the dark sun-porch and deliberately changed the atmosphere.

"Do you mind if I weep a little?" she said.

"I'm afraid I'm boring you," he responded quickly.

"You're not. I like you. But I've just had a terrible afternoon. There was a man I cared about, and this afternoon he told me out of a clear sky[5]) that he was poor as a churchmouse.[6]) He'd never even hinted it before. Does this sound horribly mundane?"[7])

"Perhaps he was afraid to tell you."

"Suppose he was," she answered. "He didn't start right. You see, if I'd thought of him as poor — well, I've been mad about loads of poor men, and fully intended to marry them all. But in this case, I hadn't thought of him that way, and my interest in him wasn't strong enough to survive the shock. As if a girl calmly informed her fiance

---

1) if they weren't … by fashionable lakes: 만일 시골 마을이 거추장스럽게 보이는 그런 곳에 있지 않고 또 호수에 모여드는 사람들의 발판으로 사용되는 그런 곳이 아니라면(고향이라 부르기에 족한 것이었다). weren't inconviently in sight=were not too easily seen from fashionable lakes=were not too near to the golf course. footstool=a low stool to put the feet on when sitting.
2) whither: where; to that city.
3) moody: sullen; ill-humored.
4) Whatever petulance she uttered in her throaty voice: 목쉰 소리로 내갈기는 어떤 급한 성미[토라짐]일지라도.
5) out of a clear sky: 청천벽력으로. (=suddenly).
6) poor as a churchmouse: very poor.
7) sound mundane: 세속적으로 들리다. mundane=earthly.

that she was a widow. He might not object to widows, but—

"Let's start right," she interrupted herself suddenly. "Who are you, anyhow?"

For a moment Dexter hesitated. Then:

"I'm nobody,"[1] he announced. "My career is largely a matter of futures."

"Are you poor?"

"No," he said frankly, "I'm probably making more money than any man my age in the Northwest. I know that's an obnoxious remark,[2] but you advised me to start right."

There was a pause. Then she smiled and the corners of her mouth drooped and an almost imperceptible sway brought her closer to him, looking up into his eyes. A lump rose in Dexter's throat, and he waited breathless for the experiment, facing the unpredictable compound that would form mysteriously from the elements of their lips.[3] Then he saw—she communicated her excitement to him, lavishly, deeply, with kisses that were not a promise but a fulfillment. They aroused in him not hunger demanding renewal but surfeit[4] that would demand more surfeit . . . kisses that were like charity, creating want by holding back nothing at all.[5]

It did not take him many hours to decide that he had wanted Judy Jones ever since he was a proud, desirous little boy.

IV

It began like that—and continued, with varying shades of intensity, on such a note right up to the dénouement.[6] Dexter surrendered a

1) nobody: insignificant person.
2) obnoxious remark: 하기 싫은 말.
3) facing the unpredictable compound … their lips: 그들 입술의 성분에서 신비적으로 만들어질 예측할 수 없는 혼합물에 직면하여.
4) surfeit: excess, esp. in eating and drinking.
5) kisses that were like charity, creating want by holding back nothing at all: 조금도 아낌없이 욕망을 채워주는, 말하자면 자선을 베푸는 것과 같은 키스.
6) dénouement: final situation; last stage.

part of himself to the most direct and unprincipled personality with which he had ever come in contact. Whatever Judy wanted, she went after[1)] with the full pressure of her charm. There was no divergence of method, no jockeying[2)] for position or premeditation of effects — there was a very little mental side to any of her affairs.[3)] She simply made men conscious to the highest degree of her physical loveliness. Dexter had no desire to change her. Her deficiencies were knit up with[4)] a passionate energy that transcended and justified them. When, as Judy's head lay against his shoulder that first night, she whispered, "I don't know what's the matter with me. Last night I thought I was in love with a man and tonight I think I'm in love with you — " — it seemed to him a beautiful and romantic thing to say. It was the exquisite excitability that for the moment he controlled and owned. But a week later he was compelled to view this same quality in a different light. She took him in her roadster[5)] to a picnic supper, and after supper she disappeared, likewise in her roadster, with another man. Dexter became enormously upset and was scarcely able to be decently civil to the other people present. When she assured him that she had not kissed the other man, he knew she was lying — yet he was glad that she had taken the trouble to[6)] lie to him.

He was, as he found before the summer ended, one of a varying dozen who circulated about her. Each of them had at one time been favored above all others — about half of them still basked in the solace of occasional sentimental revivals.[7)] Whenever one showed signs of dropping out[8)] through long neglect, she granted him a brief honeyed

---

1) went after: sought; followed.
2) jockeying: trick to get advantage.
3) her affairs: her love affairs.
4) were knit up with: ~와 결합[밀착, 유착]되고 있었다.
5) roadster: an automobile of the open car for use on ordinary roads, having a single seat for two or more persons.
6) had taken the trouble to: 하려고 애썼다.
7) about half of them still basked in the solace of occasional sentimental revivals: 지금도 그들 중 반수 가량은 가끔 (불꽃처럼) 일어나는 감상적인 부활의 위안에 몸을 녹이고 있었다.
8) dropping out: going away from her.

hour, which encouraged him to tag along[1)] for a year or so longer. Judy made these forays[2)] upon the helpless and defeated without malice, indeed half unconscious that there was anything mischievous in what she did.

When a new man came to town every one dropped out — dates were automatically cancelled.

The helpless part of trying to do anything about it was that she did it all herself. She was not a girl who could be "won" in the kinetic sense[3)] — she was proof against[4)] cleverness, she was proof against charm; if any of these assailed her too strongly she would immediately resolve[5)] the affair to a physical basis, and under the magic of her physical splendor the strong as well as the brilliant played her game and not their own. She was entertained only by the gratification of her desires and by the direct exercise of her own charm. Perhaps from so much youthful love, so many youthful lovers, she had come,[6)] in self-defense, to nourish herself wholly from within.

Succeeding Dexter's first exhilaration came restlessness and dissatisfaction. The helpless ecstasy of losing himself in her was opiate rather than tonic.[7)] It was fortunate for his work during the winter that those moments of ecstasy came infrequently. Early in their acquaintance it had seemed for a while that there was a deep and spontaneous mutual attraction that first August, for example — three days of long evenings on her dusky veranda, of strange wan[8)] kisses through the late afternoon, in shadowy alcoves or behind the protecting trellises of the garden arbors, of mornings when she was fresh as a dream and almost shy at meeting him in the clarity of the rising day. There was all the ecstasy of an engagement about it, sharpened by

---

1) tag along: follow closely.
2) forays: raids for plunder.
3) in the kinetic sense: 동적인 의미로, 행동적으로 나감으로써. kinetic=of motion.
4) proof against: not shaken by.
5) resolve ~ to: convert ~ into.
6) had come: had become.
7) was opiate rather than tonic: 그를 고무하기보다 오히려 마취시켰다. tonic= giving strengh.
8) wan: pale in the color; faint; weak.

his realization that there was no engagement. It was during those three days that, for the first time, he had asked her to marry him. She said "maybe some day," she said "kiss me," she said "I'd like to marry you," she said "I love you" — she said — nothing.

The three days were interrupted by the arrival of a New York man who visited at her house for half September. To Dexter's agony, rumor engaged them. The man was the son of the president of a great trust company. But at the end of a month it was reported that Judy was yawning. At a dance one night she sat all evening in a motor-boat with a local beau,[1] while the New Yorker searched the club for her frantically. She told the local beau that she was bored with her visitor, and two days later he left. She was seen with him at the station, and it was reported that he looked very mournful indeed.

On this note the summer ended. Dexter was twenty-four, and he found himself increasingly in a position to do as he wished. He joined two clubs in the city and lived at one of them. Though he was by no means an integral part of the stag-lines[2] at these clubs, he managed to be on hand[3] at dances where Judy Jones was likely to appear. He could have gone out socially as much as he liked — he was an eligible[4] young man, now, and popular with down-town fathers. His confessed devotion to Judy Jones had rather solidified his position. But he had no social aspirations and rather despised the dancing men who were always on tap[5] for the Thursday or Saturday parties and who filled in at dinners with the younger married set.[6] Already he was playing with the idea of going East to New York. He wanted to take Judy Jones with him. No disillusion as to the world in which she had grown up could cure his illusion as to her desirability.[7]

---

1) beau: lover; dandly.
2) stag-lines: stag=man who goes to dance and party alone or with other men.
3) to be on hand: to be present.
4) eligible: properly qualified; desirable.
5) on tap: ready.
6) married set: married group.
7) No disillusion as to the world … as to her desirability: 그녀가 자라난 세계에 대한 어떠한 환멸도 그녀를 요구하는 그의 환상을 고칠 수는 없었다. his illusion as to her desirability=the fact that he imagined she is a desirable person.

Remember that — for only in the light of it can what he did for her be understood.

Eighteen months after he first met Judy Jones he became engaged to another girl. Her name was Irene Scheerer, and her father was one of the men who had always believed in Dexter. Irene was light-haired and sweet and honorable, and a little stout, and she had two suitors[1] whom she pleasantly relinquished[2] when Dexter formally asked her to marry him.

Summer, fall, winter, spring, another summer, another fall — so much he had given of his active life to the incorrigible lips of Judy Jones. She had treated him with interest, with encouragement, with malice, with indifference, with contempt. She had inflicted on him the innumerable little slights and indignities possible in such a case[3] — as if in revenge for having ever cared for him at all. She had beckoned him and yawned at him and beckoned him again and he had responded often with bitterness and narrowed eyes. She had brought him ecstatic happiness and intolerable agony of spirit. She had caused him untold inconvenience and not a little trouble. She had insulted him, and she had ridden over him, and she had played his interest in her against his interest in his work — for fun. She had done everything to him except to criticise him — this she had not done — it seemed to him only because it might have sullied the utter indifference[4] she manifested and sincerely felt toward him.

When autumn had come and gone again it occurred to him that he could not have Judy Jones. He had to beat this into his mind but he convinced himself at last. He lay awake at night for a while and argued it over. He told himself the trouble and the pain she had caused him, he enumerated her glaring deficiencies[5] as a wife. Then he said

1) suitors: wooers.

2) relinquished: gave up.

3) She had inflicted on him the innumerable little slights and indignities possible in such a case: 그녀는 그러한 경우 될 수 있는 한 여러 가지 헤아릴 수 없는 사소한 경멸과 모욕을 그에게 주었다.

4) because it might have sullied the utter indifference: 철저한 무관심을 훼손하지 않을까 해서.

5) glaring deficiencies: 명백한 결점. glaring=conspicuous.

to himself that he loved her, and after a while he fell asleep. For a week, lest he imagined[1] her husky voice over the telephone or her eyes opposite him at lunch, he worked hard and late, and at night he went to his office and plotted out his years.

At the end of a week he went to a dance and cut in[2] on her once. For almost the first time since they had met he did not ask her to sit out[3] with him or tell her that she was lovely. It hurt him that she did not miss these things — that was all. He was not jealous when he saw that there was a new man tonight. He had been hardened against jealousy long before.

He stayed late at the dance. He sat for an hour with Irene Scheerer and talked about books and about music. He knew very little about either. But he was beginning to be master of his own time now, and he had a rather priggish notion that he — the young and already fabulously successful Dexter Green — should know more about such things.

That was in October, when he was twenty-five. In January, Dexter and Irene became engaged. It was to be announced in June, and they were to be married three months later.

The Minnesota winter prolonged itself interminably, and it was almost May when the winds came soft and the snow ran down into Black Bear Lake at last. For the first time in over a year Dexter was enjoying a certain tranquility of spirit. Judy Jones had been in Florida, and afterward in Hot Springs,[4] and somewhere she had been engaged, and somewhere she had broken it off. At first, when Dexter had definitely given her up, it had made him sad that people still linked them together and asked for news of her, but when he began to be placed at dinner next to Irene Scheerer people didn't ask him about her any more — they told him about her. He ceased to be an authority on her.[5]

May at last. Dexter walked the streets at night when the darkness

---

1) lest he imagined: lest he should imagine.
2) cut in: interrupt a dancing couple to take the place of one of them.
3) sit out: 춤을 추지 않고 쉬며 partner와 이야기를 나누는 것.
4) Hot Springs: Arkansas주의 중부에 있는 온천장.
5) authority on her: source of correct information about her.

was damp as rain, wondering that so soon, with so little done, so much of ecstasy had gone from him. May one year back had been marked[1)] by Judy's poignant, unforgivable, yet forgiven turbulence — it had been one of those rare times when he fancied she had grown to care for him. That old penny's worth of happiness he had spent for this bushel of content.[2)] He knew that Irene would be no more than a curtain spread behind him, a hand moving among gleaming tea-cups, a voice calling to children . . . fire[3)] and loveliness were gone, the magic of nights and the wonder of the varying hours and seasons . . . slender lips, down-turning, dropping to his lips and bearing him up into a heaven of eyes.[4)] . . . The thing was deep in him. He was too strong and alive for it to die lightly.

In the middle of May when the weather balanced for a few days on the thin bridge[5)] that led to deep summer he turned in one night at Irene's house. Their engagement was to be announced in a week now — no one would be surprised at it. And tonight they would sit together on the lounge at the University Club and look on for an hour at the dancers. It gave him a sense of solidity to go with her — she was so sturdily popular, so intensely "great."[6)]

He mounted the steps of the brownstone house and stepped inside.

"Irene," he called.

Mrs. Scheerer came out of the living-room to meet him.

"Dexter," she said, "Irene's gone up-stairs with a splitting headache. She wanted to go with you but I made her go to bed."

"Nothing serious, I — "

"Oh, no. She's going to play golf with you in the morning. You

---

1) had been marked: 마음에 상처를 입었다.

2) That old penny's worth of happiness he had spent for this bushel of content: 그 조그마한 옛날의 행복감을 그는 지금 이 커다란 만족감과 바꾸었던 것이다. that old penny's worth of happiness는 that little amount of happiness of last May를 말함. spent for=exchanged. this bushel of content=this large amount of content.

3) fire: passion.

4) bearing him up into a heaven of eyes: 그를 천국으로 싣고 간. slender lips에 걸린다. 말하자면 her kisses carried his soul up into heaven의 뜻.

5) thin bridge: transition of gradual change; half way between.

6) "great": fine; very good.

can spare her for just one night, can't you, Dexter?"

Her smile was kind. She and Dexter liked each other. In the living-room he talked for a moment before he said good-night.

Returning to the University Club, where he had rooms, he stood in the doorway for a moment and watched the dancers. He leaned against the door-post, nodded at a man or two — yawned.

"Hello, darling."

The familiar voice at his elbow startled him. Judy Jones had left a man and crossed the room to him — Judy Jones, a slender enamelled doll in cloth of gold: gold in a band at her head, gold in two slipper points at her dress's hem. The fragile glow of her face seemed to blossom as she smiled at him. A breeze of warmth and light blew through the room. His hands in the pockets of his dinner-jacket tightened spasmodically. He was filled with a sudden excitement.

"When did you get back?" he asked casually.

"Come here and I'll tell you about it."

She turned and he followed her. She had been away — he could have wept at the wonder of her return. She had passed through enchanted streets, doing things that were like provocative music. All mysterious happenings, all fresh and quickening hopes, had gone away with her, come back with her now.

She turned in the doorway.

"Have you a car here? If you haven't, I have."

"I have a coupé."[1)]

In then,[2)] with a rustle of golden cloth. He slammed the door. Into so many cars she had stepped — like this — like that — her back against the leather, so — her elbow resting on the door — waiting. She would have been soiled long since had there been anything to soil her — except herself — but this was her own self outpouring.

With an effort he forced himself to start the car and back into the street. This was nothing, he must remember. She had done this before, and he had put her behind him,[3)] as he would have crossed a bad

---

1) coupé: a closed, two-door automobile seating two to five people.

2) In then: Then she entered the coupé.

3) he had put her behind him: 그는 이미 그녀와의 관계를 과거지사로 돌리고 있었다.

account from his books.[1)]

He drove slowly down-town and, affecting abstraction, traversed the deserted streets of the business section, peopled here and there where a movie was giving out its crowd or where consumptive or pugilistic youth lounged in front of pool halls.[2)] The clink of glasses and the slap of hands on the bars issued from saloons, cloisters of glazed glass and dirty yellow light.

She was watching him closely and the silence was embarrassing, yet in this crisis he could find no casual word with which to profane[3)] the hour. At a convenient turning he began to zigzag back toward the University Club.

"Have you missed me?" she asked suddenly.

"Everybody missed you."

He wondered if she knew of Irene Scheerer. She had been back only a day — her absence had been almost contemporaneous[4)] with his engagement.

"What a remark!"[5)] Judy laughed sadly — without sadness. She looked at him searchingly. He became absorbed in the dashboard.[6)]

"You're handsomer than you used to be," she said thoughtfully. "Dexter, you have the most rememberable eyes."

He could have laughed at this, but he did not laugh. It was the sort of thing that was said to sophomores. Yet it stabbed at him.

"I'm awfully tired of everything, darling." She called every one darling, endowing the endearment with careless, individual comraderie. "I wish you'd marry me."

The directness of this confused him. He should have told her now that he was going to marry another girl, but he could not tell her. He could as easily have sworn that he had never loved her.

---

1) as he would have crossed a bad account from his books: 마치 장부에서 잘못된 계산을 지워버리고 말듯이. bad account=credit account which will never be paid.
2) pool halls: 공개 도박장.
3) profane: put to unworthy use.
4) contemporaneous: happening at the same time.
5) What a remark!: 그것은 인사말에 지나지 않아요라는 뜻.
6) He became absorbed in the dashboard: 그는 자동차의 계기판을 가만히 들여다보았다. dashboard=the panel with instruments and gaupes in an automobile.

"I think we'd get along,"[1] she continued, on the same note, "unless probably you've forgotten me and fallen in love with another girl."

Her confidence was obviously enormous. She had said, in effect,[2] that she found such a thing impossible to believe, that if it were true he had merely committed a childish indiscretion — and probably to show off.[3] She would forgive him, because it was not a matter of any moment[4] but rather something to be brushed aside lightly.

"Of course you could never love anybody but me," she continued. "I like the way you love me. Oh, Dexter, have you forgotten last year?"

"No, I haven't forgotten."

"Neither have I!"

Was she sincerely moved — or was she carried along by the wave of her own acting?

"I wish we could be like that again," she said, and he forced himself to answer:

"I don't think we can."

"I suppose not. . . . I hear you're giving Irene Scheerer a violent rush."

There was not the faintest emphasis on the name, yet Dexter was suddenly ashamed.

"Oh, take me home," cried Judy suddenly; "I don't want to go back to that idiotic dance — with those children."

Then, as he turned up the street that led to the residence district, Judy began to cry quietly to herself. He had never seen her cry before.

The dark street lightened, the dwellings of the rich loomed up around them, he stopped his coup in front of the great white bulk of the Mortimer Joneses' house, somnolent,[5] gorgeous, drenched with the splendor of the damp moonlight. Its solidity startled him. The strong walls, the steel of the girders,[6] the breadth and beam and pomp of it were

1) get along: agree; live socially.
2) in effect: virtually.
3) show off: make a show; display.
4) moment: importance.
5) somnolent: sleepy; drowsy.
6) girders: a main supporting beam.

there only to bring out the contrast with the young beauty beside him. It was sturdy to accentuate her slightness — as if to show what a breeze could be generated by a butterfly's wing.[1]

He sat perfectly quiet, his nerves in wild clamor, afraid that if he moved he would find her irresistibly in his arms. Two tears had rolled down her wet face and trembled on her upper lip.

"I'm more beautiful than anybody else," she said brokenly, "why can't I be happy?" Her moist eyes tore at[2] his stability — her mouth turned slowly downward with an exquisite sadness: "I'd like to marry you if you'll have me, Dexter. I suppose you think I'm not worth having, but I'll be so beautiful for you, Dexter."

A million phrases of anger, pride, passion, hatred, tenderness fought on his lips. Then a perfect wave of emotion washed over him, carrying off with it a sediment of wisdom, of convention, of doubt, of honor.[3] This was his girl who was speaking, his own, his beautiful, his pride.

"Won't you come in?" He heard her draw in her breath sharply.

Waiting.

"All right," his voice was trembling, "I'll come in."

V

It was strange that neither when it was over nor a long time afterward did he regret that night. Looking at it from the perspective of ten years,[4] the fact that Judy's flare for him endured just one month seemed of little importance. Nor did it matter that by his yielding he subjected himself to a deeper agony in the end[5] and gave serious hurt to Irene

---

1) as if to show what a breeze could be generated by a butterfly's wing: 마치 나비의 날개가 어느 정도의 산들바람을 일으키게 할 수 있는가를 나타내는 것처럼. 나비는 결혼의 상징으로 사용되므로, 그녀를 품에 안으면 어떤 행운의 정(情)을 품게 되는 것인지라는 뜻.

2) tore at: pulled hard.

3) carrying off with it … of honor: 이와 더불어 예지, 인습, 의혹, 명예의 침전물(沈澱物)은 일시에 날아가 버렸다.

4) from the perspective of ten years: 십 년의 세월을 보내고서.

5) he subjected himself to a deeper agony in the end: 결국에 가서는 더 심각한 고뇌에 빠지고 말았다.

Scheerer and to Irene's parents, who had befriended him. There was nothing sufficiently pictorial about Irene's grief to stamp itself on his mind. Dexter was at bottom hard-minded. The attitude of the city on his action was of no importance to him, not because he was going to leave the city, but because any outside attitude on the situation seemed superficial. He was completely indifferent to popular opinion. Nor, when he had seen that it was no use, that he did not possess in himself the power to move fundamentally or to hold Judy Jones, did he bear any malice toward her. He loved her, and he would love her until the day he was too old for loving — but he could not have her. So he tasted the deep pain that is reserved only for the strong, just as he had tasted for a little while the deep happiness.

Even the ultimate falsity of the grounds[1] upon which Judy terminated the engagement that she did not want to "take him away" from Irene — Judy, who had wanted nothing else — did not revolt him. He was beyond any revulsion[2] or any amusement.

He went East in February with the intention of selling out his laundries and settling in New York — but the war came to America in March and changed his plans. He returned to the West, handed over the management of the business to his partner, and went into the first officers' training-camp in late April. He was one of those young thousands who greeted the war with a certain amount of relief, welcoming the liberation from webs of tangled emotion.

VI

This story is not his biography, remember, although things creep into it which have nothing to do with those dreams he had when he was young. We are almost done with them and with him now. There is only one more incident to be related here, and it happens seven years farther on. It took place in New York, where he had done

1) falsity of the grounds: lie of the reasons.
2) was beyond any revulsion: 격한 감정의 변화는 일어나지 않았다.

well[1] — so well that there were no barriers too high for him. He was thirty-two years old, and, except for one flying trip[2] immediately after the war, he had not been West in seven years. A man named Devlin from Detroit[3] came into his office to see him in a business way, and then and there this incident occurred, and closed out, so to speak, this particular side of his life.

"So you're from the Middle West," said the man Devlin with careless curiosity. "That's funny — I thought men like you were probably born and raised on Wall Street.[4] You know — wife of one of my best friends in Detroit came from your city. I was an usher at the wedding."

Dexter waited with no apprehension of what was coming.

"Judy Simms," said Devlin with no particular interest; "Judy Jones she was once."

"Yes, I knew her." A dull impatience spread over him. He had heard, of course, that she was married — perhaps deliberately he had heard no more.

"Awfully nice girl," brooded Devlin meaninglessly, "I'm sort of[5] sorry for her."

"Why?" Something in Dexter was alert, receptive, at once.

"Oh, Lud Simms has gone to pieces[6] in a way.[7] I don't mean he ill-uses[8] her, but he drinks and runs around."[9]

"Doesn't she run around?"

"No. Stays at home with her kids."

"Oh."

"She's a little too old for him," said Devlin.

"Too old!" cried Dexter. "Why, man, she's only twenty-seven."

He was possessed with a wild notion of rushing out into the streets

---

1) had done well: 성공을 거두었었다.
2) flying trip: hasty trip.
3) Detroit: city in Michigan, famous for manufacturing automobilles.
4) Wall Street: street in downtown New York, the chief financial center of the U.S.
5) sort of: somewhat; rather; a little.
6) go to pieces: To become very nervous or sick from nervousness; become wild.
7) in a way: to some extent.
8) ill-use: treat cruelly.
9) runs around: leads wild life (and probably goes to meet other woman).

and taking a train to Detroit. He rose to his feet spasmodically.

"I guess you're busy," Devlin apologized quickly. "I didn't realize —"

"No, I'm not busy," said Dexter, steadying his voice. "I'm not busy at all. Not busy at all. Did you say she was — twenty-seven? No, I said she was twenty-seven."

"Yes, you did," agreed Devlin dryly.

"Go on, then. Go on."

"What do you mean?"

"About Judy Jones."

Devlin looked at him helplessly.

"Well, that's, I told you all there is to it.[1] He treats her like the devil. Oh, they're not going to get divorced or anything. When he's particularly outrageous she forgives him. In fact, I'm inclined to think she loves him. She was a pretty girl when she first came to Detroit."

A pretty girl! The phrase struck Dexter as ludicrous.

"Isn't she — a pretty girl, any more?"

"Oh, she's all right."

"Look here," said Dexter, sitting down suddenly, "I don't understand. You say she was a 'pretty girl' and now you say she's 'all right.' I don't understand what you mean — Judy Jones wasn't a pretty girl, at all. She was a great beauty. Why, I knew her, I knew her. She was —"

Devlin laughed pleasantly.

"I'm not trying to start a row,"[2] he said. "I think Judy's a nice girl and I like her. I can't understand how a man like Lud Simms could fall madly in love with her, but he did." Then he added: "Most of the women like her."

Dexter looked closely at Devlin, thinking wildly that there must be a reason for this, some insensitivity in the man or some private malice.

"Lots of women fade just like that," Devlin snapped his fingers. "You must have seen it happen. Perhaps I've forgotten how pretty

1) to it: about [concerning] it.

2) start a row: (Colloq.) guarrel noisily; make noise.

she was at her wedding. I've seen her so much since then, you see. She has nice eyes."

A sort of dullness settled down upon Dexter. For the first time in his life he felt like getting very drunk. He knew that he was laughing loudly at something Devlin had said, but he did not know what it was or why it was funny. When, in a few minutes, Devlin went he lay down on his lounge and looked out the window at the New York sky-line[1] into which the sun was sinking in dull lovely shades[2] of pink and gold.

He had thought that having nothing else to lose he was invulnerable at last — but he knew that he had just lost something more, as surely as if he had married Judy Jones and seen her fade away before his eyes.

The dream was gone. Something had been taken from him. In a sort of panic he pushed the palms of his hands into his eyes and tried to bring up a picture of the waters lapping on Sherry Island and the moonlit veranda, and gingham on the golf-links and the dry sun and the gold color of her neck's soft down. And her mouth damp to his kisses and her eyes plaintive with melancholy and her freshness like new fine linen[3] in the morning. Why, these things were no longer in the world! They had existed and they existed no longer.

For the first time in years the tears were streaming down his face. But they were for himself now. He did not care about mouth and eyes and moving hands. He wanted to care, and he could not care. For he had gone away and he could never go back any more. The gates were closed, the sun was gone down, and there was no beauty but the gray beauty of steel that withstands all time. Even the grief he could have borne was left behind in the country of illusion, of youth, of the richness of life, where his winter dreams had flourished.

"Long ago," he said, "long ago, there was something in me, but now that thing is gone. Now that thing is gone, that thing is gone. I cannot cry. I cannot care. That thing will come back no more."

---

1) sky-line: outline of buildings as seen against the sky.
2) lovely shades: lovely colors.
3) linen: linen shirts.

The Killers

by Ernest Hemingway

Ernest Hemingway (1899-1961) was born in Oak Park, Illinois.

He went through high school, winning some fame in boxing and football, and then became a reporter on the Kansas City *Star*. During World War I, he served on the Italian front. In postwar days, as a newspaper correspondent, he was one of the expatriates who inhabited the Left Bank in Paris. There he began to write fiction and was "discovered" by the critics in the United States. He returned to his homeland to write, going abroad now and then for travel in Europe or for big game hunting in Africa. During the Spanish Revolution and World War II he was a correspondent abroad. After the war, he lived in Cuba until he was forced to leave because of the Castro revolution. After some traveling he settled in Idaho and, following hospitalization, died of a gun-shot wound — perhaps by his own hand.

Hemingway was influenced by Mark Twain's style, which, though like oral speech, was notable for its poetic overtones. Sherwood Anderson and Gertrude Stein, whom he knew in Paris, probably encouraged him to cultivate this apparently naive colloquial style. From them, too, he may have received instruction in emphasizing basic emotions which led Oscar Cargill to classify him, as well as these two teachers of his, as "Primitivists." From Stephen Crane, by contrast, Hemingway perhaps learned something about handling symbolic or connotative details to give prose what he calls "a fourth or fifth dimension." As a result, in Hemingway's best narratives, there is a unique combination of strength — even at times brutality — with poetic subtlety and depth of sympathy which appeals to modern readers.

THE DOOR of Henry's lunchroom[1] opened and two men came in. They sat down at the counter.

"What's yours?"[2] George asked them.

"I don't know," one of the men said. "What do you want to eat, Al?"

"I don't know," said Al. "I don't know what I want to eat."

Outside it was getting dark. The street-light came on[3] outside the

---

1) lunchroom: a small, inexpensive eating place with very simple food 간이식당.

2) What's yours?: What is your order?; What do you want to eat?

3) came on: lighted.

window. The two men at the counter read the menu. From the other end of the counter Nick Adams[1] watched them. He had been talking to George when they came in.

"I'll have a roast pork tenderloin with apple sauce and mashed potatoes" the first man said.

"It isn't ready yet."

"What the hell[2] do you put it on the card[3] for?"

"That's the dinner," George explained. "You can get that at six o'clock.[4]"

George looked at the clock on the wall behind the counter.

"It's five o'clock."

"The clock says twenty minutes past five," the second man said. "It's twenty minutes fast."

"Oh, to hell with the clock[5]," the first man said. "What have you got to eat?"

"I can give you any kind of sandwiches," George said. "You can have ham and eggs, bacon and eggs, liver and bacon, or a steak."

"Give me chicken croquettes[6] with green peas and cream sauce and mashed potatoes."

"That's the dinner."

"Everything we want's the dinner, eh? That's the way you work it.[7]"

"I can give you ham and eggs, bacon and eggs liver —"

"I'll take ham and eggs," the man called Al said. He wore a derby[8] hat and a black overcoat buttoned across the chest. His face was small

---

1) Nick Adams: Hemingway 단편에 등장하는 주인공. Hemingway의 codehero이며 a stand-in.

2) What the hell: a common profanity used for emphasis.

3) card: menu; the list of available dishes with their prices.

4) six o'clock: the usual dinner hour for many American families.

5) to hell with the clock: 「제기랄 그 따위 시계는 집어치워」 앞에 go를 넣어 본다.

6) chicken croquettes: finely-chopped prices of chicken bound together by a thick white sauce, rolled in bread crumbs and then deep-fried.

7) That's the way you work it.: 그게 너희들의 장사 방식이군. work=manage. work it=영업을 하다.

8) derby: a round, stiff hat usually associated with rather formal daytime dress.

and white and he had tight lips. He wore a silk muffler[1] and gloves.

"Give me bacon and eggs," said the other man. He was about the same size as Al. Their faces were different, but they were dressed like twins. Both wore overcoats too tight for them. They sat leaning forward, their elbows on the counter.[2]

"Got anything to drink?"[3] Al asked.

"Silver beer, bevo, ginger-ale,"[4] George said. "I mean you got anything to *drink?"*

"Just those I said."

"This is a hot town,[5] "said the other. "What do they call it?"

''Summit.'

"Ever hear of it?"[6] Al asked his friend. "No," said the friend.

"What do you do here nights[7]?" Al asked.

"They eat the dinner," his friend said. "They all come here and eat the big dinner.[8]"

"That's right," George said.

"So you think that's right?" Al asked George.

"Sure."

"You're a pretty bright[9] boy, aren't you?" "Sure," said George.

"Well, You're not," said the other little man. "Is he, Al?"

"He's dumb,[10]" said Al. He turned to Nick. "What's your name?"

''Adams."

"Another bright boy," Al said. "Ain't[11] he a bright boy, Max?" "The

---

1) muffler: scarf.
2) their elbows on the counter: bad manner임을 나타냄. to keep your elbows off the table 이 good manner임.
3) Got anything to drink?: Have you got anything to drink?; Do you have anything to drink?
4) Silver beer, bevo, ginger-ale: all non-alcholic beverages. 이 이야기는 Prohibition (금주 기간, 1920-33)에 일어난 것임.
5) a hot town: a poor, good for nothing, unpleasant, uncomfortable town.
6) Ever hear of it?: Have you ever heard of it?
7) nights: at night.
8) the big dinner: table d'hote [tá:bldóut] 정식.
9) bright: clever; intelligent.
10) dumb: dull; stupid.
11) ain't: nonstandard negative form of 'be' (all persons) in the present tense. Ain't he~? =Isn't he~?

town's full of bright boys," Max said.

George put the two platters,[1] one of ham and eggs, the other of bacon and eggs, on the counter. He set down two side-dishes[2] of fried potatoes and closed the wicket[3] into the kitchen.

"Which is yours?" he asked Al.

"Don't you remember?"

"Ham and eggs."

"Just a bright boy," Max said. He leaned forward and took the ham and eggs. Both men ate with their gloves on. George watched them eat.

"What are *you* looking at?" Max looked at George.

"Nothing."

"The hell you were.[4] You were looking at me."

"Maybe the boy meant it for a joke, Max," Al said. George laughed.

"You don't have to laugh," Max said to him. "You don't have to laugh at all, see?"

"All right," said George.

"So he thinks it's all right." Max turned to Al. "He thinks it's all right. That's a good one."[5]

"Oh, he's a thinker," Al said. They went on eating.

"What's the bright boy's name down the counter?" Al asked Max.

"Hey, bright boy," Max said to Nick. "You go around on the other side of the counter with your boy friend.

"What's the idea?" Nick asked.

"There isn't any idea."

"You better go around,[6] bright boy," Al said. Nick went around behind the counter.

"What's the idea?"[7] George asked.

---

1) platter: an oval plate 쟁반, 큰 접시.
2) side-dish: a serving of potatoes, other cooked vegetables, or salad that accompany a meat dish but are served in a separate container.
3) wicket: a small window through which food is passed from the kitchen.
4) The hell you were.: I don't believe you (that you were looking at nothing).
5) That's a good one.: a cliche meaning "That statement is amusing."; here, used ironically, "That's a good joke."
6) You better go around: You had better go around.
7) What's the idea?: 뭣 때문에요?

"None of your damn business,"[1] Al said. "Who's out in the kitchen?"

"The nigger.[2]"

"What do you mean the nigger?"

"The nigger that cooks."

"Tell him to come in."

"What's the idea?"

"Tell him to come in."

"Where do you think you are?"

"We know damn well[3] where we are," the man called Max said. "Do we look silly?"

"You talk silly," Al said to him. "What the hell do you argue with this kid for? Listen," he said to George, "tell the nigger to come out here."

"What are you going to do to him?"

"Nothing. Use your head,[4] bright boy. What would we do to a nigger?"

George opened the slit[5] that opened back into the kitchen. "Sam," he called. "Come in here a minute."

The door to the kitchen opened and the nigger came in. "What was it?" he asked. The two men at the counter took a look at him.

"All right, nigger. You stand right there," Al said.

Sam, the nigger, standing in his apron, looked at the two men sitting at the counter? "Yes, sir," he said. Al got down from his stool.

"I'm going back to the kitchen with the nigger and bright boy," he said. "Go on back to the kitchen, nigger. You go with him, bright boy." The little man walked after Nick and Sam, the cook, back into the kitchen. The door shut after them. The man called Max sat at the counter opposite George. He didn't look at George but looked in the mirror that ran along back of[6] the counter. Henry's had been

---

1) None of your damn business: It is none of your own business. It is not your business. → Mind your business.
2) nigger: (Slang) an insulting term for "Negro"
3) damn well: very good.
4) use your head: think.
5) slit: a long, straight, narrow opening.
6) back of: at the back of; behind.

made over[1] from a saloon[2] into a lunch counter.

"Well, bright boy," Max said, looking into the mirror, "why don't you say something?"

"What's it all about?"

"Hey, Al," Max called, "bright boy wants to know what it's all about."

"Why don't you tell him?" Al's voice came from the kitchen.

"What do you think it's all about?"

"I don't know."

"What do you think?"

Max looked into the mirror all the time he was talking. "I wouldn't say."

"Hey, Al, bright boy says he wouldn't say what he thinks it's all about."

"I can hear you,[3] all right," Al said from the kitchen. He had propped open the slit that dishes passed through into the kitchen with a catsup[4] bottle. "Listen, bright boy," he said from the kitchen to George. "Stand a little further along the bar. You move a little to the left, Max." He was like a photographer arranging for a group picture.

"Talk to me, bright boy," Max said. "What do you think's going to happen?"

George did not say anything.

"I'll tell you," Max said. "We're going to kill a Sewde. Do you know a big Swede named Ole Andreson?"

"Yes."

"He comes here to eat every night, don't he?"[5] "Sometimes he comes here."

"He comes here at six o'clock, don't he?" "If he comes."

"We know all that, bright boy," Max said. "Talk about something

---

1) make over: alter; make different; remodel; refashion 개조하다.

2) saloon: a bar. Saloons traditionally have a long, high mirror behind the counter.

3) I can hear you: I understand what you say.

4) catsup: variant spelling of *ketchup*, a spicy tomato sauce served with hamburgers, fresh fried potatoes and some other dishes.

5) don't he: doesn't he.

else. Ever go to the movies?"

"Once in a while."

"You ought to go to the movies more. The movies are fine for a bright boy like you."

"What are you going to kill Ole Andreson for? What did he ever do to you?"

"He never had a chance to do anything to us. He never even seen us."[1]

"And he's only going to see us once," Al said from the kitchen.

"What are you going to kill him for, then?" George asked.

"We're killing him for a friend. Just to oblige a friend,[2] bright boy.'

"Shut up," said Al from the kitchen. "You talk too goddam much."

"Well, I got to keep bright boy amused. Don't I, bright boy?"

"You talk too damn much," Al said. "The nigger and my bright boy are amused by themselves. I got them tied up like a couple of girl friends in the convent.[3]"

"I suppose you were in a convent."

"You never know."

"You were in a kosher[4] convent. That's where you were."

George looked up at the clock.

"If anybody comes in you tell them the cook is off,[5] and if they keep after it,[6] you tell them you'll go back and cook yourself. Do you get that,[7] bright boy?"

"All right," George said. "What you going to do with us afterward?"

"That'll depend," Max said. "That's one of those things you never know at the time."

---

1) He never even seen us.: The omission of "has" (or "have") in the present perfect is common among uneducated people.

2) Just to oblige a friend: 친구의 청을 들어 주기 위해서일 뿐이다. oblige=do a favor for.

3) convent: a Roman Catholic institution where women who have dedicated heir lives to the church live in seclusion.

4) kosher: 여기서는 Jewish.

5) off: off duty; not working.

6) if they keep after it: 계속 조르면.

7) Do you get that: Do you understand what I say?

George looked up at the clock. It was a quarter past six. The door from the street opened. A street-car motorman[1] came in.

"Hello, George," he said. "Can I get supper?"

"Sam's gone out," George said. "He'll be back in about half an hour."

"I'd better go up the street," the motorman said. George looked at the clock. It was twenty minutes past six.

"That was nice, bright boy," Max said. "You're a regular[2] little gentleman."

"He knew I'd blow his head off," Al said from the kitchen.

"No," said Max. "It ain't that. Bright boy is nice. He's a nice boy. I like him."

At six-fifty-five George said: "He's not coming."

Two other people had been in the lunch-room. Once George had gone out to the kitchen and made a ham-and-egg sandwich "to go"[3] that a man wanted to take with him. Inside the kitchen he saw Al, his derby hat tipped back, sitting on a stool beside the wieket with the muzzle[4] of a sawed-off shotgun[5] resting on the ledge. Nick and the cook were back to back[6] in the corner, a towel tied in each of their mouths. George had cooked the sandwich, wrapped it up in oiled paper, put it in a bag, brought it in, and the man had paid for it and gone out.

"Bright boy can do everything," Max said. "He can cook and everything. You'd make some girl a nice wife, bright boy."

"Yes?" George said. "Your friend, Ole Andreson, isn't going to come."

"We'll give him ten minutes,"[7] Max said.

---

1) street-car motorman: the man who drives a street-car or tram.

2) regular: complete; perfect; undoubt.

3) to go: (Slang): to take out food from the place you bought it in order to eat somewhere else.

4) muzzle: the firing end of a gun 총구.

5) sawed-off shotgun: a weapon popular with American gangsters in the 1920's and 30's. The front end of the gun is cut off for use at short range; the gun fires a number of pellets at one time.

6) back to back: 등을 맞대고 (묶여 있다).

7) We'll give him ten minutes.: We'll wait another ten minutes for him to arrive.

Max watched the mirror and the clock. The hands of the clock marked seven o'clock, and then five minutes past seven.

"Come on, Al," said Max. "We better go. He's not coming."

"Better give him five minutes," Al said from the kitchen. In the five minutes a man came in, and George explained that the cook was sick.

"Why the hell don't you get another cook?' the man asked.

"Aren't you running a lunch-counter?" He went out.

"Come on, Al," Max said

"What about the two bright boys and the nigger?" "They're all right."

"You think so?"

"Sure. We're through with[1] it."

"I don't like it," said Al. "It's sloppy.[2] You talk too much."

"Oh, what the hell,"[3] said Max. "We got to keep amused,[4] haven't we?"

"You talk too much, all the same,[5]" Al said. He came out from the kitchen. The cut-off barrels of the shotgun made a slight bulge under the waist of his too tight-fitting overcoat. He straightened his coat with his gloved hands.

"So long,[6] bright boy," he said to George. "You got a lot of luck."

"That's the truth," Max said. "You ought to play the races,[7] bright boy."

The two of them went out the door. George watched them, through the window, pass under the arc-light[8] and across the street. In their tight overcoats and derby hats they looked like a vaudeville team. George went back through the swinging door into the kitchen and untied Nick and the cook.

"I don't want any more of that," said Sam, the cook. "I don't want

1) be through with~: have done with. ~을 끝내다, 마무리 하다.
2) sloppy: careless.
3) what the hell: 빌어먹을.
4) We got to keep amused: We have got to keep them amused.
5) all the same: notwithstanding; nevertheless.
6) So long: (Colloq.) Good-by.
7) play the races: bet money on horse races.
8) arc-light: the street light.

any more of that."

Nick stood up. He had never had a towel in his mouth before.

"Say," he said. "What the hell?" He was trying to swagger it off.[1]

"They were going to kill Ole Andreson," George said. "They were going to shoot him when he came in to eat."

"Ole Andreson?"

"Sure."

The cook felt the corners of his mouth with his thumbs. "They all gone?" he asked.

"Yeah," said George. "They're gone now."

"I don't like it," said the cook. "I don't like any of it at all."

"Listen," George said to Nick. "You better go see Ole Andreson."

"All right."

"You better not have anything to do with it at all," Sam, the cook, said. "You better stay way out of it."

"Don't go if you don't want to," George said.

"Mixing up in this ain't going to get you anywhere,[2]" the cook said. "You stay out of it."

"I'll go see him." Nick said to George. "Where does he live?" The cook turned away.

"Little boys always know what they want to do," he said.

"He lives up at Hirsch's rooming-house,[3]" George said to Nick.

"I'll go up there."

Outside the arc-light shone through the bare branches of a tree. Nick walked up the street beside the car-tracks[4] and turned at the next arc-light down a side-street. Three houses up the street was Hirsch's rooming-house. Nick walked up the two steps and pushed the bell. A woman came to the door.

"Is Ole Andreson here?"

"Do you want to see him?" "Yes, if he's in."

---

1) swagger it off: pretend to be completely unaffected by what has happened.

2) ain't going to get you anywhere: will not do anything good for you nowhere. 아무 소용없다.

3) rooming house: a private home where a person may rent a room inexpensively for a period of months or even years.

4) car-tracks: the metal rails that a street-car runs on.

Nick followed the woman up a flight of stairs and back to the end of a corridor. She knocked on the door.

"Who is it?"

"It's somebody to see you,[1] Mr. Andreson," the woman said.

"It's Nick Adams."

"Come in."

Nick opened the door and went into the room. Ole Andreson was lying on the bed with all his clothes on. He had been a heavyweight prizefighter[2] and he was too long for the bed. He lay with his head on two pillows. He did not look at Nick.

"What was it?" he asked.

"I was up at Henry's," Nick said, and two fellows came in and tied up me and the cook, and they said they were going to kill you."

It sounded silly when he said it. Ole Andreson said nothing.

"They put us out in the kitchen," Nick went on. "They were going to shoot you when you came in to supper."

Ole Andreson looked at the wall and did not say anything.

"George thought I better come and tell you about it."

"There isn't anything I can do about it," Ole Andreson said.

"I'll tell you what they were like.[3]"

"I don't want to know what they were like," Ole Andreson said. He looked at the wall. "Thanks for coming to tell me about it."

"That's all right."

Nick looked at the big man lying on the bed.

"Don't you want me to go and see the police?"

"No," Ole Andreson said. "That wouldn't do any good." "Isn't there something I could do?"

"No. There ain't anything to do."

"Maybe it was just a bluff.[4]"

"No. It ain't just a bluff."

Ole Andreson rolled over toward the wall.

---

1) It's somebody to see you: There's somebody who wants to see you.

2) heavyweight prizefighter: a professional boxer.

3) what they were like: 그들의 생김새.

4) bluff: a treat intended to get results without being carried out. 위협, 허세.

"The only thing is," he said, talking toward the wall "I just can't make up my mind to go out. I been in here[1] all day."

"Couldn't you get out of town?"

"No," Ole Andreson said. "I'm through with all that running around. "[2]

He looked at the wall.

"There ain't anything to do now."

"Couldn't you fix it up[3] some way[4]?"

"No, I got in wrong.[5]" He talked in the same flat voice. "There ain't anything to do. After a while I'll make up my mind to go out."

"I better go back and see George," Nick said.

"So long," said Ole Andreson. He did not look toward Nick.

"Thanks for coming around."

Nick went out. As he shut the door he saw Ole Andreson with all his clothes on, lying on the bed looking at the wall.

"He's been in his room all day," the landlady said downstairs.

"I guess he don't feel well. I said to him: 'Mr. Andreson, you ought to go out and take a walk on a nice fall day[6] like this,' but he didn't feel like it."

"He doesn't want to go out."

"I'm sorry he don't feel well," the woman said. "He's an awfully nice man. He was in the ring,[7] you know."

"I know it."

"You'd never know it except from the way his face is," the woman said. They stood talking just inside the street door. "He's just as gentle."[8]

"Well, good night, Mrs Hirsch," Nick said.

"I'm not Mrs. Hirsch," the woman said. "She owns the place.

---

1) I been in here: 1 have been here.
2) I'm through with all that running around.: 이제 더 도망다니지 않겠다. I'm through with~=I've done with~.
3) fix it up: come to an agreement; make compromise.
4) some way: in some way.
5) got in wrong: became involved with bad people.
6) fall day: autumn day.
7) ring: boxing ring. Ex. He was in the ring.= He was a prizefighter.
8) He is just as gentle.= He is as gentle as can be. He is very gentle.

I just look after[1] it for her. I'm Mrs. Bell."

"Well, good night, Mrs. Bell," Nick said. "Good night," the woman said.

Nick walked up the dark street to the corner under the arc-light, and then along the car-tracks to Henry's eating-house. George was inside, back of the counter. "Did you see Ole?"

"Yes," said Nick. "He's in his room and he won't go out."

The cook opened the door from the kitchen when he heard Nick's voice.

"I don't even listen to it," he said and shut the door.

"Did you tell him about it?" George asked.

"Sure. I told him but he knows what it's all about."

"What's he going to do?"

"Nothing."

"They'II kill him." "I guess they will."

"He must have got mixed up in[2] something in Chicago."

"I guess so," said Nick.

"It's a hell of a thing."[3]

"It's an awful thing," Nick said.

They did not say anything. George reached down for a towel and wiped the counter.

"I wonder what he did?" Nick said.

"Double-crossed[4] somebody. That's what they kill them for."

"I'm going to get out of this town," Nick said.

"Yes," said George. "That's a good thing to do."

"I can't stand[5] to think about him waiting in the room and knowing he's going to get it.[6] It's too damned awful."

"Well," said George, "you better not think about it."

---

1) look after: take care of; attend to.
2) got mixed up in: became involved in something bad.
3) It's a hell of a thing.: It's an awful thing.
4) double-cross: (Slang) cheat; betray.
5) stand: endure.
6) get it: (Slang) be killed; be punished.

The Gioconda[1] Smile

by Aldous Huxley

Aldous Huxley (1894-1963) was born into a family of intellectual prominence. His father, Leonard, was the son of T. H. Huxley, the famous proponent of Darwinism when it was first finding acceptance; his mother, Julia, was the niece of the poet and critic Matthew Arnold. Aldous attended Eton on a scholarship and specialized in biology, intending to become a doctor, but he contracted keratitis and soon was almost blind. However, he learned to read Braille and continued his studies under tutors. When one eye recovered enough so that he could read with a magnifying glass, he turned to English literature and philosophy at Oxford, taking a degree in 1915.

After World War I Huxley engaged in literary journalism and was on the staff of the *Athenaeum*, edited by John Middleton Murry. For the greater part of 1923-1930 he lived in Italy; after 1926 he spent much time there with D.H. and Frieda Lawrence. Lawrence was a strong influence on Huxley, particularly in his mistrust of intellect and trust in vital promptings. Huxley's early period was characterized by skeptical, brilliant portraits of a decadent society. This was the period of the novels *Crome Yellow*(1921), *Antic Hay*(1923), and *Point Counter Point*(1928). Huxley's disgust with much of the modern world became explicit in *Brave New World*(1932) and *Eyeless in Gaza*(1936). Huxley's most successful later work was *The Devils of Loudon*(1952), which dealt with the hysteria that swept a French Ursuline convent in the 17th century and the martyrdom of a priest.

"MISS SPENCE will be down directly, sir."

"Thank you," said Mr. Hutton, without turning round. Janet Spence's parlourmaid was so ugly, ugly on purpose, it always seemed to him, malignantly, criminally ugly, that he could not bear to look at her more than was necessary. The door closed. Left to himself, Mr. Hutton got up and began to wander round the room, looking with meditative eyes at the familiar objects it contained.

Photographs of Greek statuary, photographs of the Roman Forum,[2] coloured prints of Italian masterpieces, all very safe and well known.

---

1) Gioconda: Mona Lisa (Leonardo da Vinci 작은 미소를 지은 부인의 초상) Mona는 Madam의 뜻이며 Lisa는 Florence의 사람 Gioconda의 아내 이름임.

2) Forum: in ancient Rome, the place of assembly for judicial and other public business.

Poor, dear Janet, what a prig[1] — what an intellectual snob! Her real taste was illustrated in that water-colour by the pavement artist,[2] the one she had paid half-a-crown for (and thirty-five shillings for the frame). How often he had heard her tell the story, how often expatiate on[3] the beauties of that skilful imitation of an oleograph! "A real Artist in the streets," and you could hear the capital A in Artist as she spoke the words. She made you feel that part of his[4] glory had entered into Janet Spence when she tendered him that half-crown for the copy of the oleograph. She was implying a compliment to her own taste and penetration. A genuine Old Master[5] for half-a-crown. Poor, dear Janet!

Mr. Hutton came to a pause in front of a small oblong mirror. Stooping a little to get a full view of his face, he passed a white, well-manicured finger over his moustache. It was as curly, as freshly auburn[6] as it had been twenty years ago. His hair still retained its colour, and there was no sign of baldness yet — only a certain elevation of the brow. "Shakespearean,"[7] thought Mr. Hutton with a smile, as he surveyed the smooth and polished expanse of his forehead.

Others abide our question, thou art free.[8] . . . Footsteps in the sea . . . Majesty[9] . . . Shakespeare, thou shouldst be living at this hour.[10] No, that was Milton, wasn't it? Milton, the Lady of Christ's.[11] There

---

1) prig: conceited person 젠체하는 사람, 우쭐거리는 사람.
2) the pavement artist: 거리의 화가.
3) expatiate on: 장황하게 늘어 놓다.
4) his: the artist's.
5) Old Master: 특히 16~7세기의 유명한 화가를 말함.
6) auburn: golden-brown.
7) Shakespearean: 머리 벗겨진 것이 셰익스피어형(型)이라는 뜻.
8) Others abide our question, thou art free: 다른 시인들은 우리의 의문을 벗어날 수 없으나 그대만은 자유이다(즉, 의문의 여지가 없다). . 이 구절은 Matthew Arnold의 Sonnet, Shakespeare에서 인용.
9) Majesty: 장엄. 전기 Sonnet, Shakespeare에서 인용.
10) Shakespeare, ··· at this hour: 셰익스피어여, 그대는 지금 세상에 살았어야 할 걸. 이 구절은 William Wordsworth의 *National Independence and Liberty XIV*의 "London, 1802"에서 인용. 단 shakespeare는 Milton의 잘못. 원문은 "Milton! thou shouldst be living at this hour. England hath need of thee. . . ."
11) Milton, the Lady of Christ's: Miltond의 1625년 Cambridge의 Christ's College에 입학하였는데 그의 모습이 수려하였으므로 급우들이 그를 "Lady of Christ's"라고 불렀다고 함. 그리고 John Aubrey의 *Brief Lives, John Milton*에 "He was so fair that they called him the lady of Christ's College."라고 나와 있음.

was no lady about him. He was what the women would call a manly man. That was why they liked him — for the curly auburn moustache and the discreet redolence of tobacco. Mr. Hutton smiled again; he enjoyed making fun of himself. Lady of Christ's? No, no. He was the Christ of Ladies. Very pretty, very pretty.[1] The Christ of Ladies. Mr. Hutton wished there were somebody he could tell the joke[2] to. Poor, dear Janet wouldn't appreciate it, alas!

He straightened himself up, patted his hair, and resumed his peregrination.[3] Damn the Roman Forum; he hated those dreary photographs.

Suddenly he became aware that Janet Spence was in the room, standing near the door. Mr. Hutton started as though he had been taken in some felonious act. To make these silent and spectral appearances was one of Janet Spence's peculiar talents. Perhaps she had been there all the time, had seen him looking at himself in the mirror. Impossible! But, still, it was disquieting.[4]

"Oh, you gave me such a surprise," said Mr. Hutton, recovering his smile and advancing with outstretched hand to meet her.

Miss Spence was smiling too: her Gioconda smile,[5] he had once called it in a moment of half-ironical flattery. Miss Spence had taken the compliment seriously, and always tried to live up to[6] the Leonardo standard. She smiled on in silence while Mr. Hutton shook hands; that was part of the Gioconda business.

"I hope you're well," said Mr. Hutton. "You look it."

What a queer face she had! That small mouth pursed forward by the Gioconda expression into a little snout with a round hole in the middle as though for whistling — it was like a penholder seen from the front. Above the mouth a well-shaped nose, finely aquiline.[7] Eyes large, lustrous, and dark, with the largeness, lustre, and darkness that

1) Very pretty, very pretty: Hutton은 자기의 joke에 스스로 감탄하고 있음을 말함.
2) the joke: Lady of Christ's를 the Christ of Ladies라고 도치한 농을 가리킴.
3) peregrination: random walk; wandering.
4) disquieting: unquiet; anxious.
5) Gioconda smile: Leonardo da Vinci작 Mona Liza의 그 수수께끼의 미소를 가리킴.
6) live up to: ~에 따라서 살다, 행동하다.
7) aquiline: of an eagle; hooked. cf. an aquiline nose=a hooked nose.

seems to invite sties[1] and an occasional bloodshot suffusion. They were fine eyes, but unchangingly grave. The penholder might do its Gioconda trick,[2] but the eyes never altered in their earnestness. Above them, a pair of boldly arched, heavily pencilled black eyebrows lent a surprising air of power, as of a Roman matron, to the upper portion of the face. Her hair was dark and equally Roman; Agrippina[3] from the brows upward.

"I thought I'd just look in on my way home," Mr. Hutton went on. "Ah, it's good to be back here—" he indicated with a wave of his hand the flowers in the vases, the sunshine and greenery beyond the windows—"it's good to be back in the country after a stuffy day of business in town."

Miss Spence, who had sat down, pointed to a chair at her side.

"No, really, I can't sit down," Mr. Hutton protested. "I must get back to see how poor Emily is. She was rather seedy[4] this morning." He sat down, nevertheless. "It's these wretched liver chills. She's always getting them. Women—" He broke off and coughed, so as to hide the fact that he had uttered. He was about to say that women with weak digestions ought not to marry; but the remark was too cruel, and he didn't really believe it. Janet Spence, moreover, was a believer in eternal flames and spiritual attachments.[5] "She hopes to be well enough," he added, "to see you at luncheon tomorrow. Can you come? Do!" He smiled persuasively. "It's my invitation, too, you know."

She dropped her eyes, and Mr. Hutton almost thought that he detected a certain reddening of the cheek. It was a tribute; he stroked his moustache.

"I should like to come if you think Emily's really well enough to have a visitor."

---

1) sties: 다래끼. (*sing.*) sty or stye.
2) do its Gioconda trick: smile a Gioconda smile.
3) Agrippina: (A.D. 16-59) mother of the Roman Emperor Nero; poisoned her husband Gaudius and secured the throne for her son.
4) seedy: out of sorts; feeling ill.
5) a believer in eternal flames and spiritual attachments: 영원한 정열의 불과 정신적 애정을 믿는 사람. 즉 Janet가 기독교 신자라는 것을 말하는 것임. attachment=affection.

"Of course. You'll do her good. You'll do us both good. In married life three is often better company than two."

"Oh, you're cynical."

Mr. Hutton always had a desire to say "Bow-wow-wow" whenever that last word was spoken.[1] It irritated him more than any other word in the language. But instead of barking he made haste to protest.

"No, no. I'm only speaking a melancholy truth. Reality doesn't always come up to[2] the ideal, you know. But that doesn't make me believe any the less in the ideal. Indeed, I believe in it passionately: the ideal of a matrimony between two people in perfect accord. I think it's realizable. I'm sure it is."

He paused significantly, and looked at her with an arch[3] expression. A virgin of thirty-six, but still unwithered; she had her charms. And there was something really rather enigmatic about her. Miss Spence made no reply, but continued to smile. There were times when Mr. Hutton got rather bored with the Gioconda. He stood up.

"I must really be going now. Farewell, mysterious Gioconda." The smile grew intenser, focused itself, as it were, in a narrower snout. Mr. Hutton made a Cinquecento[4] gesture,[5] and kissed her extended hand. It was the first time he had done such a thing; the action seemed not to be resented. "I look forward to[6] tomorrow."

"Do you?"

For answer, Mr. Hutton once more kissed her hand, then turned to go. Miss Spence accompanied him to the porch.

"Where's your car?" she asked.

"I left it at the gate of the drive."[7]

"I'll come and see you off."

"No, no." Mr. Hutton was playful, but determined. "You must do

---

1) Mr. Hutton always had a desire … that last word was spoken: 그는 cynical이란 소리를 들으면 언제나 멍멍하고 짖어주고 싶어진다는 뜻.
2) come up to: come near to; reach.
3) arch: sly; crafty.
4) Cinquecento: 16세기. 특히 이탈리아의 예술에 대하여 씀.
5) a Cinquecento gesture: gesture after the manner of the age of Italian Renaissance.
6) look forward to: expect [anticipate] with pleasure.
7) drive: 차도.

no such thing. I simply forbid you."

"But I should like to come," Miss Spence protested, throwing a rapid Gioconda at him.

Mr. Hutton held up his hand. "No," he repeated, and then, with a gesture that was almost the blowing of a kiss, he started to run down the drive, lightly, on his toes, with long, bounding strides like a boy's. He was proud of that run; it was quite marvellously youthful. Still, he was glad the drive was no longer. At the last bend, before passing out of sight of the house, he halted and turned round. Miss Spence was still standing on the steps smiling her smile. He waved his hand, and this time quite definitely and overtly[1] wafted a kiss in her direction. Then, breaking once more into his magnificent canter,[2] he rounded the last dark promontory of trees. Once out of sight of the house he let his high paces decline to a trot, and finally to a walk. He took out his handkerchief and began wiping his neck inside his collar. What fools, what fools! Had there ever been such an ass[3] as poor, dear Janet Spence? Never, unless it was himself. Decidedly he was the more malignant fool,[4] since he, at least, was aware of his folly and still persisted in it. Why did he persist? Ah, the problem that was himself,[5] the problem that was other people . . .

He had reached the gate. A large, prosperous looking motor was standing at the side of the road.

"Home, M'Nab."[6] The chauffeur touched his cap. "And stop at the cross-roads on the way, as usual," Mr. Hutton added, as he opened the door of the car. "Well?" he said, speaking into the obscurity that lurked within.

"Oh, Teddy Bear,[7] what an age you've been!"[8] It was a fresh

1) overtly: plainly.
2) canter: easy gallop.
3) ass: fool.
4) the more malignant fool: of the two를 보충하여 생각할 것.
5) the problem that was himself: 문제는 그 자신이야.
6) M'Nab: MacNab [mnæb].
7) Teddy Bear: 장난감 곰. Doris가 Mr. Hutton에게 붙인 애칭.
8) what an age you've been!: 어쩜 그렇게도 오래 기다리게 하세요!, 정말 오래 걸렸군요!.

and childish voice that spoke the words. There was the faintest hint of Cockney impurity[1)] about the vowel sounds.

Mr. Hutton bent his large form and darted into the car with the agility of an animal regaining its burrow.[2)]

"Have I?" he said, as he shut the door. The machine began to move. "You must have missed me a lot if you found the time so long." He sat back in the low seat; a cherishing warmth enveloped him.

'Teddy Bear . . ." and with a sign of contentment a charming little head declined on to Mr. Hutton's shoulder. Ravished, he looked down sideways at the round, babyish face.

"Do you know, Doris, you look like the pictures of Louise de Kerouaille."[3)] He passed his fingers through a mass of curly hair.

"Who's Louise de Kera-whatever-it-is?"[4)] Doris spoke from remote distances.

"She was, alas! Fuit.[5)] We shall all be 'was' one of these days. Meanwhile. . . ."

Mr Hutton covered the babyish face with kisses. The car rushed smoothly along. M'Nab's back, through the front window, was stonily impassive, the back of a statue.

"Your hands," Doris whispered. "Oh, you mustn't touch me. They give me electric shocks."

Mr. Hutton adored her for the virgin imbecility of the words.[6)] How late in one's existence one makes the discovery of one's body!

"The electricity isn't in me, it's in you." He kissed her again, whispering her name several times: Doris, Doris, Doris. The scientific appellation of the sea mouse[7)] he was thinking, as he kissed the throat

---

1) Cockney impurity: 순 런던나기 말투.
2) regaining its burrow: 제 구멍에 돌아오는. burrow=hole dug in the ground by an animal for refuge or shelter.
3) Louise de Kerouaille: (1649-1734) Duchess of Portsmouth, mistress of Charles II.
4) Kera-whatever-it-is: 그 케라 뭔가 하는 사람.
5) *Fuit*: (F.) She passed away.
6) the virgin imbecility of the words: 그 처녀다운 바보 같은 말씨.
7) The scientific appellation of the sea mouse: 바다 쥐의 학명. Aphrodite aculeata라고 함. Doris의 하얀 목을 보고 연상한 것임.

she offered him, white and extended like the throat of a victim awaiting the sacrificial knife. The sea-mouse was a sausage with iridescent fur: very peculiar. Or was Doris the sea-cucumber, which turns itself inside out in moments of alarm? He would really have to go to Naples again, just to see the aquarium. These sea creatures were fabulous, unbelievably fantastic.

"Oh, Teddy Bear!" (More zoology; but he was only a land animal. His poor little jokes!) "Teddy Bear, I'm so happy."

"So am I," said Mr. Hutton. Was it true?

"But I wish I knew if it were right. Tell me, Teddy Bear, is it right or wrong?"

"Ah, my dear, that's just what I've been wondering for the last thirty years."

"Be serious, Teddy Bear. I want to know if this is right; if it's right that I should be here with you and that we should love one another, and that it should give me electric shocks when you touch me."

"Right? Well, it's certainly good that you should have electric shocks rather than sexual repressions. Read Freud;[1] repressions[2] are the devil."

"Oh, you don't help me. Why aren't you ever serious? If only you knew how miserable I am sometimes, thinking it's not right. Perhaps you know, there is a hell, and all that. I don't know what to do. Sometimes I think I ought to stop loving you."

"But could you?" asked Mr. Hutton, confident in the powers of his seduction and his moustache.

"No, Teddy Bear, you know I couldn't. But I could run away, I could hide from you, I could lock myself up and force myself not to come to you."

"Silly little thing!" He tightened his embrace.

"Oh, dear, I hope it isn't wrong. And there are times when I don't care if it is."

Mr. Hutton was touched. He had a certain protective affection for

1) Freud: Sigmund Freud (1856-1939), Austrian physician who developed a theory and technique of psychoanalysis.

2) repression: 억압.

this little creature. He laid his cheek against her hair and so, interlaced, they sat in silence, while the car, swaying and pitching a little as it hastened along, seemed to draw in[1] the white road and the dusty hedges towards it devouringly.

"Goodbye, goodbye."

The car moved on, gathered speed, vanished round a curve, and Doris was left standing by the signpost at the cross-roads, still dizzy and weak with the languor born of those kisses and the electrical touch of those gentle hands. She had to take a deep breath to draw herself up deliberately,[2] before she was strong enough to start her homeward walk. She had half a mile in which to invent the necessary lies.

Alone, Mr. Hutton suddenly found himself the prey of an appalling boredom.

Mrs. Hutton was lying on the sofa in her boudoir, playing patience.[3] In spite of the warmth of the July evening a wood fire was burning on the hearth. A black Pomeranian,[4] extenuated[5] by the heat and the fatigues of digestion, slept before the blaze.

"Phew! Isn't it rather hot in here?" Mr. Hutton asked as he entered the room.

"You know I have to keep warm, dear." The voice seemed breaking on the verge of tears.[6] "I get so shivery."

"I hope you're better this evening."

"Not much, I'm afraid."

The conversation stagnated. Mr. Hutton stood leaning his back against the mantelpiece. He looked down at the Pomeranian lying at his feet and with the toe of his right boot he rolled the little dog over and rubbed its white-flecked chest and belly. The creature lay in an inert ecstasy.[7] Mrs. Hutton continued to play patience. Arrived at

---

1) draw in: 빨아들이다. in은 *adv.*

2) draw herself up deliberately: 의식적으로 몸을 반듯하게 세우고.

3) Patience: 혼자 노는 카아드 놀이의 일종.

4) Pomeranian: 포메라니아종의 작은 개.

5) extenuated: weakened; made slender.

6) breaking on the verge of tears: 금방이라도 울음이 터질 것만 같은. verge=edge; rim; brink.

7) in an inert ecstasy: 축 늘어져 황홀한 기분으로.

an *impasse*,[1] she altered the position of one card, took back another, and went on playing. Her patiences always came out.[2]

"Dr. Libbard thinks I ought to go to Llandrindod Wells[3] this summer."

"Well, go, my dear — go, most certainly."

Mr. Hutton was thinking of the events of the afternoon: how they had driven, Doris and he, up to the hanging wood, had left the car to wait for them under the shade of the trees, and walked together out into the windless sunshine of the chalk down.[4]

"I'm to drink the waters[5] for my liver, and he thinks I ought to have massage and electric treatment, too."

Hat in hand, Doris had stalked[6] four blue butterflies that were dancing together round a scabious flower[7] with a motion that was like the flickering of blue fire. The blue fire burst and scattered into whirling sparks; she had given chase, laughing and shouting like a child.

"I'm sure it will do you good, my dear."

"I was wondering if you'd come with me, dear."

"But you know I'm going to Scotland at the end of the month."

Mrs. Hutton looked up at him entreatingly. "It's the journey," she said. "The thought of it is such a nightmare.[8] I don't know if I can manage it. And you know I can't sleep in hotels. And then there's the luggage and all the worries. I can't go alone."

"But you won't be alone. You'll have your maid with you." He spoke impatiently. The sick woman was usurping the place of the healthy one. He was being dragged back from the memory of the sunlit down and the quick, laughing girl, back to this unhealthy, overheated room

---

1) *impasse*: (F.) blind alley; deadlock 막다른 골목.
2) came out : 풀려 나왔다, 맞아 떨어졌다.
3) Llandrindod Wells: a town, urban district and health resort of Radorshire, Wales; became known for its mineral springs but only during the 19th century
4) the chalk down: chalk upland. 남부 영국의 백아질(白堊質)의 언덕. down=hill.
5) the waters: 광천(鑛泉).
6) stalked: approached steaslthily.
7) scabious flower: 체꽃.
8) such a nightmare: a very frightful nightmare.

and its complaining occupant.

"I don't think I shall be able to go."

"But you must, my dear, if the doctor tells you to. And, besides, a change[1] will do you good."

"I don't think so."

"But Libbard thinks so, and he knows what he's talking about."

"No, I can't face it. I'm too weak. I can't go alone." Mrs. Hutton pulled a handkerchief out of her black silk bag, and put it to her eyes.

"Nonsense, my dear, you must make the effort."

"I had rather be left in peace to die here." She was crying in earnest now.

"O Lord! Now do be reasonable. Listen now, please." Mrs. Hutton only sobbed more violently. "Oh, what is one to do?" He shrugged his shoulders and walked out of the room.

Mr. Hutton was aware that he had not behaved with proper patience; but he could not help it. Very early in his manhood he had discovered that not only did he not feel sympathy for the poor, the weak, the diseased, and deformed, he actually hated them. Once, as an undergraduate, he spent three days at a mission in the East End.[2] He had returned, filled with a profound and ineradicable[3] disgust. Instead of pitying, he loathed the unfortunate. It was not, he knew, a very comely emotion, and he had been ashamed of it at first. In the end he had decided that it was temperamental, inevitable, and had felt no further qualms.[4] Emily had been healthy and beautiful when he married her. He had loved her then. But now — was it his fault that she was like this?

Mr. Hutton dined alone. Food and drink left him more benevolent than he had been before dinner. To make amends for his show of exasperation he went up to his wife's room and offered to read to her. She was touched, gratefully accepted the offer, and Mr. Hutton who was particularly proud of his accent, suggested a little light reading

---

1) a change: 전지(轉地).
2) the East End: 런던 시의 동부 하층계급 사람들이 많이 사는 곳.
3) ineradicable: 뿌리 뽑기 어려운. (=deep-rooted)
4) qualms: 양심의 가책, 거리낌.

in French.

"French? I am so fond of French." Mrs. Hutton spoke of the language of Racine[1] as though it were a dish of green peas.

Mr. Hutton ran down to the library and returned with a yellow volume. He began reading. The effort of pronouncing perfectly absorbed his whole attention. But how good his accent was! The fact of its goodness seemed to improve the quality of the novel he was reading.

At the end of fifteen pages an unmistakable sound aroused him. He looked up; Mrs. Hutton had gone to sleep. He sat still for a little while, looking with a dispassionate curiosity[2] at the sleeping face. Once it had been beautiful; once, long ago, the sight of it, the recollection of it, had moved him with an emotion profounder, perhaps, than any he had felt before or since. Now it was lined and cadaverous.[3] The skin was stretched tightly over the cheekbones, across the bridge of the sharp, birdlike nose. The closed eyes were set in profound bone-rimmed sockets. The lamplight striking on the face from the side emphasized with light and shade its cavities and projections.[4] It was the face of a dead Christ by Morales.[5]

Le squelette était invisible
Au temps heureux de l'art païen.[6]

He shivered a little, and tiptoed out of the room.

On the following day Mrs. Hutton came down to luncheon. She had had some unpleasant palpitations during the night, but she was feeling better now. Besides, she wanted to do honour to her guest. Miss Spence listened to her complaints about Llandrindod Wells, and was loud in sympathy, lavish with advice.[7] Whatever she said was

1) Racine: Jean Baptiste(1639-99), 프랑스의 비극 시인.
2) a dispassionate curiosity: 아무런 감정도 없이 그저 호기심만으로.
3) cadaverous: deadly pale.
4) cavities and projections: (얼굴의) 움푹 들어간 곳과 불쑥 튀어나온 곳.
5) Morales: Luis de(1510-86), Spanish painter, called El Divino because of his emotional religious paintings, which appealed to the people.
6) *Le squelette était invisible/Au temps heureux de l'art païen.*: (F.) The skelton was invisible/At the happy times of the pagan art. 해골바가지 같은 건 눈에 뜨이지 않았다. 이단의 예술이 한창 꽃피었던 시절에.
7) lavish with advice: 아낌없이 충고를 퍼붓다.

always said with intensity. She leaned forward, aimed, so to speak, like a gun, and fired her words. Bang! the charge[1)] in her soul was ignited,[2)] the words whizzed forth at the narrow barrel of her mouth. She was a machine-gun riddling her hostess with sympathy.[3)] Mr. Hutton had undergone similar bombardments, mostly of a literary or philosophic character — bombardments of Maeterlinck,[4)] of Mrs. Besant,[5)] of Bergson,[6)] of William James. Today, the missiles were medical. She talked about insomnia, she expatiated on the virtues[7)] of harmless drugs and beneficent specialists. Under the bombardment Mrs. Hutton opened out,[8)] like a flower in the sun.

Mr. Hutton looked on[9)] in silence. The spectacle of Janet Spence evoked in him an unfailing curiosity. He was not romantic enough to imagine that every face masked an interior physiognomy[10)] of beauty or strangeness, that every woman's small talk[11)] was like a vapour hanging over mysterious gulfs. His wife, for example, and Doris; they were nothing more than what they seemed to be. But with Janet Spence it was somehow different. Here one could be sure that there was some kind of a queer face behind the Gioconda smile and the Roman eyebrows. The only question was: What exactly was there? Mr. Hutton could never quite make out.[12)]

"But perhaps you won't have to go to Llandrindod after all," Miss Spence was saying. "If you get well quickly, Dr. Libbard will let you off."[13)]

---

1) charge: 재놓은 탄약.
2) was ignited: 점화되었다. ignite=set on fire.
3) a machine gun riddling her hostess with sympathy: 동정의 총알로 여주인을 구멍투성이로 만드는, 즉 여주인을 골려 주고 있는 기관총(과 같았다).
4) Maeterlinck: Maurice(862-1949), Belgium의 극작가, 시인.
5) Mrs. Besant: Annie(1847-10933), British theosophist, the daughter of William Page Wood, married the Rev. Frank Besant.
6) Bergson: Henri(1859-1910) 아메리카의 심리학자.
7) virtues: 효능, 효용.
8) opened out: 마음이 풀렸다, 털어놓고 말했다.(=spoke out)
9) look on: be a mere spectator. 방관하다, 구경하다.
10) physiognomy: looks; features. 인상.
11) small talk: 잡담, 수다. cf. tall talk=허풍.
12) make out: understand; distinguish.
13) let you off: 놓아 주다(=excuse you), 즉 억지로 권하지 않는다.

"I only hope so. Indeed, I do really feel rather better today."

Mr. Hutton felt ashamed. How much was it his own lack of sympathy that prevented her from feeling well every day? But he comforted himself by reflecting that it was only a case of feeling, not of being better. Sympathy does not mend a diseased liver or a weak heart.

"My dear, I wouldn't eat those red currants if I were you," he said, suddenly solicitous. "You know that Libbard has banned everything with skins and pips."[1]

"But I am so fond of them," Mrs. Hutton protested, "and I feel so well today."

"Don't be a tyrant," said Miss Spence, looking first at him and then at his wife. "Let the poor invalid have what she fancies; it will do her good." She laid her hand on Mrs. Hutton's arm and patted it affectionately two or three times.

"Thank you, my dear." Mrs. Hutton helped herself to the stewed currants.

"Well, don't blame me if they make you ill again."

"Do I ever blame you, dear?"

"You have nothing to blame me for," Mr. Hutton answered playfully. "I am the perfect husband."

They sat in the garden after luncheon. From the island of shade[2] under the old cypress tree they looked out across a flat expanse of lawn, in which the parterres of flowers[3] shone with a metallic brilliance.

Mr. Hutton took a deep breath of the warm and fragrant air. "It's good to be alive," he said.

"Just to be alive," his wife echoed, stretching one pale, knot-jointed hand into the sunlight.

A maid brought the coffee; the silver pots and the little blue cups were set on a folding table near the group of chairs.

"Oh, my medicine!" exclaimed Mrs. Hutton. "Run in and fetch it, Clara, will you? The white bottle on the sideboard."

---

1) pip(s): (사과, 배 따위의) 씨.

2) the island of shade: 그늘이 져서 섬처럼 되어 있는 곳.

3) parterres of flowers: 꽃밭. parterres=level space in gardens occupied by flower-beds; flower gardens having beds arranged in apattern 화단이 있는 잔디밭.

"I'll go," said Mr. Hutton. "I've got to go and fetch a cigar in any case."

He ran in towards the house. On the threshold he turned round for an instant. The maid was walking back across the lawn. His wife was sitting up in her deck-chair, engaged in opening her white parasol. Miss Spence was bending over the table, pouring out the coffee. He passed into the cool obscurity of the house.[1)]

"Do you like sugar in your coffee?" Miss Spence inquired.

"Yes, please. Give me rather a lot. I'll drink it after my medicine to take the taste away."

Mrs. Hutton leaned back in her chair, lowering the sunshade over her eyes, so as to shut out from her vision the burning sky.

Behind her, Miss Spence was making a delicate clinking among the coffee cups.

"I've given you three large spoonfuls. That ought to take the taste away. And here comes the medicine."

Mr. Hutton had reappeared, carrying a wine-glass, half full of a pale liquid.

"It smells delicious," he said, as he handed it to his wife.

"That's only the flavouring." She drank it off at a gulp,[2)] shuddered, and made a grimace. "Ugh, it's so nasty. Give me my coffee."

Miss Spence gave her the cup; she sipped at it. "You've made it like syrup. But it's very nice, after that atrocious[3)] medicine."

At half-past three Mrs. Hutton complained that she did not feel as well as she had done, and went indoors to lie down. Her husband would have said something about the red currants, but checked himself; the triumph of an "I told you so"[4)] was too cheaply won. Instead, he was sympathetic, and gave her his arm to the house.

"A rest will do you good," he said. "By the way, I shan't[5)] be back till after dinner."

---

1) the cool obscurity of the house: 서늘하고 침침한 집안.
2) at a gulp: 한 입에, 단숨에.
3) atrocious: (Colloq.) very bad; abominable 지독한.
4) "I told you so": 거봐 내가 뭐라든.
5) I shan't: I shall not.

"But why? Where are you going?"

"I promised to go to Johnson's this evening. We have to discuss the war memorial, you know."

"Oh, I wish you weren't going." Mrs. Hutton was almost in tears. "Can't you stay? I don't like being alone in the house."

"But, my dear, I promised — weeks ago." It was a bother having to lie like this. "And now I must get back and look after[1] Miss Spence."

He kissed her on the forehead and went out again into the garden. Miss Spence received him aimed and intense.[2]

"Your wife is dreadfully ill," she fired off at him.

"I thought she cheered up so much when you came."

"That was purely nervous, purely nervous. I was watching her closely. With a heart in that condition and her digestion wrecked — yes, wrecked — anything might happen."

"Libbard doesn't take so gloomy a view of poor Emily's health." Mr. Hutton held open the gate that led from the garden into the drive; Miss Spence's car was standing by the front door.

"Libbard is only a country doctor. You ought to see a specialist."

He could not refrain from laughing. "You have a macabre[3] passion for specialists."

Miss Spence held up her hand in protest. "I am serious. I think poor Emily is in a very bad state. Anything might happen at any moment."[4]

He handed her into the car and shut the door. The chauffeur started the engine and climbed into his place, ready to drive off.

"Shall I tell him to start?" He had no desire to continue the conversation.

Miss Spence leaned forward and shot a Gioconda in his direction. "Remember, I expect you to come and see me again soon."

Mechanically he grinned, made a polite noise,[5] and, as the car

---

1) look after: ~에 배웅하다.
2) aimed and intense: (그에게 포문을) 겨누고 격하게.
3) macabre: horrible; ghastly.
4) Anything might happen … at any moment: 언제 어느 때 무슨 일이 일어날지. 커피 속에 비소를 넣은 Miss Spence의 말임에 유의할 것.
5) made a polite noise: 정중하게 인사했다.

moved forward, waved his hand. He was happy to be alone.

A few minutes afterwards Mr. Hutton himself drove away. Doris was waiting at the cross-roads. They dined together twenty miles from home, at a roadside hotel. It was one of those bad, expensive meals which are only cooked in country hotels, frequented by motorists. It revolted Mr. Hutton, but Doris enjoyed it. She always enjoyed things. Mr. Hutton ordered a not very good brand of champagne. He was wishing he had spent the evening in his library.

When they started homewards Doris was a little tipsy[1] and extremely affectionate. It was very dark inside the car, but looking forward, past the motionless form of M'Nab, they could see a bright and narrow universe of forms and colours scooped out of the night[2] by the electric head lamps.[3]

It was after eleven when Mr. Hutton reached home. Dr. Libbard met him in the hall. He was a small man with delicate hands and well-formed features that were almost feminine. His brown eyes were large and melancholy. He used to waste a great deal of time sitting at the bedside of his patients, looking sadness through those eyes and talking in a sad, low voice about nothing in particular.[4] His person exhaled a pleasing odour, decidedly antiseptic but at the same time suave[5] and discreetly delicious.

"Libbard?" said Mr. Hutton in surprise. "You here? Is my wife ill?"

"We tried to fetch you earlier," the soft, melancholy voice replied. "It was thought you were at Mr. Johnson's, but they had no news of you there."

"No, I was detained. I had a breakdown."[6] Mr. Hutton answered irritably. It was tiresome to be caught out in a lie.[7]

"Your wife wanted to see you urgently."

"Well, I can go now," Mr. Hutton moved towards the stairs.

---

1) tipsy: partially intoxicated [drunk].
2) scooped out of the night: 밤의 어둠 속에서 퍼올린 것 같은.
3) head lamps: head-lights.
4) nothing in particular: 별것이 아닌 것(얘기).
5) suave: of soft flavour.
6) I had a breakdown: 자동차가 고장이 났어.
7) be caught out in a lie: 거짓이 탄로나다, 간파되다.

Dr. Libbard laid a hand on his arm. "I am afraid it's too late."

"Too late?" He began fumbling with his watch; it wouldn't come out of the pocket.

"Mrs. Hutton passed away[1] half an hour ago."

The voice remained even[2] in its softness, the melancholy of the eyes did not deepen. Dr. Libbard spoke of death as he would speak of a local cricket match. All things were equally vain and equally deplorable.

Mr. Hutton found himself thinking of Janet Spence's words. At any moment — at any moment. She had been extraordinarily right.

"What happened?" he asked. "What was the cause?"

Dr. Libbard explained. It was heart failure[3] brought on by a violent attack of nausea,[4] caused in its turn by the eating of something of an irritant nature.[5] Red currants? Mr. Hutton suggested. Very likely. It had been too much for the heart. There was chronic valvular disease[6]: something had collapsed under the strain. It was all over; she could not have suffered much.

"It's a pity they should have chosen the day of the Eton and Harrow match[7] for the funeral," old General Grego was saying as he stood, his top hat in his hand, under the shadow of the lych gate,[8] wiping his face with his handkerchief.

Mr Hutton overheard the remark and with difficulty restrained a desire to inflict grievous[9] bodily pain on the General. He would have liked to hit the old brute in the middle of his big red face. Monstrous great mulberry, spotted with meal![10] Was there no respect for the dead?

---

1) passed away: died.
2) even: smooth.
3) heart failure: 심장마비.
4) nausea: 욕지기, 메스꺼움.(=qualm)
5) something of an irritant nature: 무슨 자극성인 것.
6) chronic valvular disease: 만성판막증(慢性瓣膜症).
7) the Eton and Harrow match: Eton과 Harrow는 전통 있는 유명한 Public School로서 양교 간에 매년 7월 cricket 시합이 있어 성황을 이룬다.
8) the lych gate: 지붕 있는 묘지 문. (=the lich gate) 여기서 목사가 오기를 기다려서 관을 묘지로 운반한다.
9) grievous: atrocious, heinous.
10) Monstrous great mulberry, spotted with meal: 점점이 흰 가루를 묻힌 엄청나게 큰 뽕나무 열매(같은 얼굴).

Did nobody care? In theory he didn't much care; let the dead bury their dead.[1] But here, at the graveside, he had found himself actually sobbing. Poor Emily, they had been pretty happy once. Now she was lying at the bottom of a seven-foot hole. And here was Grego complaining that he couldn't go to the Eton and Harrow match.

Mr. Hutton looked round at the groups of black figures that were drifting slowly out of the churchyard towards the fleet of cabs and motors assembled in the road outside. Against the brilliant background of the July grass and flowers and foliage, they had a horribly alien[2] and unnatural appearance. It pleased him to think that all these people would soon be dead, too.

That evening Mr. Hutton sat up late in his library reading the life of Milton. There was no particular reason why he should have chosen Milton; it was the book that first came to hand, that was all. It was after midnight when he had finished. He got up from his armchair, unbolted the French windows, and stepped out on to the little paved terrace. The night was quiet and clear. Mr. Hutton looked at the stars and at the holes between them, dropped his eyes to the dim lawns and hueless flowers of the garden, and let them wander over the farther landscape, black and grey under the moon.

He began to think with a kind of confused violence. There were the stars, there was Milton. A man can be somehow the peer[3] of stars and night. Greatness, nobility. But is there seriously a difference between the noble and the ignoble? Milton, the stars, death, and himself —himself. The soul, the body; the higher and the lower nature.[4] Perhaps there was something in it, after all. Milton had a god on his side and righteousness. What had he? Nothing, nothing whatever. There were only Doris's little breasts. What was the point of it all?[5] Milton, the stars, death, and Emily in her grave, Doris and himself

---

1) let the dead bury their dead: 죽은 자에게 그 죽은 자를 묻게 하여라. (St. Mathew viii, 22).
2) alien: 그런 장소에 맞지 않는.
3) peer: companion; comrade.
4) the higher and the lower nature: the soul and the body.
5) What was the point of it all?: 이런 것에 무슨 의미가 있다는 건가?.

— always himself . . .

Oh, he was a futile and disgusting being. Everything convinced him of it. It was a solemn moment. He spoke aloud: "I will, I will." The sound of his own voice in the darkness was appalling; it seemed to him that he had sworn that infernal oath[1] which binds even the gods. "I will, I will." There had been New Year's days and solemn anniversaries in the past, when he had felt the same contritions[2] and recorded similar resolutions. They had all thinned away, these resolutions, like smoke, into nothingness. But this was a greater moment and he had pronounced a more fearful oath. In the future it was to be different. Yes, he would live by reason, he would be industrious, he would curb his appetites,[3] he would devote his life to some good purpose. It was resolved and it would be so.

In practice he saw himself spending his mornings in agricultural pursuits,[4] riding round with the bailiff, seeing that[5] his land was farmed in the best modern way, silos and artificial manures and continuous cropping, and all that. The remainder of the day should be devoted to serious study. There was that book he had been intending to write for so long — *The Effect of Diseases on Civilization.*

Mr. Hutton went to bed humble and contrite, but with a sense that grace had entered into him. He slept for seven and a half hours, and woke to find the sun brilliantly shining. The emotions of the evening before had been transformed by a good night's rest into his customary cheerfulness. It was not until a good many seconds after his return to conscious life[6] that he remembered his resolution, his Stygian oath.[7] Milton and death seemed somehow different in the sunlight. As for the stars, they were not there. But the resolutions were good; even in the daytime he could see that. He had his horse saddled after breakfast,

1) infernal oath: 지옥의 맹세, 터무니없는 서약.
2) contritions: 뉘우침. (*v.*) contrite.
3) curb his appetites: 욕망을 억제하다. curb=restrain; cheek.
4) agricultural pursuits: 농사 일.
5) seeing that~: making sure that~.
6) his return to conscious life: 잠에서 깨다.
7) Stygian oath: dreadful oath; inferal oath. Stygian <Styx=infernal river; river encompassing Hades>.

and rode round the farm with the bailiff. After luncheon he read Thucydides[1] on the plague at Athens. In the evening he made a few notes on malaria in Southern Italy. While he was undressing he remembered that there was a good anecdote in Skelton's[2] jest-book about the Sweating Sickness.[3] He would have made a note of it if only he could have found a pencil.

On the sixth morning of his new life Mr. Hutton found among his correspondence an envelope addressed in that peculiarly vulgar handwriting which he knew to be Doris's. He opened it, and began to read. She didn't know what to say; words were so inadequate. His wife dying like that, and so suddenly — it was too terrible. Mr. Hutton sighed, but his interest revived somewhat as he read on:

"Death is so frightening, I never think of it when I can help it. But when something like this happens, or when I am feeling ill or depressed, then I can't help remembering it is there so close, and I think about all the wicked things I have done and about you and me, and I wonder what will happen, and I am so frightened. I am so lonely, Teddy Bear, and so unhappy, and I don't know what to do. I can't get rid of the idea of dying. I am so wretched and helpless without you. I didn't mean to write to you; I meant to wait till you were out of mourning[4] and could come and see me again, but I was so lonely and miserable, Teddy Bear, I had to write. I couldn't help it. Forgive me, I want you so much; I have nobody in the world but you. You are so good and gentle and understanding; there is nobody like you. I shall never forget how good and kind you have been to me, and you are so clever and know so much, I can't understand how you ever came to pay any attention to me, I am so dull and stupid, much less like me and love me, because you do love me a little, don't you, Teddy Bear?"

Mr. Hutton was touched with shame and remorse. To be thanked like this, worshipped for having seduced the girl — it was too much.

1) Thucydides: (460?-400? B.C.) 그리스의 역사가.
2) Skelton: John(1460?-1529), 영국의 풍자시인.
3) the Sweating Sickness: (15~6세기에 유행한) 전염성 발한열병(發汗熱病.)
4) out of mourning: 탈상(脫喪).

It had just been a piece of imbecile wantonness.[1] Imbecile, idiotic: there was no other way to describe it. For, when all was said,[2] he had derived very little pleasure from it. Taking all things together,[3] he had probably been more bored than amused. Once upon a time he had believed himself to be a hedonist. But to be a hedonist implies a certain process of reasoning, a deliberate choice of known pleasures, a rejection of known pains. This had been done without reason, against it.[4] For he knew beforehand — so well, so well — that there was no interest or pleasure to be derived from these wretched affairs. And yet each time the vague itch[5] came upon[6] him he succumbed, involving himself once more in the old stupidity. There had been Maggie, his wife's maid, and Edith, the girl on the farm, and Mrs. Pringle, and the waitress in London, and others — there seemed to be dozens of them. It had all been so stale and boring. He knew it would be; he always knew. And yet, and yet . . . Experience doesn't teach.

Poor little Doris! He would write to her kindly, comfortingly, but he wouldn't see her again. A servant came to tell him that his horse was saddled and waiting. He mounted and rode off. That morning the old bailiff was more irritating than usual.

Five days later Doris and Mr. Hutton were sitting together on the pier at Southend;[7] Doris, in white muslin with pink garnishings,[8] radiated happiness; Mr. Hutton, legs outstretched and chair tilted, had pushed the panama back from his forehead and was trying to feel like a tripper.[9] That night, when Doris was asleep, breathing and warm by his side, he recaptured, in this moment of darkness and physical fatigue, the rather cosmic emotion which had possessed him that

1) a piece of imbecile wantonness: 어리석은 변덕. imbecile=weak in intellect; stupid; foolish.
2) when all was said: after all.
3) Taking all things together: Considering everything.
4) against it: against reason.
5) the vague itch: 막연한 충동. itch=restless desire; hankering.
6) came upon: attacked.
7) Southend: 영국 남동부 Essex주 Thames강 어구에 있는 항구·요양지.
8) garnishings: decorations.
9) tripper: tourist; excursionist.

evening, not a fortnight ago, when he had made his great resolution. And so his solemn oath had already gone the way of so many other resolutions.[1] Unreason had triumphed; at the first itch of desire he had given way. He was hopeless, hopeless.

For a long time he lay with closed eyes, ruminating[2] his humiliation. The girl stirred in her sleep. Mr. Hutton turned over and looked in her direction. Enough faint light crept in between the half-drawn curtains to show her bare arm and shoulder, her neck, and the dark tangle of hair on the pillow. She was beautiful, desirable. Why did he lie there moaning over his sins? What did it matter? If he were hopeless, then so be it;[3] he would make the best of[4] his hopelessness. A glorious sense of irresponsibility suddenly filled him. He was free, magnificently free. In a kind of exaltation he drew the girl towards him. She woke, bewildered, almost frightened under his rough kisses.

The storm of his desire subsided into a kind of serene merriment.[5] The whole atmosphere seemed to be quivering with enormous silent laughter.

"Could anyone love you as much as I do, Teddy Bear?" The question came faintly from distant worlds of love.

"I think I know somebody who does," Mr. Hutton replied. The submarine laughter[6] was swelling, rising, ready to break the surface of silence and resound.

"Who? Tell me. What do you mean?" The voice had come very close; charged with[7] suspicion, anguish, indignation, it belonged to this immediate world.[8]

"A-ah!"

---

1) had already gone the way of so many other resolutions: 이미 다른 결심들과 똑같은 길을 걸었다.
2) ruminating: ruminate=ponder; meditate.
3) so be it: 할 수 없다, 도리가 없지 않는가. (=let it be so)
4) make the best of: 되도록 활용하다.
5) serene merriment: 조용한 즐거운.
6) The submarine laughter: 표면에 나타나지 않는 웃음소리.
7) charged with: filled with.
8) this immediate world: 이 현세에 세계, 직접 눈 앞에 있는 세계. 앞에 나온 distant world of love와 대조됨.

"Who?"

"You'll never guess." Mr. Hutton kept up the joke until it began to grow tedious, and then pronounced the name: "Janet Spence."

Doris was incredulous. "Miss Spence of the Manor? That old woman?" It was too ridiculous. Mr. Hutton laughed, too.

"But it's quite true," he said. "She adores me." Oh, the vast joke! He would go and see her as soon as he returned — see and conquer.[1)] "I believe she wants to marry me," he added.

"But you wouldn't. . . you don't intend. . ."

The air was fairly crepitating[2)] with humour. Mr. Hutton laughed aloud. "I intend to marry you," he said. It seemed to him the best joke he had ever made in his life.

When Mr. Hutton left Southend he was once more a married man. It was agreed that, for the time being, the fact should be kept secret. In the autumn they would go abroad together, and the world should be informed.[3)] Meanwhile he was to go back to his own house and Doris to hers.

The day after his return he walked over in the afternoon to see Miss Spence. She received him with the old Gioconda.

"I was expecting you to come."

"I couldn't keep away," Mr. Hutton gallantly replied.

They sat in the summerhouse.[4)] It was a pleasant place — a little old stucco temple bowered[5)] among dense bushes of evergreen. Miss Spence had left her mark on it by hanging up over the seat a blue-and-white Della Robbia plaque.[6)]

"I am thinking of going to Italy this autumn," said Mr. Hutton. He felt like a ginger-beer bottle, ready to pop with bubbling humorous

---

1) see and conquer: cf. "veni, vidi, vici," i.e. "I came, I saw, I conquered." Julius Caesar가 로마의 원로원에 승전을 보고했을 때(47 B.C.)의 간결한 편지.

2) crepitating: making crackling noise.

3) be informed: be informed of the marriage.

4) summerhouse: (정원, 공원 안에 있는) 정자, (미국) 하계별장.

5) bowered: bowery, shady.

6) Della Robbia plaque: Robbia(1400?-82), 이탈리아의 조각가. plaque는 장식판, 액자, 현판.

excitement.[1]

"Italy. . ." Miss Spence closed her eyes ecstatically. "I feel drawn there, too."

"Why not let yourself be drawn?"

"I don't know. One somehow hasn't the energy and initiative to set out alone."

"Alone. . ." Ah, sound of guitars and throaty[2] singing! "Yes, travelling alone isn't much fun."

Miss Spence lay back in her chair without speaking. Her eyes were still closed. Mr. Hutton stroked his moustache. The silence prolonged itself for what seemed a very long time.

Pressed to stay to dinner, Mr. Hutton did not refuse. The fun had hardly started. The table was laid in the loggia.[3] Through its arches they looked out on to the sloping garden, to the valley below and the farther hills. Light ebbed away; the heat and silence were oppressive. A huge cloud was mounting up the sky, and there were distant breathings of thunder.[4] The thunder drew nearer, a wind began to blow, and the first drops of rain fell. The table was cleared. Miss Spence and Mr. Hutton sat on in the growing darkness.

Miss Spence broke a long silence by saying meditatively:

"I think everyone has a right to a certain amount of happiness, don't you?"

"Most certainly." But what was she leading up to?[5] Nobody makes generalizations about life unless they mean to talk about themselves. Happiness: he looked back on his own life, and saw a cheerful, placid existence disturbed by no great griefs or discomforts or alarms. He had always had money and freedom; he had been able to do very much as he wanted. Yes, he supposed he had been happy, happier than most men. And now he was not merely happy; he had discovered

---

1) ready to pop … humorous excitement: 웃음이 부글부글 끓어서 언제 펑하고 터져 나올지 모를 지경.

2) throaty: hoarse.

3) loggia: gallery or arcade open to the air on at least one side.

4) distant breathings of thunder: 멀리서 들려오는 뇌성.

5) what was she leading up to: 도대체 무슨 말을 하려는 걸까?.

in irresponsibility the secret of gaiety. He was about to say something about his happiness when Miss Spence went on speaking.

"People like you and me have a right to be happy some time in our lives."

"Me?" said Mr. Hutton, surprised.

"Poor Henry! Fate hasn't treated either of us very well."

"Oh, well, it might have treated me worse."

"You're being cheerful. That's brave of you.[1] But don't think I can't see behind the mask."[2]

Miss Spence spoke louder and louder as the rain came down more and more heavily. Periodically the thunder cut across[3] her utterances. She talked on, shouting against the noise.

"I have understood you so well and for so long."

A flash[4] revealed her, aimed and intent, leaning towards him. Her eyes were two profound and menacing gun barrels. The darkness reengulfed her.

"You were a lonely soul seeking a companion soul. I could sympathize with you in your solitude. Your marriage. . . ."

The thunder cut short[5] the sentence. Miss Spence's voice became audible once more with the words:

". . . could offer no companionship to a man of your stamp.[6] You needed a soul mate."[7]

A soul mate — he! a soul mate! It was incredibly fantastic. "Georgette Leblanc,[8] the ex-soul mate of Maurice Maeterlinck." He had seen that in the paper a few days ago. So it was thus that Janet Spence had painted him in her imagination — as a soul-mater.[9] And for Doris

1) That's brave of you: You are brave in that point.
2) the mask: 쾌활을 가장한 가면을 말함.
3) cut across: 가로채다.
4) flash: (번갯불의) 번쩍이는 빛.
5) cut short: interrupted.
6) a man of your stamp: a man of your type.
7) a soul mate: a platonic friend of the opposite sex 영혼의 배필.
8) Georgette Leblanc: 프랑스의 여배우. 작가 Maeterlinck와 1901년에 결혼, 1918년 이혼.
9) soul-mater: 영혼의 배필을 구하는 사람.

he was a picture of goodness and the cleverest man in the world. And actually, really, he was what? — Who knows?

"My heart went out to you. I could understand; I was lonely, too." Miss Spence laid her hand on his knee. "You were so patient." Another flash. She was still aimed, dangerously. "You never complained. But I could guess — I could guess."

"How wonderful of you!" So he was an *âme incomprise.*[1] "Only a woman's intuition. . ."

The thunder crashed and rumbled, died away, and only the sound of the rain was left. The thunder was his laughter, magnified, externalized. Flash and crash, there it was again,[2] right on top of them.

"Don't you feel that you have within you something that is akin to this storm?" He could imagine her leaning forward as she uttered the words. "Passion makes one the equal of the elements."[3]

What was his gambit[4] now? Why, obviously, he should have said "yes," and ventured on some unequivocal[5] gesture. But Mr. Hutton suddenly took fright. The ginger beer in him had gone flat.[6] The woman was serious — terribly serious. He was appalled.

Passion? "No," he desperately answered. "I am without passion." But his remark was either unheard or unheeded, for Miss Spence went on with a growing exaltation, speaking so rapidly, however, and in such a burningly intimate whisper that Mr. Hutton found it very difficult to distinguish what she was saying. She was telling him, as far as he could make out, the story of her life. The lightning was less frequent now, and there were long intervals of darkness. But at each flash he saw her still aiming towards him, still yearning forward with a terrifying intensity. Darkness, the rain, and then flash! her face was there, close at hand. A pale mask, greenish white; the large eyes, the narrow barrel

1) *âme incomprise*: (F.) incomprehensible soul.
2) there it was again: 또 시작이다.
3) the elements: earth, water, air, fire의 the four elements을 말함.
4) gambit: (chess) 수(手), 첫수, 선수.
5) unequivocal: not ambiguous; clear.
6) The ginger beer … gone flat: 진저 비어 같은 기분은 김이 빠져 버렸다. flat=dull; lifeless.

of the mouth, the heavy eyebrows. Agrippina, or wasn't it rather — yes, wasn't it rather George Robey?[1)]

He began devising absurd plans for escaping. He might suddenly jump up, pretending he had seen a burglar — Stop thief! stop thief! — and dash off into the night in pursuit.[2)] Or should he say that he felt faint, a heart attack?[3)] or that he had seen a ghost — Emily's ghost — in the garden? Absorbed in his childish plotting, he had ceased to pay any attention to Miss Spence's words. The spasmodic clutching of her hand recalled his thoughts.[4)]

"I honoured you for that, Henry," she was saying.

Honoured him for what?[5)]

"Marriage is a sacred tie, and your respect for it, even when the marriage was, as it was in your case, an unhappy one, made me respect you and admire you, and — shall I dare say the word? — "

Oh, the burglar, the ghost in the garden! But it was too late.

". . . yes, love you, Henry, all the more. But we're free now, Henry."

Free? There was a movement in the dark, and she was kneeling on the floor by his chair.

"Oh, Henry, Henry, I have been unhappy, too."

Her arms embraced him, and by the shaking of her body he could feel that she was sobbing. She might have been a suppliant crying for mercy.

"You mustn't, Janet," he protested. Those tears were terrible, terrible. "Not now, not now! You must be calm; you must go to bed." He patted her shoulder, then got up, disengaging himself from her embrace. He left her still crouching on the floor beside the chair on which he had been sitting.

Groping his way into the hall, and without waiting to look for his hat, he went out of the house, taking infinite pains to close the front door noiselessly behind him. The clouds had blown over, and the moon

---

1) George Robey: 영국의 희극배우 George Wade(1869-?)의 예명.
2) in pursuit: pursuing; in the pursuit of the burglar.
3) a heart attack: 심장병의 발작.
4) The spasmodic clutching … his thoughts: 그녀의 손이 발작적으로 그의 손을 꽉 쥐는 바람에 그는 번쩍 정신이 들었다. spasmodic=convulsive; fitful.
5) Honoured him for what?: For what did she honored him?.

was shining from a clear sky. There were puddles all along the road, and a noise of running water rose from the gutters and ditches. Mr. Hutton splashed along, not caring if he got wet.

How heart-rendingly[1] she had sobbed! With the emotions of pity and remorse that the recollection evoked[2] in him there was a certain resentment: why couldn't she have played the game that he was playing, the heartless, amusing game? Yes, but he had known all the time that she wouldn't, she couldn't, play that game; he had known and persisted.

What had she said about passion and the elements? Something absurdly stale, but true, true. There she was, a cloud[3] black-bosomed and charged with thunder, and he, like some absurd little Benjamin Franklin,[4] had sent up a kite into the heart of the menace. Now he was complaining that his toy[5] had drawn the lightning.

She was probably still kneeling by that chair in the loggia, crying.

But why hadn't he been able to keep up[6] the game? Why had his irresponsibility deserted him, leaving him suddenly sober in a cold world? There were no answers to any of his questions. One idea burned steady and luminous in his mind, the idea of flight. He must get away at once.

"What are you thinking about, Teddy Bear?"

"Nothing."

There was a silence. Mr. Hutton remained motionless, his elbows on the parapet of the terrace, his chin in his hands, looking down over Florence. He had taken a villa on one of the hilltops to the south of the city. From a little raised terrace at the end of the garden one looked down a long fertile valley on to the town and beyond it to the bleak mass of Monte Morello[7] and, eastward of it, to the peopled

---

1) heart-rendingly: terribly; distressingly; grievously.
2) evoked: called up; excited.
3) a cloud: 바로 앞의 she와 동격.
4) Benjamin Franklin: (1706-1790) American statesman, diplomat, writer and scientist. He discovered the identity of lightning and electricity(1752), framed a kite and sent it to the sky for the experiment of his theory. He also invented the lightning rod.
5) his toy: the kite.
6) keep up: continue.
7) Monte Morello: 프로렌스 부근의 산 이름.

hill of Fiesole,[1] dotted with white houses. Everything was clear and luminous in the September sunshine.

"Are you worried about anything?"

"No, thank you."

"Tell me, Teddy Bear."

"But, my dear, there's nothing to tell." Mr. Hutton turned round, smiled and patted the girl's hand. "I think you'd better go in and have your siesta.[2] It's too hot for you here."

"Very well, Teddy Bear. Are you coming, too?"

"When I've finished my cigar."

"All right. But do hurry up and finish it, Teddy Bear." Slowly, reluctantly, she descended the steps of the terrace and walked towards the house.

Mr. Hutton continued his contemplation[3] of Florence. He had need to be alone. It was good sometimes to escape from Doris and the restless solicitude of her passion.[4] He had never known the pains of loving hopelessly,[5] but he was experiencing now the pains of being loved. These last weeks had been a period of growing discomfort. Doris was always with him, like an obsession, like a guilty conscience. Yes, it was good to be alone.

He pulled an envelope out of his pocket and opened it, not without reluctance. He hated letters; they always contained something unpleasant nowadays, since his second marriage. This was from his sister. He began skimming through[6] the insulting home-truths of which it was composed.[7] The words "indecent haste," "social suicide," "scarcely cold in her grave,"[8] "person of the lower classes," all occurred. They were inevitable now in any communication from a well-meaning[9]

1) Fiesole: 프로렌스 지방의 마을 이름.
2) siesta: mid-day rest usual in hot countries.
3) contemplation: steady gaze; meditation.
4) the restless solicitude of her passion: 그녀의 귀찮을 정도의 정열적인 배려.
5) the pains of loving hopelessly: 짝사랑(실연)의 괴로운.
6) skimming through: 빼고 읽다, 대충 읽다.
7) the insulting home-truths … composed: 아픈 데(급소)를 찌른 모욕적인 귀절.
8) scarcely cold in her grave: 매장된 처의 시체가 무덤 속에서 아직 싸늘해지기도 전에.
9) well-meaning: 선의의, 악의가 없는.

and right-thinking[1]) relative. Impatient, he was about to tear the stupid letter to pieces when his eye fell on a sentence at the bottom of the third page. His heart beat with uncomfortable violence as he read it. It was too monstrous! Janet Spence was going about telling everyone that he had poisoned his wife in order to marry Doris. What damnable malice! Ordinarily a man of the suavest temper, Mr. Hutton found himself trembling with rage. He took the childish satisfaction of calling names[2]) — he cursed the woman.

The suddenly he saw the ridiculous side of the situation. The notion that he should have murdered anyone in order to marry Doris! If they only knew how miserably bored he was. Poor, dear Janet! She had tried to be malicious; she had only succeeded in being stupid.

A sound of footsteps aroused him; he looked round. In the garden below the little terrace the servant girl of the house was picking fruit. A Neapolitan, strayed somehow as far north as Florence,[3]) she was a specimen of the classical type a little debased.[4]) Her profile might have been taken from a Sicilian coin of a bad period.[5]) Her features, features, carved floridly in the grand tradition, expressed an almost perfect stupidity. Her mouth was the most beautiful thing about her; the calligraphic hand of nature[6]) had richly curved it into an expression of mulish bad temper. . . . Under her hideous black clothes, Mr. Hutton divined a powerful body, firm and massive. He had looked at her before with a vague interest and curiosity. Today the curiosity defined and focused itself into a desire.[7]) An idyll of Theocritus.[8]) Here was the woman;[9]) he, alas, was not precisely like a goatherd[10]) on the volcanic hills. He called to her.

---

1) right-thinking: right-minded; noble-minded.
2) calling names: 욕설을 하다. (=speak ill or one). names 험담, 욕설.
3) A Neapolitan, strayed … as Florence: 프로렌스와 같은 먼 북쪽 지방까지 흘러온 나폴리 태생의 이 여자.
4) a little debased: 약간 격이 떨어진다.
5) a bad period: 퇴폐한 시대.
6) the calligraphic hand of nature: 조물주의 서예[붓] 솜씨.
7) focused itself into a desire: 집결하여 하나의 욕망을 이루다.
8) Theocritus: Grecian idyll poet about 3 cent. B.C.
9) the woman: Theocritus의 시에 나오는 여인.
10) goatherd: 양치는 사람.

"Armida!"

The smile with which she answered him was so provocative, attested so easy a virtue,[1] that Mr. Hutton took fright. He was on the brink once more — on the brink. He must draw back, oh! quickly, quickly, before it was too late. The girl continued to look up at him.

"*Ha chiamato*?"[2] she asked at last.

Stupidity or reason? Oh, there was no choice now. It was imbecility every time.

"*Scendo*,"[3] he called back to her. Twelve steps led from the garden to the terrace. Mr. Hutton counted them. Down, down, down, down . . . He saw a vision of himself descending from one circle of the inferno to the next,[4] from a darkness full of wind and hail to an abyss of stinking mud.

For a good many days the Hutton case had a place on the front page of every newspaper. There had been no more popular murder trial since George Smith[5] had temporarily eclipsed the European War[6] by drowning in a warm bath his seventh bride. The public imagination was stirred by this tale of a murder brought to light months after the date of the crime. Here, it was felt, was one of those incidents in human life, so notable because they are so rare, which do definitely justify the ways of God to man.[7] A wicked man had been moved by an illicit passion[8] to kill his wife. For months he had lived in sin and fancied security,[9] only to be dashed at last more horribly

---

1) attested so easy a virtue: 손만 벌리면 언제든지 응하겠다는 바람둥이 여자의 태도를 말함. attested=proved.

2) *Ha chiamato*? : (It.) Did you call me?.

3) *Scendo*: (It.) I'll descend.; I shall come down.

4) from one circle of the inferno to the next: 지옥의 한 영역에서 다른 영역으로. Dante가 그린 지옥에는 nine circles가 있다.

5) George Smith: 재산을 목적으로 결혼하여 아내를 여러 명 죽인 사나이.

6) eclipsed the European War: 유럽 대전을 무색케 하였다. eclipse=surpass; outline.

7) justify the ways of God to man: Milton의 *Paradise Lost* 제 1권의 26행을 인용한 것임.

8) an illicit passion: 불의의 정열, 불륜의 정.

9) fancied security: 안전하다고 생각했다.

into the pit he had prepared for himself. "Murder will out,"[1] and here was a case of it. The readers of the newspapers were in a position[2] to follow every movement of the hand of God. There had been vague, but persistent rumours in the neighbourhood; the police had taken action[3] at last. Then came the exhumation order,[4] the post mortem examination,[5] the inquest,[6] the evidence of the experts,[7] the verdict of the coroner's jury,[8] the trial, the condemnation.[9] For once[10] Providence had done its duty, obviously, grossly, didactically, as in a melodrama. The newspapers were right in making of the case the staple intellectual food[11] of a whole season.

Mr. Hutton's first emotion when he was summoned from Italy to give evidence at the inquest was one of indignation. It was a monstrous, a scandalous thing that the police should take such idle,[12] malicious gossip seriously. When the inquest was over he would bring an action for malicious prosecution[13] against[14] the Chief Constable; he would sue the Spence woman for slander.

The inquest was opened; the astonishing evidence unrolled itself. The experts had examined the body, and had found traces of arsenic;[15] they were of opinion that the late Mrs. Hutton had died of arsenic poisoning.

Arsenic poisoning . . . Emily had died of arsenic poisoning? After that, Mr. Hutton learned with surprise that there was enough arsenicated

---

1) Murder will out: 살인은 반드시 탄로난다. Chaucer의 *The Canterbury Tales*에 나오는 귀절.
2) be in a position: be able to; can.
3) take action: 조치를 강구하다.
4) the exhumation order: 시체 발굴 명령.
5) post mortem examination: 검시해부(檢屍解剖).
6) the inquest: 심문.
7) evidence of the experts: 감정인의 증언.
8) the coroner's jury: 검시 배심원.
9) condemnation: 형의 선고.
10) For once: 이번만은.
11) staple intellectual food: 지적(知的) 주식(主食).
12) idle: 밑도 끝도 없는.
13) malicious prosecution: 악의적인 고소.
14) bring an action against: ~을 상대로 소송을 제기하다.
15) arsenic: 비소.

insecticide in his greenhouses to poison an army.

It was now, quite suddenly, that he saw it[1]: there was a case against him.[2] Fascinated he watched it growing, growing, like some monstrous tropical plant. It was enveloping him, surrounding him; he was lost in a tangled forest.

When was the poison administered? The experts agreed that it must have been swallowed eight or nine hours before death. About lunchtime? Yes, about lunchtime. Clara, the parlormaid, was called. Mrs. Hutton, she remembered, had asked her to go and fetch her medicine. Mr. Hutton had volunteered to go instead; he had gone alone. Miss Spence —ah, the memory of the storm, the white face! the horror of it all! —Miss Spence confirmed Clara's statement, and added that Mr. Hutton had come back with the medicine already poured out in a wineglass, not in the bottle.

Mr. Hutton's indignation evaporated. He was dismayed, frightened. It was all too fantastic to be taken seriously, and yet this nightmare was fact, it was actually happening.

M'Nab had seen them kissing, often. He had taken them for a drive on the day of Mrs. Hutton's death. He could see them reflected in the wind screen,[3] sometimes out of the tail of his eye.[4]

The inquest was adjourned. That evening Doris went to bed with a headache. When he went to her room after dinner, Mr. Hutton found her crying.

"What's the matter?" He sat down on the edge of her bed and began to stroke her hair. For a long time she did not answer, and he went on stroking her hair mechanically, almost unconsciously; sometimes, even, he bent down and kissed her bare shoulder. He had his own affairs, however, to think about. What had happened? How was it that the stupid gossip had actually come true? Emily had died of arsenic poisoning. It was absurd, impossible. The order of things had been broken, and he was at the mercy of an irresponsibility. What had

1) It was now … he saw it: 이제야 사태를 깨닫게 되었다.
2) a case against him: 그에게 불리한 사건.
3) wind screen: windshield.
4) out of the tail of his eye: 곁눈으로.

happened, what was going to happen? He was interrupted in the midst of his thoughts.

"It's my fault, it's my fault!" Doris suddenly sobbed out. "I shouldn't have loved you; I oughtn't to have let you love me. Why was I ever born?"

Mr. Hutton didn't say anything, but looked down in silence at the abject figure of misery lying on the bed.

"If they do anything to you I shall kill myself."

She sat up, held him for a moment at arm's length,[1] and looked at him with a kind of violence, as though she were never to see him again.

"I love you, I love you, I love you." She drew him, inert and passive,[2] towards her, clasped him, pressed herself against him. "I didn't know you loved me as much as that, Teddy Bear. But why did you do it, why did you do it?"

Mr. Hutton undid[3] her clasping arms and got up. His face became very red. "You seem to take it for granted[4] that I murdered my wife," he said. "It's really too grotesque. What do you all take me for?[5] A cinema hero?" He had begun to lose his temper. All the exasperation, all the fear and bewilderment of the day, was transformed into a violent anger against her. "It's all such damned[6] stupidity. Haven't you any conception of a civilized man's mentality? Do I look the sort of man who'd go about slaughtering people? I suppose you imagined I was so insanely in love with you that I could commit any folly. When will you women understand that one isn't insanely in love? All one asks for is a quiet life, which you won't allow one to have. I don't know what the devil ever induced me to marry you. It was all a damned stupid, practical joke.[7] And now you go about saying I'm a murderer. I won't stand it."

---

1) held him … at arm's length: 그를 가까이 하지 않았다, 쌀쌀하게 대했다.
2) inert and passive: 완전히 피동적인, 상대편이 하는 대로 몸을 내맡기고 있는.
3) undid: released.
4) take it for granted: 그대로 받아들여 의심치 않는다.
5) What do you all take me for: 도대체 나를 어떻게 생각하고 있는 거야.
6) damned: very; extremely.
7) practical joke: 못된 장난, 입에 발린 농담.

Mr. Hutton stamped towards the door. He had said horrible things, he knew, odious things that he ought speedily to unsay. But he wouldn't. He closed the door behind him.

"Teddy Bear!" He turned the handle; the latch clicked into place. "Teddy Bear!" The voice that came to him through the closed door was agonized. Should he go back? He ought to go back. He touched the handle, then withdrew his fingers and quickly walked away. When he was half-way down the stairs he halted. She might try to do something silly — throw herself out of the window or God knows what! He listened attentively; there was no sound. But he pictured her very clearly tiptoeing across the room, lifting the sash as high as it would go, leaning out into the cold night air. It was raining a little. Under the window lay the paved terrace. How far below? Twenty-five or thirty feet? Once, when he was walking along Piccadilly,[1] a dog had jumped out of a third-storey window of the Ritz.[2] He had seen it fall; he had heard it strike the pavement. Should he go back? He was damned if he would; he hated her.

He sat for a long time in the library. What had happened? What was happening? He turned the question over and over in his mind and could find no answer. Suppose the nightmare dreamed itself out[3] to its horrible conclusion. Death was waiting for him. His eyes filled with tears; he wanted so passionately to live. "Just to live." Poor Emily had wished it, too, he remembered: "Just to be alive." There were still so many places in this astonishing world unvisited, so many queer delightful people still unknown, so many lovely women never so much as seen. The huge white oxen would still be dragging their wains along the Tuscan roads, the cypresses would still go up, straight as pillars, to the blue heaven; but he would not be there to see them. And the sweet southern wines — Tears of Christ and Blood of Judas[4] — others would drink them, not he. Others would walk down the obscure and narrow lanes between the bookshelves in the London Library, sniffing

1) Piccadilly: 런던 중심부의 번화한 거리의 이름.
2) the Ritz: 세계적으로 유명한 런던에 있는 호텔 이름.
3) the nightmare dreamed itself out: 이 악몽이 끝까지 깨지 않고.
4) Tears of Christ and Blood of Judas: 둘 다 포도주의 이름임.

the dusty perfume of good literature,[1] peering at strange titles, discovering unknown names, exploring the fringes of vast domains of knowledge. He would be lying in a hole in the ground. And why, why? Confusedly he felt that some extraordinary kind of justice was being done. In the past he had been wanton and imbecile and irresponsible. Now Fate was playing as wantonly, as irresponsibly with him. It was tit for tat,[2] and God existed after all.

He felt that he would like to pray. Forty years ago he used to kneel by his bed every evening. The nightly formula[3] of his childhood came to him almost unsought from some long unopened chamber of the memory. "God bless Father and Mother, Tom and Cissie and the Baby, Mademoiselle and Nurse, and everyone that I love, and make me a good boy. Amen." They were all dead now all except Cissie.

His mind seemed to soften and dissolve; a great calm descended upon his spirit. He went upstairs to ask Doris's forgiveness. He found her lying on the couch at the foot of the bed. On the floor beside her stood a blue bottle of liniment,[4] marked "NOT TO BE TAKEN",[5] she seemed to have drunk about half of it.

"You didn't love me," was all she said when she opened her eyes to find him bending over her.

Dr. Libbard arrived in time to prevent any very serious consequences. "You mustn't do this again," he said while Mr. Hutton was out of the room.

"What's to prevent me?"[6] she asked defiantly.

Dr. Libbard looked at her with his large, sad eyes. "There's nothing to prevent you," he said. "Only yourself and your baby. Isn't it rather bad luck on your baby, not allowing it to come into the world because you want to go out of it?"

Doris was silent for a time. "All right," she whispered. "I won't."

---

1) good literature: 훌륭한 서적.
2) tit for tat: 보복, 오는 말에 가는 말.
3) formula: (의식 같은 데서 사용하는) 판에 박은 문구.
4) liniment: 바르는 약.
5) Not to be taken: 내복(內服)을 금함.
6) What's to prevent me?: Nothing can prevent me.

Mr. Hutton sat by her bedside for the rest of the night. He felt himself now to be indeed a murderer. For a time he persuaded himself that he loved this pitiable child. Dozing in his chair, he woke up, stiff and cold, to find himself drained dry, as it were, of every emotion.[1) He had become nothing but a tired and suffering carcass. At six o'clock he undressed and went to bed for a couple of hours' sleep. In the course of the same afternoon the coroner's jury brought in a verdict of "Willful Murder,"[2) and Mr. Hutton was committed for trial.[3)

Miss Spence was not at all well. She had found her public appearances in the witness box very trying,[4) and when it was all over she had something that was very nearly a breakdown. She slept badly, and suffered from nervous indigestion. Dr. Libbard used to call every other day. She talked to him a great deal, mostly about the Hutton case. . . . Her moral indignation was always on the boil.[5) Wasn't it appalling to think that one had had a murderer in one's house? Wasn't it extraordinary that one could have been for so long mistaken about the man's character? (But she had had an inkling[6) from the first.) And then the girl he had gone off with — so low class, so little better than a prostitute. The news that the second Mrs. Hutton was expecting a baby — the posthumous child[7) of a condemned and executed crimina l[8) — revolted her; the thing was shocking, an obscenity.[9) Dr. Libbard answered her gently and vaguely, and prescribed bromide.

One morning he interrupted her in the midst of her customary tirade.[10) "By the way," he said in his soft, melancholy voice, "I suppose it was really you who poisoned Mrs. Hutton."

Miss Spence stared at him for two or three seconds with enormous

1) find himself drained dry … of every emotion: 모든 감정이 메말라 붙어버린 것 같은 기분이 들다.
2) Willful Murder: 고의의 살인, 모살(謀殺).
3) was committed for trial: 재판에 회부되었다.
4) trying: hard to bear; painful; afflicting.
5) on the boil: boiling.
6) inkling: slight suspicion of.
7) the posthumous child: 유복자.
8) a condemned and executed criminal: 사형수.
9) shocking, an obscenity: 끔찍하고 더러운 일.
10) customary tirade: 여느 때의 독설.

eyes, and then quietly said, "Yes." After that she started to cry.

"In the coffee, I suppose."

She seemed to nod assent. Dr. Libbard took out his fountain pen, and in his neat, meticulous[1] calligraphy wrote out[2] a prescription for a sleeping draught.[3]

---

1) meticulous: overscrupulous.
2) wrote out: 정서하다.
3) a prescription for a sleeping draught: 수면제의 처방.

Araby[1)]

by James Joyce

James Joyce(1882-1941) was born in Dublin, and first won fame with his collection of stories called *Dubliners*. The title is significant, for in all his subsequent works, including the celebrated *Ulysses* and *Finnegan's Wake*, the city of Dublin is the vital fact. Joyce's influence has been prodigious, and some critics are inclined to rate him as the most significant novelist of the century.

NORTH RICHMOND Street,[2)] being blind,[3)] was a quiet street except at the hour when the Christian Brothers' School[4)] set the boys free. An uninhabited house of two stories stood at the blind end, detached from its neighbours in a square ground.[5)] The other houses of the street, conscious of decent lives within them, gazed at one another with brown imperturbable[6)] faces.

The former tenant of our house, a priest, had died in the back drawing-room. Air, musty from having been long enclosed, hung in all the rooms, and the waste room behind the kitchen was littered with old useless papers. Among these I found a few paper-covered books, the pages of which were curled and damp: *The Abbot*,[7)] by Walter Scott, *The Devout Communicant*,[8)] and *The Memoirs of Vidocq*.[9)]

---

1) Araby: (Arabian) 1894년 5월에 프랑스에서 열렸던 bazaar.
2) North Richmond Street: Dublin시 북쪽 끝에 있는 거리 이름. 실지로 Joyce가 소년 시절에 산 곳임.
3) blind: with only one opening 막다른.
4) Christian Brothers' School: 가톨릭의 초등학교.
5) square ground: 네모난 땅.
6) imperturbable: unexcitable; not easily excited; calm.
7) *The Abbot*: 스코틀랜드의 소설가시인인 Walter Scott(1771-1832)의 1820년 작품. Mary Stwart가 유폐당했던 시대를 다루었음. abbot=man at the head of an abbey of monks.
8) *The Devout Communicant* : 경건한 성찬 배수자. 1813년에 나온 책.
9) *The Memoirs of Vidocq* : 프랑스의 탐정가. 비도크의 회고록. 1828년경에 나왔음.

I liked the last best because its leaves[1)] were yellow. The wild garden behind the house contained a central apple-tree and a few straggling bushes, under one of which I found the late tenant's rusty bicycle-pump. He had been a very charitable priest; in his will[2)] he had left all his money to institutions and the furniture of his house to his sister.

When the short days of winter came, dusk fell before we had well eaten our dinners. When we met in the street the houses had grown sombre. The space of sky above us was the colour of everchanging violet and towards it the lamps of the street lifted their feeble lanterns. The cold air stung us and we played till our bodies glowed. Our shouts echoed in the silent street. The career[3)] of our play brought us through the dark muddy lanes behind the houses, where we ran the gauntlet[4)] of the rough tribes from the cottages, to the back doors of the dark dripping gardens where odours arose from the ashpits, to the dark odorous stables where a coachman smoothed and combed the horse or shook music from the buckled harness.[5)] When we returned to the street, light from the kitchen windows had filled the areas. If my uncle was seen turning the corner, we hid in the shadow until we had seen him safely housed.[6)] Or if Mangan's sister came out on the doorstep to call her brother in to his tea, we watched her from our shadow peer up and down the street. We waited to see whether she would remain or go in and, if she remained, we left our shadow and walked up to Mangan's steps[7)] resignedly. She was waiting for us, her figure defined by the light from the half-opened door. Her brother always teased her before he obeyed, and I stood by the railings looking at her. Her dress swung as she moved her body, and the soft rope of

---

1) leaves: 책장. leaf=a sheet of paper.

2) will: a legal statement of a person's wishes about what shall be done with his property after he is dead.

3) career: course.

4) ran the gauntlet: ran the gantlet; ran between two rows of men who stirke the victim as he passes. 태형을 당하다, 가혹한 공격을 받다.

5) shook music from the buckled harness: 죄임쇠가 달린 마구(馬韭)를 듣기좋게 달랑거리다.

6) had seen him safely housed: 그가 어김없이 집안에 들어간 것을 보았다.

7) Mangan's steps: the steps of Mangan's house.

her hair tossed from side to side.

Every morning I lay on the floor in the front parlour watching her door. The blind was pulled down to within an inch of the sash so that I could not be seen. When she came out on the doorstep my heart leaped. I ran to the hall, seized my books and followed her. I kept her brown figure always in my eye and, when we came near the point at which our ways diverged, I quickened my pace and passed her. This happened morning after morning. I had never spoken to her, except for a few casual words, and yet her name was like a summons to all my foolish blood.1)

Her image accompanied me even in places the most hostile to romance. On Saturday evenings when my aunt went marketing I had to go to carry some of the parcels. We walked through the flaring streets,2) jostled by drunken men and bargaining women, amid the curses of labourers, the shrill litanies3) of shop-boys who stood on guard by the barrels of pigs' cheeks,4) the nasal chanting of street-singers, who sang a *come-all-you* about O'Donovan Rossa,5) or a ballad about the troubles in our native land. These noises converged in a single sensation of life for me: I imagined that I bore my chalice6) safely through a throng7) of foes. Her name sprang to my lips at moments in strange prayers and praises which I myself did not understand. My eyes were often full of tears (I could not tell why) and at times a flood from my heart seemed to pour itself out into my bosom. I thought little of the future. I did not know whether I would ever speak to her or not or, if I spoke to her, how I could tell her of my confused

1) a summons to all my foolish blood: 나의 어리석은 피를 온통 불러 모으는 소환장.
2) the flaring streets: 번지르르한 거리.
3) litanies: series of prayers by the minister with responses by the congregation. 연도(連禱).
4) stand on guard by the barrels of pigs' cheeks: 돼지의 볼살을 절여 넣은 통 옆에서 망보다.
5) a *come-all-you* about O'Donovan Rossa: O'Donovan Rossa에 관한 <모두들 오라>라는 노래, O'Donovan Rossa는 아일랜드의 정치가이며 피니언 비밀결사를 창설하였다. *come-all-you*는 "Come all you gallant Irishmen, and listen to my song"으로 시작된다.
6) chalice: the cup used in a sacrament of the Lord's Super.
7) throng: crowd.

adoration.[1] But my body was like a harp and her words and gestures were like fingers running upon the wires.[2]

One evening I went into the back drawing-room in which the priest had died. It was a dark rainy evening and there was no sound in the house. Through one of the broken panes I heard the rain impinge[3] upon the earth, the fine incessant needles of water[4] playing in the sodden beds.[5] Some distant lamp or lighted window gleamed below me. I was thankful that I could see so little. All my senses seemed to desire to veil themselves and, feeling that I was about to slip from them,[6] I pressed the palms of my hands together until they trembled, murmuring: '*O love! O love!*' many times.

At last she spoke to me. When she addressed the first words to me I was so confused that I did not know what to answer. She asked me was I going to *Araby*. I forgot whether I answered yes or no. It would be a splendid bazaar; she said she would love to go.

'And why can't you?' I asked.

While she spoke she turned a silver bracelet round and round her wrist. She could not go, she said, because there would be a retreat[7] that week in her convent. Her brother and two other boys were fighting for their caps, and I was alone at the railings. She held one of the spikes, bowing her head towards me. The light from the lamp opposite our door caught the white curve of her neck, lit up her hair that rested there and, falling, lit up the hand upon the railing. It fell over one side of her dress and caught the white border of a petticoat, just visible as she stood at ease.

'It's well for you,' she said.

'If I go,' I said, 'I will bring you something.'

---

1) confused adoration: 혼란스러운 사랑.
2) fingers running upon the wires: harp의 줄을 튕기는 손가락.
3) impinge: hit; strike.
4) fine incessant needles of water: 끊임없이 내리는 바늘과 같은 실비.
5) sodden beds: 흠뻑 젖은 화단, bed=piece of ground (of flowers, vegetable).
6) feeling that I was about to slip from them: 내 자신이 그러한 감각에서 빠져나오려 하고 있다고 느끼면서.
7) retreat: (Catholic) 묵상(시간).

What innumerable follies[1)] laid waste my waking and sleeping thoughts after that evening! I wished to annihilate the tedious intervening days.[2)] I chafed against the work of school.[3)] At night in my bedroom and by day in the classroom her image came between me and the page I strove to read. The syllables of the word *Araby* were called to me through the silence in which my soul luxuriated[4)] and cast an Eastern enchantment over me.[5)] I asked for leave[6)] to go to the bazaar on Saturday night. My aunt was surprised, and hoped it was not some Freemason affair.[7)] I answered few questions in class. I watched my master's face pass from amiability to sternness[8)]; he hoped I was not beginning to idle. I could not call my wandering thoughts together. I had hardly any patience with the serious work of life which, now that[9)] it stood between me and my desire, seemed to me child's play, ugly monotonous child's play.[10)]

On Saturday morning I reminded my uncle that I wished to go to the bazaar in the evening. He was fussing at the hallstand, looking for the hatbrush, and answered me curtly:

'Yes, boy, I know.'

As he was in the hall I could not go into the front parlour and lie at the window. I felt the house in bad humour and walked slowly towards the school. The air was pitilessly raw and already my heart misgave me.[11)]

When I came home to dinner my uncle had not yet been home.

---

1) innumerable follies: (very) many foolish ideas. 이 글은 어른이 된 후의 추억담이라는 점을 유의할 것.
2) the tedious intervening days: bazaar가 열리기까지의 지루한 나날.
3) chafed against the work of school: 학교 공부가 짜증났다.
4) through the silence in which my soul luxuriated: 내 영혼이 탐닉했던 침묵을 통해. luxuriate=indulge.
5) cast an Eastern enchantment over me: 동양적인 마법을 내게 걸었다.
6) leave: permission.
7) some Freemason affair: some secret society organized by persons who are united for fraternal purposed.
8) pass from amiability to sternness: 상냥한 표정이 냉혹하게 굳어지다.
9) now that: since.
10) ugly monotonous child's play: 추하고 단조로운 어린애 장난.
11) my heart misgave me: 나는 불안해졌다. misgive=cause to feel doubt, suspicion or anxiety.

Still it was early. I sat staring at the clock for some time and, when its ticking began to irritate me, I left the room. I mounted the staircase and gained[1] the upper part of the house. The high, cold, empty, gloomy rooms liberated me and I went from room to room singing. From the front window I saw my companions playing below in the street. Their cries reached me weakened and indistinct and, leaning my forehead against the cool glass, I looked over at the dark house where she lived. I may have stood there for an hour, seeing nothing but the brown-clad figure[2] cast by my imagination, touched discreetly by the lamplight at the curved neck, at the hand upon the railings and at the border[3] below the dress.

When I came downstairs again I found Mrs Mercer sitting at the fire. She was an old, garrulous woman, a pawn-broker's[4] widow, who collected used stamps for some pious purpose.[5] I had to endure the gossip of the tea-table. The meal was prolonged beyond an hour and still my uncle did not come. Mrs Mercer stood up to go: she was sorry she couldn't wait any longer, but it was after eight o'clock and she did not like to be out late, as the night air was bad for her. When she had gone I began to walk up and down the room, clenching my fists. My aunt said:

'I'm afraid you may put off your bazaar for this night of Our Lord.'[6]

At nine o'clock I heard my uncle's latchkey in the hall door. I heard him talking to himself and heard the hallstand[7] rocking when it had received the weight of his overcoat. I could interpret these signs. When he was midway through his dinner[8] I asked him to give me the money to go to the bazaar. He had forgotten.

'The people are in bed and after their first sleep now,' he said.

I did not smile. My aunt said to him energetically:

---

1) gain: arrive at, get to.
2) brown-clad figure: i.e. of the girl.
3) border: ornamental strip of woman's clothing.
4) pawn-broker: 전당포 주인.
5) for some pious purpose: 무슨 종교적인 목적으로.
6) for this night of Our Lord: a pious way of expressing "tonight".
7) hallstand: piece of furniture for hats, coats, umbrellas, etc.
8) midway through his dinner: 저녁 식사 도중에.

'Can't you give him the money and let him go? You've kept him late enough as it is.'

My uncle said he was very sorry he had forgotten. He said he believed in the old saying: 'All work and no play makes Jack[1] a dull boy.' He asked me where I was going and, when I told him a second time, he asked me did I know *The Arab's Farewell to his Steed*.[2] When I left the kitchen he was about to recite the opening lines of the piece[3] to my aunt.

I held a florin[4] tightly in my hand as I strode down Buckingham Street towards the station. The sight of the streets thronged with buyers and glaring with gas[5] recalled to me the purpose of my journey. I took my seat in a third-class carriage of a deserted train.[6] After an intolerable delay the train moved out of the station slowly. It crept onward among ruinous houses[7] and over the twinkling river. At Westland Row Station[8] a crowd of people pressed[9] to the carriage doors; but the porters moved them back, saying that it was a special train for the bazaar. I remained alone in the bare carriage. In a few minutes the train drew up[10] beside an improvised wooden platform.[11] I passed out on to the road and saw by the lighted dial of a clock that it was ten minutes to ten. In front of me was a large building which displayed the magical name.

I could not find any sixpenny entrance[12] and, fearing that the bazaar would be closed, I passed in quickly through a turnstile, handing a

1) Jack: boy; fellow.
2) *The Arab's Farewell to his Steed*: 아랍의 장수가 사랑하는 말을 팔고 읊은 석별의 시. 작자는 Caroline Elizabeth Saraph Norton(1808-1877). 어떤 아랍인이 가난하여 자기 말을 팔아 버렸으나 그 말을 잊지 못하여 돈을 써가며 말을 찾아 다녔다. 그러나 찾지를 못해 그 말을 찾아주는 사람에게 그 말을 주겠다고 했다는 내용.
3) opening lines of the piece: 그 시(詩)의 서두.
4) florin: an English silver coin worth 2 shillings.
5) gas: 가스등.
6) deserted train: 텅빈 기차.
7) ruinous houses: 황폐한 집들.
8) Westland Row Station: railroad station near College Park in Dubline
9) pressed: 밀어닥쳤다.
10) drew up: pulled up.
11) improvised wooden platform: 나무로 된 임시 플랫폼.
12) sixpenny entrance: 6펜스를 주고 들어가는 출입구.

shilling to a weary-looking man. I found myself in a big hall girded at half its height by a gallery. Nearly all the stalls were closed and the greater part of the hall was in darkness. I recognized a silence like that which pervades a church after a service. I walked into the centre of the bazaar timidly. A few people were gathered about the stalls which were still open. Before a curtain, over which the words *Café Chantant*[1] were written in coloured lamps, two men were counting money on a salver.[2] I listened to the fall of the coins.

Remembering with difficulty why I had come, I went over to one of the stalls and examined porcelain vases and flowered tea-sets.[3] At the door of the stall a young lady was talking and laughing with two young gentlemen. I remarked their English accents and listened vaguely to their conversation.

'O, I never said such a thing!'

'O, but you did!'

'O, but I didn't!'

'Didn't she say that?'

'Yes. I heard her.'

'O, there's a. . . fib!'[4]

Observing me, the young lady came over and asked me did I wish to buy anything. The tone of her voice was not encouraging; she seemed to have spoken to me out of a sense of duty.[5] I looked humbly at the great jars that stood like eastern guards at either side of the dark entrance to the stall and murmured:

'No, thank you.'

The young lady changed the position of one of the vases and went back to the two young men. They began to talk of the same subject. Once or twice the young lady glanced at me over her shoulder.

I lingered before her stall, though I knew my stay was useless, to make my interest in her wares seem the more real. Then I turned

---

1) *Café Chantant*: (Fr.) 노래와 음악이 있는 카페.
2) salver: tray.
3) flowered tea-sets: 꽃 무늬가 있는 찻잔 세트.
4) fib: lie about some small matter.
5) out of a sense of duty: 의무감에서.

away slowly and walked down the middle of the bazaar. I allowed the two pennies to fall against the sixpence in my pocket. I heard a voice call from one end of the gallery that the light was out. The upper part of the hall was now completely dark.

Gazing up into the darkness I saw myself as a creature driven and derided by vanity;[1] and my eyes burned with anguish and anger.

1) a creature driven and … by vanity: 허영에 쫓기고 또 농락당한 인간.

The Lottery[1)]

by Shirley Jackson

Shirley Jackson (1919-1965) was born in San Francisco and spent her youth in California. In *Life Among the Savages* (1953) and *Raising Demons* (1956), she humorously described life in North Bennington, Vermont with her husband, the literary critic Stanley Edgar Hyman, and their four children. She died quietly of heart failure at the age of 46.

A prolific writer, Miss Jackson was a regular contributor to *The New Yorker* for ten years. "The Lottery" first appeared in that magazine and has subsequently been reprinted in numerous anthologies, and has been dramatized for radio and television. Miss Jackson's husband reports that "She was always proud that the Union of South Africa banned 'The Lottery' and she felt that *they* at least understood the story."

She is best known for her stories and novels in the genre known as "Gothic," which typically involves a seemingly-innocent heroine who is nonetheless implicated in at least one violent death, often that of a close relative. The atmosphere is always one of horror and mystery in the midst of genteel surroundings and, as in Collier's work, there are often supernatural elements. Miss Jackson's highly successful novel *We Have Always Lived in the Castle* (1962) exemplifies this style.

THE MORNING of June 27th was clear and sunny, with the fresh warmth of a full-summer day; the flowers were blossoming profusely and the grass was richly green. The people of the village began to gather in the square, between the post office and the bank, around ten o'clock; in some towns there were so many people that the lottery took two days and had to be started on June 26th, but in this village, where there were only about three hundred people, the whole lottery took less than two hours, so it could begin at ten o'clock in the morning and still be through in time[2)] to allow the villagers to get home for noon dinner.

The children assembled first, of course. School was recently over for the summer, and the feeling of liberty sat uneasily on most of

---

1) lottery: a contest in which tickets are distributed or sold; the winning ticker or tickets are selected in a chance drawing(drawn by lot).

2) in time: a little early; sooner than necessary enough.

them; they tended to gather together quietly for a while before they broke into[1)] boisterous[2)] play, and their talk was still of the classroom and the teacher, of books and reprimands.[3)] Bobby Martin had already stuffed his pockets full of stones, and the other boys soon followed his example, selecting the smoothest and roundest stones; Bobby and Harry Jones and Dickie Delacroix — the villagers pronounced this name "Dellacroy" — eventually made a great pile of stones in one corner of the square and guarded it against the raids of the other boys. The girls stood aside, talking among themselves, looking over their shoulders at the boys, and the very small children rolled in the dust or clung[4)] to the hands of their older brothers or sisters.

Soon the men began to gather, surveying their own children, speaking of planting and rain, tractors and taxes. They stood together, away from the pile of stones in the corner, and their jokes were quiet and they smiled rather than laughed. The women, wearing faded house dresses[5)] and sweaters, came shortly after their menfolk. They greeted one another and exchanged bits of gossip as they went to join their husbands. Soon the women, standing by their husbands, began to call to their children, and the children came reluctantly, having to be called four or five times. Bobby Martin ducked[6)] under his mother's grasping hand and ran, laughing, back to the pile of stones. His father spoke up sharply, and Bobby came quickly and took his place between his father and his oldest brother.

The lottery was conducted — as were the square dances,[7)] the teen-age club, the Halloween[8)] program — by Mr. Summers. who had time

1) break into: to begin suddenly.
2) boisterous: noisy and active.
3) reprimand: a reproof; faultfinding, sharp words(from the teacher).
4) clung: past tense of cling "hold tightly"; always followed by *to* and a noun.
5) house dress: a simple, inexpensive cotton dress worn for doing housework, rather than for social occasions.
6) ducked: rapidly moved down and to one side.
7) square dances: an American fork dance, done with four couples facing each other in a square.
8) Halloween: October 31, the eve of All Saints' Day(All Hallows' Day). American children celebrate it by dressing up in costume, carving pumpkins, and playing harmless tricks.

and energy to devote to civic activities. He was a round-faced, jovial man and he ran the coal business,[1] and people were sorry for him. because he had no children and his wife was a scold.[2] When he arrived in the square, carrying the black wooden box, there was a murmur of conversation among the villagers, and he waved and called. "Little late today, folks." The postmaster, Mr. Graves, followed him, carrying a three-legged stool, and the stool was put in the center of the square and Mr. Summers set the black box down on it. The villagers kept their distance,[3] leaving a space between themselves and the stool. and when Mr. Summers said, "Some of you fellows want to give me a hand?"[4] there was a hesitation before two men. Mr. Martin and his oldest son, Baxter, came forward to hold the box steady on the stool while Mr. Summers stirred up the papers inside it.

The original paraphernalia[5] for the lottery had been lost long ago, and the black box now resting on the stool had been put into use even before Old Man Warner, the oldest man in town, was born. Mr. Summers spoke frequently to the villagers about making a new box, but no one liked to upset[6] even as much tradition as was represented by the black box. There was a story that the present box had been made with some pieces of the box that had preceded it, the one that had been constructed when the first people settled down to make a village here. Every year, after the lottery, Mr. Summers began talking again about a new box, but every year the subject was allowed to fade off without anything's[7] being done. The black box grew shabbier[8] each year; by now it was no longer completely black but splintered[9] badly along one side to show the original wood color, and in some places faded or stained.

---

1) coal business: selling coal to the townspeople for heating their homes.
2) scold: a bad-tempered woman.
3) kept their distance: were hesitant to approach; stayed away.
4) give me a hand: help me.
5) paraphernalia: equipment.
6) upset: overthrow.
7) anything's: The addition of 's is a rural colloquialism.
8) shabbier: more worn-out; in worse condition.
9) splintered: with the wood split and coming off in narrow, sharp pieces.

Mr. Martin and his oldest son, Baxter, held the black box securely on the stool until Mr. Summers had stirred the papers thoroughly with his hand. Because so much of the ritual had been forgotten or discarded, Mr. Summers had been successful in having slips of paper substituted for the chips[1] of wood that had been used for generations. Chips of wood, Mr. Summers had argued, had been all very well[2] when the village was tiny, but now that the population was more than three hundred and likely to keep on growing, it was necessary to use something that would fit more easily into the black box. The night before the lottery, Mr. Summers and Mr. Graves made up the slips of paper and put them in the box, and it was then taken to the safe of Mr. Summers' coal company and locked up until Mr. Summers was ready to take it to the square next morning. The rest of the year, the box was put way, sometimes one place, sometimes another; it had spent one year in Mr. Graves's barn and another year underfoot in the post office, and sometimes it was set on a shelf in the Martin grocery and left there.

There was a great deal of fussing[3] to be done before Mr. Summers declared the lottery open. There were the lists to make up — of heads of families, heads of households[4] in each family, members of each household in each family. There was the proper swearing-in[5] of Mr. Summers by the postmaster, as the official of the lottery; at one time, some people remembered, there had been a recital of some sort, performed by the official of the lottery, a perfunctory. tuneless chant that had been rattled off[6] duly[7] each year; some people believed that the official of the lottery used to stand just so[8] when he said or sang it, others believed that he was supposed to walk among the people,

1) chip: small, flat piece.
2) all very well: satisfactory.
3) fussing: paying attention to small details.
4) households: those people living as a separate economic unit.
5) swearing-in: the ceremony in which a public official takes his oath of office, formally promising to carry out his duties to the best of his ability.
6) rattled off: said mechanically, without thought.
7) duly: in the proper manner and at the proper time; adverbial form of due.
8) just so: in a precise manner.

but years and years ago this part of the ritual had been allowed to lapse.[1] There had been, also, a ritual salute, which the official of the lottery had had to use in addressing each person who came up to draw from the box, but this also had changed with time, until now it was felt necessary only for the official to speak to each person approaching. Mr. Summers was very good at all this; in his clean white shirt and blue jeans. with one hand resting carelessly on the black box. he seemed very proper and important as he talked interminably to Mr. Graves and the Martins.

Just as Mr. Summers finally left off[2] talking and turned to the assembled villagers, Mrs. Hutchinson came hurriedly along the path to the square, her sweater thrown over her shoulders, and slid into place in the back of the crowd. "Clean[3] forgot what day it was," she said to Mrs. Delacroix, who stood next to her, and they both laughed softly. "Thought my old man[4] was out back[5] stacking wood," Mrs. Hutchinson went on. "and then I looked out the window and the kids was gone, and then I remembered it was the twenty-seventh and came a-running."[6] She dried her hands on her apron, and Mrs. Delacroix said, "You're in time, though. They're still talking away up there."

Mrs. Hutchinson craned her neck to see through the crowd and found her husband and children standing near the front. She tapped Mrs. Delacroix on the arm as a farewell and began to make her way through the crowd. The people separated good-humoredly to let her through; two or three people said, in voices just loud enough to be heard across the crowd, "Here comes your Missus,[7] Hutchinson," and "Bill, she made it after all." Mrs. Hutchinson reached her husband, and Mr. Summers, who had been waiting, said cheerfully. "Thought

1) lapse: end without being renewed.
2) left off: stopped.
3) clean: (Rural) completely.
4) my old man: (Informal) my husband.
5) out back: in the back yard, behind the house.
6) a-running: (Archaic) old-fashioned verb form; the a-is a verbal prefix meaning "to be in the act of".
7) your, Missus: (Informal) your wife.

we were going to have to get on[1] without you, Tessie." Mrs. Hutchinson said, grinning, "Wouldn't have me leave m'dishes[2] in the sink, now, would you, Joe?," and soft laughter ran through the crowd as the people stirred back into position after Mrs. Hutchinson's arrival.

"Well, now." Mr. Summers said soberly, "guess we better get started, get this over with,[3] so's[4] we can go back to work. Anybody ain't here?"

"Dunbar." several people said. "Dunbar. Dunbar."

Mr. Summers consulted his list. "Clyde Dunbar." he said. "That's right. He's broke[5] his leg, hasn't he? Who's drawing for him?"

"Me. I guess," a woman said, and Mr. Summers turned to look at her. "Wife draws for her husband." Mr. Summers said. "Don't you have a grown boy to do it for you, Janey?" Although Mr. Summers and everyone else in the village knew the answer perfectly well, it was the business of the official of the lottery to ask such questions formally. Mr. Summers waited with an expression of polite interest while Mrs. Dunbar answered.

"Horace's not but[6] sixteen yet." Mrs. Dunbar said regretfully. "Guess I gotta fill in for the old man[7] this year."

"Right." Sr. Summers said. He made a note on the list he was holding. Then he asked, "Watson boy drawing this year?"

A tall boy in the crowd raised his hand. "Here," he said. "I'm drawing for m'mother and me." He blinked his eyes nervously and ducked[8] his head as several voices in the crowd said things like "Good fellow, lack." and "Glad to see your mother's got a man to do it."

"Well," Mr. Summers said, "guess that's everyone. Old Man Warner

---

1) get on: begin.
2) m'dishes: my dishes.
3) we better get started, get this over with: 곧 시작해서 끝내는 게 낫겠다. better=had better; should. get ~ over with=finish.
4) so's: (Rural) so that.
5) broke: broken.
6) not but: only.
7) gotta fill in for the old man: have got to(=have to) substitute for the old man 남편 대신하지 않으면 안 된다.
8) ducked: rapidly moved down and to one side. ducked his head=lowered his head in embarrassment.

make it?"

"Here," a voice said. and Mr. Summers nodded.

A sudden hush fell on the crowd[1] as Mr. Summers cleared his throat and looked at the list. "All ready?" he called. "Now, I'll read the names — heads of families first — and the men come up and take a paper out of the box. Keep the paper folded in your hand without looking at it until everyone has had a turn. Everything clear?"

The people had done it so many times that they only half listened to the directions: most of them were quiet, wetting their lips, not looking around. Then Mr. Summers raised one hand high and said, "Adams." A man disengaged himself[2] from the crowd and came forward. "Hi. Steve." Mr. Summers said, and Mr. Adams said. "Hi. Joe." They grinned at one another humorlessly and nervously. Then Mr. Adams reached into the black box and took out a folded paper. He held it firmly by one corner as he turned and went hastily back[3] to his place in the crowd, where he stood a little apart from his family, not looking down at his hand.

"Allen," Mr. Summers said. "Anderson. . . . Bentham."

"Seems like there's no time at all between lotteries any more," Mrs. Delacroix said to Mrs. Graves in the back row. Seems like we got through with[4] the last one only last week."

"Time sure goes fast. Mrs. Graves said.

"Clark. . . . Delacroix"

"There goes my old man." Mrs. Delacroix said. She held her breath[5] while her husband went forward.

"Dunbar," Mr. Summers said, and Mrs. Dunbar went steadily to the box while one of the women said. "Go on. Janey," and another said, "There she goes."

"We're next." Mrs. Graves said. She watched while Mr. Graves

---

1) a sudden hush fell on the crowd: the crowd was suddenly quiet; the crowd suddenly grew quiet.
2) disengaged himself: left, removed.
3) went hastily back: hurried.
4) got through with: finished.
5) held (her) breath: didn't breathe for several seconds.

came around from the side of the box, greeted Mr. Summers gravely and selected a slip of paper from the box. By now, all through the crowd there were men holding the small folded papers in their large hand, turning them over and over nervously Mrs. Dunbar and her two sons stood together, Mrs. Dunbar holding the slip of paper.

"Harburt. . . . Hutchinson."

"Get up there,[1] Bill," Mrs. Hutchinson said, and the people near her laughed.

"Jones."

"They do say," Mr. Adams said to Old Man Warner, who stood next to him, "that over in the north village they're talking of giving up the lottery."

Old Man Warner snorted.[2] "Pack of crazy fools," he said. "Listening to the young folks, nothing's good enough for *them.* Next thing you know, they'll be wanting to go back to living in caves, nobody work any more, live *that* way for a while. Used to be a saying about 'Lottery in June, corn be heavy soon.' First thing you know, we'd all be eating stewed[3] chickweed[4] and acorns.[5] There's *always* been a lottery," he added petulantly.[6] "Bad enough to see young Joe Summers up there joking with everybody."

"Some places have already quit lotteries." Mrs. Adams said.

"Nothing but trouble in *that,*" Old Man Warner said stoutly.[7] "Pack of young fools."

"Martin." And Bobby Martin watched his father go forward.

"Overdyke. . . . Percy."

"I wish they'd hurry," Mrs. Dunbar said to her older son. "I wish they'd hurry."

"They're almost through," her son said.

"You get ready to run tell Dad," Mrs. Dunbar said.

---

1) get up there: go (agead).
2) snorted: made a sound of disgust.
3) stewed: cooked slowly in water for a long period of time.
4) chickweed: a low, weedy plant, eaten by chickens.
5) acorns: the fruit of the oak tree, eaten by animals, but not normally by humans.
6) petulantly: with unreasonable irritation.
7) stoutly: with great conviction, with strong belief.

Mr. Summers called his own name and then stepped forward precisely and selected a slip from the box. Then he called, "Warner."

"Seventy-seventh year I been in the lottery," Old Man Warner said as he went through the crowd. "Seventy-seventh time."

"Watson." The tall boy came awkwardly through the crowd. Someone said, "Don't be nervous, Jack," and Mr. Summers said, "Take your time,[1] son."[2]

"Zanini."

After that, there was a long pause, a breathless pause, until Mr. Summers, holding his slip of paper in the air, said, "All right, fellows." For a minute, no one moved, and then all the slips of paper were opened. Suddenly, all the women began to speak at once, saving. "Who is it?," "Who's got it?," "Is it the Dunbars?," "Is it the Watsons?" Then the voices began to say, "It's Hutchinson. It's Bill," "Bill Hutchinson's got it."

"Go tell your father," Mrs. Dunbar said to her older son.

People began to look around to see the Hutchinsons. Bill Hutchinson was standing quiet, staring down at the paper in his hand. Suddenly. Tessie Hutchinson shouted to Mr. Summers. "You didn't give him time enough to take any paper he wanted. I saw you. It wasn't fair!"

"Be a good sport, Tessie." Mrs. Delacroix called, and Mrs. Graves said, "All of us took the same chance."

"Shut up, Tessie," Bill Hutchinson said.

"Well, everyone," Mr. Summers said, "that was done pretty fast, and now we've got to be hurrying[3] a little more to get done in time." He consulted his next list. "Bill," he said, "you draw for the Hutchinson family. You got any other households in the Hutchinsons?"

"There's Don and Eva," Mrs. Hutchinson yelled. "Make them take their chance!"

"Daughters draw with their husbands' families, Tessie," Mr. Summers

1) Take your time: Don't hurry.

2) son: a common way for an lod person to address a boy; *sonny* is used with younger boys.

3) we've got to be hurrying: we have to hurry; the use of *be* plus the present participle after *got* to is now rare except in the phrase "We've [I've] got to be going now."

said gently. "You know that as well as anyone else."

"It wasn't fair," Tessie said.

"I guess not, Joe." Bill Hutchinson said regretfully. "My daughter draws with her husband's family, that's only fair. And I've got no other family except the kids."

"Then, as far as drawing for families is concerned, it's you," Mr. Summers said in explanation, "and as far as drawing for households is concerned, that's you, too. Right?"

"Right," Bill Hutchinson said.

"How many kids, Bill?" Mr. Summers asked formally.

"Three," Bill Hutchinson said.

"There's Bill, Jr., and Nancy, and little Dave. And Tessie and me."

"All right, then," Mr. Summers said. "Harry, you got their tickets back?"

Mr. Graves nodded and held up the slips of paper. "Put them in the box, then," Mr. Summers directed. "Take Bill's and put it in."

"I think we ought to start over," Mrs. Hutchinson said, as quietly as she could. "I tell you it wasn't *fair*. You didn't give him time enough to choose. *Every*body saw that."

Mr. Graves had selected the five slips and put them in the box. and he dropped all the papers but those onto the ground, where the breeze caught them and lifted them off.

"Listen, everybody," Mrs. Hutchinson was saying to the people around her.

"Ready, Bill?" Mr. Summers asked. and Bill Hutchinson, with one quick glance around at his wife and children, nodded.

"Remember," Mr. Summers said. "take the slips and keep them folded until each person has taken one. Harry, you help little Dave." Mr. Graves took the hand of the little boy, who came willingly with him up to the box. "Take a paper out of the box, Davy." Mr. Summers said. Davy put his hand into the box and laughed. "Take just *one* paper." Mr. Summers said. "Harry, you hold it for him." Mr. Graves took the child's hand and removed the folded paper from the tight fist and held it while little Dave stood next to him and looked up at him wonderingly.

"Nancy next," Mr. Summers said. Nancy was twelve, and her school friends breathed heavily as she went forward switching[1] her skirt, and took a slip daintily[2] from the box "Bill, Jr.," Mr. Summers said, and Billy, his face red and his feet overlarge, nearly knocked the box over as he got a paper out. "Tessie," Mr. Summers said. She hesitated for a minute, looking around defiantly, and then set her lips[3] and went up to the box. She snatched a paper out and held it behind her.

"Bill," Mr. Summers said, and Bill Hutchinson reached into the box and felt around, bringing his hand out at last with the slip of paper in it.

The crowd was quiet. A girl whispered, "I hope it's not Nancy," and the sound of the whisper reached the edges of the crowd.

"It's not the way it used to be."[4] Old Man Warner said clearly. "People ain't the way they used to be."[5]

"All right," Mr. Summers said. "Open the papers. Harry, you open little Dave's."

Mr. Graves opened the slip of paper and there was a general sigh through the crowd as he held it up and everyone could see that it was blank. Nancy and Bill. Jr. . opened theirs at the same time. and both beamed[6] and laughed, turning around to the crowd and holding their slips of paper above their heads.

"Tessie," Mr. Summers said. There was a pause, and then Mr. Summers looked at Bill Hutchinson, and Bill unfolded his paper and showed it. It was blank.

"It's Tessie," Mr. Summers said, and his voice was hushed. "Show us her paper. Bill."

Bill Hutchinson went over to his wife and forced the slip of paper out of her hand. It had a black spot on it, the black spot Mr. Summers

---

1) switching: casually brushing her skit with her hand so that it moved as she walked.
2) daintily: delicately, in a lady-like fashion.
3) set her lips: didn't allow her lips to move; assumed a determined expression.
4) "It's not the way it used to be": "Things aren't the way it used to be."
5) "People ain't the way they used to be.": a common complaint among older people.
6) beamed: smiled very happily.

had made the night before with the heavy pencil in the coal company office. Bill Hutchinson held it up, and there was a stir in the crowd.

"All right, folks." Mr. Summers said. "Let's finish quickly."

Although the villagers had forgotten the ritual and lost the original black box, they still remembered to use stones. The pile of stones the boys had made earlier was ready; there were stones on the ground with the blowing scraps of paper that had come out of the box Delacroix selected a stone so large she had to pick it up with both hands and turned to Mrs. Dunbar. "Come on," she said. "Hurry up."

Mr. Dunbar had small stones in both hands, and she said. gasping for breath. "I can't run at all. You'll have to go ahead and I'll catch up with[1] you."

The children had stones already. And someone gave little Davy Hutchinson few pebbles.[2]

Tessie Hutchinson was in the center of a cleared space by now, and she held her hands out desperately as the villagers moved in on her. "It isn't fair," she said. A stone hit her on the side of the head.

Old Man Warner was saying, "Come on, come on, everyone." Steve Adams was in the front of the crowd of villagers, with Mrs. Graves beside him.

"It isn't fair, it isn't right," Mrs. Hutchinson screamed, and then they were upon her.

---

1) catch up with: go fast enough so as not to be behind; overtake; come even.

2) pebbles: a tiny stone, such as one finds on a beach.

The Horse Dealer's Daughter

by D. H. Lawrence

D.H. Lawrence (1885-1903) was born in Nottinghamshire, England, the son of a coal miner. For a time he taught in elementary school, trying to find himself as a painter and writer. With recognition, he became a wanderer, partly from curiosity and restlessness, and partly in the vain attempt to cure his tuberculosis, travelling in Europe, Mexico, Australia, and the United States. He was an enormously versatile writer, producing stories and novels, books of travel, criticism and essays, and poetry. By the time of his death, in Vence, France, his reputation seemed permanently established.

'Well, Mabel, and what are you going to do with yourself?' asked Joe, with foolish flippancy. He felt quite safe himself. Without listening for an answer, he turned aside, worked a grain of tobacco to the tip of his tongue, and spat it out.[1] He did not care about anything, since he felt safe himself.

The three brothers and the sister sat round the desolate breakfast table, attempting some sort of desultory consultation. The morning's post had given the final tap to the family fortunes, and all was over. The dreary dining-room itself, with its heavy mahogany furniture, looked as if it were waiting to be done away with.[2]

But the consultation amounted to nothing. There was a strange air of ineffectuality[3] about the three men, as they sprawled at table, smoking and reflecting vaguely on their own condition. The girl was alone, a rather short, sullen-looking young woman of twenty-seven. She did not share the same life as her brothers. She would have been good-looking, save for the impassive fixity of her face,[4] 'bull-dog',

---

1) worked a grain of tobacco to the tip of his tongue, and spat it out: 혀 끝에 모아 탁 뱉았다.

2) done away with: abolish.

3) a strange air of ineffectuality: 이상 야릇한 무기력.

4) save for the impassive fixity of her face: 아무런 감각도 없는 늘 똑같은 표정을 지닌 얼굴(표정)만 아니었다면 save for=except for.

as her brothers called it.

There was a confused tramping of horses' feet outside. The three men all sprawled round in their chairs to watch. Beyond the dark holly bushes that separated the strip of lawn from the high-road, they could see a cavalcade[1] of shire horses[2] swinging out of their own yard, being taken for exercise. This was the last time. These were the last horses that would go through their hands. The young men watched with critical, callous look. They were all frightened at the collapse of their lives, and the sense of disaster in which they were involved left them no inner freedom.

Yet they were three fine, well-set fellows enough. Joe, the eldest, was a man of thirty-five, broad and handsome in a hot flushed way. His face was red, he twisted his black moustache over a thick finger, his eyes were shallow and restless. He had a sensual way of uncovering his teeth[3] when he laughed, and his bearing was stupid. Now he watched the horses with a glazed look of helplessness in his eyes, a certain stupor of downfall.[4]

The great draught-horses[5] swung past. They were tied head to tail, four of them, and they heaved along to where a lane branched off from the high-road, planting their great roofs floutingly in the fine black mud,[6] swinging their great rounded haunches sumptuously, and trotting a few sudden steps as they were led into the lane, round the corner. Every movement showed a massive, slumbrous strength, and a stupidity which held them in subjection.[7] The groom at the head looked back, jerking the leading rope. And the cavalcade moved out of sight up the lane, the tail of the last horse, bobbed up tight and stiff,[8] held out taut from the swinging great haunches as they rocked[9]

1) cavalcade: procession of persons riding on horses.
2) shire horses: 영국 중부 지방산의 마차 끄는 말.
3) had a sensual way of uncovering his teeth: 육감적으로 이빨을 드러내곤 했다.
4) a certain stupor of downfall: 몰락에서 온 얼빠진 표정. stupor=a dazed condition.
5) draught-horses: draft-horses 짐 끄는 말.
6) planting their great roofs floutingly in the fine black mud: 커다란 발굽을 검은 진흙 속에 조롱하듯 쿵쿵 내리박으며.
7) a stupidity which held them in subjection: 순종케 하는 우둔함.
8) bobbed up tight and stiff: 꼿꼿하게 일어선.
9) rock: move backward or forward.

behind the hedges in a motion-like sleep.

Joe watched with glazed hopeless eyes. The horses were almost like his own body to him. He felt he was done for[1] now. Luckily he was engaged to a woman as old as himself, and therefore her father, who was steward of a neighbouring estate, would provide him with a job. He would marry and go into harness. His life was over, he would be a subject animal now.

He turned uneasily aside, the retreating steps of the horses echoing in his ears. Then, with foolish restlessness, he reached for the scraps of bacon-rind from the plates, and making a faint whistling sound, flung them to the terrier that lay against the fender. He watched the dog swallow them, and waited till the creature looked into his eyes. Then a faint grin came on his face, and in a high, foolish voice he said:

"You won't get much more bacon, shall you, you little bitch?"

The dog faintly and dismally wagged its tail, then lowered its haunches, circled round, and lay down again.

There was another hopeless silence at the table. Joe sprawled uneasily in his seat, not willing to go till the family conclave was dissolved.[2] Fred Henry, the second brother, was erect, clean-limbed, alert. He had watched the passing of the horses with more sang-froid.[3] If he was an animal, like Joe, he was an animal which controls, not one which is controlled. He was master of any horse, and he carried himself with a well-tempered air of mastery.[4] But he was not master of the situation of life. He pushed his coarse brown moustache upwards, off his lip, and glanced irritably at his sister, who sat impassive and inscrutable.

"You'll go and stop with Lucy for a bit,[5] shan't you?" he asked. The girl did not answer.

"I don't see what else you can do," persisted Fred Henry.

---

1) do for: to cause the death or ruin of; cause to fail.

2) till the family conclave was dissolved: 가족회의가 해산될 때까지 conclave=a private meeting.

3) sang-froid: coolness of mind; calmness.

4) he carried himself with a well-tempered air of mastery: 그는 잘 단련된 대가연(大家然)한 태도로 자처했다.

5) for a bit: for a short time.

"Go as a skivvy,"[1] Joe interpolated laconically.

The girl did not move a muscle.

"If I was her, I should go in for[2] training for a nurse," said Malcolm, the youngest of them all. He was the baby of the family, a young man of twenty-two, with a fresh, jaunty *museau*.[3]

But Mabel did not take any notice of him. They had talked at her and round her for so many years, that she hardly heard them at all.

The marble clock on the mantel piece softly chimed the halfhour, the dog rose uneasily from the hearthrug and looked at the party at the breakfast-table. But still they sat on in ineffectual conclave.

"Oh, all right," said Joe suddenly, apropos of nothing.[4] "I'll get a move on."[5]

He pushed back his chair, straddled his knees with a downward jerk,[6] to get them free, in horsey fashion,[7] and went to the fire. Still, he did not go out of the room; he was curious to know what the others would do or say. He began to charge his pipe, looking down at the dog and saying in a high affected voice:

"Going wi' me? Going wi' me are ter? Tha'rt goin' further than that counts on just now, dost hear?"[8]

The dog faintly wagged its tail, the man stuck out his jaw and covered his pipe with his hands, and puffed intently, losing himself in the tobacco, looking down all the while at the dog with an absent brown eye. The dog looked up at him in mournful distrust. Joe stood with his knees stuck out, in real horsey fashion.

"Have you had a letter from Lucy?" Fred Henry asked of his sister.

"Last week," came the neutral reply.

---

1) skivvy: 하녀.
2) go in for: try to di; take part in; take pleasure in.
3) jaunty *museau*: 미끈한 콧마루.
4) apropos of nothing: 아닌 밤중에 홍두깨 격으로.
5) I'll get a move on: I'll have to move on.
6) straddled his knees with a downward jerk: 양 무릎을 짝 아래로 벌리고는.
7) in horsey fashion: 말 타는 식으로, 말을 좋아하는 식으로. horsey=horsy; fond of horse.
8) Tha'rt goin' further than that counts on just now, dost hear?': 넌 네가 생각하는 것 보다 더 멀리 가게 될 거다, 알겠니?.

"And what does she say?"

There was no answer.

"Does she ask you to go and stop there?" persisted Fred Henry.

"She says I can if I like."

"Well, then, you'd better. Tell her you'll come on Monday."

This was received in silence.

"That's what you'll do then, is it?" said Fred Henry, in some exasperation.[1]

But she made no answer. There was a silence of futility and irritation in the room.[2] Malcolm grinned fatuously.

"You'll have to make up your mind between now and next Wednesday," said Joe loudly, "or else find your lodgings on the kerbstone."[3]

The face of the young woman darkened, but she sat on immutable.

"Here's Jack Fergusson!" exclaimed Malcolm, who was looking aimlessly out of the window.

"Where?" exclaimed Joe loudly.

"Just gone past."

"Coming in?"

Malcolm craned his neck to see the gate.

"Yes," he said.

There was a silence. Mabel sat on like one condemned, at the head of the table. Then a whistle was heard from the kitchen. The dog got up and barked sharply. Joe opened the door and shouted: "Come on."

After a moment a young man entered. He was muffled up[4] in overcoat and a purple woollen scarf, and his tweed cap, which he did not remove, was pulled down on his head. He was of medium height, his face was rather long and pale, his eyes looked tired.

"Hello, Jack! Well, Jack!" exclaimed Malcolm and Joe. Fred Henry

---

1) in some exasperation: 다소 성을 내며.

2) There was a silence of futility and irritation in the room: 방안에는 이상 더 말해도 소용없다는 초조한 적막감이 감돌았다.

3) find your lodgings on the kerbstone: 길거리에서 잘 신세가 될 거다.
kerbstone=curbstone; a stone set along a margin as a limit and protection.

4) muffled up: wrap or cover up in order to keep warm.

merely said: "Jack."

"What's doing?" asked the newcomer, evidently addressing Fred Henry.

"Same. We've got to be out[1] by Wednesday. Got a cold?"

"I have — got it bad, too."

"Why don't you stop in?"

"*Me* stop in? When I can't stand on my legs, perhaps I shall have a chance." The young man spoke huskily. He had a slight Scotch accent.

"It's a knock-out, isn't it," said Joe, boisterously, "if a doctor goes round croaking with a cold.[2] Looks bad for the patients, doesn't it?"

The young doctor looked at him slowly.

"Anything the matter with *you* then?" he asked sarcastically.

"Not as I know of. Damn your eyes, I hope not.[3] Why?"

"I thought you were very concerned about the patients, wondered if you might be one yourself."

"Damn it, no, I've never been a patient to no flaming[4] doctor, and hope I never shall be," returned Joe.

At this point Mabel rose from the table, and they all seemed to become aware of her existence. She began putting the dishes together. The young doctor looked at her, but did not address her. He had not greeted her. She went out the room with the tray, her face impassive and unchanged.

"When are you off[5] then, all of you?" asked the doctor.

"I'm catching the eleven-forty," replied Malcolm. "Are you goin" down wi' th' trap, Joe?"

"Yes, I've told you I'm going down wi' th' trap, haven't I?"

"We'd better be getting her in then.[6] So long, Jack, if I don't see you before I go," said Malcolm, shaking hands.

---

1) We've got to be out: We have to be out.
2) goes round croaking with a cold: 감기에 걸려 쿨룩거리며 돌아다니다.
3) Damn your eyes, I hope not.: 제발 그런 눈으로 보지 마라.
4) flaming: very bright; brilliant.
5) be off: go away; leave quickly.
6) We'd better be getting her in then: 그러면 누리를 태우는 게 낫겠다.

He went out, followed by Joe, who seemed to have his tail between his legs.[1)]

"Well, this is the devil's own," exclaimed the doctor, when he was left alone with Fred Henry. "Going before Wednesday, are you?"

"That's the orders," replied the other.

"Where, to Northampton?"

"That's it."

"The devil!"[2)] exclaimed Fergusson, with quiet chagrin.[3)]

And there was silence between the two.

"All settled up, are you?" asked Fergusson.

"About."

There was another pause.

"Well, I shall miss yer,[4)] Freddy, boy," said the young doctor.

"And I shall miss thee, Jack," returned the other.

"Miss you like hell," mused[5)] the doctor.

Fred Henry turned aside. There was nothing to say. Mabel came in again, to finish clearing the table.

"What are *you* going to do, then, Miss Pervin?" asked Fergusson. "Going to your sister's, are you?"

Mabel looked at him with her steady, dangerous eyes, that always made him uncomfortable, unsettling his superficial ease.[6)]

"No," she said.

"Well, what in the name of fortune are you going to do? Say what you mean to do," cried Fred Henry, with futile intensity.

But she only averted her head, and continued her work. She folded the white table-cloth, and put on the chenille cloth.

"The sulkiest bitch that ever trod" muttered her brother.

But she finished her task with perfectly impassive face, the young

---

1) tail between his legs: state of feeling beaten, ashamed, or very obedient, as after a scolding or a whipping.

2) The devil!: Exclamation of disgust, anger, etc.

3) chagrin: a felling of disappintment, failure, or humiliation.

4) yer: you.

5) mused: said thoughtfully.

6) that always made him uncomfortable, unsettling his superficial ease: 언제나 그를 불안하게 하며, 그의 표면적인 안이감을 뒤흔들어 놓은(그런 눈초리였다).

doctor watching her interestedly all the while. Then she went out.

Fred Henry stared after her, clenching his lips, his blue eyes fixing in sharp antagonism,[1] as he made a grimace of sour exasperation.[2]

"You could bray her into bits,[3] and that's all you'd get out of her," he said, in a small, narrowed tone.

The doctor smiled faintly.

"What's she *going* to do, then?" he asked.

"Strike me if *I* know!" returned the other.

There was a pause. Then the doctor stirred.

"I'll be seeing you tonight, shall I?" he said to his friend.

"Ay — where's it to be? Are we going over to Jessdale?"

"I don't know. I've got such a cold on me. I'll come round to the "Moon and Stars", anyway."

"Let Lizzie and May miss their night for once, eh?"

"That's it — if I feel as I do now."

"All's one — "

The two young men went through the passage and down to the back door together. The house was large, but it was servantless now, and desolate. At the back was a small bricked house-yard and beyond that a big square, gravelled fine and red, and having stables on two sides. Sloping, dank, winter-dark fields stretched away on the open sides.

But the stables were empty. Joseph Pervin, the father of the family, had been a man of no education, who had become a fairly large horse-dealer. The stables had been full of horses, there was a great turmoil and come-and-go of horses and of dealers and grooms. Then the kitchen was full of servants. But of late[4] things had declined. The old man had married a second time, to retrieve his fortunes. Now he was dead and everything was gone to the dogs,[5] there was nothing but debt and threatening.

---

1) his blue eyes fixing in sharp antagonism: 무서운 적대심에 파란 눈을 깜박거리지도 않고.

2) as he made a grimace of sour exasperation: 몹시 불쾌하고 격분하여 얼굴을 찌푸리며. exasperation=extreme annoyance; irritation; anger.

3) bray ~ into bits: ~을 갈래갈래 찢어 버리다.

4) of late: recently.

5) go to the dogs: be ruined.

For months, Mabel had been servantless in the big house, keeping the home together in penury[1] for her ineffectual brothers. She had kept house for ten years. But previously it was with unstinted means. Then, however brutal and coarse everything was, the sense of money had kept her proud, confident. The men might be foul-mouthed, the women in the kitchen might have bad reputations, her brothers might have illegitimate children. But so long as there was money, the girl felt herself established, and brutally proud, reserved.[2]

No company came to the house, save dealers and coarse men. Mabel had no associates of her own sex, after her sister went away. But she did not mind. She went regularly to church, she attended to[3] her father. And she lived in the memory of her mother, who had died when she was fourteen, and whom she had loved. She had loved her father, too, in a different way, depending upon him, and feeling secure in him, until at the age of fifty-four he married again. And then she had set hard against him.[4] Now he had died and left them all hopelessly in debt.

She had suffered badly during the period of poverty. Nothing, however, could shake the curious, sullen, animal pride that dominated each member of the family. Now, for Mabel, the end had come. Still she would not cast about her. She would follow her own way just the same. She would always hold the keys of her own situation. Mindless and persistent, she endured from day to day. Why should she think? Why should she answer anybody? It was enough that this was the end, and there was no way out. She need not pass any more darkly along the main street of the small town, avoiding every eye. She need not demean herself any more,[5] going into the shops and buying the cheapest food. This was at an end. She thought of nobody, not even

---

1) keeping the home together in penury: 궁핍 속에서 집안 살림을 꾸려 나가면서.
2) the girl felt herself established, and brutally proud, reserved: 그녀는 마음 든든히 여겼고 무섭게 잘난 체하고 말이 없었다.
3) attended to: wait on; care for; tend.
4) she had set hard against him: 그녀는 아버지에게 반감을 품게 되었다. set~ against=make unfriendly or hostile toward.
5) She need not demean herself any more: 더 이상 자신을 천하게 굴 필요는 없다.

herself. Mindless and persistent, she seemed in a sort of ecstasy[1] to be coming nearer to her fulfilment, her own glorification, approaching her dead mother, who was glorified.

In the afternoon she took a little bag, with shears and sponge and a small scrubbingbrush, and went out. It was a grey, wintry day, with saddened, dark green fields and an atmosphere blackened by the smoke of foundries not far off. She went quickly, darkly along the causeway, heeding nobody, through the town to the churchyard.

There she always felt secure, as if no one could see her, although as a matter of fact she was exposed to the stare of everyone who passed along the churchyard wall. Nevertheless, once under the shadow of the great looming church,[2] among the graves, she felt immune from the world,[3] reserved within the thick churchyard wall as in another country.

Carefully she clipped the grass from the grave, and arranged the pinky white, small chrysanthemums in the tin cross. When this was done, she took an empty jar from a neighbouring grave, brought water, and carefully, most scrupulously sponged the marble headstone and the coping-stone.

It gave her sincere satisfaction to do this. She felt in immediate contact with the world of her mother. She took minute pains,[4] went through the park in a state bordering on pure happiness,[5] as if in performing this task she came into a subtle, intimate connection with her mother. For the life she followed here in the world was far less real than the world of death she inherited from her mother.

The doctor's house was just by the church. Fergusson, being a mere hired assistant, was slave to the country-side. As he hurried now to attend to the outpatients[6] in the surgery, glancing across the graveyard

---

1) in a sort of ecstasy: 일종의 황홀경에 잠겨.

2) once under the shadow of the great looming church: 크게 어렴풋이 나타나는 교회의 그림자 속에 일단 들어가면.

3) felt immune from the world: 이 세상과는 멀리 격해 있다고 느꼈다.

4) took minute pains: 세심한 애를 썼다, 세심한 정성을 들였다.

5) in a state bordering on pure happiness: 순결한 행복감과 비슷한 상태에서. border on=be close to; resemble.

6) outpatients: patient receiving treatment at a hospital but not staying there.

with his quick eye, he saw the girl at task at the grave. She seemed so intent and remote, it was looking into another world. Some mystical element was touched in him. He slowed down as he walked, watching her as if spell-bound.[1)]

She lifted her eyes, feeling him looking. Their eyes met. And each looked again at once, each feeling, in some way, found out by the other. He lifted his cap and passed on down the road. There remained distinct in consciousness, like a vision, the memory of her face, lifted from the tombstone in the churchyard, and looking at him with slow, large, portentous eyes. It *was* portentous, her face.[2)] It seemed to mesmerise[3)] him. There was a heavy power in her eyes which laid hold of his whole being,[4)] as if he had drunk some powerful drug. He had been feeling weak and done[5)] before. Now the life came back into him, he felt delivered from his own fretted, daily self.

He finished his duties at the surgery as quickly as might be, hastily filling up the bottles of the waiting people with cheap drugs. Then, in perpetual haste, he set off again to visit several cases in another part of his round, before tea-time. At all times he preferred to walk if he could, but particularly, when he was not well. He fancied the motion restored him.

The afternoon was falling. It was grey, deadened, and wintry, with a slow, moist, heavy coldness sinking in and deadening all the faculties. But why should he think or notice? He hastily climbed the hill and turned across the dark green fields, following the black cinder-track. In the distance, across a shallow dip[6)] in the country, the small town was clustered like smouldering ash,[7)] a tower, a spire, a heap of low, raw, extinct houses. And on the nearest fringe of the town, sloping

---

1) as if spell-bound: as if (he were) fascinated [enchanted].

2) It *was* portentous, her face: 그녀의 얼굴은 그야말로 흉조의 얼굴이었다. portentous=ominous; threatening.

3) mesmerise: hypnotize.

4) laid hold of his whole being: 그의 전 존재를 꽉 붙잡았다.

5) done: exhausted.

6) a shallow dip: 얕은 경사지.

7) the small town was clustered like smouldering ash: 조그만 마을은 그을려 타고 있는 잿더미처럼 옹기종기 모여 있었다.

into the dip, was Oldmeadow, the Pervins' house. He could see the stables and the outbuildings distinctly, as they lay towards him on the slope.[1] Well, he would not go there many more times! Another resource would be lost to him, another place gone: the only company he cared for in the alien, ugly little town he was losing.[2] Nothing but work, drudgery, constant hastening from dwelling to dwelling among the colliers and the iron-workers. It wore him out, but at the same time he had a craving[3] for it. It was a stimulant to him to be in the homes of the working people, moving, as it were, through the innermost body of their life.[4] His nerves were excited and gratified. He could come so near, into the very lives of the rough, inarticulate, powerfully emotional men and women. He grumbled, he said he hated the hellish hole. But as a matter of fact it excited him, the contact with the rough, strongly-feeling people was a stimulant applied direct to his nerves.

Below Old meadow, in the green, shallow, soddened hollow of fields, lay a square, deep pond. Roving across the landscape, the doctor's quick eye detected a figure in black passing through the gate of the field, down towards the pond. He looked again. It would be Mabel Pervin. His mind suddenly became alive and attentive.

Why was she going down there? He pulled up on the path on the slope above,[5] and stood staring. He could just make sure of the small black figure moving in the hollow of the failing day. He seemed to see her in the midst of such obscurity, that he was like a clairvoyant, seeing rather with the mind's eye than with ordinary sight. Yet he could see her positively enough, whilst he kept his eye attentive. He felt, if he looked away from her, in the thick, ugly falling dusk, he would lose her altogether.

He followed her minutely as she moved, direct and intent, like

---

1) as they lay towards him on the slope: (마구간이니 창고 따위가) 그가 향한 비탈에서 있었기 때문에.
2) he was losing: 목적어는 the only company~.
3) craving: strang desire; longing.
4) moving, as it were, through the innermost body of their life: 말하자면 그들 생활의 가장 깊은 내부를 뚫고 들어가는 것.
5) pulled up on the path on the slope above: 비탈길을 따라 위로 올라갔다.

something transmitted rather than stirring in voluntary activity,[1] straight down the field towards the pond. There she stood on the bank for a moment. She never raised her head. Then she waded slowly into the water.

He stood motionless as the small black figure walked slowly and deliberately towards the centre of the pond, very slowly, gradually moving deeper into the motionless water, and still moving forward as the water got up to her breast. Then he could see her no more in the dusk of the dead afternoon.

"There!" he exclaimed. "Would you believe it?"

And he hastened straight down, running over the wet, soddened fields, pushing through the hedges, down into the depression of callous wintry obscurity.[2] It took him several minutes to come to the pond. He stood on the bank, breathing heavily. He could see nothing. His eyes seemed to penetrate the dead water. Yes, perhaps that was the dark shadow of her black clothing beneath the surface of water.

He slowly ventured[3] into the pond. The bottom was deep, soft clay, he sank in, and the water clasped dead cold round his legs. As he stirred he could smell the cold, rotten clay that fouled[4] up into the water. It was objectionable in his lungs. Still, repelled and yet not heeding, he moved deeper into the pond. The cold water rose over his thighs, over his loins, upon his abdomen The lower part of body was all sunk in the hideous cold element. And the bottom was so deeply soft and uncertain, he was afraid of pitching with his mouth underneath.[5] He could not swim, and was afraid.

He crouched a little, spreading his hands under the water and moving them round, trying to feel for her. The dead cold pond swayed upon his chest. He moved again, a little deeper, and again, with his hands

1) like something transmitted rather than stirring in voluntary activity: 자발적인 활동에서 움직이고 있다기보다 무엇에 홀린 것처럼.
2) down into the depression of callous wintry obscurity: 침울하고 쌀쌀한 어둠이 깔린 움푹한 곳으로. depression=a low place; hollow.
3) venture: dare to go.
4) foul: make dirty.
5) uncertain, he was afraid of pitching with his mouth underneath: 거꾸로 곤두박질 하지 않을까 싶어 겁이 났다.

underneath, he felt all around under the water. And he touched her clothing. But it evaded his fingers. He made a desperate effort to grasp it.

And so doing he lost his balance and went under, horribly, suffocating in the foul earthy water, struggling madly for a few moments. At last, after what seemed an eternity, he got his footing, rose again into the air and looked around. He gasped, and knew he was in the world. Then he looked at the water. She had risen near him. He grasped her clothing, and drawing her nearer, turned to take his way to land again.

He went very slowly, carefully, absorbed in the slow progress.[1] He rose higher, climbing out of the pond. The water was now only about his legs; he was thankful, full of relief to be out of the clutches of the pond.[2] He lifted her and staggered on to the bank, out of the horror of wet, grey clay.

He laid her down on the bank. She was quite unconscious and running with water. He made the water come from her mouth, he worked to restore her. He did not have to work very long before he could feel the breathing begin again in her; she was breathing heavily naturally. He worked a little longer. He could feel her live beneath his hands; she was coming back. He wiped her face, wrapped her in his overcoat, looked round into the dim, dark grey world, then lifted her and staggered down the bank and across the fields.

It seemed an unthinkably long way, and his burden so heavy he felt he would never get to the house. But at last he was in the stable-yard, and then in the house-yard. He opened the door and went into the house. In the kitchen he laid her down on the hearthrug and called. The house was empty. But the fire was burning in the grate.

Then again he kneeled to attend to her. She was breathing regularly, her eyes wide open and as if conscious, but there seemed something missing in her look. She was conscious in herself, but unconscious of her surroundings.

---

1) absorbed in the slow progress: 천천히 나아가는 데만 정신이 팔린 채.

2) (was) full of relief to be out of the clutches of the pond: 못의 마수(魔手)에서 벗어난 안도감에 가득 찼다.

He ran upstairs, took blankets from a bed and put them before the fire to warm. Then he removed her saturated,[1] earthy-smelling clothing, rubbed her dry with a towel, and wrapped her naked in the blankets. Then he went into the dining-room, to look for spirits.[2] There was a little whisky. He drank a gulp himself, and put some into her mouth.

The effect was instantaneous. She looked full into his face, as if she had been seeing him for some time, and yet had only just become conscious of him.

"Dr. Fergusson?" she said.

"What?" he answered.

He was divesting himself of his coat,[3] intending to find some dry clothing upstairs. He could not bear the smell of the dead, clayey water, and he was mortally afraid for his own health.

"What did I do?" she asked.

"Walked into the pond," he replied. He had begun to shudder like one sick, and could hardly attend to her. Her eyes remained full on him, he seemed to be going dark in his mind, looking back at her helplessly. The shuddering became quieter in him, his life came back to him, dark and unknowing, but strong again.

"Was I out of my mind?"[4] she asked, while her eyes were fixed on him all the time.[5]

"Maybe, for the moment," he replied. He felt quiet, because his strength had come back. The strange fretful strain had left him.

"Am I out of my mind now?" she asked.

"Are you?" he reflected a moment. "No," he answered truthfully, "I don't see that you are." He turned his face aside. He was afraid now, because he felt dazed, and felt dimly that her power was stronger that his, in this issue. And she continued to look at him fixedly all the time. "Can you tell me where I shall find some dry things to put on?" he asked.

---

1) saturated: soaked thoroughly
2) spirits: strong alcoholic liquor
3) He was divesting himself of his coat: He was taking off his coat
4) out of my mind: out of my head; out of my senses
5) all the time: all the while; during the whole period; through the whole time

"Did you dive into the pond for me?" she asked.

"No," he answered. "I walked in. But I went in overhead as well."

There was silence for a moment. He hesitated. He very much wanted to go upstairs to get into dry clothing. But there was another desire in him. And she seemed to hold him. His will seemed to have gone to sleep, and left him, standing there slack before her. But he felt warm inside himself. He did not shudder at all, though his clothes were sodden on him.

"Why did you?" she asked.

"Because I didn't want you to do such a foolish thing," he said.

"It wasn't foolish," she said, still gazing at him as she lay on the floor, with a sofa cushion under her head. "It was the right thing to do. I knew best, then."

"I'll go and shift these wet things," he said. But still he had not the power to move out of her presence, until she sent him. It was as if she had the life of his body in her hands, and he could not extricate[1] himself. Or perhaps he did not want to.

Suddenly she sat up. Then she became aware of her own immediate condition. She felt the blankets about her, she knew her own limbs. For a moment it seemed as if her reason were going. She looked round, with wild eye, as if seeking something. He stood still with fear. She saw her clothing lying scattered.

"Who undressed me?" she asked, her eyes resting full and inevitable on his face.[2]

"I did," he replied, "to bring you round."

For some moments she sat and gazed at him awfully, her lips parted.

"Do you love me, then?" she asked.

He only stood and stared at her, fascinated. His soul seemed to melt.

She shuffled forward on her knees, and put her arms round him, round his legs, as he stood there, pressing her breasts against his knees and thighs, clutching him with strange, convulsive certainty, pressing his thighs against her, drawing him to her face, her throat, as she looked

---

1) extricate: set free; release

2) her eyes resting full and inevitable on his face: 그의 얼굴을 뚫어지게 쳐다보면서.

up at him with flaring, humble eyes and transfiguration, triumphant in first possession.[1)]

"You love me," she murmured, in strange transport, yearning and triumphant and confident. "You love me. I know you love me, I know."

And she was passionately kissing his knees, through the wet clothing, passionately and indiscriminately kissing his knees, his legs, as if unaware of everything.

He looked down at the tangled wet hair, the wild, bare, animal shoulders. He was amazed, bewildered and afraid. He had never thought of loving her. He had never wanted to love her. When he rescued her and restored her, he was a doctor, and she was a patient. He had had no single personal thought of her. Nay, this introduction of the personal element was very distasteful to him, a violation of his professional honour. It was horrible to have her there embracing his knees. It was horrible. He revolted from it, violently. And yet — and yet — he had not the power to break away.

She looked at him again, with the same supplication of powerful love,[2)] and that same transcendent, frightening light of triumph. In view of the delicate flame which seemed to come from her face like a light, he was powerless. And yet he had never intended to love her. He had never intended. And something stubborn in him could not give way.[3)]

"You love me," she repeated, in a murmur of deep, rhapsodic assurance. "You love me."

Her hands were drawing him, drawing him down to her. He was afraid, even a little horrified. For he had, really, no intention of loving her. Yet her hands were drawing him towards her. He put out his hand quickly to steady himself, and grasped her bare shoulder. He had no intention of loving her: his whole will was against his yielding. It was horrible. And yet wonderful was the touch of her shoulders,

---

1) she looked up at him … first possession: 그녀는 처음으로 남자를 차지한 데 의기양양한 듯 확 달라진 모습으로 너울너울 불타는 겸손한 눈초리를 그에게 던졌다.

2) with the same supplication of powerful love: 여전히 애원하는 열렬한 사랑으로.

3) And something stubborn in him could not give way: 그리고 그의 마음속에 간직한 어떤 완강한 것이 무너질 수도 없었다. give way = break down: yield; retreat.

beautiful the shining of her face. Was she perhaps mad? He had a horror of yielding to her. Yet something in him ached also.

He had been staring away at the door, away from her. But his hand remained on her shoulder. She had gone suddenly very still. He looked down at her. Her eyes were now wide with fear, with doubt, the light was dying from her face, a shadow of terrible greyness was returning. He could not bear the touch of her eyes' question upon him, and the look of death behind the question.

With an inward groan he gave way, and let his heart yield towards her. A sudden gentle smile came on his face. And her eyes, which never left his face, slowly, slowly filled with tears. He watched the strange water rise in her eyes, like some slow fountain coming up. And his heart seemed to burn and melt away in his breast.

He could not bear to look at her any more. He dropped on his knees and caught her head. with his arms and pressed her face against his throat. She was very still. His heart, which seemed to have broken, was burning with a kind of agony in his breast. And he felt her slow, hot tears wetting his throat. But he could not move.

He felt the hot tears wet his neck and the hollows of his neck, and he remained motionless, suspended through one of man's eternities. Only now it had become indispensable to him to have her face pressed close to him; he could never let her go[1] again. He could never let her head go away from the close clutch of his arm. He wanted to remain like that for ever, with his heart hurting him in a pain that was also life to him. Without knowing, he was looking down on her damp, soft brown hair.

Then, as it were suddenly, he smelt the horrid stagnant smell of that water. And at the same moment she drew away from him and looked at him. Her eyes were wistful and unfathomable. He was afraid of them, and he fell to kissing her, not knowing what he was doing. He wanted her eyes not to have that terrible, wistful, unfathomable look.

When she turned her face to him again, a faint delicate flush was

---

1) let go: release the hold on.

glowing, and there was again dawning that terrible shining of joy in her eyes, which really terrified him, and yet which he now wanted to see, because he feared the look of doubt still more.

"You love me?" she said, rather faltering.

"Yes." The word cost him a painful effort. Not because it wasn't true. But because it was too newly true, the *saying* seemed to tear open again his newly-torn heart. And he hardly wanted it to be true, even now.

She lifted her face to him, and he bent forward and kissed her on the mouth, gently, with the one kiss that is an eternal pledge. And as he kissed her his heart strained again in his breast. He never intended to love her. But now it was over. He had crossed over the gulf to her, and all that he had left behind had shrivelled and become void.

After the kiss, her eyes again slowly filled with tears. She sat still, away from him, with her face drooped aside, and her hands folded in her lap. The tears fell very slowly. There was complete silence. He too sat there motionless and silent on the hearthrug. The strange pain of his heart that was broken seemed to consume him. That he should love her? That this was love! That he should be ripped open in this way! Him, a doctor! How they would all jeer if they knew! It was agony to him to think they might know.

In the curious naked pain of the thought he looked again to her. She was sitting there drooped into a muse. He saw a tear fall, and his heart flared hot. He saw for the first time that one of her shoulders was quite uncovered, one arm bare, he could see one of her small breasts; dimly, because it had become almost dark in the room.

"Why are you crying?" he asked, in an altered voice.

She looked up at him, and behind her tears the consciousness of her situation for the first time brought a dark look of shame to her eyes.

"I'm not crying, really," she said, watching him, half-frightened.

He reached his hand, and softly closed it on her bare arm.

"I love you! I love you!" he said in a soft, low vibrating voice, unlike himself.

She shrank, and dropped her head. The soft, penetrating grip of his hand on her arm distressed her. She looked up at him.

"I want to go," she said. "I want to go and get you some dry things."

"Why?" he said. "I'm all right."

"But I want to go," she said. "And I want you to change your things."

He released her arm, and she wrapped herself in the blanket, looking at him rather frightened. And still she did not rise.

"Kiss me," she said wistfully.

He kissed her, but briefly, half in anger.

Then, after a second, she rose nervously, all mixed up in the blanket. He watched her in her confusion as she tried to extricate herself and wrap herself up so that she could walk. He watched her relentlessly, as she knew. And as she went, the blanket trailing, and he saw a glimpse of her feet and her white leg, he tried to remember her as she was when he had wrapped her up in the blanket. But then he didn't want to remember, because she had been nothing to him then, and his nature revolted from remembering her as she was when she was nothing to him.

A tumbling, muffled noise from within the dark house startled him. Then he heard her voice: "There are clothes." He rose and went to the foot of the stairs, and gathered up the garments she had thrown down. Then he came back to the fire, to rub himself down and dress. He grinned at his own appearance when he had finished.

The fire was sinking, so he put on coal. The house was now quite dark, save for the light of a street-lamp that shone in faintly from beyond the holly trees. He lit the gas with matches he found on the mantelpiece. Then he emptied the pockets of his own clothes, and threw all his wet things in a heap into the scullery. After which he gathered up her sodden clothes, gently, and put them in a separate heap on the copper-top in the scullery.

It was six o'clock on the clock. His own watch had stopped. He ought to go back to the surgery. He waited, and still she did not come down. So he went to the foot of the stairs and called:

"I shall have to go."

Almost immediately he heard her coming down. She had on her

best dress of black voile, and her hair was tidy, but still damp. She looked at him — and in spite of herself, smiled.

"I don't like you in those clothes," she said.

"Do I look a sight?" he answered.

They were shy of one another.

"I'll make you some tea," she said.

"No, I must go."

"Must you?" And she looked at him again with the wide, strained, doubtful eyes. And again, from the pain of his breast, he knew how he loved her. He went and bent to kiss her, gently, passionately, with his heart's painful kiss.

"And my hair smells so horrible," she murmured in distraction. "And I'm so awful, I'm so awful! Oh no, I'm too awful." And she broke into bitter, heart-broken sobbing. "You can't want to love me, I'm horrible."

"Don't be silly, don't be silly," he said, trying to comfort her, kissing her, holding her in his arms. "I want you, I want to marry you, we're going to be married, quickly, quickly — tomorrow if I can."

But she only sobbed terribly, and cried:

"I feel awful. I feel awful. I feel I'm horrible to you."

"No, I want you, I want you," was all he answered, blindly, with that terrible intonation which frightened her almost more than her horror lest he should *not* want her.[1)]

---

1) with that terrible intonation … lest he should *not* want her: 그가 그녀를 원치 않을까 하는 그녀의 공포보다 더욱 그녀를 무섭게 한 그런 무서운 어조로.

Marriage à la Mode[1)]

by Katherine Mansfield

Katherine Mansfield (1888-1923) was born in Wellington, New Zealand, with the name of Kathleen Mansfield Beauchamp. She attended Queen's College, in London, edited the college magazine, studied music and became a competent cellist, and later toured as a super in opera. Her first stories appeared when she was twenty-two. She married John Middleton Murry, the critic, collaborated with him and D.H. Lawrence in founding a review, *The Signature*, and continued her own writing. By 1920 with the publication of the volume *Bliss and Other Stories*, her reputation was made. For several years she had been suffering from tuberculosis, and died at the age of thirty-five, in France, where she had gone for treatment.

ON HIS way to the station William remembered with a fresh pang of disappointment that he was taking nothing down to the kiddies.[2)] Poor little chaps![3)] It was hard lines on them.[4)] Their first words always were as they ran to greet him, "What have you got for me,[5)] daddy?" and he had nothing. He would have to buy them some sweets at the station. But that was what he had done for the past four Saturdays; their faces had fallen last time when they saw the same old boxes produced again.

And Paddy had said, "I had red ribbing[6)] on mine *bee*-fore!"

And Johnny had said, "It's always pink on mine. I hate pink."

But what was William to do? The affair wasn't so easily settled. In the old days, of course, he would have taken a taxi off to a decent toyshop and chosen them something in five minutes. But nowadays

1) Marriage à la Mode: Marriage accordings to the fashion; Fashional Marriage.
2) kiddies: children; youngsters.
3) chap: fellow; man; boy.
4) It was hard lines on them: (아무것도 안 사오다니) 그들에겐 절망이겠다라는 뜻. lines=처지, 운(명).
5) What have you got for me?: What do you have for me?.
6) ribbing: ribbon.

they had Russian toys, French toys, Serbian toys — toys from God knows where. It was over a year since Isabel had scrapped the old donkeys and engines and so on because they were so "dreadfully sentimental" and "so appallingly bad for the babies' sense of form."[1)]

"It's so important," the new Isabel had explained, "that they should like the right things from the very beginning. It saves so much time later on. Really, if the poor pets have to spend their infant years staring at these horrors, one can imagine them growing up and asking to be taken to the Royal Academy."

And she spoke as though a visit to the Royal Academy was certain immediate death to any one . . . .

"Well, I don't know," said William slowly. "When I was their age I used to go to bed hugging an old towel with a knot in it."

The new Isabel looked at him, her eyes narrowed, her lips apart.

"*Dear* William! I'm sure you did!" She laughed in the new way.

Sweets it would have to be, however,[2)] thought William gloomily, fishing in his pocket for[3)] change for the taxi-man. And he saw the kiddies handing the boxes round — they were awfully generous little chaps — while Isabel's precious friends didn't hesitate to help themselves.[4)] . . .

What about fruit? William hovered before a stall just inside the station. What about a melon each? Would they have to share that, too? Or a pineapple, for Pad, and a melon for Johnny? Isabel's friends could hardly go sneaking up to the nursery at the children's meal-times. All the same, as he bought the melon William had a horrible vision of one of Isabel's young poets lapping up a slice,[5)] for some reason, behind the nursery door.

With his two very awkward parcels he strode off to his train. The

---

1) so appallingly bad for the babies' sense of form: 아이들의 형태감을 조성하는 데 무섭게도 나쁘다.

2) Sweets it would have to be, however: 그래도 사탕과자라야 할 걸.

3) fishing ~ for: to try to get or to find out.

4) help themselves: to take what they want; take rather than ask or wait to be given.

5) lapping up a slice: 한 조각을 핥아 먹고 있는. lap up=drink by lifting up with the tongue.

platform was crowded, the train was in. Doors banged open and shut. There came such a loud hissing from the engine that people looked dazed as they scurried[1] to and fro. William made straight for[2] a first-class smoker,[3] stowed away his suit-case and parcels, and taking a huge wad[4] of papers out of his inner pocket, he flung down in the corner and began to read.

"Our client moreover is positive .... We are inclined to reconsider ... in the event of — " Ah, that was better. William pressed back his flattened hair and stretched his legs across the carriage floor. The familiar dull gnawing in his breast quietened down.[5] "With regard to[6] our decision — " He took out a blue pencil and scored a paragraph slowly.

Two men came in, stepped across him, and made for the farther corner. A young fellow swung his golf clubs into the rack and sat down opposite. The train gave a gentle lurch, they were off. William glanced up and saw the hot, bright station slipping away. A red-faced girl raced along by the carriages, there was something strained and almost desperate in the way she waved and called. "Hysterical!" thought William dully. Then a greasy, blackfaced workman at the end of the platform grinned at the passing train. And William thought, "A filthy life!" and went back to his papers.

When he looked up again there were fields, and beasts standing for shelter under the dark trees. A wide river, with naked children splashing in the shallows, glided into sight and was gone again. The sky shone pale, and one bird drifted high like a dark fleck in a jewel.[7]

"We have examined our client's correspondence files. . . ." The last sentence he had read echoed in his mind. "We have examined . . ."

---

1) scurry: hurry.
2) made straight for: went directly toward.
3) smoker: smoking car.
4) wad: a tight roll; compact bundle or mass.
5) The familiar dull gnawing … down: 가슴 속에 에이듯이 자리잡고 있던 지루함이 차츰 가라앉았다. gnawing=pain.
6) with regard to: about; concerning; relating to.
7) one bird drifted high like a dark fleck in a jewel: 한 마리의 작은 새가 보석 속의 검은 티와도 같이 하늘 높이 날며 떠돌고 있었다.

William hung on to[1] that sentence, but it was no good; it snapped in the middle, and the fields, the sky, the sailing bird, the water, all said, "Isabel." The same thing happened every Saturday afternoon. When he was on his way to meet Isabel there began those countless imaginary meetings. She was at the station, standing just a little apart from everybody else; she was sitting in the open taxi outside; she was at the garden gate; walking across the parched grass; at the door, or just inside the hall.

And her clear, light voice said, "It's William," or "Hillo, William!" or "So William has come!" He touched her cool hand, her cool cheek.

The exquisite freshness of Isabel! When he had been a little boy, it was his delight to run into the garden after a shower of rain and shake the rosebush over him. Isabel was that rosebush, petal-soft, sparkling and cool. And he was still that little boy. But there was no running into the garden now, no laughing and shaking. The dull, persistent gnawing in his breast started again. He drew up his legs, tossed the papers aside, and shut his eyes.

"What is it, Isabel? What is it?" he said tenderly. They were in their bedroom in the new house. Isabel sat on a painted stool before the dressing-table that was strewn[2] with little black and green boxes.

"What is what, William?" And she bent forward, and her fine light hair fell over her cheeks.

"Ah, you know!" He stood in the middle of the room and he felt a stranger. At that Isabel wheeled round quickly and faced him.

"Oh, William!" she cried imploringly, and she held up the hair-brush: "Please! Please don't be so dreadfully stuffy and — tragic. You're always saying or looking or hinting that I've changed. Just because I've got to know really congenial people, and go about more, and am frightfully keen[3] on — on everything, you behave as though I'd — " Isabel tossed back her hair and laughed — "killed our love or something. It's so awfully absurd" — she bit her lip — "and it's so maddening, William.

1) hang on to: to hold tightly; keep firmly.
2) strewn: (=strewed) scattered; sprinkled.
3) keen: eager; full of enthusiasm.

Even this new house and the servants you grudge[1] me."

"Isabel!"

"Yes, yes, it's true in a way," said Isabel quickly. "You think they are another bad sign. Oh, I know you do. I feel it," she said softly, "every time you come up the stairs. But we couldn't have gone on living in that other poky little hole, William. Be practical, at least! Why, there wasn't enough room for the babies even."

No, it was true. Every morning when he came back from chambers it was to find the babies with Isabel in the back drawing-room. They were having rides on the leopard skin thrown over the sofa back, or they were playing shops with Isabel's desk for a counter, or Pad was sitting on the hearthrug rowing away for dear life[2] with a little brass fire shovel, while Johnny shot at pirates with the tongs. Every evening they each had a pick-a-back up the narrow stairs[3] to their fat old Nanny.

Yes, he supposed it was a poky little house. A little white house with blue curtains and a windowbox of petunias. William met their friends at the door with "Seen our petunias? Pretty terrific for London, don't you think?"

But the imbecile thing, the absolutely extraordinary thing was that he hadn't the slightest idea[4] the Isabel wasn't as happy as he. God, what blindness! He hadn't the remotest notion in those days that she really hated the inconvenient little house, that she thought the fat Nanny was ruining the babies, that she was desperately lonely, pining for[5] new people and new music and pictures and so on. If they hadn't gone to that studio party at Moira Morrison's — if Moira Morrison hadn't said as they were leaving, "I'm going to rescue your wife, selfish man. She's like an exquisite little Titania[6]" — if Isabel hadn't gone

1) grudge: feel anger or dislike toward (a person) because of (something).
2) for dear life: 죽을 힘을 다하여.
3) they each had a pick-a-back up the narrow stairs: 애들은 하나씩 등에 업혀서 좁은 층계를 올라갔다. pick-a-back=on the back or shoulders.
4) he hadn't the slightest idea: he hadn't the remotest notion과 같이 he didn't know anything의 뜻.
5) pining for: longing eagerly for; yearning.
6) Titania: in Shakespeare's *Midsummer Night's Dream*, the queen of the fairies.

with Moira to Paris — if — if . . .

The train stopped at another station. Bettingford. Good heavens! They'd be there in ten minutes. William stuffed the papers back into his pockets; the young man opposite had long since disappeared. Now the other two got out. The late afternoon sun shone on women in cotton frocks and little sunburnt, barefoot children. It blazed on a silky yellow flower with coarse leaves which sprawled over a bank of rock. The air ruffling through the window smelled of the sea. Had Isabel the same crowd with her this week-end, wondered William?

And he remembered the holidays they used to have, the four of them, with a little farm girl, Rose, to look after the babies. Isabel wore a jersey[1)] and her hair in a plait; she looked about fourteen. Lord! how his nose used to peel! And the amount they ate, and the amount they slept in that immense feather bed with their feet locked together. . . . William couldn't help a grim smile as he thought of Isabel's horror if she knew the full extent of his sentimentality.

* *

"Hillo, William!" She was at the station after all, standing just as he had imagined, apart from the others, and — William's heart leapt — she was alone.

"Hallo, Isabel!" William stared. He thought she looked so beautiful that he had to say something, "You look very cool."

"Do I?" said Isabel. "I don't feel very cool. Come along, your horrid old train is late. The taxi's outside." She put her hand lightly on his arm as they passed the ticket collector. "We've all come to meet you," she said. "But we've left Bobby Kane at the sweet shop, to be called for."[2)]

"Oh!" said William. It was all he could say for the moment.

There in the glare waited the taxi, with Bill Hunt and Dennis Green sprawling on one side, their hats tilted over their faces, while on the other, Moira Morrison, in a bonnet like a huge strawberry, jumped up and down.

---

1) jersey: a close fitting sweater.

2) called for: go and get; stop and get.

"No ice! No ice! No ice!" she shouted gaily.

And Dennis chimed in[1] from under his hat. "*Only* to be had from the fishmonger's."

And Bill Hunt, emerging, added, "With *whole* fish in it."

"Oh, what a bore!"[2] wailed Isabel. And she explained to William how they had been chasing round the town for ice while she waited for him. "Simply everything is running down the steep cliffs into the sea, beginning with the butter."

"We shall have to anoint ourselves with butter," said Dennis. "May thy head, William, lack not ointment."

"Look here," said William, "how are we going to sit? I'd better get up by the driver."

"No, Bobby Kane's by the driver," said Isabel. "You're to sit between Moira and me." The taxi started. "What have you got in those mysterious parcels?"

"De-cap-it-ated[3] heads!" said Bill Hunt, shuddering beneath his hat.

"Oh, fruit!" Isabel sounded very pleased. "Wise William! A melon and a pineapple. How too nice!"

"No, wait a bit," said William, smiling. But he really was anxious. "I brought them down for the kiddies."

"Oh, my dear!" Isabel laughed, and slipped her hand through his arm. "They'd be rolling in agonies[4] if they were to eat them. No" — she patted his hand — "you must bring them something next time. I refuse to part with[5] my pineapple."

"Cruel Isabel! Do let me smell it!" said Moira. She flung her arms across William appealingly. "Oh!" The strawberry bonnet fell forward: she sounded quite faint.

"A Lady in Love with a Pineapple," said Dennis, as the taxi drew up[6] before a little shop with a striped blind. Out came Bobby Kane,

---

1) chime in: join in.
2) what a bore!: 참 따분한 얘기군!
3) De-cap-it-ated: beheaded; cut off the head of.
4) They'd be rolling in agonies: 애들이 (이걸 먹다가는) 배가 아파서 펄펄 뛸 거다.
5) part with: give up; let go.
6) drew up: stopped.

his arms full of little packets.

"I do hope they'll be good. I've chosen them because of the colours. There are some round things which really look too divine.[1] And just look at this nougat,[2]" he cried ecstatically, "Just look at it! It's a perfect little ballet."

But at that moment the shopman appeared. "Oh, I forgot. They're none of them paid for," said Bobby, looking frightened. Isabel gave the shopman a note, and Bobby was radiant again. "Hallo, William! I'm sitting by the driver." And bareheaded, all in white, with his sleeves rolled up to the shoulders, he leapt into his place. "Avanti![3]" he cried.

. . .

After tea the others went off to bathe, while William stayed and made his peace with the kiddies. But Johnny and Paddy were asleep, the rose-red glow had paled, bats were flying, and still the bathers had not returned. As William wandered downstairs, the maid crossed the hall carrying a lamp. He followed her into the sitting-room. It was a long room, coloured yellow. On the wall opposite William some one had painted a young man, over life-size,[4] with very wobbly legs, offering a wide-eyed daisy to a young woman who had one very short arm and one very long, thin one. Over the chairs and sofa there hung strips of black material, covered with big splashes like broken eggs, and everywhere one looked there seemed to be an ash-tray full of cigarette ends. William sat down in one of the arm-chairs. Nowadays, when one felt with one hand down the sides, it wasn't to come upon a sheep with three legs or a cow that had lost one horn, or a very fat dove out of the Noah's Ark.[5] One fished up yet another little paper-covered book of smudged-looking poems. . . . He thought of the wad of papers in his pocket, but he was too hungry and tired to read. The door was open; sounds came from the kitchen. The servants were

---

1) too divine: very excellent.
2) nougat: a king of soft candy containing nuts.
3) Avanti!: 떠나자! 라는 뜻.
4) life-size: as big as the living person.
5) Noah's Ark: the vessel in which Noah and his family were preserved during the Deluge (*Gen.* vi).

talking as if they were alone in the house. Suddenly there came a loud screech of laughter and an equally loud "Sh!" They had remembered him. William got up and went through the French windows into the garden, and as he stood there in the shadow he heard the bathers coming up the sandy road; their voices rang through the quiet.

"I think its up to[1] Moira to use her little arts and wiles."

A tragic moan from Moira.

"We ought to have a gramophone for the weekends that played 'The Maid of the Mountains.'"

"Oh no! Oh no!" cried Isabel's voice. "That's not fair to William. Be nice to him, my children! He's only staying until tomorrow evening."

"Leave him to me," cried Bobby Kane. "I'm awfully good at looking after people."

The gate swung open and shut. William moved on the terrace; they had seen him. "Hallo, William!" And Bobby Kane, flapping his towel, began to leap and pirouette on the parched lawn. "Pity you didn't come, William. The water was divine. And we all went to a little pub afterwards and had sloe gin."[2]

The others had reached the house. "I say, Isabel," called Bobby, "would you like me to wear my Nijinsky[3] dress tonight?"

"No," said Isabel, "nobody's going to dress. We're all starving. William's starving, too. Come along, *mes amis*,[4] let's begin with sardines."

"I've found the sardines," said Moira, and she ran into the hall, holding a box high in the air.

"A Lady with a Box of Sardines," said Dennis gravely.

"Well, William, and how's London?" asked Bill Hunt, drawing the cork out of a bottle of whisky.

"Oh, London's not much changed," answered William.

"Good old London," said Bobby, very hearty, spearing a sardine.

---

1) up to: facing as a duty; to be chosen or decided by; depending on.
2) sloe gin: an alcoholic beverage flavored with sloe(=a dark-purpled, plum-like fruit).
3) Nijinsky: (1890-1950) Russian ballet dancer.
4) *mes amis*: (F.) my friends.

But a moment later William was forgotten. Moira Morrison began wondering what colour one's legs really were under water.

"Mine are the palest, palest mushroom colour."

Bill and Dennis ate enormously. And Isabel filled glasses, and changed plates, and found matches, smiling blissfully. At one moment, she said, "I do wish, Bill, you'd paint it."

"Paint what?" said Bill loudly, stuffing his mouth with bread.

"Us," said Isabel, "round the table. It would be so fascinating in twenty years' time."

Bill screwed up his eyes and chewed. "Light's wrong," he said rudely, "far too much yellow"; and went on eating. And that seemed to charm Isabel, too.

But after supper they were all so tired they could do nothing but yawn until it was late enough to go to bed. . . .

It was not until William was waiting for his taxi the next afternoon that he found himself alone with Isabel. When he brought his suit-case down into the hall, Isabel left the others and went over to him. She stooped down and picked up the suit-case. "What a weight!" she said, and she gave a little awkward laugh. "Let me carry it! To the gate."

"No, why should you?" said William. "Of course, not. Give it to me."

"Oh, please, do let me," said Isabel. "I want to, really." They walked together silently. William felt there was nothing to say now.

"There," said Isabel triumphantly, setting the suit-case down, and she looked anxiously along the sandy road. "I hardly seem to have seen you this time," she said breathlessly. "It's so short, isn't it? I feel you've only just come. Next time — " The taxi came into sight. "I hope they look after you properly in London. I'm so sorry the babies have been out all day, but Miss Neil had arranged it. They'll hate missing you. Poor William, going back to London." The taxi turned. "Goodbye!" She gave him a little hurried kiss; she was gone.

Fields, trees, hedges streamed by. They shook through the empty, blind-looking little town, ground up the steep pull to the station.[1)]

---

1) ground up the steep pull to the station: 정거장에 이르는 가파른 비탈을 열심히 올라갔다. pull=uphill. An ascent requiring effort; as, a long pull.

The train was in. William made straight for a first-class smoker, flung back into the corner, but this time he let the papers alone. He folded his arms against the dull, persistent gnawing,[1] and began in his mind to write a letter to Isabel.

* *

The post was late as usual. They sat outside the house in long chairs under coloured parasols. Only Bobby Kane lay on the turf at Isabel's feet. It was dull, stifling; the day drooped like a flag.

"Do you think there will be Mondays in Heaven?" asked Bobby childishly.

And Dennis murmured, "Heaven will be one long Monday."

But Isabel couldn't help wondering what had happened to the salmon they had for supper last night. She had meant to have fish mayonnaise for lunch and now . . .

Moira was asleep. Sleeping was her latest discovery. "It's *so* wonderful. One simply shuts one's eyes, that's all. It's so delicious."

When the old ruddy postman came beating along the sandy road on his tricycle one felt the handle-bars ought to have been oars.

Bill Hunt put down his book. "Letter," he said complacently, and they all waited. But, heartless postman — O malignant world! There was only one, a fat one for Isabel. Not even a paper.

"And mine's only from William," said Isabel mournfully.

"From William — already?"

"He's sending you back your marriage lines[2] as a gentle reminder."

"Does everybody have marriage lines? I thought they were only for servants."

"Pages and pages! Look at her! A Lady reading a Letter," said Dennis.

My darling, precious Isabel. Pages and pages there were. As Isabel read on her feeling of astonishment changed to a stifled feeling. What on earth had induced William . . .? How extraordinary it was. . . . What could have made him . . .? She felt confused, more and more excited,

1) folded his arms against the dull, persistent gnawing: 지루하고도 집요하게 스며드는 마음의 괴로움을 지워버리려고 팔짱을 꼈다.

2) marriage lines: marriage certificate.

even frightened. It was just like William. Was it? It was absurd, of course, it must be absurd, ridiculous. "Ha, ha, ha! Oh dear!" What was she to do? Isabel flung back in her chair and laughed till she couldn't stop laughing.

"Do, do tell us," said the others. "You must tell us."

"I'm longing to," gurgled Isabel. She sat up, gathered the letter, and waved it at them. "Gather round," she said. "Listen, it's too marvellous. A love-letter!"

"A love-letter! But how divine!" *Darling, precious Isabel.* But she had hardly begun before their laughter interrupted her.

"Go on, Isabel, it's perfect."

"It's the most marvellous find.[1)]"

"Oh, do go on, Isabel!"

God forbid, my darling, that I should be a drag on your happiness.[2)]

"Oh! oh! oh!"

"Sh! sh! sh!"

And Isabel went on. When she reached the end they were hysterical: Bobby rolled on the turf and almost sobbed.

"You must let me have it just as it is, entire, for my new book," said Dennis firmly. "I shall give it a whole chapter."

"Oh, Isabel," moaned Moira, "that wonderful bit[3)] about holding you in his arms!"

"I always thought those letters in divorce cases[4)] were made up. But they pale[5)] before this."

"Let me hold it. Let me read it, mine own self," said Bobby Kane.

But, to their surprise, Isabel crushed the letter in her hand. She was laughing no longer. She glanced quickly at them all; she looked exhausted. "No, not just now. Not just now," she stammered.

---

1) find: (*n.*) a finding; thing found.

2) *God forbid, my darling, that I should be a drag on your happiness*: 사랑하는 그대요, 내가 당신의 행복에 방해가 되기를 하나님도 허락하지 않으시지요. drag=anything that holds back; hindrance.

3) that wonderful bit: 그 놀라운 광경. bit=(풍경화의) 소품. a small part or role, as in a motion picture의 뜻이 있음.

4) divorce cases: 이혼 소송.

5) pale: turn pale.

And before they could recover she had run into the house, through the hall, up the stairs into her bedroom. Down she sat on the side of the bed. "How vile, odious, abominable, vulgar," muttered Isabel. She pressed her eyes with her knuckles and rocked to and fro. And again she saw them, but not four, more like forty, laughing, sneering, jeering, stretching out their hands while she read them William's letter. Oh, what a loathsome thing to have done. How could she have done it! *God forbid, my darling, that I should be a drag on your happiness.* William! Isabel pressed her face into the pillow. But she felt that even the grave bedroom knew her for what she was, shallow, tinkling, vain.[1)] . . .

Presently from the garden below there came voices.

"Isabel, we're all going for a bathe. Do come!"

"Come, thou wife of William!"

"Call her once before you go, call once yet!"

Isabel sat up. Now was the moment, now she must decide. Would she go with them, or stay here and write to William. Which, which should it be? "I must make up my mind." Oh, but how could there be any question? Of course she would stay here and write.

"Titania!" piped Moira.

"Isa-bel?"

No, it was too difficult. "I'll — I'll go with them, and write to William later. Some other time. Later. Not now. But I shall *certainly* write," thought Isabel hurriedly.

And, laughing, in the new way, she ran down the stairs.

1) the grave bedroom knew her for what she was, shallow, tinkling, vain . . .: 무덤같이 엄숙한 침실까지도 자기가 어떤 여자였던가를, 천박하고 겉만 번지르르한 속이 빈 여자인 것을 알고 있으리라고 느꼈다.

The Little Wife

by William March

William March (1894-1954) was born in Mobile, Alabama. He began to write short stories in 1928. His novels and short stories-many of them set in Alabama-treat small-town Southern life with something of Faulkner's starkness and artistry. But March was not an imitator, nor did he write within any fixed framework or tradition.

JOE HINCKLEY selected a seat on the shady side of the train and carefully stowed away[1] his traveling bag and his heavy, black catalogue. It was unsually hot for early June. Outside the heat waves shimmered and danced above the hot slag roadbed[2] and the muddy river that ran by the station was low between its red banks. "If it's as hot as this in June, it sure will be awful in August," he thought. He looked at his watch: 2.28-the train was five minutes late in getting out.[3] If he had known the 2.23 was going to be late he might have had time to pack his sample trunk and get it to the station, but he couldn't have anticipated that, of course. He had had so little time after getting that telegram from Mrs. Thompkins: barely time to pack his bag and check out of the hotel. Joe loosened his belt and swabbed his neck with a limp handkerchief. "It don't matter[4] so much about the trunk," he thought; "one of the boys at the hotel can express[5] it to me, or I can pick it up on my way back."

Joe noticed that one end of his catalogue case protruded slightly. With his foot he shoved it farther under the seat. It was a battered, black case, made strongly to withstand constant traveling, and

1) stowed away: hid (on a train) to get a free ride.
2) roadbed: foundation of a railroad.
3) getting out: going out.
4) don't matter: doesn't matter.
5) express: send by express.

reenforced at its corners with heavy copper cleats. One of the handles had been broken and mended with newer leather. On the front of the case there had once been stamped in gilt[1)] the firm name of Boy-kin & Rosen, Wholesale Hardware, Chattanooga, Tenn., but time had long since worn away the gold lettering.[2)]

The telegram had upset Joe: it had come so suddenly, so unexpectedly. He felt vaguely that somebody was playing a joke on[3)] him. He felt confused and helpless. It was difficult to believe that Bessie was so desperately sick. He sat for a time staring at his finger nails. Suddenly he remembered an appointment at four o'clock with the buyer for Snowdown and Sims and he rose quickly from his seat with some dim idea of telephoning or sending a message to explain his absence. Then he realized that the train was already in motion. "I'll write him a letter when I get to Mobile," said Joe to himself; "he'll understand all right when I explain the circumstances. He won't blame me for breaking that date when I tell him about my wife being so sick." He sat down heavily in his seat and again looked at his hands.

Ahead of him two young girls were leaning out of the window and waving to their friends. Their eyes were shining and their cheeks were flushed and they were laughing with excitement at the prospect of going away.

Across the aisle sat a gaunt farm-woman. Her redveined eyes protruded. Her neck was swollen with a goiter.[4)] In her arms she held a bouquet of red crêpe-myrtle[5)] which was already wilting in the heat. Beside her she had placed her straw suitcase and several bulky, paper-wrapped parcels. She gazed steadily out of the window as if afraid that someone would catch her eye and try to talk to her.

It was very hot in the coach. The small electric fan at the end of the car droned and wheezed sleepily but succeeded only in stirring

---

1) in gilt: in a thin layer of gold. 금박으로.
2) time had long since worn away the gold lettering: 금박으로 쓴 문자가 닳아 없어진지 이미 오래였었다.
3) play joke on: make fun of.
4) goiter: disease of the thyroid gland, that often cause a large swelling in the neck.
5) crêpe-myrtle: 식물이름.

up the hot air.

Joe took from his pocket the telegram that he had received from his mother-in-law and read it again: "J. G. Hinckley, American Hotel, Montgomery, Ala.[1] Come home at once. Doctor says Bessie not expected live through day. Will wire again if necessary. It was a boy. Mother."

Joe's hands clenched suddenly and then relaxed. It had all happened so suddenly; he couldn't quite get it through his head, even yet. He had taken a buyer to lunch that day and they had laughed and talked and told each other stories. Then at two o'clock he had gone back to the hotel to freshen up and the clerk had reached in his box and taken out the key to his room and the telegram. The telegram had been waiting for him for two hours the clerk said. Joe read it through twice and then looked at the address to make sure that the message was really for him. He hadn't understood. Bessie was getting along so nicely — she had had no trouble at all — and the baby wasn't expected for a month. He had arranged his itinerary[2] so that he would be with her when the baby was born. They had gone over all that and had arranged everything. And now everything was upset. He thought: "I was out talking and laughing with that buyer and the telegram was waiting here all the time." That thought hurt him. He stood repeating stupidly: "I was out laughing and selling smutty stories and that telegram was here all the time."

Joe leaned his head against the red plush of the seat. He felt numb and very tired. At first the signature "Mother" had puzzled him. He couldn't understand what his mother would be doing in Mobile with Bessie; then he realized that it was Bessie's mother who had sent the telegram. He had never thought of Bessie's mother by any name except Mrs. Thompkins.

When he had married Bessie her mother had come to live with them as a matter of course. He was rather glad of that arrangement; he was really fond of the old lady in an impersonal sort of way. Then, too, it was pleasant for Bessie to have someone with her while he

1) Ala: Alabama; a Southern State of the United States. Capital: Montgomery.
2) itinerary: route of travel; plan of travel.

was on the road.[1] His work made it impossible for him to get home oftener than every other week-end, and many times it was difficult for him to get home that often, but he had always managed to make it, one way or another. He couldn't disappoint Bessie, no matter what happened. Their year of married life had been the happiest that he had ever known. And Bessie had been happy too. Suddenly he had a clear picture of her lying on their bed, her face white with suffering, and a quick panic gripped his heart. To reassure himself he whispered: "Those doctors don't know everything. She'll be all right. Mrs. Thompkins was just excited and frightened. Everything's going to be all right!"

Ahead of him a white-haired old gentleman opened his bag and took out a traveling cap. He had some difficulty in fastening the catch while holding his straw hat in his hand, but his wife, sitting with him, took the bag and fastened it at once. Then she took his hat and held it on her lap. The wife was reading a magazine. She did not look up from the magazine when she fastened the bag.

Down the aisle came the Negro porter. He had a telegram in his hand. When he reached the center of the coach he stopped and called out: "Telegram for Mr. J. G. Hinckley!" Joe let him call the name three times before he claimed the message. The porter explained that the telegram had been delivered to the train by a messenger from the American Hotel just as the train was getting under way.[2] Joe gave the porter twenty-five cents for a tip and went back to his seat.

The country woman looked up for an instant and then turned her eyes away. The young girls giggled and whispered and looked boldly at Joe, and the old gentleman, after settling his cap firmly on his head, took a cigar from his case and went to the smoking-room.

Joe's throat felt tight and he noticed that his hands were shaking. He wanted to put his head on the window-sill but he was afraid that people would think him sick and try to talk to him. He placed the unopened telegram on the seat beside him and stared at it for a long time. At last he re-read the first telegram very slowly. "It must be

1) on the road: travelling, esp. as a salesman.
2) under way: going on; in motion.

from Mrs. Thompkins, all right," he thought, "she said she'd wire again if— " Then he thought: "It may not be from Mrs. Thompkins at all; it may be from somebody else; it may be from Boykin & Rosen about that cancellation in Meridian.[1] That's who it's from: it's from the House, it's not from Mrs. Thompkins at all!" He looked up quickly and saw that the two young girls had turned around and were watching him, making laughing remarks to each other behind their hands.

He arose from his seat feeling weak and slightly nauseated, the unopened telegram in his hand. He passed through several coaches until he reached the end of the train and went out on the rear vestibule. He had a sudden wish to jump from the end of the train and run off into the woods, but a brakeman was there tinkering with a red lantern and Joe realized that such an act would look very strange. When the brakeman looked up and saw Joe's face he put down his lantern and asked: "Are you feeling all right, mister?" Joe said, "Yes, I'm feeling all right but it's a little hot, though." Finally the brakeman finished his job and left and Joe was very glad of that. He wanted to be alone. He didn't want anybody around him.

The rails clicked rhythmically and the wilted country-side flew past. A little Negro girl . . . in a patched pink dress . . . ran down to the track . . . and waved her hand. A lame old country man . . . ploughing in his stumpy field . . . pulled up his mangy mule . . . to stare at the passing train. The rails clattered and clicked and the train flew over the hot slag roadbed. "There's no need of going so fast," thought Joe, "we've got all the time in the world." He felt sick. In the polished metal of the car he caught a distorted glimpse of his face. It was white and terrified. He thought: "No wonder that brakeman asked me how I was feeling." Then he thought: "Do I look so bad that people can tell it?" That worried him. He didn't' want people to notice him or to talk to him. There was nothing that anybody could say, after all.

He kept turning the telegram over in his hand thinking: "I've got to open it now; I've got to open it and read it." Finally he said aloud:

---

1) in Meridian: at noon.

"It's not true! I don't believe it!" He repeated these words a number of times and then he said: "It's from the House about that cancellation in Meridian — it isn't from Mrs. Thompkins at all." He tore the unopened telegram into tiny bits and threw the pieces from the end of the train. A wind fluttered and shimmered the yellow fragments before they settled down lightly on the hard, hot roadbed. He thought: "They look like a cloud of yellow butterflies dancing and settling that way." Immediately he felt better. He drew back his shoulders and sucked in lungfuls of the country air.[1] "Everything's all right," he said. "I'm going home to see the little wife and everything's all right." He laughed happily. He felt like a man who has just escaped some terrible calamity. When he could no longer see the scraps of paper on the track he went back to his seat humming a tune. He felt very gay and immensely relieved.

Joe reached his seat just as the conductor came through the train. He nodded pleasantly as he gave up[2] his ticket.

"Don't let anybody talk you out of a free ride,[3]" he said. "No chance of that, Cap![4]" said the conductor.

Joe laughed with ringing heartiness and the conductor looked at him in surprise. Then he laughed a little himself. "You sure are in a good humor, considering how hot it is," he said.

"And why shouldn't I be in a good humor?" asked Joe. "I'm going home to see the little wife." Then he whispered, as if it were a great secret, "It's a boy!"

"That's fine, that's simply fine!" said the conductor. He put his papers and his tickets on the seat and shook Joe's hand. Joe blushed and laughed again. As the conductor moved off he nudged Joe's ribs and said: "Give my regards to the madam."

"I sure will," said Joe happily.

Joe was sorry that the conductor couldn't stay longer. He felt an imperative[5] need of talking to someone. He felt that he must talk

---

1) sucked in lungfuls of the country air: 맑은 공기를 가슴 깊이 들여 마셨다.
2) gave up: handed over.
3) a free ride: 무임승차.
4) Cap: Captain; A train conductor.
5) imperative: urgent.

about Bessie to someone. He looked around the car to see if he knew anybody on the train. The two young girls smiled at him. Joe understood perfectly; they were just two nice kids going on a trip. Either one, alone, would never think of smiling at a strange man but being together changed things all the way around. That made it an exciting adventure, something to be laughed over and discussed later with their friends. Joe decided that he would go over and talk to them. He walked over casually and seated himself.

"Well, where are you young ladies going?" he asked.

"Don't you think that you have a great deal of nerve?[1]" asked the black-eyed girl.

"Sure I have. I wouldn't be the best hardware salesman on the road if I didn't have a lot of nerve," said Joe pleasantly.

Both of the girls laughed at that and Joe knew that everything was all right. He decided that the blue-eyed girl was the prettier of the two but the black-eyed girl had more snap.[2]

"We're getting off at Flomaton," said the blue-eyed girl.

"We've been in school in Montgomery," said the black-eyed girl.

"We're going home for the summer vacation."

"And we want the cock-eyed[3] world to know we're glad of it!"

Joe looked at them gravely. "Don't make a mistake, young ladies; get all the education you can. You'll regret it later on if you don't."

Both the girls started laughing. They put their arms around each other and laughed until tears came into their eyes. Joe laughed too although he wondered what the joke was. After a while the girls stopped laughing, but a sudden giggle from the blue-eyed girl set them off again, worse than before.

"This is awfully silly!" said the black-eyed girl.

"Please don't think us rude," gasped the blue-eyed girl.

"What's the joke?" asked Joe, who was really laughing as much as either of the girls.

---

1) nerve: (Slang) courage; guts.
2) snap: (Colloq.) liveliness; dash; vim.
3) cock-eyed: (Slang) foolish; silly.

"You sounded so — so — " explained the blue-eyed girl.

"So damned *fatherly*!" finished the black-eyed girl.

They went off into another whirlwind of mirth, laughing and hugging each other. The old lady across the aisle put down her magazine and started laughing too, but the woman with the goiter held her bouquet of crêpe-myrtle rigidly and stared out of the window.

Joe waited until the girls had exhausted themselves. Finally they wiped their eyes and opened their vanity cases[1] to look at themselves in their mirrors and to repowder their faces. He said:

"Well, I guess I ought to sound fatherly: I just got a telegram saying that I was a parent for the first time."

That interested the young girls and they crowded him with questions: they wanted to know all about it. Joe felt very happy. As he started to talk he noticed that the old lady had been listening and that she had moved over in her seat in order to hear better. Joe felt friendly toward everybody: "Won't you come over and join us?" he asked.

"Yes, indeed," said the old lady and Joe moved over and made a place for her.

"Now tell us all about it!" demanded the blue-eyed girl.

"You must be very happy," said the old lady.

"I sure am happy," said Joe. Then he added: "There's not a whole lot to tell except that I got a telegram from Mrs. Thompkins — Mrs. Thompkins is my mother-in-law — saying that Bessie had given birth to a fine boy and that both of them were doing just fine: the doctor said that he'd never seen anybody do so well before, but of course my wife wanted me to be with her and so I just dropped everything and here I am. You see Bessie and I have only been married for a year. We've been very happy. The only bad thing is that I don't get home very often, but it wouldn't do to have everything perfect in the world, would it? She sure is the finest little wife a man ever had. She don't complain at all about my being away so much, but some day we hope to have things different."

"There isn't anything nicer than a baby," said the blue-eyed girl.

1) vanity case: case containing a small mirror, powder, rouge, etc., carried by women.

"What are you going to name him?" asked the old lady.

"Well, Bessie wants to name him for me, but I can't see much sense in that. My first name's Joe and I think that's a little common don't you? But I'll leave the naming part up to Bessie. She can name him anything she wants to. She sure has been a fine little wife to me."

Joe started talking rapidly. He told in detail of the first time he had met Bessie. It had been in the home of Jack Barnes, one of the boys he had met on the road, and he had been invited over for dinner and a little stud poker later. Mrs. Barnes didn't play poker so Bessie, who lived across the street, had been invited over to keep Mrs. Barnes company while the men played. He had liked Bessie at once and the boys had kidded him about not keeping his mind on the game. He had never told anybody this before, but when the boys started kidding him he made up his mind not to look at Bessie again as he didn't want her to think that he was fresh,[1)] but he couldn't stop looking at her and every time he caught her eye she would smile in a sweet, friendly sort of way. Finally everybody noticed it and they started joking Bessie too, but she hadn't minded at all. He had lost $14.50 that night, but he had met Bessie. You couldn't call Bessie exactly beautiful but she was sweet and nice. Bessie was the sort of girl that any man would want to marry.

He told of their courtship. He quoted whole paragraphs from letters that she had written to prove a particular point which he had brought up. Bessie hadn't liked him especially, not right at first, at any rate; of course she had liked him as a friend from the first but not in any serious way. There were one or two other fellows hanging around, too. Bessie had a great deal of attention; she could have gone out every night with a different man if she had wanted to. Being on the road all the time had been pretty much of a disadvantage. He didn't have an opportunity to see her often. Or maybe that was an advantage —anyway he wrote her every day. Then, finally, they had become engaged. She hadn't even let him kiss her until then. He knew from

1) fresh: (Slang) too bold; impudent.

the first that she would make a wonderful little wife but he was still puzzled why a girl as superior as Bessie would want to marry *him.*

He talked on and on, rapidly—feverishly. He told how he had once determined not to get married at all, but that was before he had met Bessie. She had changed all that. Two hours passed before he knew it. His audience was getting bored, but Joe didn't realize it.

Finally the old gentleman with the cap came back from the smoking-room and his wife, glad of a chance to get away, made her excuses and went over to sit with him. Joe smiled and nodded, but paused only a moment in his story. He was in the midst of a long description of Mrs. Thompkins. Mrs. Thompkins wasn't at all like the comic supplement mother-in-law. Quite the contrary. He didn't see how he and Bessie would get along without her. To show you the sort of woman she really was, she always took his side in any dispute —not that he and Bessie ever quarreled! Oh, no! But occasionally they had little friendly discussions like all other married couples and Mrs. Thompkins always took his side of the argument. That was unusual, wasn't it? Joe talked and talked and talked, totally unconscious of the passing of time.

Finally the train reached Flomaton and the porter came to help the girls off with their bags. They were very glad to get away. They were getting a little nervous. There was something about Joe that they couldn't understand. At first they had thought him just jolly and high spirited, but after a time they came to the conclusion that he must be a little drunk, or, possibly, slightly demented. For the past hour they had been nudging each other significantly.

Joe helped them off the train and on to the station platform. Just as the train pulled out the black-eyed girl waved her hand and said: "Give my love to Bessie and the son and heir," and the blue-eyed girl said: "Be sure and kiss the baby for me."

"I sure will," said Joe.

After the train had passed the girls looked at each other for a moment. Then they started laughing. Finally the black-eyed girl said: "Well, Bessie certainly has him roped and tied." The blue-eyed girl said: "Did you ever see anything like that in your life before?"

Joe came into the coach again "Just a couple of nice kids," he thought to himself. He looked at his watch. It was 5.25. He was surprised. The time had passed very quickly. "It won't be long now before I'm in Mobile," he thought.

He went back to his seat, but he was restless. He decided that he would have a cigarette. He found three men in the smoker. One of them was an old man with a tuft of gray whiskers. His face was yellow and sunken and blue veins stood out on his hands. He was chewing tobacco gravely and spitting into the brass cuspidor.[1] The second man was large and flabby. When he laughed his eyes disappeared entirely and his fat belly shook. His finger nails were swollen and his underlip hung down in a petulant droop. The third man was dark and nervous looking. He had on his little finger a ring with a diamond much too large.

They were telling jokes and laughing when Joe came in. Joe wanted to talk to them about Bessie, but he couldn't bring her name up in such an atmosphere. Suddenly he thought: "I was laughing and telling smutty[2] stories with that buyer in Montgomery and the telegram was there all the time." His face contracted with pain. He crushed the thought from his mind. Quickly he threw away his cigarette and went back to his seat.

A bright-skinned waiter came through the train announcing the first call for dinner. At first Joe thought that he would have his dinner on the train as that would break the monotony of the trip and help pass the time, but immediately he remembered that Mrs. Thompkins would have dinner for him at home — a specially prepared dinner with all of the things that he liked. "I'll wait until I get home," thought Joe. "I wouldn't disappoint Mrs. Thompkins and the little wife for the world after they went to all that trouble for me."

Again he felt that curious, compulsive need of talking about Bessie to someone. He had a feeling that as long as he talked about her she would remain safe. He saw the old lady and her husband in their seat eating a lunch which they had brought and he decided to go

1) cuspidor: container to spit into; spittoon.

2) smutty: dirty; indecent; obscene.

over and talk with them. "Can I come over and talk to you folks?" asked Joe.

"Certainly, sir," said the old gentleman with the cap. Then, in order to make conversation he said: "My wife has been telling me that you are going home to see your new son."

"That's right," said Joe, "that's right." He started talking rap, hardly pausing for breath. The old lady looked at her husband reproachfully. "Now see what you started!" her glance seemed to say.

Joe talked of his wedding. It had been very quiet. Bessie was the sort of a girl who didn't go in for[1] a lot of show. There had been present only a few members of the family and one or two close friends. George Orcutt who traveled a line of rugs[2] out of New York had been his best man.[3] Bessie was afraid that someone would try to play a joke on them: something like tying tin cans to the automobile that was to take them to the station or marking their baggage with chalk. But everything had gone off smoothly. The Barneses had been at the wedding, of course: he had met Bessie in their home and they were such close neighbors that they couldn't overlook them, but almost nobody else outside the family was there.

Then he told of the honeymoon they had spent in New Orleans; all the places they had visited there and just what Bessie had thought and said about each one. He talked on and on and on. He told of the first weeks of their married life and how happy they were. He told what a splendid cook Bessie was and what an excellent house, how much she had loved the home he had bought for her and her delight when she knew that she was going to have a baby.

The old gentleman was staring at Joe in a puzzled manner. He was wondering if he hadn't better call the conductor as it was his private opinion that Joe had a shot of cocaine in him. The old lady had folded her hands like a martyr. She continued to look at her husband with an "I-told-you-so!" expression.

Joe had lost all idea of time. He talked on and on, rapidly, excitedly.

---

1) go in for: (Colloq.) try to do; take part in; spend time and energy at.
2) who traveled a line of rugs: 한 줄의 융단을 팔고 다녔던.
3) best man: chief attendant of the bridegroom at a wedding.

He had got as far as Bessie's plans for the child's education when the porter touched him on the arm and told him that they were pulling into the station at Mobile. He came to himself with a start and looked at his watch: 7.35! He didn't believe it possible that two hours had passed so quickly.

"It sure has been a pleasure talking to you folks," said Joe.

"Oh, that's all right," said the man with the cap.

Joe gave the porter a tip and stepped off the train jauntily. As he turned to pick up his bag he saw that the woman with the goiter was staring at him. He walked over to the window that framed her gaunt face. "Good-bye, lady; I hope you have a nice trip." The woman answered: "The doctors said it wasn't no use operating on me. I waited too long." "Well that's fine! — That sure is fine!" said Joe. He laughed gaily and waved his hand. He picked up his bag and his catalogue case and followed the people through the gate. The woman with the goiter stared at him until he was out of sight.

On the other side of the iron fence Joe saw Mrs. Thompkins. She was dressed in black and she wore a black veil. Joe went over to her briskly and Mrs. Thompkins put her arms around him and kissed him twice. "Poor Joe!" she said. Then she looked at his smiling, excited face with amazement. Joe noticed that her eyes were red and swollen.

"Didn't you get my telegram?" she asked. Joe wrinlked his brow in an effort to remember. Finally he said: "Oh, sure. I got it at the hotel."

"Did you get my second telegram?" insisted Mrs. Thompkins.

She looked steadily into Joe's eyes. A feeling of terror swept over him. He knew that he could no longer lie to himself. He could no longer keep Bessie alive by talking about her. His face was suddenly twisted with pain and his jaw trembled like a child's. He leaned against the iron fence for support and Mrs. Thompkins held his hand and said: "You can't give in.[1] You got to be a man. You can't give in like that, Joe!"

Finally he said: "I didn't read your telegram. I didn't want to know

1) give in: yield, surrender.

that she was dead. I wanted to keep her alive a little longer." He sat down on an empty baggage truck and hid his face in his hands. He sat there for a long time while Mrs. Thompkins stood guard over him, her black veil trailing across his shoulder.

"Joe!" she said patiently. . . "Joe! . . ."

A man in a dirty uniform came up. "I'm sorry, Mister, but you'll have to move. We got to use that truck." Joe picked up his catalogue case and his bag and followed Mrs. Thompkins out of the station.

Mr. Know-All[1)]

by William Somerset Maugham

William Somerset Maugham (1874-1965) was born in Paris, on Jan. 25, 1874, where his father was solicitor to the British embassy, Somerset Maugham was orphaned by the death of his mother when he was 2 and of his father when he was 8. He was reared by a paternal uncle, a clergyman, and at 13 was sent to King's school, Cambridge, intended for Oxford and preparation for the Church. Wanting to write, he obtained his uncle' s permission to go to Heidelberg for a time. He chose the profession of medicine and spent 6 years in training at a London hospital. A year as an intern in the Lambeth slums followed, but he never practiced. For 10 years he wrote and lived in poverty in Paris.

The titles of some of Maugham's early novels were familiar to a whole generation of readers: *Of Human Bondage* (1915) *The Moon and Six pence* (1919), *Ashenden;* or, *The British Agent* (1938), and *Cakes and Ale:* or, *The Skeleton in the Cupboard* (1930). A later novel that had something of the same success was *The Razor"s Edge* (1944). Among his plays, perhaps best known and much produced was *Rain* (1922). An early auto biograph is *The Summing Up* (1938). Praised by some critics for his craftsmanship and professionalism, he wrote much on the subject of fiction: *Essays-Great Novelists and Their Novels* (1948); *A Writer's Notebook* (1949); and *The Art of Fiction* (1955). His *Travel Books* appeared in 1955; *The Magician, A Novel, Together with a Fragment of Auto-biography* in 1956; and essays titled *Points of View* in 1958. In his last years he worked on an auto biograph to be published posthumously.

I WAS prepared to dislike[2)] Max Kelada even before I knew him. The war had just finished and the passenger traffic in the ocean-going liners[3)] was heavy.[4)] Accommodation[5)] was very hard to get and you had to put up with[6)] whatever the agents chose to offer you. You

1) know-all: 무엇이나 아는 체하는 사람. (=know-it-all)
2) I was prepared to dislike: 그를 싫어하게끔 되어 있었다.
3) the ocean-going liners: 대양횡단 정기여객선.
4) was heavy: 승객이 많았다.
5) accommodation: traveling space as in a railroad, train, ship or airplane. 여기서는 선실.
6) put up with: endure, bear with patience; tolerate.

could not hope for a cabin to yourself[1] and I was thankful to be given one in which there were only two berths. But when I was told the name of my companion my heart sank. It suggested closed port-holes and the night air rigidly excluded. It was bad enough to share a cabin for fourteen days with anyone (I was going from San Francisco to Yokohama), but I should have looked upon it with less dismay if my fellow passenger's name had been Smith or Brown.[2]

When I went on board I found Mr. Kelada's luggage already below.[3] I did not like the look of it; there were too many labels on the suitcases, and the wardrobe trunk was too big. He had unpacked his toilet things, and I observed that he was a patron of the excellent Monsieur Coty,[4] for I saw on the washing-stand his scent,[5] his hairwash and his brilliantine.[6] Mr. Kelada's brushes, ebony with his monogram in gold, would have been all the better for a scrub.[7] I did not at all l like Mr. Kelada. I made my way into the smoking-room. I called for a pack of cards and began to play patience.[8] I had scarcely started before a man came up to me and asked me if he was right in thinking my name was so-and-so.

"I am Mr. Kelada," he added, with a smile that showed a row of flashing teeth, and sat down.

"Oh, yes, we're sharing a cabin, I think."

"Bit of luck, I call it. You never know who you're going to be put in with. I was jolly glad when I heard you were English. I'm all for[9] us English sticking together when we're abroad, if you understand what I mean."

I blinked.

---

1) a cabin to yourself: 혼자 쓰는 선실.
2) Smith or Brown: 영미에서 가장 흔한 이름.
3) below: 선실에 운반되어.
4) the excellent Monsieur Coty: 코티회사의 고급 화장품.
5) scent: perfume.
6) brilliantine: an oily liquid used to make the hair glossy.
7) would have been all the better for a scrub: 마룻바닥을 문지르는데 쓰는 편이 더 알맞다. 그만큼 큰 머릿솔이라는 뜻.
8) patience: solitaire 혼자 노는 카드놀이, 카드 점.
9) I'm all for: 절대 찬성이다.

"Are you English?" I asked, perhaps tactlessly.

"Rather.[1] You don't think I look like an American, do you? British to the backbone,[2] that's what I am."

To prove it, Mr. Kelada took out of his pocket a passport and airily waved it under my nose.

King George has many strange subjects. Mr. Kelada was short and of sturdy build, clean-shaven and dark-skinned, with a fleshy, hooked nose and very large, lustrous and liquid eyes. His long black hair was sleek and curly. He spoke with a fluency in which there was nothing English[3] and his gestures were exuberant. I felt pretty sure that a closer inspection of that British passport would have betrayed the fact that Mr. Kelada was born under a bluer sky[4] than is generally seen in England.

"What will you have?" he asked me.

I looked at him doubtfully. Prohibition was in force[5] and to all appearances the ship was bone-dry.[6] When I am not thirsty I do not know which I dislike more, ginger-ale or lemon squash. But Mr. Kelada flashed an oriental smile at me.

"Whisky and soda or a dry Martini,[7] you have only to say the word."

From each of his hip-pockets he fished a flask and laid them on the table before me. I chose the Martini, and calling the steward he ordered a tumbler of ice and a couple of glasses.

"A very good cocktail," I said.

"Well, there are plenty more where that came from, and if you've got any friends on board, you tell them you've got a pal[8] who's got all the liquor in the world."

Mr. Kelada was chatty. He talked of New York and of San Francisco.

---

1) Rather: Yes, indeed!; Certainly!; Very much so!.
2) to the backbone: 뼈 끝까지.
3) there was nothing English: 영국인이 말하는 영어다운 곳은 전혀 없다.
4) under a bluer sky: 지중해 연안의 제국을 말함.
5) Prohibition was in force: 금주법이 실시 중이었다.
6) bone-dry: dry as a bone; completely dry; with no intoxicating drink whatever.
7) dry Martini: cocktail의 일종.
8) pal: intimate friend.

He discussed plays, pictures and politics. He was patriotic. The Union Jack is an impressive piece of drapery, but when it is flourished by a gentleman from Alexandria[1] or Beirut,[2] I cannot but feel that it loses somewhat in dignity. Mr. Kelada was familiar. I do not wish to put on airs,[3] but I cannot help feeling that it is seemly[4] in a total stranger to put mister before my name when he addresses me. Mr. Kelada, doubtless to set me at my ease, used no such formality. I did not like Mr. Kelada. I had put aside the cards when he sat down, but now, thinking that for this first occasion our conversation had lasted long enough, I went on with my game.

"The three on the four,"[5] said Mr. Kelada.

There is nothing more exasperating when you are playing patience than to be told where to put the card you have turned up before you have had a chance to look for yourself.

"It's coming out,[6] it's coming out," he cried. "The ten in the knave[7]"

With rage and hatred in my heart I finished. Then he seized the pack.

"Do you like card tricks?"

"No, I hate card tricks," I answered.

"Well, I'll just show you this one."

He showed me three. Then I said I would go down to the dining room and get my seat at table.

"Oh, that's all right," he said. "I've already taken a seat for you. I thought that as we were in the same state-room we might just as well sit at the same table."

I did not like Mr. Kelada.

I not only shared a cabin with him and ate three meals a day at the same table, but I could not walk on the deck without his joining me.

---

1) Alexandria: Egypt. 도시.
2) Beirut: Lebanon의 수도.
3) put on airs: 거만하게 굴다.
4) seemly: suitable; proper.
5) The three on the four: Put the three on the four.
6) It's coming out: 싹수가 보인다.
7) knave: the jack, a playing card with a picture of a servant or soldier on it.

It was impossible to snub him.[1] It never occurred to him that he was not wanted. He was certain that you were as glad to see him as he was to see you. In your own house you might have kicked him downstairs and slammed the door in his face without the suspicion dawning on him that[2] he was not a welcome visitor. He was a good mixer,[3] and in three days knew everyone on board. He ran[4] everything. He managed the sweeps,[5] conducted the auctions, collected money for prizes at the sports, got up[6] quoit[7] and golf matches, organized the concert and arranged the fancy dress ball. He was everywhere and always. He was certainly the best-hated man[8] in the ship. We called him Mr. Know-All, even to his face. He took it as a compliment. But it was at meal time that he was most intolerable. For the better part of an hour then he had us at his mercy.[9] He was hearty, jovial, loquacious and argumentative. He knew everything better than anybody else, and it was an affront to his overweening vanity that you should disagree with him. He would not drop a subject, however unimportant, till he had brought you round[10] to his way of thinking. The possibility that he could be mistaken never occurred to him. He was the chap who knew. We sat at the doctor's table. Mr. Kelada would certainly have had it all his own way, for the doctor was lazy and I was frigidly indifferent, except for a man called Ramsay who sat there also. He was as dogmatic as Mr. Kelada and resented bitterly the Levantine's[11] cocksureness. The discussions they had were acrimonious and

---

1) It was impossible to snub him: It was impossible to treat him coldly, scornfully, or with contempt.
2) without the suspicion dawning on him that: 꿈에도 그런 의혹은 품지 않고.
3) good mixer: 사교가.
4) ran: managed.
5) sweeps: sweepstakes; a lottery in which each person puts up a stake of money in a common fund which is given as the prize to the winner.
6) got up: organized.
7) quoit: a game in which players throw rings at a peg in the ground.
8) the best-hated man: the most hated man.
9) he had us at his mercy: 그는 우리를 마음대로 했다. at his mercy=in his power.
10) brought you round: bring round=convince; persuade.
11) Levantine: 레반트 사람. Levant는 동부 지중해의 여러 섬과 연안 제국, 특히 시리아, 레바논, 이스라엘을 말한다.

interminable.

Ramsay was in the American Consular Service, and was stationed at Kobe.[1] He was a great heavy fellow from the Middle West, with loose fat under a tight skin, and he bulged out of his ready-made clothes.

He was on his way back to resume his post, having been on a flying visit to New York to fetch his wife, who had been spending a year at home. Mrs. Ramsay was a very pretty little thing, with pleasant manners and a sense of humour. The Consular Service is ill paid,[2] and she was dressed always very simply; but she knew how to wear her clothes. She achieved an effect of quiet distinction. I should not have paid any particular attention to her but that she possessed a quality that may be common enough in women, but nowadays is not obvious in their demeanour. You could not look at her without being struck by her modesty. It shone in her like a flower on a coat.

One evening at dinner the conversation by chance drifted to the subject of pearls. There had been in the papers a good deal of talk about the culture pearls[3] which the cunning Japanese were making, and the doctor remarked that they must inevitably diminish the value of real ones. They were very good already; they would soon be perfect. Mr. Kelada, as was his habit, rushed the new topic. He told us all that was to be known about pearls. I do not believe Ramsay knew anything about them at all, but he could not resist the opportunity to have a fling at[4] the Levantine, and in five minutes we were in the middle of a heated argument. I had seen Mr.Kelada vehement and voluble before, but never so voluble and vehement as now. At last something that Ramsay said stung him, for he thumped the table and shouted:

"Well, I ought to know what I am talking about. I'm going to Japan just to look into[5] this Japanese pearl business. I'm in the trade and there's not a man in it who won't tell you that what I say about pearls

1) Kobe: 일본의 항구 도시(神戶).
2) is ill paid: 보수가 좋지 않다.
3) culture pearl: 양식 진주.
4) have a fling at: ~와 한판 해 보다.
5) look into: inspect; examine.

goes.[1] I know all the best pearls in the world, and what I don't know about pearls isn't worth knowing."

Here was news for us, for Mr. Kelada, with all his loquacity[2] had never told anyone what his business was. We only knew vaguely that he was going to Japan on some commercial errand. He looked round the table triumphantly.

"They'll never be able to get a culture pearl that an expert like me can't tell with half an eye."[3] He pointed to a chain that Mrs. Ramsay wore. "You take my word for it,[4] Mrs. Ramsay, that chain you're wearing will never be worth a cent less than it is now."

Mrs. Ramsay in her modest way flushed a little and slipped the chain inside her dress. Ramsay leaned forward. He gave us all a look and a smile flickered in his eyes.

"That's a pretty chain of Mrs. Ramsay's, isn't it?"

"I noticed it at once," answered Mr. Kelada. "Gee, I said to myself, those are pearls all right."

"I didn't buy it myself, of course. I'd be interested to know how much you think it cost."

"Oh, in the trade[5] somewhere round[6] fifteen thousand dollars.

But if it was bought on Fifth Avenue[7] I shouldn't be surprised to hear that anything up to thirty thousand was paid for it."

Ramsay smiled grimly.

"You'll be surprised to hear that Mrs. Ramsay bought that string at a department store the day before we left New York, for eighteen dollars."

Mr. Kelada flushed.

"Rot.[8] It's not only real, but it's as fine a string for its size as I've ever seen."

---

1) go: contribute 도움이 되다.
2) loquacity: talkativeness.
3) with half an eye: 얼핏 보아.
4) You take my word for it: 내 말을 믿으시오.
5) the trade: 동업자.
6) somewhere round: 대충 ~쯤.
7) Fifth Avenue: New York의 번화가.
8) Rot: Nonsense.

"Will you bet on it? I'll bet you a hundred dollars its imitation."

"Done."[1]

"Oh, Elmer, you can't bet on a certainty," said Mrs. Ramsay. She had a little smile on her lips and her tone was gently deprecating.

"Can't I? If I get a chance of easy money like that I should be all sorts of a fool not to take it."

"But how can it be proved?" she continued. "It's only my word against Mr. Kelada's."

"Let me look at the chain, and if it's imitation I'll tell you quickly enough. I can afford to lose a hundred dollars," said Mr. Kelada.

"Take it off, dear. Let the gentleman look at it as much as he wants."

Mrs. Ramsay hesitated a moment. She put her hands to the clasp.

"I can't undo it," she said, "Mr. Kelada will just have to take my word for it."

I had a sudden suspicion that something unfortunate was about to occur, but I could think of nothing to say.

Ramsay jumped up.

"I'll undo it."

He handed the chain to Mr. Kelada. The Levantine took a magnifying glass from his pocket and closely examined it. A smile of triumph spread over his smooth and swarthy face. He handed back the chain. He was about to speak. Suddenly he caught sight of Mrs. Ramsay's face. It was so white that she looked as though she were about to faint. She was staring at him with wide and terrified eyes. They held a desperate appeal; it was so clear that I wondered why her husband did not see it.

Mr. Kelada stopped with his mouth open. He flushed deeply. You could almost see the effort he was making over himself.[2]

"I was mistaken," he said. "It's a very good imitation, but of course as soon as I looked through my glass I saw that it wasn't real. I think eighteen dollars is just about as much as the damned thing's worth."

He took out his pocket-book and from it a hundred-dollar note. He handed it to Ramsay without a word.

1) Done: "Will you bet on it?"에 대해서 "Agree!"의 뜻.

2) the effort he was making over himself: 자제하려는 노력.

"Perhaps that'll teach you not to be so cocksure another time, my young friend," said Ramsay as he took the note.

I noticed that Mr. Kelada's hands were trembling.

The story spread over the ship as stories do,[1] and he had to put up with a good deal of chaff[2] that evening. It was a fine joke that Mr. Know-All had been caught out.[3] But Mrs. Ramsay retired to her state-room[4] with a headache.

Next morning I got up and began to shave. Mr. Kelada lay on his bed smoking a cigarette. Suddenly there was a small scraping sound and I saw a letter pushed under the door. I opened the door and looked out. There was nobody there. I picked up the letter and saw that it was addressed to Max Kelada. The name was written in block letters.[5] I handed it to him.

"Who's this from?" He opened it. "Oh!"

He took out of the envelope, not a letter, but a hundred dollar note. He looked at me and again he reddened. He tore the envelope into little bits and gave them to me.

"Do you mind just throwing them out of the porthole?"

I did as he asked, and then I looked at him with a smile.

"No one likes being made to look a perfect damned fool," he said.

"Were the pearls real?"

"If I had a pretty little wife I shouldn't let her spend a year in New York while I stayed at Kobe," said he.

At that moment I did not entirely dislike Mr. Kelada. He reached out for[6] his pocket-book and carefully put in it the hundred-dollar note.

1) as stories do: 모든 이야기가 그렇듯이.
2) chaff: 놀림.
3) had been caught out: 꼬리가 잡혔다.
4) state-room: a private room on a ship.
5) in block letters: 활자체로 (필적을 알 수 없게 하려고).
6) reached out for: 팔을 뻗어 ~을 잡았다.

The Sojourner

by Carson McCullers

Carson McCullers (1917-67), born in Columbia, Georgia, often is compared with such diverse writers of the South as William Faulkner and Katherine Anne Porter — proof that she writes in a unique way. Expecting to have a carrier in music, she studied in the Juilliard School of Music and Columbia University. She broke off her schooling, took up writing, and at the precocious age of twenty-two published her first novel. Immediately she was recognized as an important new talent, and readers have eagerly awaited her relatively infrequent, subsequent works. Her second novel, *Reflections in a Golden Eye,* an account of a grotesque adventure into the underworld of the emotions, was ranked high among writings in the new Gothic school. Her third novel, *The Member of the Wedding,* charmingly and wistfully portrayed a Southern family, in particular the adolescent girl through whose eyes the events were seen. Critics abroad as well as in the United States have praised Mrs. McCullers' sense of construction and character, her feeling, her lucidity, and her poetic symbolism.

THE TWILIGHT border between sleep and waking was a Roman one this morning: splashing fountains and arched, narrow streets, the golden lavish city[1] of blossoms and agesoft stone. Sometimes in this semi-consciousness he sojourned again in Paris, or war German rubble,[2] or Swiss skiing and a snow hotel. Sometimes, also, in a fallow Georgia field[3] at hunting dawn. Rome it was this morning in the yearless region of dreams.

John Ferris awoke in a room in a New York hotel. He had the feeling that something unpleasant was awaiting him — what it was, he did not know. The feeling, submerged by matinal necessities,[4] lingered even after he had dressed and gone downstairs. It was a

---

1) the golden lavish city: 호화찬란한 도시.
2) war German rubble: 독일의 전쟁 폐허.
3) a fallow Georgia field: 조지아주의 휴한지(休閑地). fallow=plowed and left unseeded for a season or more; uncultivated; inactive.
4) submerged by matinal necessities: 아침의 일과 때문에 가라앉은.

cloudless autumn day and the pale sunlight sliced between the pastel skyscrapers. Ferris went into the next-door drugstore and sat at the end booth next to the window glass that overlooked the sidewalk. He ordered an American breakfast with scrambled eggs and sausage.

Ferris had come from Paris to his father's funeral which had taken place the week before in his home town in Georgia. The shock of death had made him aware of youth already passed. His hair was receding[1] and the veins in his now naked temples were pulsing and prominent and his body was spare except for an incipient belly bulge.[2] Ferris had loved his father and the bond between them had once been extraordinarily close — but the years had somehow unraveled this filial devotion;[3] the death, expected for a long time, had left him with an unforeseen dismay. He had stayed as long as possible to be near his mother and brothers at home. His plane for Paris was to leave the next morning.

Ferris pulled out his address book to verify a number. He turned the pages with growing attentiveness. Names and addresses from New York, the capitals of Europe, a few faint ones from his home state in the South. Faded, printed names, sprawled drunken ones.[4] Betty Wills: a random love, married now. Charlie Williams: wounded in the Hurtgen Forest, unheard of since. Grand old Williams — did he live or die? Don Walker: a B.T.O. in television, getting rich. Henry Green: hit the skids[5] after the war, in a sanitarium now, they say. Cozie Hall: he had heard that she was dead. Heedless, laughing Cozie — it was strange to think that she too, silly girl, could die. As Ferris closed the address book, he suffered a sense of hazard, transience,[6] almost of fear.

---

1) His hair was receding: 이마가 벗겨지고 있었다.

2) his body was spare except for an incipient belly bulge: 그의 몸집은 배가 나오기 시작하지 않았더라면 여윈 편이었다. except for=~이 없다면. incipient=just beginning; in an early stage.

3) the years had somehow unraveled this filial devotion: 세월이 흘러감에 아버지에 대한 사랑이 어떻게 된 셈인지 식어 버렸다. unravel=pull apart; come apart.

4) sprawled drunken ones: 술 취한 듯 비틀비틀한 이름들. ones는 names.

5) hit the skids: headed for dismissal, failure, or other disaster 몰락한.

6) transience: also transiency. quality or state of being transient 무상, 덧없음.

It was then that his body jerked suddenly. He was staring out of the window when there, on the sidewalk, passing by, was his ex-wife. Elizabeth passed quite close to him, walking slowly. He could not understand the wild quiver of his heart, nor the following sense of recklessness and grace[1] that lingered after she was gone.

Quickly Ferris paid his check and rushed out to the sidewalk. Elizabeth stood on the corner waiting to cross Fifth Avenue. He hurried toward her meaning to speak,[2] but the lights changed as she crossed the street before he reached her. Ferris followed. On the other side he could easily have overtaken her, but he found himself lagging unaccountably. Her fair brown hair was plainly rolled, and as he watched her Ferris recalled that once his father had remarked that Elizabeth had a "beautiful carriage."[3] She turned at the next corner and Ferris followed, although by now his intention to overtake her had disappeared. Ferris questioned the bodily disturbance that the sight of Elizabeth aroused in him, the dampness of his hands, the hard heartstrokes.[4]

It was eight years since Ferris had last seen his ex-wife. He knew that long ago she had married again. And there were children. During recent years he had seldom thought of her. But at first, after the divorce, the loss had almost destroyed him. Then after the anodyne of time,[5] he had loved again, and then again. Jeannine, she was now. Certainly his love for his ex-wife was long since past. So why the unhinged body, the shaken mind? He knew only that his clouded heart was oddly dissonant with[6] the sunny, candid autumn day. Ferris wheeled suddenly, and walking with long strides, almost running, hurried back to the hotel.

Ferris poured himself a drink, although it was not yet eleven o'clock. He sprawled out in an armchair like a man exhausted, nursing[7] his glass of bourbon[8] and water. He had a full day ahead of him as

1) the following sense of recklessness and grace: 뒤따르는 들뜨고 훈훈한 기분.
2) meaning to speak: 말을 걸려고.
3) 'beautiful carriage': carriage=act of carrying the head and body; bearing.
4) heartstrokes: throbs or beats of the heart.
5) after the anodyne of time: 시간이라는 진통제를 먹고 나자.
6) dissonant with: out of harmony with.
7) nurse: hold closely; clasp fondly.
8) bourbon: kind of whisky.

he was leaving by plane the next morning for Paris. He checked over his obligations: take luggage to Air France, lunch with his boss, buy shoes and an overcoat. And something — wasn't there something else? Ferris finished his drink and opened the telephone directory.

His decision to call his ex-wife was impulsive. The number was under Bailey, the husband's name, and he called before he had much time for self-debate. He and Elizabeth had exchanged cards at Christmastime, and Ferris had sent a carving set when he received the announcement of her wedding. There was no reason not to call. But as he waited, listening to the ring at the other end, misgiving fretted him.[1]

Elizabeth answered; her familiar voice was a fresh shock to him. Twice he had to repeat his name, but when he was identified, she sounded glad. He explained he was only in town for that day. They had a theater engagement, she said — but she wondered if he would come by for an early dinner. Ferris said he would be delighted.

As he went from one engagement to another, he was still bothered at odd moments[2] by the feeling that something necessary was forgotten. Ferris bathed and changed in the late afternoon, often thinking about Jeannine; he would be with her the following night. "Jeannine," he would say, "I happened to run into my ex-wife when I was in New York. Had dinner with her. And her husband, of course. It was strange seeing her after all these years."

Elizabeth lived in the East Fifties, and as Ferris taxied uptown he glimpsed at intersections[3] the lingering sunset, but by the time he reached his destination it was already autumn dark. The place was a building with a marquee and a doorman, and the apartment was on the seventh floor.

"Come in, Mr. Ferris."

Braced for[4] Elizabeth or even the unimagined husband, Ferris was

---

1) misgiving fretted him: 불안이 그를 초조하게 만들었다; 조마조마했다. misgiving=a feeling of doubt, suspicion, or anxiety.

2) at odd moments: 이따금씩.

3) at intersections: at the crossing [crossroad].

4) Braced for: Having braced for ~를 기대하여 긴장해 있었으므로.

astonished by the freckled red-haired child; he had known of the children, but his mind had failed somehow to acknowledge them. Surprise made him step back awkwardly.

"This is our apartment," the child said politely. "Aren't you Mr. Ferris? I'm Billy. Come in."

In the living room beyond the hall, the husband provided another surprise; he too had not been acknowledged emotionally. Bailey was a lumbering red-haired man with a deliberate manner. He rose and extended a welcoming hand.

"I'm Bill Bailey. Glad to see you. Elizabeth will be in, in a minute. She's finishing dressing."

The last words struck a gliding series of vibrations,[1] memories of the other years. Fair Elizabeth, rosy and naked before her bath. Half-dressed before the mirror of her dressing table, brushing her fine, chestnut hair. Sweet, casual intimacy, the soft-fleshed loveliness indisputably possessed.[2] Ferris shrank from the unbidden memories[3] and compelled himself to meet Bill Bailey's gaze.

"Billy, will you please bring that tray of drinks from the kitchen table?"

The child obeyed promptly, and when he was gone Ferris remarked conversationally, "Fine boy you have there."

"We think so."

Flat[4] silence until the child returned with a tray of glasses and a cocktail shaker of Martinis. With the priming drinks[5] they pumped up conversation: Russia, they spoke of, and the New York rain-makin g,[6] and the apartment situation in Manhattan and Paris.

"Mr. Ferris is flying all the way across the ocean tomorrow," Bailey said to the little boy who was perched[7] on the arm of his chair, quiet

---

1) struck a gliding series of vibrations: 연속적인 여운(餘韻)을 일으켰다.
2) Sweet, casual intimacy ~ possessed: 부드러운 살결의 아름다움이 명백히 지닌 포근한 다정감.
3) shrank from the unbidden memories: 본의 아닌 회상을 물리쳤다.
4) Flat: 멋없는.
5) With the priming drinks: 술을 들면서. prime=~에게 충분히 먹이다(마시게 하다)
6) rain-making: 인공 강우.
7) perched: sit on.

and well behaved. "I bet you would like to be a stowaway[1] in his suitcase."

Billy pushed back his limp bangs. "I want to fly in an airplane and be a newspaperman like Mr. Ferris." He added with sudden assurance, "That's what I would like to do when I am big."

Bailey said," I thought you wanted to be a doctor."

"I do!" said Billy. "I would like to be both. I want to be a atom-bomb scientist too."

Elizabeth came in carrying in her arms a baby girl.

"Oh, John!" she said. She settled the baby in the father's lap. "It's grand to see you. I'm awfully glad you could come."

The little girl sat demurely on Bailey's knees. She wore a pale pink crepe de Chine frock,[2] smocked around the yoke with rose, and a matching silk hair ribbon tying back her pale soft curls. Her skin was summer tanned and her brown eyes flecked with gold and laughing. When she reached up and fingered her father's horn-rimmed glasses, he took them off and let her look through them a moment. "How's my old Candy?"

Elizabeth was very beautiful, more beautiful perhaps than he had ever realized. Her straight clean hair was shining. Her face was softer, glowing and serene. It was a madonna loveliness, dependent on the family ambiance.[3]

"You've hardly changed at all," Elizabeth said, "but it has been a long time."

"Eight years." His hand touched his thinning hair selfconsciously while further amenities were exchanged.

Ferris felt himself suddenly a spectator — an interloper among these Baileys. Why had he come? He suffered. His own life seemed so solitary, a fragile column supporting nothing amidst the wreckage of the years.

---

1) stowaway: person who hides on a ship, train, etc., to get a free passage or to escape secretly.

2) a pale pink crepe de Chine frock: 엷은 핑크색의 크레프 비단옷. crepe de Chine=a fairly sheer silk crepe, and the soft but heavier silk.

3) It was a madonna loveliness, dependent on the family ambiance: 그것은 가정의 분위기에 따른(와 일치하는) 마돈나의 아름다움이었다. ambiance=environment; surroundings.

He felt he could not bear much longer to stay in the family room.

He glanced at his watch. "You're going to the theater?"

"It's a shame,[1]" Elizabeth said, "but we've had this engagment for more than a month. But surely, John, you'll be staying home one of these days before long. You're not going to be an expatriate, are you?"

"Expatriate," Ferris repeated. "I don't much like the word."

"What's a better word?" she asked.

He thought for a moment. "Sojourner might do."

Ferris glanced again at his watch, and again Elizabeth apologized. "If only we had know ahead of time —"

"I just had this day in town. I came home unexpectedly. You see, Papa died last week."

"Papa Ferris is dead?"

"Yes, at Johns-Hopkins. He had been sick there nearly a year. The funeral was down home in Georgia."

"Oh, I'm so sorry, John. Papa Ferris was always one of my favorite people."

The little boy moved from behind the chair so that he could look into his mother's face. He asked, "Who is dead?"

Ferris was oblivious to apprehension;[2] he was thinking of his father's death. He saw again the outstretched body on the quilted silk within the coffin. The corpse flesh was bizarrely rouged and the familiar hands lay massive and joined above a spread of funeral roses. The memory closed and Ferris awakened to Elizabeth's calm voice.

"Mr. Ferris' father, Billy. A really grand person. Somebody you didn't know."

"But why did you call him *Papa* Ferris?"

Bailey and Elizabeth exchanged a trapped look.[3] It was Bailey who answered the questioning child. "A long time ago," he said, "your mother and Mr. Ferris were once married. Before you were born — a long time ago."

---

1) shame: fact to be sorry about.
2) was oblivious to apprehension: 조바심을 잊었다.
3) a trapped look: 난처한 시선.

"Mr. Ferris?"

The little boy stared at Ferris, amazed and unbelieving. And Ferris' eyes, as he returned the gaze, were somehow unbelieving too. Was it indeed true that at one time he had called this stranger, Elizabeth, Little Butterduck[1] during nights of love, that they had lived together, shared perhaps a thousand days and nights and — finally — endured in the misery of sudden solitude the fiber by fiber (jealousy, alcohol and money quarrels) destruction of the fabric of married love.[2]

Bailey said to the children, "It's somebody's suppertime. Come on now."

"But Daddy! Mama and Mr. Ferris — I — "

Billy's everlasting eyes — perplexed and with a glimmer of hostility — reminded Ferris of the gaze of another child. It was the young son of Jeannine — a boy of seven with a shadowed little face and nobby knees whom Ferris avoided and usually forgot.

"Quick march!" Bailey gently turned Billy toward the door. "Say good night now, son."

"Good night, Mr. Ferris." He added resentfully, "I thought I was staying up for the cake."

"You can come in afterward for the cake," Elizabeth said. "Run along now with Daddy for your supper."

Ferris and Elizabeth were alone. The weight of the situation descended on those first moments of silence. Ferris asked permission to pour himself another drink and Elizabeth set the cocktail shaker on the table at his side. He looked at the grand piano and noticed the music[3] on the rack.

"Do you still play as beautifully as you used to?"

"I still enjoy it."

"Please play, Elizabeth."

Elizabeth arose immediately. Her readiness to perform when asked had always been one of her amiabilities; she never hung back,

---

1) Little Butterduck: 귀여운 오리.

2) the fiber by fiber destruction of the fabric of married love: 부부애의 조직을 한 가닥씩 파괴하는 것.

3) the music: 악보.

apologized. Now as she approached the piano there was the added readiness of relief.

She began with a Bach prelude and fugue.[1] The prelude was as gaily iridescent[2] as a prism in a morning room. The first voice of the fugue, an announcement pure and solitary,[3] was repeated intermingling with a second voice, and again repeated within an elaborated frame, the multiple music, horizontal and serene, flowed with unhurried majesty. The principal melody was woven with two other voices, embellished with countless ingenuities[4] — now dominant, again submerged, it had the sublimity of a single thing that does not fear surrender to the whole. Toward the end, the density of the material[5] gathered for the last enriched insistence on the dominant first motif[6] and with a chorded final statement[7] the fugue ended. Ferris rested his head on the chair back and closed his eyes. In the following silence a clear, high voice came from the room down the hall.

"Daddy, how *could* Mama and Mr. Ferris — " A door was closed.

The piano began again — what was this music? Unplaced,[8] familiar, the limpid melody had lain a long while dormant[9] in his heart. Now it spoke to him of another time, another place — it was the music Elizabeth used to play. The delicate air summoned a wilderness of memory. Ferris was lost in the riot of[10] past longings, conflicts, ambivalent desires. Strange that the music, catalyst for this tumultuous anarchy,[11] was so serene and clear. The singing melody was broken off by the appearance of the maid.

---

1) a Bach prelude and fugue: 바하의 전주곡과 둔주곡(遁走曲). Bach=Johann Sebastian(1685-1750), German composer of music and organist.
2) iridescent: 무지갯빛의, 진주빛의.
3) an announcement pure and solitary: 맑고 고독한 음조.
4) embellished with countless ingenuities: 헤아릴 수 없는 교묘함으로 윤색된; 교묘한 윤색을 수없이 받으며.
5) the density of the material: 음의 밀도.
6) gathered for the last … motif: 최고도로 올라가 첫 주제를 강조했다.
7) with a chorded final statement: 최종 화음(和音)의 절미로.
8) unplaced: unidentified.
9) dormant: sleeping.
10) was lost in the riot of: ~의 격동 속에 빠졌다.
11) catalyst for this tumultuous anarchy: 이 시끄러운 무질서에 대한 촉매(인 음악).

"Miz Bailey, dinner is out on the table now."

Even after Ferris was seated at the table between his host and hostess, the unfinished music still overcast his mood. He was a little drunk.

"*L'improvisation de la vie humaine*,"[1] he said. "There's nothing that makes you so aware of the improvisation of human existence as a song unfinished. Or an old address book."

"Address book?" repeated Bailey. Then he stopped, noncommittal and polite.

"You're still the same old boy, Johnny," Elizabeth said with a trace of the old tenderness.[2]

It was a Southern dinner that evening, and the dishes were his old favorites. They had fried chicken and corn pudding and rich, glazed candied sweet potatoes. During the meal Elizabeth kept alive a conversation when the silences were overlong. And it came about[3] that Ferris was led to speak of Jeannine.

"I first knew Jeannine last autumn — about this time of the year — in Italy. She's a singer and she had an engagement in Rome. I expect we will be married soon."

The words seemed so true, inevitable, that Ferris did not at first acknowledge to himself the lie. He and Jeannine had never in that year spoken of marriage. And indeed, she was still married — to a White Russian money-changer in Paris from whom she had been separated for five years. But it was too late to correct the lie. Already Elizabeth was saying: "This really makes me glad to know. Congratulations, Johnny."

He tried to make amends with truth. "The Roman autumn is so beautiful. Balmy and blossoming." He added. "Jeannine has a little boy of seven. A curious trilingual[4] little fellow. We go to the Tuileries sometimes."

A lie again. He had taken the boy once to the gardens. The sallow

1) *L'improvisation de la vie humaine*: the improvisation of human existence. 인간 존재의 즉석 연주.

2) with a trace of the old tenderness: 예전의 애정을 풍기면서.

3) came about: happened; took place; occurred.

4) trilingual: familiar with three languages. *cf.* bilingual.

foreign child in shorts that bared his spindly legs had sailed his boat in the concrete pond and ridden the pony. The child had wanted to go in to the puppet show. But there was not time, for Ferris had an engagement at the Scribe Hotel. He had promised they would go to the guignol[1] another afternoon. Only once had he taken Valentin to the Tuileries.

There was a stir. The maid brought in a white-frosted cake with pink candles. The children entered in their night clothes. Ferris still did not understand.

"Happy birthday, John," Elizabeth said. "Blow out the candles."

Ferris recognized his birthday date. The candles blew out lingeringly and there was the smell of burning wax. Ferris was thirty-eight years old. The veins in his temples darkened and pulsed visibly.

"It's time you started for the theater."

Ferris thanked Elizabeth for the birthday dinner and said the appropriate good-byes. The whole family saw him to the door.

A high, thin moon shone above the jagged, dark skyscrapers. The streets were windy, cold. Ferris hurried to Third Avenue and hailed a cab. He gazed at the nocturnal city with the deliberate attentiveness of departure and perhaps farewell.[2] He was alone. He longed for flight time and the coming journey.

The next day, he looked down on the city from the air, burnished in sunlight, toylike, precise. Then America was left behind and there was only the Atlantic and the distant European shore. The ocean was milky pale and placid beneath the clouds. Ferris dozed most of the day. Toward dark he was thinking of Elizabeth and the visit of the previous evening. He thought of Elizabeth among her family with longing, gentle envy and inexplicable regret. He sought the melody, the unfinished air,[3] that had so moved him. The cadence, some unrelated tones, were all that remained;[4] the melody itself evaded

1) the guignol: 기놀관(舘).
2) the nocturnal city … farewell: 자기의 출발과 아마도 최후의 작별을 신중히 지켜보는 밤의 도시. nocturnal=of or in the night.
3) the unfinished air: 미완성의 곡.
4) The cadence, some unrelated tones, were all that remained: 남아 있는 것은 어느 단편적인 음조와 여운뿐이었다.

him. He had found instead the first voice of the fugue that Elizabeth had played — it came to him, inverted mockingly and in a minor key. Suspended above the ocean the anxieties of transience and solitude no longer troubled him and he thought of his father's death with equanimity. During the dinner hour the plane reached the shore of France.

At midnight Ferris was in a taxi crossing Paris. It was a clouded night and mist wreathed the lights of the Place de la Concorde. The midnight bistros[1] gleamed on the wet pavements. As always after a transocean flight the change of continents was too sudden. New York at morning, this midnight Paris. Ferris glimpsed the disorder of his life: the succession of cities, the transitory loves; and time, the sinister glissando of the years,[2] time always.

"*Vite! Vite!*"[3] he called in terror. "*Dépêchez-vous.*"[4]

Valentin opened the door to him. The little boy wore pajamas and an outgrown red robe. His gray eyes were shadowed and, as Ferris passed into the flat, they flickered momentarily.

"*J'attends Maman.*"[5]

Jeannine was singing in a night club. She would not be home before another hour. Valentin returned to a drawing, squatting with his crayons over the paper on the floor. Ferris looked down at the drawing — it was a banjo[6] player with notes and wavy lines inside a comic-strip[7] balloon.

"We will go again to the Tuileries."

The child looked up and Ferris drew him closer to his knees. The melody, the unfinished music that Elizabeth had played, came to him suddenly, Unsought, the load of memory jettisoned — this time bringing only recognition and sudden joy.

---

1) bistros: a small wineshop or eating place.

2) the sinister glissando of the years: 세월의 불길한 글리싼도. glissando=(음악용어로서) 악곡의 활주 주음부(奏音部).

3) *Vite*: (F.) 빨리.

4) *Dépêchez-vous*: (F.) 빨리 갑시다.

5) *J'attends Maman*: (F.) 엄마 기다리고 있어요.

6) banjo: a stringed musical instrument of the guitar class, played with the fingers.

7) comic-strip: series of drawings, sometimes humorous, presenting an adventure.

"Monsieur Jean," the child said, "did you see him?"

Confused, Ferris thought only of another child — the freckled, family-loved boy. "See who, Valentin?"

"Your dead papa in Georgia." The child added, "Was he okay?"

Ferris spoke with rapid urgency: "We will go often to the Tuileries. Ride the pony and we will go into the guignol. We will see the puppet show and never be in a hurry any more."

"Monsieur Jean," Valentin said. "The guignol is now closed."

Again, the terror the acknowledgement of wasted years and death. Valentin, responsive and confident, still nestled in his arms. His cheek touched the soft cheek and felt the brush of the delicate eyelashes. With inner desperation he pressed the child close — as though an emotion as protean as his love[1] could dominate the pulse of time.

---

1) an emotion as protean as his love: 그의 애정처럼 변화무쌍한 감정. protean= exceedingly variable.

My Oedipus Complex[1)]

by Frank O'Conner

Frank O'Conner (1903-) was born in Cork, Ireland, and attended the Christian Brothers School there, but was too poor to go to the university. He began to write early, worked as a librarian to maintain himself, and attracted the attention of literary men like Yeats and AE (George Russell). His reputation is based on his stories, but he has also written verse and a critical study of Turgenev.

The readers have been delighted, amused and suprised by his statement of the human condition. The readers have found his sense of humor equalled only by his sense of his reality and the warmth and richness of his character delineation.

FATHER WAS in the army all through the war — the first war, I mean — so, up to the age of five, I never saw much of him, and what I saw did not worry me. Sometimes I woke and there was a big figure in khaki peering down at me in the candlelight. Sometimes in the early morning I heard the slamming of the front door and the clatter of nailed boots down the cobbles of the lane. These were Father's entrances and exits. Like Santa Claus[2)] he came and went mysteriously.

In fact, I rather liked his visits, though it was an uncomfortable squeeze between Mother and him when I got into the big bed in the early morning. He smoked, which gave him a pleasant musty smell, and shaved, an operation of astounding interest. Each time he left a trail of souvenirs — model tanks and Gurkha knives with handles made of bullet cases, and German helmets and cap badges and button sticks, and all sorts of military equipment — carefully stowed away[3)]

---

1) Oedipus Complex: an early and morbidly strong attachment to the parent of the opposite sex, accompanied by dislike for the other parent. Oedipus=(Greek legend) king who unknowingly killed his father and married his mother.

2) Santa Claus: Saint Nicholas, the saint of Christmas-giving, according to modern conception, a jolly old man with a white beard, clad in a fur-trimmed red costume.

3) stowed away: pack or store away.

in a long box on top of the wardrobe, in case they ever came in handy. There was a bit of the magpie[1] about Father; he expected everything to come in handy.[2] When his back was turned, Mother let me get a chair and rummage through his treasures. She didn't seem to think so highly of[3] them as he did.

The war was the most peaceful period of my life. The window of my attic faced southeast. My mother had curtained it, but that had small effect. I always woke with the first light and, with all the responsibilities of the previous day melted,[4] feeling myself rather like the sun, ready to illumine and rejoice. Life never seemed so simple and clear and full of possibilities as then. I put my feet out from under the clothes — I called them Mrs. Left and Mrs. Right — and invented dramatic situations for them in which they discussed the problems of the day.[5] At least Mrs. Right did; she was very demonstrative, but I hadn't the same control of Mrs. Left, so she mostly contented[6] herself with nodding agreement.

They discussed what Mother and I should do during the day, what Santa Claus should give a fellow for Christmas, and what steps should be taken[7] to brighten the home. There was that little matter of the baby, for instance. Mother and I could never agree about that. Ours was the only house in the terrace without a new baby, and Mother said we couldn't afford one till Father came back from the war because they cost seventeen and six.

That showed how simple she was. The Geneys up the road had a baby, and everyone knew they couldn't afford seventeen and six. It was probably a cheap baby, and Mother wanted something really

---

1) magpie: person who chatters.
2) come in handy: prove useful.
3) think so highly of: think that (something or someone) is important or valuable.
4) with all the responsibilities of the previous day melted: 그 전날의 무거운 짐은 온통 녹아 버린 채.
5) and invented dramatic situations … the problems of the day: 오늘 하루의 문제를 토의하는 극적인 장면을 꾸며냈다.
6) contented: satisfy; please; make easy in mind.
7) what steps should be taken: 무슨 수단을 강구해야 하는가. take steps=begin to make plans or arrangements; make parations; give orders.

good, but I felt she was too exclusive. The Geneys' baby would have done us fine.[1]

Having settled my plans for the day, I got up, put a chair under the attic window, and lifted the frame high enough to stick out my head. The window overlooked the front gardens of the terrace behind ours, and beyond these it looked over a deep valley to the tall, red brick houses terraced up the opposite hillside, which were all still in shadow, while those at our side of the valley were all lit up, though with long strange shadows that made them seem unfamiliar; rigid and painted.

After that I went into Mother's room and climbed into the big bed. She woke and I began to tell her of my schemes. By this time, though I never seemed to have noticed it, I was petrified[2] in my nightshirt, and I thawed[3] as I talked until, the last frost melted, I fell asleep beside her and woke again only when I heard her below in the kitchen, making the breakfast.

After breakfast we went into town; heard Mass[4] at St. Augustine's and said a prayer for Father, and did the shopping. If the afternoon was fine we either went for a walk in the country or a visit to Mother's great friend in the convent, Mother Saint Dominic. Mother had them all praying for Father, and every night, going to bed, I asked God to send him back safe from the war to us. Little, indeed, did I know what I was praying for!

One morning, I got into the big bed, and there, sure enough, was Father in his usual Santa Claus manner, but later, instead of uniform, he put on his best blue suit, and Mother was as pleased as anything. I saw nothing to be pleased about, because, out of uniform, Father was altogether less interesting, but she only beamed, and explained that our prayers had been answered, and off we went to Mass to thank God for having brought Father safely home.

1) The Geneys' baby would have done us fine: 제니스네 어린애 정도면 우리에게 충분할 터인데.
2) petrifify: harden; stiffen; deaden; turn into stone; become stone.
3) thaw: melt.
4) Mass: central service of worship in the Roman Catholic Church.

The irony of it! That very day when he came in to dinner he took off his boots and put on his slippers, donned the dirty old cap he wore about the house to save him from colds, crossed his legs, and began to talk gravely to Mother, who looked anxious. Naturally, I disliked her looking anxious, because it destroyed her good looks, so I interrupted him.

"Just a moment, Larry!" she said gently. This was only what she said when we had boring visitors, so I attached no importance to it and went on talking. "Do be quiet, Larry!" she said impatiently. "Don't you hear me talking to Daddy?"

This was the first time I had heard those ominous words, "talking to Daddy," and I couldn't help feeling that if this was how God answered prayers, he couldn't listen to them very attentively."Why are you talking to Daddy?" I asked with as great a show of indifference as I could muster.[1] "Because Daddy and I have business to discuss. Now, don't interrupt again!"

In the afternoon, at Mother's request, Father took me for a walk. This time we went into town instead of out in the country, and I thought at first, in my usual optimistic way, that it might be an improvement. It was nothing of the sort. Father and I had quite different notions of a walk in town. He had no proper interest in trams, ships, and horses, and the only thing that seemed to divert him was talking to fellows as old as himself. When I wanted to stop he simply went on, dragging me behind him by the hand; when he wanted to stop I had no alternative but to do the same.[2] I noticed that it seemed to be a sign that he wanted to stop for a long time whenever he leaned against a wall. The second time I saw him do it I got wild. He seemed to be settling himself forever. I pulled him by the coat and trousers, but, unlike Mother who, if you were too persistent, got into a wax[3] and said: "Larry, if you don't behave yourself, I'll give you a good

1) with as great a show of indifference as I could muster: 될 수 있는 한 태연한 태도를 취하면서.

2) I had no alternative but to do the same: 꼭 같은 짓을 할 수밖에 별 도리가 없었다.

3) get into a wax: 발끈 화를 내다, 분통이 터지다. wax=(Colloq.) anger; fury.

slap," Father had an extraordinary capacity for amiable inattention.[1)] I sized him up[2)] and wondered would I cry, but he seemed to be too remote to be annoyed even by that. Really, it was like going for a walk with a mountain! He either ignored the wrenching and pummeling entirely, or else glanced down with a grin of amusement from his peak. I had never met anyone so absorbed in himself as he seemed.

At teatime, "talking to Daddy" began again, complicated this time by the fact that he had an evening paper, and every few minutes he put it down and told Mother something new out of it. I felt this was foul play. Man for man, I was prepared to compete with him any time for Mother's attention, but when he had it all made up for him by other people it left me no chance. Several times I tried to change the subject without success. "You must be quiet while Daddy is reading, Larry," Mother said impatiently.

It was clear that she either genuinely liked talking to Father better than talking to me, or else that he had some terrible hold[3)] on her which made her afraid to admit the truth. "Mummy," I said that night when she was tucking me up, "do you think if I prayed hard God would send Daddy back to the war?"

She seemed to think about that for a moment. "No, dear," she said with a smile. "I don't think He would." "Why wouldn't He, Mummy?" "Because there isn't a war any longer, dear." "But, Mummy, couldn't God make another war, if He liked?" "He wouldn't like to, dear. It's not God who makes wars, but bad people." "Oh!" I said. I was disappointed about that. I began to think that God wasn't quite what He was cracked up[4)] to be.

Next morning I woke at my usual hour, feeling like a bottle of champagne. I put out my feet and invented a long conversation in which Mrs. Right talked of the trouble she had with her own father

1) Father had an extraordinary capacity for amiable inattention: 아빠는 마음씨 곱게도 조금도 개의치 않는 비범한 재능을 지니고 있었다.
2) sized up: estimate; form an opinion of.
3) hold: a controlling force or influence.
4) crack up: (Colloq.) praise.

till she put him in the Home. I didn't quite know what the Home was but it sounded the right place for Father. Then I got my chair and stuck my head out of the attic window. Dawn was just breaking, with a guilty air that made me feel I had caught it in the act. My head bursting with stories and schemes, I stumbled[1] in next door, and in the half-darkness scrambled into the big bed. There was no room at Mother's side so I had to get between her and Father. For the time being I had forgotten about him, and for several minutes I sat bolt upright,[2] racking my brains to know what I could do with him. He was taking up more than his fair share of the bed, and I couldn't get comfortable, so I gave him several kicks that made him grunt and stretch. He made room all right, though. Mother waked and felt for me. I settled back comfortably in the warmth of the bed with my thumb in my mouth.

"Mummy!" I hummed, loudly and contentedly.

"Sssh! dear," she whispered. "Don't wake Daddy!"

This was a new development, which threatened to be even more serious than "talking to Daddy." Life without my early-morning conferences was unthinkable.

"Why?" I asked severely.

"Because poor Daddy is tired."

This seemed to me a quite inadequate reason, and I was sickened by the sentimentality of her "poor Daddy." I never liked that sort of gush;[3] it always struck me as insincere.

"Oh!" I said lightly. Then in my most winning tone: "Do you know where I want to go with you today, Mummy?"

"No, dear," she sighed.

"I want to go down the Glen and fish for thornybacks with my new net, and then I want to go out to the Fox and Hounds, and — "

"Don't-wake-Daddy!" she hissed angrily, clapping her hand across my mouth.

---

1) stumble: walk unsteadily.
2) bolt upright: stiff and straight.
3) gush: (Colloq.) silly, emotional talk.

But it was too late. He was awake, or nearly so. He grunted and reached for the matches. Then he stared incredulously at his watch.

"Like a cup of tea, dear?" asked Mother in a meek, hushed voice I had never heard her use before. It sounded almost as though she were afraid.

"Tea?" he exclaimed indignantly. "Do you know what the time is?"

"And after that I want to go up the Rathcooney Road," I said loudly, afraid I'd forget something in all those interruptions.

"Go to sleep at once, Larry!" she said sharply.

I began to snivel.[1] I couldn't concentrate, the way that pair went on,[2] and smothering my early-morning schemes was like burying a family from the cradle. Father said nothing, but lit his pipe and sucked it, looking out into the shadows without minding Mother or me. I knew he was mad. Every time I made a remark Mother hushed me irritably. I was mortified.[3] I felt it wasn't fair; there was even something sinister in it. Every time I had pointed out to her the waste of making two beds when we could both sleep in one, she had told me it was healthier like that, and now here was this man, this stranger, sleeping with her without the least regard for her health! He got up early and made tea, but though he brought Mother a cup he brought none for me.

"Mummy," I shouted, "I want a cup of tea, too."

"Yes, dear," she said patiently. "You can drink from Mummy's saucer."

That settled it. Either Father or I would have to leave the house. I didn't want to drink from Mother's saucer; I wanted to be treated as an equal in my own home, so, just to spite[4] her, I drank it all and left none for her. She took that quietly, too. But that night when she was putting me to bed she said gently:

"Larry, I want you to promise me something."

"What is it?" I asked.

---

1) snivel: cry with sniffling; put on a show of grief; whine.
2) the way that pair went on: 엄마와 아빠가 해가고 있듯이.
3) mortify: make ashamed; humiliate.
4) spite: show ill will toward; annoy.

"Not to come in and disturb poor Daddy in the morning. Promise?"

"Poor Daddy" again! I was becoming suspicious of everything involving that quite impossible man.

"Why?" I asked.

"Because poor Daddy is worried and tired and he doesn't sleep well."

"Why doesn't he, Mummy?"

"Well, you know, don't you, that while he was at the war Mummy got the pennies from the post office?"

"From Miss MacCarthy?"

"That's right. But now, you see, Miss MacCarthy hasn't any more pennies, so Daddy must go out and find us some. You know what would happen if he couldn't?"

"No," I said, "tell us."

"Well, I think we might have to go out and beg for them like the poor old woman on Fridays. We wouldn't like that, would we?"

"No," I agreed. "We wouldn't."

"So you'll promise not to come in and wake him?"

"Promise."

Mind you, I meant that. I knew pennies were a serious matter, and I was all against having to go out and beg like the old woman on Fridays. Mother laid out[1] all my toys in a complete ring round the bed so that, whatever way I got out, I was bound to fall over one of them.

When I woke I remembered my promise all right. I got up and sat on the floor and played — for hours, it seemed to me. Then I got my chair and looked out the attic window for more hours. I wished it was time for Father to wake; I wished someone would make me a cup of tea. I didn't feel in the least like the sun; instead, I was bored and so very, very cold! I simply longed for the warmth and depth of the big feather bed.

At last I could stand it no longer. I went into the next room. As there was still no room at Mother's side I climbed over her and she woke with a start.

---

1) laid out: spread out.

"Larry," she whispered, gripping my arm very tightly, "what did you promise?"

"But I did, Mummy," I wailed, caught in the very act.[1] "I was quiet for ever so long."

"Oh, dear, and you're perished!" she said sadly, feeling me all over. "Now, if I let you stay will you promise not to talk?"

"But I want to talk, Mummy," I wailed.

"That has nothing to do with it," she said with a firmness that was new to me. "Daddy wants to sleep. Now, do you understand that?"

I understood it only too well. I wanted to talk, he wanted to sleep —whose house was it, anyway?

"Mummy," I said with equal firmness, "I think it would be healthier for Daddy to sleep in his own bed."

That seemed to stagger[2] her, because she said nothing for a while. "Now, once for all,"[3] she went on, "you're to be perfectly quiet or go back to your own bed. Which is it to be?"

The injustice of it got me down.[4] I had convicted her out of her own mouth of inconsistency and unreasonableness,[5] and she hadn't even attempted to reply. Full of spite, I gave Father a kick, which she didn't notice but which made him grunt and open his eyes in alarm.

"What time is it?" he asked in a panic-stricken voice, not looking at Mother but at the door, as if he saw someone there.

"It's early yet," she replied soothingly. "It's only the child. Go to sleep again. . . . Now, Larry," she added, getting out of bed, "you've wakened Daddy and you must go back."

This time, for[6] all her quiet air, I knew she meant it, and knew that my principal rights and privileges were as good as lost unless I asserted them at once. As she lifted me, I gave a screech, enough to wake the dead, not to mind Father. He groaned.

1) caught in the very act: 현행범으로 잡힌 채.
2) stagger: confuse or astonish greatly.
3) once for all: finally or decisively.
4) The injustice of it got me down: 이 부당한 처사가 나를 실망케 했다.
5) I had convicted her out of her own mouth of inconsistency and unreasonableness: 나는 엄마의 말이 그야말로 모순이며 부당하다는 판결을 이미 내렸던 것이다.
6) for: in spite of.

"That damn child! Doesn't he ever sleep?"

"It's only a habit, dear," she said quietly, though I could see she was vexed.[1)]

"Well, it's time he got out of it," shouted Father, beginning to heave in the bed. He suddenly gathered all the bedclothes about him, turned to the wall, and then looked back over his shoulder with nothing showing only two small, spiteful, dark eyes. The man looked very wicked.

To open the bedroom door, Mother had to let me down, and I broke free and dashed for the farthest corner, screeching. Father sat bolt upright in bed.

"Shut up, you little puppy,[2)]" he said in a choking voice.

I was so astonished that I stopped screeching. Never, never had anyone spoken to me in that tone before. I looked at him incredulously and saw his face convulsed with rage. It was only then that I fully realized how God had codded[3)] me, listening to my prayers for the safe return of this monster.

"Shut up, you!" I bawled, beside myself.

"What's that you said?" shouted Father, making a wild leap out of the bed.

"Mick, Mick!" cried Mother. "Don't you see the child isn't used to you?"

"I see he's better fed than taught," snarled Father, waving his arms wildly. "He wants his bottom smacked."

All his previous shouting was as nothing to these obscene words referring to my person.[4)] They really made my blood boil.

"Smack your own!" I screamed hysterically. "Smack your own! Shut up! Shut up!"

At this he lost his patience and let fly at me.[5)] He did it with the lack of conviction you'd expect of a man under Mother's horrified

---

1) vexed: angry; disturbed.

2) puppy: a silly, conceited young man.

3) cod: (*v.*) 속이다, 조롱하다.

4) was as nothing to these obscene words referring to my person: 나의 인격에 관계되는 이런 추악한 말에 비하면 아무것도 아니었다.

5) let fly at me: began to bawl out at me. fly at. ~에게 달려들다, ~을 야단치다, 공격하다.

eyes, and it ended up as a mere tap, but the sheer indignity of being struck at all by a stranger, a total stranger who had cajoled his way back from the war into our big bed as a result of my innocent intercession, made me completely dotty.[1] I shrieked and shrieked, and danced in my bare feet, and Father, looking awkward and hairy in nothing but a short gray army shirt, glared down at me like a mountain out for murder. I think it must have been then that I realized he was jealous too. And there stood Mother in her nightdress, looking as if her heart was broken between us. I hoped she felt as she looked. It seemed to me that she deserved it all.

From that morning out my life was a hell. Father and I were enemies, open and avowed. We conducted a series of skirmishes against one another, he trying to steal my time with Mother and I his. When she was sitting on my bed, telling me a story, he took to[2] looking for some pair of old boots which he alleged[3] he had left behind him at the beginning of the war. While he talked to Mother I played loudly with my toys to show my total lack of concern. He created a terrible scene one evening when he came in from work and found me at his box, playing with his regimental badges, Gurkha knives and button sticks. Mother got up and took the box from me.

"You mustn't play with Daddy's toys unless he lets you, Larry," she said severely. "Daddy doesn't play with yours."

For some reason Father looked at her as if she had struck him and then turned away with a scowl.[4]

"Those are not toys," he growled, taking down the box again to see had I lifted anything. "Some of those curios are very rare and valuable."

But as time went on I saw more and more how he managed to alienate Mother and me. What made it worse was that I couldn't grasp his method or see what attraction he had for Mother. In every possible way he was less winning than I. He had a common accent and made

1) dotty: half-witted; partly insane.
2) take to: form a liking for; become fond of.
3) allege: state positively.
4) with a scowl: with an angry, sullen look.

noises at his tea. I thought for a while that it might be the newspapers she was interested in, so I made up bits of news of my own to read to her. Then I thought it might be the smoking, which I personally thought attractive, and took his pipes and went round the house dribbling into them till he caught me. I even made noises at my tea, but Mother only told me I was disgusting. It all seemed to hinge round that unhealthy habit of sleeping together, so I made a point of dropping into their bedroom and nosing round, talking to myself, so that they wouldn't know I was watching them, but they were never up to anything that I could see. In the end it beat me. It seemed to depend on being grown-up and giving people rings, and I realized I'd have to wait.

But at the same time I wanted him to see that I was only waiting, not giving up the fight. One evening when he was being particularly obnoxious, chattering away well above my head, I let him have it.

"Mummy," I said, "do you know what I'm going to do when I grow up?"

"No, dear," she replied. "What?"

"I'm going to marry you," I said quietly.

Father gave a great guffaw out of him,[1] but he didn't take me in.[2] I knew it must only be pretence. And Mother, in spite of everything, was pleased. I felt she was probably relieved to know that one day Father's hold on her would be broken.

"Won't that be nice?" she said with a smile.

"It'll be very nice," I said confidently. "Because we're going to have lots and lots of babies."

"That's right, dear," she said placidly. "I think we'll have one soon, and then you'll have plenty of company."

I was no end pleased about that because it showed that in spite of the way she gave in to[3] Father she still considered my wishes. Besides, it would put the Geneys in their place.[4]

---

1) gave a great guffaw out of him: 허허하고 너털웃음을 웃었다.
2) take in: receive; admit; understand.
3) give in to: ~에게 굴복(항복)하다.
4) put the Geneys in their place: 제니 가(家)의 주제넘은 짓을 타이르다(분수를 알게 하다).

It didn't turn out like that, though. To begin with, she was very preoccupied — I supposed about where she would get the seventeen and six — and though Father took to staying out late in the evenings it did me no particular good. She stopped taking me for walks, became as touchy as blazes,[1] and smacked me for nothing at all. Sometimes I wished I'd never mentioned the confounded baby — I seemed to have a genius for bringing calamity on myself.

And calamity it was! Sonny arrived in the most appalling hullabaloo[2] — even that much he couldn't do without a fuss — and from the first moment I disliked him. He was a difficult child — so far as I was concerned he was always difficult — and demanded far too much attention. Mother was simply silly about him, and couldn't see when he was only showing off.[3] As company he was worse than useless. He slept all day, and I had to go round the house on tiptoe to avoid waking him. It wasn't any longer a question of not waking Father. The slogan now was "Don't-wake-Sonny!" I couldn't understand why the child wouldn't sleep at the proper time, so whenever Mother's back was turned I woke him. Sometimes to keep him awake I pinched him as well. Mother caught me at it one day and gave me a most unmerciful flaking.

One evening, when Father was coming in from work, I was playing trains in the front garden. I let on[4] not to notice him; instead, I pretended to be talking to myself, and said in a loud voice: "If another bloody baby comes into this house, I'm going out."

Father stopped dead[5] and looked at me over his shoulder. "What's that you said?" he asked sternly. "I was only talking to myself," I replied, trying to conceal my panic. "It's private."

He turned and went in without a word. Mind you, I intended it as a solemn warning, but its effect was quite different. Father started

---

1) became as touchy as blazes: 성미가 불길처럼 날카로워졌다.

2) arrived in the most appalling hullabaloo: 간담을 서늘하게 하는 응애 소리를 지르며 세상에 태어났다. hullabaloo=uproar.

3) show off: make a show.

4) let on: (Colloq.) allow to be known; pretend.

5) dead: (*adv.*) completely; absolutely.

being quite nice to me. I could understand that, of course. Mother was quite sickening about Sonny. Even at mealtimes she'd get up and gawk[1] at him in the cradle with an idiotic smile, and tell Father to do the same. He was always polite about it, but he looked so puzzled you could see he didn't know what she was talking about. He complained of the way Sonny cried at night, but she only got cross and said that Sonny never cried except when there was something up with him[2] — which was a flaming lie, because Sonny never had anything up with him, and only cried for attention. It was really painful to see how simpleminded she was. Father wasn't attractive, but he had a fine intelligence. He saw through Sonny, and now he knew that I saw through him as well.

One night I woke with a start. There was someone beside me in the bed. For one wild moment I felt sure it must be Mother, having come to her senses and left Father for good, but then I heard Sonny in convulsions in the next room, and Mother saying: "There! There! There!" and I knew it wasn't she. It was Father. He was lying beside me, wide-awake, breathing hard and apparently as mad as hell.

After a while it came to me what he was mad about. It was his turn now. After turning me out of the big bed, he had been turned out himself. Mother had no consideration now for anyone but that poisonous pup, Sonny.

I couldn't help feeling sorry for Father. I had been through it all myself, and even at that age I was magnanimous. I began to stroke him down and say: "There! There!" He wasn't exactly responsive.

"Aren't you asleep either?" he snarled.

"Ah, come on and put your arm around us, can't you?" I said, and he did, in a sort of way. Gingerly,[3] I suppose, is how you'd describe it. He was very bony but better than nothing.

At Christmas he went out of his way to buy me a really nice model railway.

---

1) gawk: (Colloq.) stare rudely or stupidly.

2) there was something up with him: 그에게 무슨 탈이 있다. up=in process of going on or happening.

3) gingerly: with extreme care or caution.

Innocence

by Sean O'Faolain

Sean O'Faolain (1900-) was born in Cork, Ireland. He was educated at the University College, Cork, and served in the Irish Republican Army. From 1933 he became a full-time writer.

He has become one of the best known interpreters of modern Irish life, and his writings on Ireland and its people are widely praised outside Ireland as realistic and sympathetic interpretations.

Beginning with romantic stories that try to deal objectively with his experience as a revolutionary, he moved on to stories that reveal the emergence of a distinctive, pessimistic point of view. The central issue is the plight of the individual in a stag, post-revolutionary society.

ALL THIS month the nuns have been preparing my little boy for his first Confession. In a few days he will go in a crocodile[1] from the school to the parish church; enter the strange-looking cabinet in the corner of the aisle and see in the dusk of this secretive box an old priest's face behind a grille. He will acknowledge his wickedness to this pale, criss-crossed[2] face. He will be a little frightened but he will enjoy it too, because he does not really believe any of it — for him it is a kind of game that the nuns and the priest are playing between them.

How could he believe it? The nuns tell him that the Infant Jesus is sad when he is wicked. But he is never wicked, so what can it matter? If they told him instead of the sorrow he causes the Weasel, or Two Toes, or the Robin in the Cow's Ear, all of which live in the fields below our house, he would believe it in just the same way. To be sure he tells lies, he is a terrible liar, and when he plays Rummy[3]

1) in a crocodile: 열을 지어.

2) criss-crossed: marked or covered with lines.

3) Rummy: a kind of card game.

with me he cheats as often as he can, and when he is slow and I flurry him he flies into furious rages and his eyes swim with tears and he dashes the cards down and calls me A Pig. For this I love him so much that I hug him, because it is so transparent and innocent; and at night if I remember his tears I want to go into his room and hold his fat, sweaty hand that lies on the coverlet clutching some such treasure as an empty reel. How, then, can he believe that God could be angry with him because he tells lies or calls his daddy A Pig?

Yet, I hate to see him being prepared for his first Confession because one day he will really do something wicked, and I know the fear that will come over him on that day — and cannot prevent it.

I have never forgotten the first time I knew that I had committed sin. I had been going to Confession for years, ever since I was Seven, as he is now, telling the same things time after time just as he will do. 'Father, I told a lie... Father, I forgot to say my morning prayers. .. Father, I was disobedient to my parents... And that is all, Father.' It was always quite true: I had done these things; but, as with him, it was only true as a fable or a mock-battle[1] is true since none of these things were any more sinful than childish lies and rages. Until, one dim, wintry after-noon, not long after Christmas, when I went as usual to Confession in an old, dark, windy church called Saint Augustine's, down a side-lane, away from the city's traffic, a place as cold and damp and smelly as a tomb. It has since been pulled down and if they had not pulled it down it must soon have fallen down. It was the sort of church where there was always a beggar or two sheltering from the weather in the porch or in the dusky part under the back gallery; and always some poor shawled woman sighing her prayers in a corner like the wind fluttering in the slates.[2] The paint was always clean and fresh, but the floor and the benches and the woodwork were battered and worn by the generations. The priests dressed in the usual black Augustinian garment with a cowl and a leather cincture. Altogether, a stranger would have found it a gloomy

1) mock-battle: not real (copying; sham; imitation) battle. 모의전.

2) slates: a bluish-gray rock that splits easily into thin, smooth layers. Slate is used to cover roofs.

place. But I was familiar with it ever since my mother brought me there to dedicate me to Saint Monica, the mother of Augustine, and I loved the bright candles before her picture, and the dark nooks under the galleries, and the painted tondos[1] on the ceiling, and the stuffy confessional boxes with their heavy purple curtains, underneath which the heels of the penitents stuck out when they knelt to the grille.

There I was, glad to be out of the January cold, kneeling before Saint Monica, brilliant with the candles of her mendicants.[2] I was reading down through the lists of sins in my penny prayerbook heeding the ones I knew, passing over the ones I didn't know, when I suddenly stopped at the name of a sin that I had hitherto passed by as having nothing to do with me.

As I write down these words I again feel the terror that crept into me like a snake as I realized that I knew that sin. I knew it well. No criminal who feels the sudden grip of a policeman on his arm can have felt more fear than I did as I stared at the horrible words. . . .

I joined the long silent queue[3] of penitents seated against the wall. I went, at last, into the dark confessional. I told my usual innocent litany.[4] I whispered the sin.

Now, the old priest inside the confessional was a very aged man. He was so old and feeble that the community rarely allowed him to do anything but say Mass and hear Confessions. Whenever they let him preach he would ramble on and on for an hour; people would get up and go away; the sacristan[5] would peep out in despair through the sacristy[6] door; and in the end an altar-boy[7] would be sent out to ring the great gong on the altar-steps to make him stop. I have seen the boy come out three times to the gong before the old man could be lured down from the pulpit.

When this old priest heard what I said to him he gave a groan

1) tondo: (It.) 둥근 바탕 위에 그린 그림. 양각(陽刻).
2) mendicant: (begging) friar. 탁발 수도자.
3) queue: a long line of people.
4) litany: a repeated series. 연도(連禱).
5) sacristan: person in charge of a sacristy.
6) sacristy: place where the sacred vessels, robes, etc., of a church are kept.
7) altar-boy: person who helps a priest during certain religious services, esp. Mass

that must have been heard in the farthest corner of the church. He leaned his face against the wire and called me his 'child,' as all priests in the confessional call every penitent. Then he began to question me about the details. I had not counted on this. I had thought that I would say my sin and be forgiven: for up to this every priest had merely told me that I was a very good little boy and asked me to pray for him as if I were a little angel whose prayers had a special efficacy, and then I would be dismissed jumping with joy.

To his questions I replied tremulously that it had happened 'more than once' — How soon we begin to evade the truth! — and, I said, 'Yes, Father, it was with another.' At this he let out another groan so that I wanted to beg him to be quiet or the people outside would hear him. Then he asked me a question that made my clasped hands sweat and shake on the ledge of the grille. He asked me if any harm had been done to me. At first I didn't know what he meant. Then horrible shapes of understanding came creeping towards me along the dark road of my ignorance, as, in some indistinct manner, I recognized that he was mistaking me for a girl! I cried out that nothing at all had happened, Father. Nothing! Nothing! Nothing! But he only sighed like the south wind and said:

'Ah, my poor child, you won't know for several months.'

I now had no desire but to escape. I was ready to tell him any story, any lie, if he would only stop his questions. What I did say I don't know but in some fashion I must have made the old man understand that I was a male sinner. For his next question, which utterly broke me, was:

'I see, I see. Well, tell me, my poor child. Was she married or unmarried?'

I need hardly say that as I remember this now I laugh at it for an absurd misadventure, and I have sometimes made my friends laugh at his questions and his groans, and at me with my two skinny heels sticking out under the curtains and knocking like castanets,[1] and the

1) castanet: a pair, or one of a pair, of instruments of hard wood or ivory like little symbals, held in the hand and clicked together to beat time for dancing or music.

next penitents wondering what on earth was going on inside the box. But, then, I was like a pup caught in a bramble bush,[1] recanting[2] and retracting[3] and trying to get to the point where he would say the blessed words '*Absolvo te . . .*'[4] and tell me what my penance would be.

What I said I cannot recall. All I remember distinctly is how I emerged under the eyes of the queue, walked up the aisle, as far away as I could get from the brightness of Saint Monica into the darkest corner under the gallery where the poorest of the poor crowd on Sundays. I saw everything through smoke. The scarlet eye of the sanctuary lamp — the only illumination apart from the candles before the shrine — stared at me. The shawled woman sighed at me. The wind under my bare knees crept away from me. A beggar in a corner, picking his nose and scratching himself, was Purity itself compared to me.

In the streets the building stood dark and wet against the after-Christmas pallor of the sky. High up over the city there was one tiny star. It was as bright and remote as lost innocence. The blank windows that held the winter sky were sullen. The wet cement walls were black, I walked around for hours. When I crept in home my mother demanded angrily where I had been all these hours and I told her lies that were lies, because I wanted to deceive her, and I knew that from this on I would always be deceiving everybody because I had something inside me that nobody must ever know. I was afraid of the dark night before me. And I still had to face another Confession when I would have to confess all these fresh lies that I had just told the old priest and my mother.

It's forty years ago, now: something long since put in its unimportant place. Yet, somehow, when I look across at this small kid clutching his penny prayer-book in his sweaty hands and wrinkling up his nose at the hard words — I cannot laugh. It does not even comfort me when

---

1) like a pup caught in a bramble bush: 가시덤불 속에 붙잡힌 강아지처럼.
2) recant: withdraw; renounce (a statement, opinion, etc.).
3) retract: draw back or in.
4) *Absolvo te*. . . : absolve to. . . ~을 면제하다. absolve= declare (a person) free from sin, guilt, or blame.

I think of that second Confession, after I had carefully examined those lists of sins for the proper name of my sin. For, what I said to the next priest was: 'Father, I committed adultery.' With infinite tenderness he assured me that I was mistaken, and that I would not know anything about that sin for many years to come, indeed, that I would have to be married before I could commit it — and then asked me to pray for him, and said I was a very good little boy and sent me away jumping with joy. When I think of that and look at this small Adam he becomes like that indescribably remote and tender star, and I sigh like that old, dead priest, and it does not help to know that he is playing a fable of — 'Father, I told lies. . . Father, I forgot to say my morning prayers. . . . Father, I called my daddy A Pig.'

The Open Window

by SAKI (H. H. Munro)

SAKI (Hector Hugh Munro, 1970-1916): writer of fiction, began his literary career as a political satirist for *the Westminster Gazette,* and during 1902-8 was correspondent in Russia and subsequently in Paris of *the Morning Post. Reginald,* his first characteristic collection of short stories, was published under the pseudonym Saki in 1904, and was followed by *Reginald in Russia* (1910), *The Chronicles of Clovis* (1911), and *Beasts and Superbeasts* (1914). *The Unbearable Bassington,* a novel, appeared in 1912.

"MY AUNT will be down presently, Mr. Nuttel," said a very self-possessed[1] young lady of fifteen; "in the meantime you must try and put up with[2] me."

Framton Nuttel endeavoured to say the correct something which should duly flatter the niece of the moment without unduly discounting the aunt that was to come. Privately he doubted more than ever whether these formal visits on a succession of total strangers[3] would do much towards helping the nerve cure which he was supposed to be undergoing.[4]

"I know how it will be," his sister had said when he was preparing to migrate to this rural retreat[5]; "you will bury yourself down there and not speak to a living soul, and your nerves will be worse than ever from moping.[6] I shall just give you letters of introduction to all the people I know there. Some of them, as far as I can remember, were quite nice."

---

1) self-possessed: calm.

2) put up with: bear with patience; tolerate.

3) these formal visits on a succession of total strangers: 전혀 낯선 사람들을 연달아 정식으로 방문하는 것.

4) whether ~ would do much towards helping the nerve cure which he was supposed to be undergoing: 자기의 고질이라고 생각되는 신경병 치료에 크게 효험이 있을지. undergo=go through; suffer.

5) rural retreat: 벽지.

6) moping: being gloomly and sad.

Framton wondered whether Mrs. Sappleton, the lady to whom he was presenting one of the letters of introduction came into the nice division.

"Do you know many of the people round here?" asked the niece, when she judged that they had had sufficient silent communion.

"Hardly a soul," said Framton. "My sister was staying here, at the rectory,[1] you know, some four years ago, and she gave me letters of introduction to some of the people here."

He made the last statement in a tone of distinct regret.

"Then you know practically nothing about my aunt?" pursued the self-possessed young lady.

"Only her name and address," admitted the caller. He was wondering whether Mrs. Sappleton was in the married or widowed state. An undefinable something about the room seemed to suggest masculine habitation.[2]

"Her great tragedy happened just three years ago," said the child; "that would be since your sister's time."

"Her tragedy?" asked Framton; somehow in this restful country spot tragedies seemed out of place.[3]

"You may wonder why we keep that window wide open on an October afternoon," said the niece, indicating a large French window that opened on to a lawn.

"It is quite warm for the time of the year," said Framton; "but has that window got anything to do with the tragedy?"

"Out through that window, three years ago to a day, her husband and her two young brothers went off for their day's shooting. They never came back. In crossing the moor to their favourite snipe-shooting ground they were all three engulfed in a treacherous piece of bog.[4] It had been that dreadful wet summer, you know, and places that were safe in other years gave way[5] suddenly without warning. Their

1) rectory: rector's house.
2) seemed to suggest masculine habitation: 남자와의 동거(同居)를 암시하는 것 같다.
3) out of place: inappropriate or ill-timed.
4) were ~ engulfed in a treacherous piece of bog: 배반적인 수렁 속에 삼켜졌다(파묻혀 버렸다). bog=marsh; swamp.
5) gave way: collapsed; failed. *Ex.* The river was so high that the dam gave away. (There was so much water that it broke the dam.)

bodies were never recovered. That was the dreadful part of it." Here the child's voice lost its self-possessed note and became falteringly human. "Poor aunt always thinks that they will come back someday, they and the little brown spaniel that was lost with them, and walk in at that window just as they used to do. That is why the window is kept open every evening till it is quite dusk. Poor dear aunt, she has often told me how they went out, her husband with his white waterproof coat over his arm, and Ronnie, her youngest brother, singing 'Bertie, why do you bound?' as he always did to tease her, because she said it got on her nerves.[1] Do you know, sometimes on still, quiet evenings like this, I almost get a creepy feeling that they will all walk in through that window — "

She broke off[2] with a little shudder. It was a relief to Framton when the aunt bustled into the room with a whirl of apologies[3] for being late in making her appearance.

"I hope Vera has been amusing you?" she said.

"She has been very interesting," said Framton.

"I hope you don't mind the open window," said Mrs. Sappleton briskly; "my husband and brothers will be home directly from shooting, and they always come in this way. They've been out for snipe in the marshes today, so they'll make a fine mess[4] over my poor carpets. So like you menfolk, isn't it?"[5]

She rattled on[6] cheerfully about the shooting and the scarcity of birds, and the prospects for duck in the winter. To Framton it was all purely horrible. He made a desperate but only partially successful effort to turn the talk on to a less ghastly topic, he was conscious that his hostess was giving him only a fragment of her attention, and her eyes were constantly straying past him to the open window and the lawn beyond. It was certainly an unfortunate coincidence that he

1) got on her nerves: made her nervous.
2) broke off: stopped suddenly.
3) with a whirl of apologies: 미안하다는 수다를 떨면서.
4) make a mess: make dirty or untidy.
5) So like you menfolk, isn't it?: 남자들이란 으레 그렇지 않아요?
6) rattled on: talked quickly, on and on.

should have paid his visit on this tragic anniversary.

"The doctors agree in ordering me complete rest, an absence of mental excitement, and avoidance of anything in the nature of violent physical exercise," announced Framton, who laboured under the tolerably widespread delusion[1] that total strangers and chance acquaintances[2] are hungry for[3] the least detail of one's ailments and infirmities, their cause and cure. "On the matter of diet they are not so much in agreement," he continued.

"No?" said Mrs. Sappleton, in a voice which only replaced a yawn at the last moment. Then she suddenly brightened into alert attention — but not to what Framton was saying.

"Here they are at last!" she cried. "Just in time for tea, and don't they look as if they were muddy up to the eyes!"

Framton shivered slightly and turned towards the niece with a look intended to convey sympathetic comprehension. The child was staring out through the open window with a dazed horror in her eyes. In a chill shock of nameless fear[4] Framton swung round in his seat and looked in the same direction.

In the deepening twilight three figures were walking across the lawn towards the window, they all carried guns under their arms, and one of them was additionally burdened with a white coat hung over his shoulders. A tired brown spaniel kept close at their heels. Noiselessly they neared the house, and then a hoarse young voice chanted out of the dusk: "I said, Bertie, why do you bound?"

Framton grabbed wildly at his stick and hat; the hall door, the gravel drive, and the front gate were dimly noted stages in his headlong retreat.[5] A cyclist coming along the road had to run into the hedge to avoid imminent collision.

"Here we are, my dear," said the bearer of the white mackintosh,

---

1) who laboured under the tolerably widespread delusion: 꽤 깊은 착각으로 괴로워했던(고민했던).
2) chance acquaintances: 우연히 알게 된 사람들.
3) are hungry for: have a strong desire or craving for; eager.
4) in a chill shock of nameless fear: 야릇한 공포에 오싹 떨며.
5) were dimly noted stages in his headlong retreat: 쏜살같이 도망을 치는 그의 눈에 희미하게 띄었다.

coming in through the window, "fairly muddy, but most of it's dry. Who was that who bolted out as we came up?"[1)]

"A most extraordinary man, a Mr. Nuttel," said Mrs. Sappleton; "could only talk about his illnesses, and dashed off without a word of goodby or apology when you arrived. One would think he had seen a ghost."

"I expect it was the spaniel," said the niece calmly; "he told me he had a horror of dogs. He was once hunted into a cemetery somewhere on the banks of the Ganges by a pack of pariah dogs, and had to spend the night in a newly dug grave with the creatures snarling and grinning and foaming just above him. Enough to make anyone lose their nerve."

Romance at short notice was her speciality.[2)]

---

1) Who was that who bolted out as we came up?: 우리가 들어올 때 뛰어나간 사람이 누구요? bolt out=dish away; run away.

2) Romance at short notice was her speciality: 즉석 로맨스는 그녀의 특기였다.

Uncle Wiggily in Connecticut

by J.D. Salinger

J.D. Salinger (1919-) has been one of the most talked about but also one of the most retiring of contemporary authors. He has taken care to keep his private life out of view of reporters and photographers. He was born in New York City and went to school in that area. During World War II he served in France. He published his first story at the age of twenty-one and has since published frequently in *The New Yorker* and other magazines. Although his works are few in contrast to those by other well-known authors, they have been the subject of numerous critical and scholarly articles. Salinger's works deal in many instances with the world of sensitive children and adolescents who see through the "phony" exterior of the adults in the world around them.

IT WAS almost three o'clock when Mary Jane finally found Eloise's house. She explained to Eloise, who had come out to the driveway to meet her, that everything had been absolutely *perfect*, that she had remembered the way *exactly*, until she had turned off the Merrick Parkway. Eloise said, "*Merritt* Parkway, baby," and reminded Mary Jane that she had found the house twice before, but Mary Jane just wailed something ambiguous, something about her box of Kleenex,[1] and rushed back to her convertible.[2] Eloise turned up the collar of her camel's-hair coat, put her back to the wind, and waited. Mary Jane was back in a minute using a leaf of Kleenex and still looking upset,[3] even fouled. Eloise said cheerfully that the *whole* damn lunch was burned — sweetbreads, everything — but Mary Jane said she'd eaten anyway, on the road. As the two walked toward the house, Eloise asked Mary Jane how it happened she had the day off.[4] Mary Jane said she didn't have the whole day off; it was just that Mr.

---

1) Kleenex: 부드러운 인조직물의 일종으로, 주로 손수건·휴지용으로 쓰임.
2) convertible: an automobile, having a top that may be folded down.
3) upset: disturbed; disordered.
4) off: without work.

Weyinburg had a hernia[1] and was home in Larchmont, and she had to bring him his mail and take a couple of letters every afternoon. She asked Eloise, "Just exactly what is a hernia, anyway?" Eloise, dropping her cigarette on the soiled snow underfoot, said she didn't *actually* know but that Mary Jane didn't have to worry much about getting one. Mary Jane said, "Oh," and the two girls entered the house.

Twenty minutes later, they were finishing their first highball in the living room and were talking in the manner peculiar, probably limited, to former college roommates. They had an even stronger bond between them; neither of them had graduated. Eloise had left college in the middle of her sophomore year, in 1942, a week after she had been caught with a soldier in a closed elevator on the third floor of her residence hall. Mary Jane had left — same year, same class, almost the same month — to marry an aviation cadet stationed in Jacksonville, Florida, a lean, air-minded boy from Dill, Mississippi, who had spent two of the three months Mary Jane had been married to him in jail for stabbing an M.P. .

"No," Eloise was saying. "It was actually *red*." She was stretched out on the couch, her thin but very pretty legs crossed at the ankles.

"I heard it was blond," Mary Jane repeated. She was seated in the blue straight chair. "Wuddayacallit swore up and down[2] it was blond."

"Uh-uh. Definitely." Eloise yawned. "I was almost in the *room* with her when she dyed it. What's the matter? Aren't there any cigarettes in there?"

"It's all right. I have a whole pack," Mary Jane said. "Somewhere." She searched through her handbag.

"That dopey[3] maid," Eloise said without moving from the couch. "I dropped two brand-new[4] cartons in front of her nose about an hour ago. She'll be in, any minute, to ask me what to do with them.

---

1) hernia: protrusion of a part of the intestine or some other organ through a break in its surrounding walls; rupture 탈장.

2) Wuddayacallit swore up and down ~: Would you call it ~. 누구든가(뭔가) 이름은 잊었지만 온통 금발이라고 단언하더라.

3) dopey: (Slang) affected by "dope"; esp., sluggish or dull as if doped.

4) brand-new: very new; entirely new.

Where the hell was I?"[1)]

"Thieringer," Mary Jane prompted, lighting one of her own cigarettes.

"Oh, yeah. I remember exactly. She dyed it the *night* before she married that Frank Henke. You remember him at all?"

"Just sort of.[2)] Little ole private?[3)] Terribly unattractive?"

"Unattractive. God! He looked like an unwashed Bela Lugosi."

Mary Jane threw back her head and roared. "Marvellous," she said, coming back into drinking position.

"Gimme[4)] your glass," Eloise said, swinging her stockinged feet to the floor and standing up. "Honestly, that *dope*. I did everything but get Lew to make love to her to get her to come out here with us. Now I'm sorry I — Where'd you get that thing?"

"*This*?" said Mary Jane, touching a cameo brooch at her throat. "I had it at school, for goodness sake. It was Mother's."

"God," Eloise said, with the empty glasses in her hands. "I don't have one damn thing holy to wear. If Lew's mother ever dies — ha, ha — she'll probably leave me some old monogrammed[5)] icepick or something."

"How're you getting along with her these days, anyway?"

"Don't be funny,"[6)] Eloise said on her way to the kitchen.

"This is positively the last one for me!" Mary Jane called after her.

"Like hell it is. *Who* called *who*? And who came two hours late? You're gonna[7)] stick around[8)] till I'm sick of you. The hell with your lousy career."[9)]

Mary Jane threw back her head and roared again, but Eloise had already gone into the kitchen.

---

1) Where the hell was I?: 얘기를 어디까지 했더라?
2) sort of: (Colloq.) some what; rather.
3) little ole private?: Little old common soldier, not an officer?
4) gimme: give me.
5) monogrammed: with a person's initials combined in one design. monogram=(성명 첫 글자 따위의) 짜맞춘 글자.
6) Don't be funny: 농담 말라.
7) gonna: going to.
8) stick around: (Slang) stay or wait neardy.
9) The hell with your lousy career.: 그놈의 직업이 문제야.

With little or no wherewithal[1] for being left alone in a room, Mary Jane stood up and walked over to the window. She drew aside the curtain and leaned her wrist on one of the crosspieces between panes, but, feeling grit, she removed it, rubbed it clean with her other hand, and stood up more erectly. Outside, the filthy slush was visibly turning to ice. Mary Jane let go[2] the curtain and wandered back to the blue chair, passing two heavily stocked bookcases without glancing at any of the titles. Seated, she opened her handbag and used the mirror to look at her teeth. She closed her lips and ran her tongue hard over her upper front teeth, then took another look.

"It's getting so *icy* out," she said, turning. "God, that was quick. Didn't you put any soda in them?"

Eloise, with a fresh drink in each hand, stopped short.[3] She extended both index fingers, gun-muzzle style,[4] and said, "Don't nobody move. I got the whole damn place surrounded."

Mary Jane laughed and put away her mirror.

Eloise came forward with the drinks. She placed Mary Jane's insecurely in its coaster[5] but kept her own in hand. She stretched out on the couch again. "Wuddaya[6] think she's doing out there?" she said. "She's sitting on her big, black butt[7] reading `The Robe.' I dropped the ice trays taking them out. She actually looked up annoyed."

"This is my last. And I mean it," Mary Jane said, picking up her drink. "Oh, listen! You know who I saw last week? On the main floor of Lord & Taylor's?"

"Mm-hm," said Eloise, adjusting a pillow under her head. "Akim Tamiroff."

"*Who*?" said Mary Jane. "Who's he?"

---

1) With little or no wherewithal: 무료하기도 하여. wherewithal=means; supplies.
2) let go: release the hold on. 놓다.
3) short: abruptly; suddenly.
4) gun-muzzle style: 총구(銃口) 모양(으로). muzzle=nose, mouth and jaws of an animal.
5) coaster: a little tray to hold a glass or bottles.
6) Wuddaya: Would you.
7) butt: a large barrel for wine or beer.

"Akim Tamiroff. He's in the movies. He always says, `You make beeg joke — hah?' I love him. . . . There isn't one damn pillow in this house that I can stand. Who'd you see?"

"Jackson. She was — "

"Which one?"

"I don't know. The one that was in our Psych[1] class, that always — "

"Both of them were in our Psych class."

"Well. The one with the terrific — "

"Marcia Louise. I ran into her once, too. She talk your ear off?[2]"

"God, yes. But you know what she told me, though? Dr. Whiting's dead. She said she had a letter from Barbara Hill saying Whiting got cancer last summer and died and all. She only weighed sixty-two pounds. When she died. Isn't that terrible?"

"No."

"Eloise, you're getting hard as nails.[3]"

"Mm. What else'd she say?"

"Oh, she just got back from Europe. Her husband was stationed in Germany or something, and she was with him. They had a forty-seven-room house, she said, just with one other couple, and about ten servants. Her own horse, and the groom they had, used to be Hitler's own private riding master or something. Oh, and she started to tell me how she almost got raped by a colored soldier. *Right* on the main floor of Lord & Taylor's she started to tell me — you know Jackson. She said he was her husband's chauffeur, and he was driving her to market or something one morning. She said she was so scared she didn't even — "

"Wait just a second." Eloise raised her head and her voice. "Is that you, Ramona?"

"Yes," a small child's voice answered.

"Close the front door after you, please," Eloise called.

"Is that Ramona? Oh, I'm dying to see her. Do you realize I haven't

1) Psych: (Psycho.) mind, as in psychoanalysis. Psych class=심리학 교실.
2) She talk your ear off?: 귀청이 떨어지게 떠들어대지?
3) hard as nails: tough and strong; not mild or gentle; rough; stern.

seen her since she had her — "

"Ramona," Eloise shouted, with her eyes shut, "go out in the kitchen and let Grace take your galoshes[1] off."

"All right," said Ramona. "C'mon, Jimmy."

"Oh, I'm dying to see her," Mary Jane said. "Oh, *God*! Look what I did. I'm *ter*ribly sorry, El."

"Leave it. *Leave* it," said Eloise. "I hate this damn rug anyway. I'll get you another."

"No, look, I have more than half left!" Mary Jane held up her glass.

"Sure?" said Eloise. "Gimme a cigarette."

Mary Jane extended her pack of cigarettes, saying "Oh, I'm dying to see her. Who does she look like now?"

Eloise struck a light. "Akim Tamiroff."

"No, seriously."

"Lew. She looks like Lew. When his mother comes over, the three of them look like triplets.[2]" Without sitting up, Eloise reached for a stack of ashtrays on the far side of the cigarette table. She successfully lifted off the top one and set it down on her stomach. "What I need is a cocker spaniel[3] or something," she said. "Somebody that looks like me."

"How're her eyes now?" Mary Jane asked. "I mean they're not any worse or anything, are they?"

"God! Not that I know of."

"Can she see at all without her glasses? I mean if she gets up in the night to go to the john[4] or something.

"She won't tell anybody. She's lousy with secrets.[5]"

Mary Jane turned around in her chair. "Well, hel*lo*, Ramona!" she said. "Oh, what a *pretty* dress!" She set down her drink. "I'll bet you don't even remember me, Ramona."

---

1) galoshes: rubber overshoe covering the ankle, worn in wet or snowy weather.
2) triplets: one of three children born at the same time from the same mother.
3) cocker spaniel: any of a breed of small dogs with long, silky hair and drooping ears.
4) go to the john: go to the toilet. (esp. a public toilet for males).
5) She's lousy with secrets.: She is well supplied with secrets. 비밀투성이다.

"Certainly she does. Who's the lady, Ramona?"

"Mary Jane," said Ramona, and scratched herself.

"Marvellous!" said Mary Jane. "Ramona, will you give me a little kiss?"

"Stop that," Eloise said to Ramona.

Ramona stopped scratching herself.

"Will you give me a little kiss, Ramona?" Mary Jane asked again.

"I don't like to kiss people."

Eloise snorted, and asked, "Where's Jimmy?"

"He's here."

"Who's Jimmy?" Mary Jane asked Eloise.

"Oh, God! Her beau.[1] Goes where she goes. Does what she does. All very hoopla.[2]"

"*Really*?" said Mary Jane enthusiastically. She leaned forward. "Do you have a beau, Ramona?"

Ramona's eyes, behind thick, counter-myopia lenses,[3] did not reflect even the smallest part of Mary Jane's enthusiasm.

"Mary Jane asked you a question, Ramona," Eloise said.

Ramona inserted a finger into her small, broad nose.

"Stop that," Eloise said. "Mary Jane asked you if you have a beau."

"Yes," said Ramona, busy with her nose.

"Ramona," Eloise said. "Cut that out.[4] But immediately."

Ramona put her hand down.

"Well, I think that's just wonderful," Mary Jane said. "What's his name? Will you tell me his name, Ramona? Or is it a big secret?"

"Jimmy," Ramona said.

"Jimmy? Oh, I love the name Jimmy! Jimmy what, Ramona?"

"Jimmy Jimmereeno," said Ramona.

"Stand still," said Eloise.

"Well! That's quite a name. Where is Jimmy? Will you tell me, Ramona?"

---

1) beau: lover; dandy.
2) All very hoopla: 야단법석이다. hoopla: 법석, 헛선전.
3) counter-myopia lenses: 근시 안경.
4) Cut that out.: Stop doing that.

"Here," said Ramona.

Mary Jane looked around, then looked back at Ramona, smiling as provocatively as possible. "Here where, honey?"

"*Here,*" said Ramona. "I'm holding his *hand.*"

"I don't get it," Mary Jane said to Eloise, who was finishing her drink.

"Don't look at *me,*" said Eloise.

Mary Jane looked back at Ramona. "Oh, I see. Jimmy's just a make-believe[1] little boy. Marvellous." Mary Jane leaned forward cordially. "How do you *do,* Jimmy?" she said.

"He won't talk to you," said Eloise. "Ramona, tell Mary Jane about Jimmy."

"Tell her *what*?"

"Stand up, please. . . . Tell Mary Jane how Jimmy looks."

"He has green eyes and black hair."

"What else?"

"No mommy and no daddy."[2]

"What else?"

"No freckles."[3]

"What else?"

"A sword."

"What else?"

"I don't know," said Ramona, and began to scratch herself again.

"He sounds *beau*tiful!" Mary Jane said, and leaned even farther forward in her chair. "Ramona. Tell me. Did Jimmy take off *his* galoshes, too, when you came *in*?"

"He has boots," Ramona said.

"Marvellous," Mary Jane said to Eloise.

"You just think so. I get it all day long. Jimmy eats with her. Takes a bath with her. Sleeps with her. She sleeps way over to one side of the bed, so's not to roll over and hurt him."

Looking absorbed and delighted with this information, Mary Jane

1) make-believe: pretended.
2) mommy and no daddy: mama(mamma) and dad; mother and father.
3) freckles: a small, light-brown spot on the skin.

took in[1] her lower lip, then released it to ask, "Where'd he get that name, though?"

"Jimmy Jimmereeno? God knows."

"Probably from some little boy in the neighborhood."

Eloise, yawning, shook her head. "There are no little boys in the neighborhood. No children at all. They call me Fertile Fanny[2] behind my — "

"Mommy," Ramona said, "can I go out and play?"

Eloise looked at her. "You just came in," she said.

"Jimmy wants to go out again."

"Why, may I ask?"

"He left his sword outside."

"Oh, him and his goddam sword," Eloise said. "Well. Go ahead. Put your galoshes back on."

"Can I have this?" Ramona said, taking a burned match out of the ashtray.

"*May* I have this. Yes. Stay out of the street, please."

"Goodbye, Ramona!" Mary Jane said musically.

"Bye," said Ramona. "C'mon,[3] Jimmy."

Eloise lunged suddenly to her feet. "Gimme your glass," she said.

"No, really, El. I'm supposed to be in *Larchmont*. I mean Mr. Weyinburg's so sweet, I hate to — "

"Call up[4] and say you were killed. Let go of[5] that damn glass."

"No, honestly, El. I mean it's getting so *terribly* icy. I have hardly any anti-freeze[6] in the car. I mean if I don't — "

"Let it freeze. Go phone. Say you're dead," said Eloise. "Gimme that."

"Well... Where's the phone?"

"It went,"[7] said Eloise, carrying the empty glasses and walking

1) took in: make smaller.
2) Fertile Fanny: 수정부(受精婦). fertile=productive.
3) C'mon: Come on.
4) call up: telephone to.
5) Let go of: 놓아라.
6) anti-freeze: substance added to a liquid to prevent it from freezing 부동액.
7) It went: It broke down. 고장났다.

toward the dining room, "— this-a-way."[1] She stopped short on the floor board between the living room and the dining room and executed a grind[2] and a bump. Mary Jane giggled.

"I mean you didn't really *know* Walt," said Eloise at a quarter of five, lying on her back on the floor, a drink balanced upright on her small-breasted chest. "He was the only boy I ever knew that could make me laugh. I mean *really* laugh." She looked over at Mary Jane. "You remember that night — our last year — when that crazy Louise Hermanson busted[3] in the room wearing that black brassiere she bought in Chicago?"

Mary Jane giggled. She was lying on her stomach on the couch, her chin on the armrest, facing Eloise. Her drink was on the floor, within reach.

"Well, he could make me laugh *that* way," Eloise said. "He could do it when he talked to me. He could do it over the phone. He could even do it in a letter. And the best thing about it was that he didn't even try to be funny — he just *was* funny." She turned her head slightly toward Mary Jane. "Hey, how 'bout throwing me a cigarette?"

"I can't reach 'em," Mary Jane said.

"Nuts[4] to you." Eloise looked up at the ceiling again. "Once," she said, "I fell down. I used to wait for him at the bus stop, right outside the PX, and he showed up late once, just as the bus was pulling out. We started to run for it, and I fell and twisted my ankle. He said, `Poor Uncle Wiggily.' He meant my ankle. Poor old Uncle Wiggily, he called it. . . . God, he was nice."

"Doesn't Lew have a sense of humor?" Mary Jane said.

"What?"

"Doesn't Lew have a sense of humor?"

"Oh, God! Who knows? Yes. I guess so. He laughs at cartoons and stuff." Eloise raised her head, lifted her drink from her chest, and drank from it.

"Well," Mary Jane said. "That isn't everything. I mean that isn't

1) this-a-way: 이 모양으로.
2) executed a grind: 한 바퀴 빙 돌았다.
3) bust: (*v.*) burst; spree; go, come, do, stc., by force or suddenly.
4) Nuts: (Slang) insane; crazy.

everything."

"What isn't?"

"Oh. . . you know. Laughing and stuff."

"Who says it isn't?" Eloise said. "Listen, if you're not gonna be a nun or something, you might as well laugh."

Mary Jane giggled. "You're *terrible*," she said.

"Ah, God, he was nice," Eloise said. "He was either funny or sweet. Not that damn little-boy sweet, either. It was a special kind of sweet. You know what he did once?"

"Uh-uh," Mary Jane said.

"We were on the train going from Trenton to New York — it was just right after he was drafted. It was cold in the car and I had my coat sort of over us. I remember I had Joyce Morrow's cardigan[1] on underneath — you remember that darling blue cardigan she had?"

Mary Jane nodded, but Eloise didn't look over to get the nod.

"Well, he sort of had his hand on my stomach. You know. Anyway, all of a sudden he said my stomach was so beautiful he wished some officer would come up and order him to stick his other hand through the window.

He said he wanted to do what was fair. Then he took his hand away and told the conductor to throw his shoulders back. He told him if there was one thing he couldn't stand it was a man who didn't look proud of his uniform. The conductor just told him to go back to sleep." Eloise reflected a moment, then said, "It wasn't always what he said, but how he said it. You know."

"Have you ever told Lew about him — I mean, at all?"

"Oh," Eloise said, "I started to, once. But the first thing he asked me was what his rank was."

"What was his rank?"

"Ha!" said Eloise.

"No, I just meant — "

Eloise laughed suddenly, from her diaphragm.[2] "You know what

1) cardigan: cardigan jacket; a knitted worsted jacket.

2) from her diaphragm: 옆구리를 쥐어짜면서. diaphragm=a partition of muscles and tendons separating the cavity of the chest from the cavity of the abdomen.

he said once? He said he felt he was advancing in the Army, but in a different direction from everybody else. He said that when he'd get his first promotion, instead of getting stripes[1] he'd have his sleeves taken away from him. He said when he'd get to be a general, he'd be stark[2] naked. All he'd be wearing would be a little infantry button in his navel." Eloise looked over at Mary Jane, who wasn't laughing. "Don't you think that's funny?"

"Yes. Only, why don't you tell Lew about him sometime, though?"

"Why? Because he's too damn unintelligent, that's why," Eloise said. "Besides. Listen to me, career girl.[3] If you ever get married again, don't tell your husband *any*thing. Do you hear me?"

"Why?" said Mary Jane.

"Because I say so, that's why," said Eloise. "They wanna[4] think you spent your whole life vomiting every time a boy came near you. I'm not kidding, either. Oh, you can tell them stuff. But never honestly. I mean never *honestly*. If you tell 'em you once knew a handsome boy, you gotta[5] say in the same breath he was *too* handsome. And if you tell 'em you knew a witty boy, you gotta tell 'em he was kind of a smart aleck,[6] though, or a wise guy. If you *don't*, they hit you over the head with the poor boy every time they get a chance." Eloise paused to drink from her glass and to think. "Oh," she said, "they'll listen very *maturely* and all that. They'll even look intelligent as hell. But don't let it fool[7] you. Believe me. You'll go through *hell*[8] if you ever give 'em any credit for intelligence. Take my word.[9]"

Mary Jane, looking depressed, raised her chin from the armrest of

---

1) stripes: number of combination of strios of braid on te sleeve of a uniform to show rank, length o service, etc.
2) stark: completely; entirely.
3) career girl: girl who has a job(profession, occupation).
4) wanna: want to.
5) gotta: have(has) got to; have to.
6) aleck: guy. Aleck는 남자 이름(Alexandea의 애칭). smart aleck: (Colloq.) 젠체하는 녀석.
7) fool: deceive.
8) go through *hell*: go through danger or trouble. 죽을 고생을 하다.
9) Take my word: Believe my word.

the couch. For a change, she supported her chin on her forearm. She thought over Eloise's advice. "You can't call Lew not intelligent," she said aloud.

"*Who* can't?"

"I mean isn't he intelligent?" Mary Jane said innocently.

"Oh," said Eloise, "what's the use of talking? Let's drop[1] it. I'll just depress you. Shut me up.[2]"

"Well, wudga marry him for,[3] then?" Mary Jane said.

"Oh, God! I don't know. He told me he loved Jane Austen.[4] He told me her books meant a great deal to him. That's exactly what he said. I found out after we were married that he hadn't even read *one* of her books. You know who his favorite author is?"

Mary Jane shook her head.

"L. Manning Vines. Ever hear of him?"

"Uh-uh."

"Neither did I. Neither did anybody else. He wrote a book about four men that starved to death in Alaska. Lew doesn't remember the name of it, but it's the most beautifully *written* book he's ever read. *Christ*! He isn't even honest enough to come right out and say he liked it because it was about four guys that starved to death in an igloo[5] or something. He has to say it was beautifully *written*."

"You're too critical," Mary Jane said. "I mean you're too critical. Maybe it *was* a good — "

"Take my word for it, it couldn't've been," Eloise said. She thought for a moment, then added, "At least, you have a job. I mean at least you — "

"But listen, though," said Mary Jane. "Do you think you'll ever tell him Walt was killed, even? I mean he wouldn't be jealous, would he, if he knew Walt was — you know. Killed and everything."

"Oh, lover! You poor, innocent little career girl," said Eloise. "He'd

---

1) drop: stop; end.
2) Shut up: (Colloq.) stop talking.
3) wudga marry him for?: 뭣 때문에 결혼했어?
4) Jane Austen: (1775-1817) Engligh novelist.
5) igloo: a dome-shaped hut used by Eskimos, often built of blocks of hard snow.

be worse. He'd be a *ghoul.*[1] Listen. All he knows is that I went around with somebody named Walt — some *wisecracking*[2] G. I.[3] The last thing I'd do would be to tell him he was killed. But the last thing. And if I *did* — which I wouldn't — but if I did, I'd tell him he was killed in action.[4]"

Mary Jane pushed her chin farther forward over the edge of her forearm.

"El. . ." she said.

"Why won't you tell me how he was killed? I *swear* I won't tell anybody. Honestly. Please."

"No."

"Please. Honestly. I won't tell anybody."

Eloise finished her drink and replaced the empty glass upright on her chest. "You'd tell Akim Tamiroff," she said.

"No, I wouldn't! I mean I wouldn't tell any — "

"Oh," said Eloise, "his regiment was resting someplace. It was between battles or something, this friend of his said that wrote me. Walt and some other boy were putting this little Japanese stove in a package. Some colonel wanted to send it home. Or they were taking it *out* of the package to rewrap it — I don't know exactly. Anyway, it was all full of gasoline and junk[5] and it exploded in their faces. The other boy just lost an eye." Eloise began to cry. She put her hand around the empty glass on her chest to steady it.

Mary Jane slid off the couch and, on her knees, took three steps over to Eloise and began to stroke her forehead. "Don't cry, El. Don't cry."

"Who's crying?" Eloise said.

"I know, but don't. I mean it isn't worth it or anything.

The front door opened.

---

1) *ghoul*: a horrible demon in Oriental stories, believed to feed on corpses; person who robs graves or corpses.

2) *wisecracking*: smart remarking.

3) G. I.: (Colloq.) an enlisted soldier; serviceman.

4) in action: in a minor battle.

5) junk: old metal, paper, rags, etc.; rubbish; trash.

"That's Ramona back," Eloise said nasally. "Do me a favor. Go out in the kitchen and tell whosis[1] to give her her dinner early. Willya?[2]"

"All right, if you promise not to cry, though."

"I promise. Go on. I don't feel like going out to that damn kitchen right this minute."

Mary Jane stood up, losing and recovering her balance, and left the room.

She was back in less than two minutes, with Ramona running ahead of her. Ramona ran as flat-footed[3] as possible, trying to get the maximum noise out of her open galoshes.

"She wouldn't let me take her galoshes off," Mary Jane said.

Eloise, still lying on her back on the floor, was using her handkerchief. She spoke into it, addressing Ramona. "Go out and tell Grace to take your galoshes off. You know you're not supposed to come into the —"

"She's in the lavatory,[4]" Ramona said.

Eloise put away her handkerchief and hoisted herself to a sitting position. "Gimme your foot," she said. "Sit down, first, please. . . . Not *there* — *here*. God!"

On her knees, looking under the table for her cigarettes, Mary Jane said, "Hey. Guess what happened to Jimmy."

"No idea. Other foot. *Other* foot."

"He got runned over,[5]" said Mary Jane. "Isn't that tragic?"

"I saw Skipper with a bone," Ramona told Eloise.

"What happened to Jimmy?" Eloise said to her.

"He got runned over and killed. I saw Skipper with a bone, and he wouldn't —"

"Gimme your forehead a second," Eloise said. She reached out and

---

1) whosis: whozis. (Who is this?)에서 any person or object whose name is unknown or forgotten.
2) Willya: Will you?
3) flat-footed: having feet with flattened arches.
4) lavatory: bathroom; toilet.
5) got runned over: 차에 치었다.

felt Ramona's forehead. "You feel a little feverish. Go tell Grace you're to have your dinner upstairs. Then you're to go straight to bed. I'll be up later. Go on, now, please. Take these *with* you."

Ramona slowly giant-stepped her way out of the room.

"Throw me one," Eloise said to Mary Jane. "Let's have another drink."

Mary Jane carried a cigarette over to Eloise. "Isn't that something? About Jimmy? What an imagination!"

"Mm. You go get[1] the drinks, huh? And bring the bottle. . . I don't wanna go out there. The whole damn place smells like orange juice."

At five minutes past seven, the phone rang. Eloise got up from the window seat and felt in the dark for her shoes. She couldn't find them. In her stocking feet, she walked steadily, almost languidly, toward the phone. The ringing didn't disturb Mary Jane, who was asleep on the couch, face down.

"Hello," Eloise said into the phone, without having turned the overhead light on. "Look, I can't meet you. Mary Jane's here. She's got her car parked right in front of me and she can't find the key. I can't get out. We spent about twenty minutes looking for it in the wuddayacallit[2] — the snow and stuff. Maybe you can get a lift with Dick and Mildred." She listened. "Oh. Well, that's tough, kid. Why don't you boys form a platoon and march home? You can say that hut-hopehoop-hoop business.[3] You can be the big shot.[4]" She listened again. "I'm not funny," she said. "Really, I'm not. It's just my face.[5]" She hung up.

She walked, less steadily, back into the living room. At the window seat, she poured what was left in the bottle of Scotch into her glass. It made about a finger.[6] She drank it off, shivered, and sat down.

When Grace turned on the light in the dining room, Eloise jumped.

---

1) go get: go and get; go to get.

2) wuddayacallit: would you call it. 뭔가. lift=free ride.

3) that hut-hopehoop-hoop business: 군대행진 식으로 하나 둘 셋 넷 하는 일.

4) big shot: an important person; a leader; a high official; a person of high rank. big cheese or big gun or big wheel or big wig라고도 함.

5) It's just my face: 그건 바로 나의 체면이다. face=dignity; prestige.

6) It made about a finger: 손가락 하나의 깊이만큼 찼다.

Without getting up, she called in to Grace, "You better not serve until eight, Grace. Mr. Wengler'll be a little late."

Grace appeared in the dining-room light but didn't come forward. "The lady go?" she said.

"She's resting."

"Oh," said Grace. "Miz Wengler,[1)] I wondered if it'd be all right if my husband passed the evenin' here. I got plentya[2)] room in my room, and he don't have to be back in New York till tomorrow mornin', and it's so *bad* out."

"Your husband? Where is he?"

"Well, right now," Grace said, "he's in the kitchen."

"Well, I'm afraid he can't spend the night here, Grace."

"Ma'am?"

"I say I'm afraid he can't spend the night here. I'm not running[3)] a hotel."

Grace stood for a moment, then said, "Yes, Ma'am," and went out to the kitchen.

Eloise left the living room and climbed the stairs, which were lighted very faintly by the overglow from the dining room. One of Ramona's galoshes was lying on the landing. Eloise picked it up and threw it, with as much force as possible, over the side of the banister; it struck the foyer floor with a violent thump.

She snapped on the light in Ramona's room and held on to the switch, as if for support. She stood still for a moment looking at Ramona. Then she let go of the light switch and went quickly over to the bed. "Ramona. Wake up. Wake *up*."

Ramona was sleeping far over on one side of the bed, her right buttock off the edge. Her glasses were on a little Donald Duck night table, folded neatly and laid stems down.

"*Ramona!*"

The child awoke with a sharp intake of breath.[4)] Her eyes opened

---

1) Miz Wengler: Mrs. Wengler.

2) plentya: plenty of.

3) run: conduct; manage.

4) with a sharp intake of breath: 숨을 꿀꺽 들이키며.

wide, but she narrowed them almost at once. "Mommy?"

"I thought you told me Jimmy Jimmereeno was run over and killed."

"What?"

"You heard me," Eloise said. "Why are you sleeping way over here?"

"Because," said Ramona.

"Because why? Ramona, I don't feel like— "

"Because I don't want to hurt Mickey."

"*Who*?"

"Mickey," said Ramona, rubbing her nose. "Mickey Mickeranno."

Eloise raised her voice to a shriek. "You get in the center of that bed. *Go on*.[1]"

Ramona, extremely frightened, just looked up at Eloise.

"All right." Eloise grabbed Ramona's ankles and half lifted and half pulled her over to the middle of the bed. Ramona neither struggled nor cried; she let herself be moved without actually submitting to it.[2]

"Now go to sleep," Eloise said, breathing heavily. "Close your eyes. . . . You heard me, *close* them."

Ramona closed her eyes.

Eloise went over to the light switch and flicked it off. But she stood for a long time in the doorway. Then, suddenly, she rushed, in the dark, over to the night table, banging her knee against the foot of the bed, but too full of purpose to feel pain. She picked up Ramona's glasses and, holding them in both hands, pressed them against her cheek. Tears rolled down her face, wetting the lenses. "Poor Uncle Wiggily," she said over and over again. Finally, she put the glasses back on the night table, lenses down.

She stooped over, losing her balance, and began to tuck in[3] the blankets of Ramona's bed. Ramona was awake. She was crying and had been crying. Eloise kissed her wetly on the mouth and wiped the hair out of her eyes and then left the room.

She went downstairs, staggering now very badly, and wakened Mary

---

1) *Go on*: 어서.

2) she let herself be moved without actually submitting to it: 복종하는 것도 아니고 그저 끌리는 대로 내맡기고 있었다.

3) tuck in: thrust the edge closely into place.

Jane.

"*Wuzzat?*[1] Who? *Huh*?" said Mary Jane, sitting bolt upright on the couch.[2]

"Mary Jane. Listen. Please," Eloise said, sobbing. "You remember our freshman year, and I had that brawn-and-yellow dress I bought in Boise, and Miriam Ball told me nobody wore those kind of dresses in New York, and I cried all night?" Eloise shook Mary Jane's arm. "I was a nice girl," she pleaded, "wasn't I?"

---

1) *Wuzzat?*: Who is that?

2) sitting bolt upright on the couch: 침상 의자에 벌떡 일어나 앉으며.

Flowering Judas

by Katherine Anne Porter

Katherine Anne Porter (1894-1980) was born in Indiana Creek, Texas, the great-great-great-granddaughter of Daniel Boone and spent her early life in Texas and Louisiana. She was educated in various convent schools of the South. She married in 1933 and was soon divorced; in 1938 she married Albert Russel Erskine, Jr., and they were divorced in 1942. Miss Porter has lived in various parts of the world: in the South, in New York City, in Europe, in Mexico. Using details from her experiences, she has therefore employed a variety of backgrounds in her fiction. She was awarded a Guggenheim Fellowship and again in 1938. In 1944 she was Fellow of Regional American Literature in the Library of Congress, and in 1958she was writer in residence at the University of Virginia. Although *Ship of Fools* is her major novel, she has written primarily short stories and novelettes.

Throughout her career Miss Porter has worked scrupulously and painstakingly, refusing to print anything until completely satisfied with it. Her devotion to her craft has been richly rewarded, for, although she has published comparatively little, she has achieved high distinction in the art of fiction.

BRAGGIONI SITS heaped upon[1] the edge of a straight-backed chair much too small for him, and sings to Laura in a furry, mournful voice. Laura has begun to find reasons for avoiding her own house until the latest possible moment, for Braggioni is there almost every night. No matter how late she is, he will be sitting there with a surly, waiting expression, pulling at his kinky yellow hair, thumbing the strings of his guitar, snarling a tune under his breath.[2] Lupe the Indian maid meets Laura at the door, and says with a flicker of a glance towards the upper room, "He waits."

Laura wishes to lie down, she is tired of her hairpins and the feel of her long tight sleeves, but she says to him, "Have you a new song for me this evening?" If he says yes, she asks him to sing it. If he

1) sit heaped upon: ~에 더미를 쌓아올린 듯 앉아 있다.
2) snarl a tune under his breath: 흥얼흥얼 콧노래를 부르다.

says no, she remembers his favorite one, and asks him to sing it again. Lupe brings her a cup of chocolate and a plate of rice, and Laura eats at the small table under the lamp, first inviting Brag, whose answer is always the same: "I have eaten, and besides, chocolate thickens the voice.[1]"

Laura says, "Sing, then." and Braggioni heaves himself into song. He scratches the guitar familiarly as though it were a pet animal, and sings passionately off key, taking the high notes in a prolonged painful squea1.[2] Laura, who haunts the markets listening to the ballad singers, and stops every day to hear the blind boy playing his reed-flute in Sixteenth of September Street, listens to Braggioni with pitiless courtesy,[3] because she dares not smile at his miserable performance. Nobody dares to smile at him. Braggioni is cruel to everyone, with a kind of specializd insolence,[4] but he is so vain of his talents, and so sensitive to slights, it would require a cruelty and vanity greater than his own to lay a finger on the vast cureless wound of his self-esteem. It would require courage, too, for it is dangerous to offend him, and nobody has this courage.

Braggioni loves himself with such tenderness and amplitude and eternal chairity that his followers-for he is a leader of men, a skilled revolutionist, and his skin has been punctured in honorable warfare[5] -warm themselves in the reflected glow, and say to each other:

"He has a real nobility, a love of humanity raised above mere personal affections." The excess of this self-love has flowed out, inconveniently for her, over Laura, who, with so many others, owes her comfortable situation and her salary to him. When he is in a very good humor, he tells her, "I am tempted to forgive you for being a *gringa.*[6] *Gringita*[7]!"

---

1) chocolate thickens the voice: 초콜릿을 먹으면 목소리가 탁해진다.
2) squeal: a long, sharp, shrill cry.
3) with pitiless courtesy: 쌀쌀한 태도로.
4) with a kind of specialized insolence: 일종의 특수한 오만으로. insolence= bold rudeness; insulting behavior or speech.
5) his skin has been punctured in honorable warfare: 그의 피부에는 명예로운 투쟁의 자국이 남아 있었다.
6) *gringa*: 이방인(異邦人).
7) *Gringita*: 이방인의 여인.

and Laura, burning, imagines herself leaning forward suddenly, and with a sound back-handed slap[1)] wiping the suety smile from his face. If he notices her eyes at these moments he gives no sign.

She knows what Braggioni would offer her, and she must resist tenaciously without appearing to resist, and if she could avoid it she would not admit even to herself the slow drift of his intention. During these long evenings which have spoiled a long month for her, she sits in her deep chair with an open book on her knees, resting her eyes on the consoling rigidity of the printed page[2)] when the sight and sound of Braggioni singing threaten to identify themselves with all her remembered afflictions and to add their weight to her uneasy premonitions of the future. The gluttonous[3)] bulk of Bragginoi has become a symbol of her many disillusions, for a revolutionist should be lean, animated by heroic faith, a vessel of abstract virtues. This is nonsense, she knows it now and is ashamed of it. Revolution must have leaders, and leadership is a career for energetic men. She is, her comrades tell her, full of romantic error, for what she defines as cynicism in them is merely "a developed sense of reality." She is almost too willing to say, "I am wrong, I suppose I don't really understand the principles," and afterward she makes a secret truce with herself determined not to surrender her will to such expedient[4)] logic. But she cannot help feeling that she has been betrayed irreparably by the disunion[5)] between her way of living and her feeling of what life should be, and at times she is almost contented to rest in this sense of grievance[6)] as a private store of consolation.[7)] Sometimes she wishes to run away, but she stays. Now she longs to fly out of this room, down the narrow stairs, and into the street where the houses lean together like conspirators

1) with a sound back-handed slap: 철썩 한 대를 갈겨 주어.

2) resting her eyes on the consoling rigidity of the printed page: 마음을 위로해 주는 딱딱한 활자에 눈을 던지며.

3) gluttonous: greedy about food.

4) expedient: suitable or desirable.

5) disunion: disagreement; separation.

6) contented to rest in this sense of grievance: 이러한 불만(슬픔)에 잠기는 것에 만족했다. grievance=cause for complaint.

7) consolation: comfort.

under a single mottled lamp, and leave Braggioni singing to himself.

Instead she looks at Braggioni, frankly and clearly, like a good child who understands the rules of behavior. Her knees cling together under sound[1)] blue serge, and her round white collar is not purposely nun-like. She wears the uniform of an idea,[2)] and has renounced vanities. She was born Roman Catholic, and in spite of her fear of being seen by someone who might make a scandal of it, she slips now and again into some crumbling little church, kneels on the chilly stone, and says a Hail Mary[3)] on the gold rosary[4)] she bought in Tehuantepec. It is no good and she ends by examining the altar with its tinsel flowers and ragged brocades, and feels tender about the battered doll-shape of some male saint[5)] whose white, lacetrimmed drawers hang limply around his ankles below the hieratic dignity of his velvet robe.[6)] She has encased[7)] herself in a set of principles derived from her early training, leaving no detail of gesture or of personal taste untouched,[8)] and for this reason she will not wear lace made on machines. This is her private heresy, for in her special group the machine is sacred, and will be the salvation of the workers. She loves fine lace, and there is a tiny edge of fluted cobweb on this collar, which is one of twenty precisely alike, folded in blue tissue paper in the upper drawer of her clothes chest.

Braggioni catches her glance solidly as if he had been waiting for it, leans forward, balancing his paunch[9)] between his spread knees, and sings with tremendous emphasis, weighing his words. He has, the song relates,[10)] no father and no mother, nor even a friend to console

1) sound: solid. 딱 달라붙은.
2) the uniform of an idea: 하나의 관념을 나타내는 제복.
3) says a Hail Mary: 아베 마리아를 부르다.
4) rosary: string of beads for keeping count in saying a series of prayers.
5) feels tender about the battered doll-shape of some male saint: 부서진 인형과 같은 모양의, 어느 어느 남자의 성상(聖像)에 마음의 부드러움을 느낀다.
6) whose white, lace-trimmed drawers hang . . . of his velvet robe: 그 상(像)의 발목 주위, 정직자의 위엄을 갖춘 빌로오드의 법의(法衣) 밑에는 레이스의 주름잡힌 속바지가 축 늘어져 있었다.
7) encase: incase; cover completely; enclose.
8) leaving no detail . . . untouched: 강화의 흔적을 남기지 않은 것이 없다.
9) paunch: belly; stomach.
10) the song relates: 노래는 말한다, 이런 뜻의 노래이다.

him; lonely as a wave of the sea he comes and goes, lonely as a wave. His mouth opens round and yearns sideways, his balloon cheeks grow oily with the labor of song. He bulges marvelously in his expensive garments. Over his lavender collar, crushed upon a purple necktie, held by a diamond hoop: over his ammunition belt of tooled leather worked in silver,[1] bucked cruelly around his gasping middle:[2] over the tops of his glossy yellow shoes Braggioni swells with ominous ripeness, his mauve silk hose stretched taut,[3] his ankles bound with the stout leather thongs of his shoes.[4]

When he stretches his eyelids at Laura she notes again that his eyes are the true tawny yellow cat's eyes. He is rich, not in money, he tells her, but in power, and this power brings with it the blame]?s ownership of things, and the right to indulge his love of small luxuries.[5] "I have a taste for the elegant refinements," he said once, flourishing a yellow silk handkerchief before her nose. "Smell that? It is Jockey Club, imported from New York." Nonetheless he is wounded by life. He will say so presently. "It is true everything truns to dust in the hand, to gall on the tongue,[6]" He sighs and his leather belt creaks like a saddle girth. "I am disappointed in everything as it comes. Everything." He shakes his head. "You, poor thing, you will be disappointed too. You are born for it. We are more alike than you realize in some things. Wait and see. Some day you will remember what I have told you, you will know that Braggioni was your friend."

Laura feels a slow chill, a purely physical sense of danger, a warning in her blood that violence, mutilation, a shocking death, wait for her

---

1) over his ammunition belt of tooled leatber worked in silver: 은 세공의 장식을 단 압형(押型) 가죽의 탄약대(彈藥帶)에서도.

2) bucked cruelly around his gasping middle: 헐떡거리는 배를 잔인하리만큼 졸라맨. middle=waist.

3) his mauve silk hose stretched taut: 엷은 자주빛 양말은 팽팽히 당겨져 있었다. hose=stockings. taut=tightly drawn.

4) his ankles bound with the stout leather thongs of his shoes: 그의 발목은 튼튼한 가죽 구두끈으로 꽉 동여져 있다.

5) the right to indulge his love of small luxuries: 사소한 사치욕(奢侈欲)을 만족시키는 권리.

6) (turns) to gall on the tongue: 혀 끝에 닿으면(무엇이건) 쓰디쓰게 된다. gall=anything very bitter or harsh.

with lessening patience.[1] She has translated this fear into something homely, immediate, and sometimes hesitates before crossing the street. "My personal fate is nothing, except as the test imony of a mental attitude," she reminds herself, quoting from some forgotten philosophic primer,[2] and is sensible enough to add, "Anyhow, I shall not be killed by an automobile if I can help it."

"It may be true I am as corrupt, in another way, as Braggioni," she thinks in spite of herself, "as callous, as incomplete," and if this is so, any kind of death seems preferable. Still she sits quietly, she does not run. Where could she go? Uninvited she has promised herself to this place; she can no longer imagine herself as living in another country, and there is no pleasure in remembering her life before she came here.

Precisely what is the nature of this devotion, its true motives, and what are its obligations? Laura cannot say. She spends part of her days in Xochimilco, near by, teaching Indian children to say in English, "The cat is on the mat." When she appears in the classroom they crowd about her with smiles on their wise, innocent, clay-colored faces, crying, "Good morning, my titcher!" in immaculate voices, and they make of her desk a fresh garden of flowers every day.

During her leisure she goes to union meetings and listens to busy important voices quarreling over tactics, methods, internal politics. She visits the prisoners of her own political faith in their cells, where they entertain themselves with counting cockroaches, repenting of their indiscretions, composing their memoirs. writing out manifestoes and plans for their comrades who are still walking about free, hands in pockets. sniffing fresh air. Laura brings them food and cigarettes and a little money, and she brings messages disguised in equivocal phrases[3] from the men outside who dare not set foot in the prison for fear of disappearing into the cells kept empty for them. If the prisoners confuse night and day, and com, "Dear little Laura, time doesn't pass in this infernal hole, and I won't know when it is time to sleep unless

1) with lessening patience: 차츰 참을 수 없게.
2) primer: a first book in reading. 입문서.
3) messages disguised in equivocal phrases: 애매한 문구로 얼버무린 메시지.

I have a remind?," she brings them their favorite narcotics,[1] and says in a tone that does not wound them with pity,[2] "Tonight will really be night for you," and though her Spanish amuses them, they find her comforting, useful. If they lose patience and all faith, and curse the slowness of their friends in coming to their rescue with money and influence, they trust her not to repeat everything, and if she inquires, "Where do you think we can find money, or influence?" they are certain to answer, "Well, there is Braggioni, why doesn't he do something?"

She smuggles letters from headquarters to men hiding from firing squads in back streets in mildewed houses, where they sit in tumbled beds and talk bitterly as if all Mexico were at their heels, when Laura knows positively they might appear at the band concert in the Alameda on Sunday morning, and no one would notice them. But Braggioni says, "Let them sweat[3] a little. The next time they may be careful. It is very restful to have them out of the way[4] for a while." She is not afraid to knock on any door in any street after midnight, and enter in the darkness, and say to one of these men who is really in danger: "They will be looking for you—seriously—tomorrow morning after six. Here is some money from Vicente. Go to Vera Cruz and wait."

She borrows money from the Roumanian agitator to give to his bitter enemy the Polish agitator. The favor of Braggioni is their disputed territory,[5] and Braggioni holds the balance nicely, for he can use them both. The Polish agitator talks love to her over cafe tables, hoping to exploit what he believes is her secret sentimental preference for him,[6] and he gives her misinformation which he begs her to repeat

---

1) narcotics: drug that produces drowsiness, sleep, dullness and lessens pain by dulling the nerves.

2) in a tone that does not wound them with pity: 상대편의 마음을 상하게 하지 않는 동정어린 말투로.

3) sweat: (Colloq.) suffer from anxiety, impatience, etc.

4) out of the way: so as not to be an obstacle, hindrance, etc.

5) The favor of Braggioni is their disputed territory: Braggioni의 호의를 사려고 그들은 서로 다투고 있다.

6) hoping to exploit what he believes is her secret sentimental preference for him: 그녀가 남몰래 자기에게만 호의를 베풀고 있는 줄로 믿어 그것을 이용하고자.

as the solemn truth to certain persons. The Roumanian is more adroit. He is generous with his money in all good causes, and lies to her with an air of ingenuous candor,[1] as if he were her good friend and confidant. She never repeats anything they may say. Braggioni never asks question. He has other ways to discover all that he wishes to know about them.

Nobody touches her, but all praise her gray eyes, and the soft, round under lip which promises gayety, yet is always grave, nearly always firmly closed: and they cannot understand why she is in Mexico. She walks back and forth on her errands, with puzzled eyebrows, carrying her little folder of drawings and music and school papers. No dancer dances more beautifully than Laura walks, and she inspires some amusing, unexpected ardors, which cause little gossip, because nothing comes of them. A young captain who had been a soldier in Zapata's army attempted, during a horseback ride near Cuernavaca, to express his desire for her with the noble simplicity befitting a rude folk-hero[2]: but gently, because he was gentle. This gentleness was his defeat, for when he alighted, and removed her foot from the stirrup, and essayed[3] to draw her down into his arms, her horse, ordinarily a tame one, shied[4] fiercely, reared and plunged away. The young hero's horse careered blindly after his stable-mate, and the hero did not return to the hotel until rather late that evening. At breakfast he came to her table in full charro dress, gray buckskin jacket and trousers with strings of silver buttons down the leg, and he was in a humorous, careless mood. "May I sit with you?" and "You are a wonderful rider. was terrified that you might be thrown and dragged. I should never have forgiven myself. But I cannot admire you enough for your riding!"

"I learned to ride in Arizona," said Laura.

"If you will ride with me again this morning, I promise you a horse that will not shy with you," he said. But Laura remembered that she

---

1) with an air of ingenuous candor: 꾸밈없는 (솔직한) 담담한 태도로.

2) with the noble simplicity befitting a rude folk-hero: 소박한 민중의 영웅답게 단도직입적으로.

3) essay: try; attempt.

4) shied: pt. and pp. of shy. shy=(*v.*) start back or aside suddenly.

must return to Mexico City at noon.

Next morning the children made a eeleration and spent their playtime writing on the blackboard, "We lov ar ticher,"[1] and with tinted chalks they drew wreaths of flowers around the words. The young hero wrote her a letter: "I am a very foolish, wasteful, impulsive man. I should have first said I love you, and then you would not have run away. But you shall see me again." Laura thought, "I must send him a box of colored crayons," but she was trying to forgive herself for having spurred her horse at the wrong moment.

A brown, shock-haired youth came and stood in her patio[2] one night and sang like a lost soul for two hours, but Laura could think of nothing to do about it. The moonlight spread a wash of gauzy silver over the clear spaces of the garden, and the shadows were cobalt blue. The scarlet blossoms of the Judas tree were dull purple, and the names of the colors repeated themselves automatically in her mind, while she watched not the boy, but his shadow, fall? like a dark garment across the fountain rim, trailing in the water. Lupe came silently and whispered expert counsel in her ear: "If you will throw him one little flower, he will sing another song or two and go away." Laura threw the flower, and he sang a last song and went away with the flower tucked in the band of his hat. Lupe said, "He is one of the organizers of the Typographers Union, and before that he sold corridos in the Merced market, and before that, he came from Guanajuato, where I was born. I would not trust any man, but I trust least those from Guanajuato."

She did not tell Laura that he would be back again the next night, and the next, nor that he would follow her at a certain fixed distance[3] around the Merced market, through the Zocolo, up Francisco J. Madero A venue, and so along the Paseo de la Reforma to Chapultepec Park, and into the Philosopher's Foot,[4] still with that flower withering in his hat, and an indivisible attention in his eyes.[5]

---

1) We lov ar ticher: We love our teacher.
2) patio: an inner court or yard open to the sky.
3) of a certain fixed distance: 일정한 간격을 두고.
4) Philosopher's Footpath: 명상의 오솔길.
5) (with) an indivisible attention in his eyes: 심각한 표정을 지으면서.

Now Laura is accustomed to him, it means nothing except that he is nineteen years old and is observing a convention with all propriety, as though it were founded on a law of nature, which in the end it might well prove to be. He is beginning to write poems which he prints on a wooden press, and he leaves them stuck like handbills in her door. She is pleasantly disturbed by the abstract, unhurried watchfulness of his black eyes which will in time turn easily towards another object. She tells herself that throwing the flower was a mistake, for she is twenty-two years old and knows better; but she refuses to regret it, and persuades herself that her negation of all external events as they occur[1] is a sign that she is gradually perfecting herself in the stoicism she strives to cultivate against that disaster she fears, though she cannot name it.

She is not at home in the world. Every day she teaches children who remain strangers to her, though she loves their tender round hands and their charming opportunist savagery.[2] She knocks at unfamiliar doors not knowing whether a friend or a stranger shall answer, and even if a known face emerges from the sour gloom of that unknown interior, still it is the face of a stranger. No matter what this stranger says to her, nor what her message to him, the very cells of her flesh reject knowledge and kinship in one monotonous word. No. No. No. She draws her strength from this one holy talismanic word which does not suffer her to be led into evil. Denying everything, she may walk anywhere in safety, she looks at everything without amazement.

No, repeats this firm unchanging voice of her blood; and she looks at Braggioni without amazement. He is a great man, he wishes to impress this simple girl who covers her great round breasts with thick dark cloth, and who hides long, invaluably beautiful legs under a heavy skirt. She is almost thin except, for[3] the incomprehensible fullness of her breasts, like a nursing mother's,[4] and Braggioni, who considers himself a judge of women, speculates again on the puzzle of her

1) her negation of all external events as they occur: (주위에서) 일어나는 온갖 외적 사건을 받아들이지 않는 것.

2) their charming opportunist savagery: 기회만 있으면 뛰놀고자 덤비는 그 애들의 귀여운 야만성.

3) except for: but for; without; with the exception of.

4) like a nursing mother's: 젖꼭지를 물리고 있는 애엄마(의 젖)처럼.

notorious virginity,[1] and takes the liberty of speech[2] which she permits without a sign of modesty, indeed, without any sort of sign, which is disconcert.[3]

"You think you are so cold, *gringita*! Wait and see. You will surprise yourself some day! May I be there to advise you!" He stretches his eyelids at her, and his ill-humored eat's eyes waver in a separate glance for the two points of light marking the opposite ends of a smoothly drawn path between the swollen curve of her breasts. He is not put off by that blue serge, nor by her resolutely fixed gaze. There is all the time in the world. His cheeks are bellying with the wind of song. "O girl with the dark eyes," he sings, and reconsiders. "But yours are not dark. I can change all that. O girl with the green eyes, you have stolen my heart away!" then his mind wanders to the song, and Laura feels the weight of his attention being shifted elsewhere. Singing thus, he seems harmless, he is quite harmless, there is nothing to do but sit patiently and say "No," when the moment comes. She draws a full breath, and her mind wanders also, but not far. She dares not wander too far.

Not for nothing[4] has Braggioni taken pains to be a good revolutionist and a professional lover of humanity. He will never die of it. He has the malice, the cleverness, the wickedness, the sharpness of wit, the hardness of heart, stipulated for loving the world profitably. *He will never die of it.* He will live to see himself kicked out from his feeding trough[5] by other hungry world saviors. Traditionally he must sing in spite of his life which drives him to bloodshed, he tells Laura, for his father was a Tuscany[6] peasant who drifted to Yucatan[7] and married

1) the puzzle of her notorious virginity: 그녀가 독신 생활을 지키고 있다고 널리 알려진 그 수수께끼.
2) takes the liberty of speech: 함부로 입을 놀리다. take liberties=to act toward in too close or friendly a manner.
3) disconcert: disturb the self-possession of; confuse; upset.
4) Not for nothing: ~한 것도 목적하는 바 없는 것은 아니었다.
5) He will live to see himself kicked out from his feeding trough: 그의 밥통에서 채어 굴러 떨어지는 한이 있더라도 살아남을 사나이다. feeding trough=a long, narrow container for holding food.
6) Tuscany: 이탈리아 서해안의 주.
7) Yucatan: 멕시코 동남부의 주.

a Maya woman: a woman of race, an aristocrat. They gave him the love and knowledge of music, thus: and under the rip of his thumbnail, the strings of the instrument complain like exposed nerves.

Once he was called Delgadito[1] by all the girls and married women who ran after him; he was so scrawny all his bones showed under his thin cotton clothing, and he could squeeze his emptiness to the very backbone with his two hands.[2] He was a poet and the revolution was only a dream then; too many women loved him and sapped away his youth, and he could never find enough to eat anywhere, anywhere! Now he is a leader of men, crafty men who whisper in his ear, hungry men who wait for hours outside his office for a word with him, emaciated men with wild faces who waylay[3] him at the street gate with a timid, "Comrade, let me tell you. . ." and they blow the foul breath from their empty stomachs in his face.

He is always sympathetic. He gives them handfuls of small coins from his own pocket, he promises them work, there will be demonstrations, they must join the unions and attend the meet, above all they must be on the watch for spies. They are closer to him than his own brothers, without them he can do nothing — until tomorrow, comrade!

Until tomorrow. "They are stupid, they are lazy, they are treach, they would cut my throat for nothing," he says to Laura. He has good food and abundant drink, he hires an automobile and drives in the Paseo on Sunday morning, and enjoys plenty of sleep in a soft bed beside a wife who dares not disturb him; and he sits pampering his bones in easy billows of fat,[4] singing to Laura, who knows and thinks these things about him. When he was fifteen, he tried to drown himself because he loved a girl, his first love, and she laughed at him. "A thousand women have paid for that," and his tight little mouth turns down at the corners. Now he perfumes his hair with Jockey Club,

---

1) Deigadito: 골피씨(骨皮氏).

2) he could squeeze his emptiness to the very backbone. . . . : 배가 고픈 때에는 두 손으로 배를 움켜쥐면 뱃가죽을 등뼈에 찰떡같이 붙일 수 있었다.

3) waylay: lie in wait for; attack on the way.

4) he sits pampering his bones in easy billows of fat: 토실토실 살찐 몸으로 기분좋게 (의자에) 앉는다.

and confides to Laura: "One woman is really as good as another for me, in the dark. I prefer them all."

His wife organizes unions among the girls in the cigarette factories, and walks in picket lines,[1] and even speaks at meetings in the evening. But she cannot be brought to acknowledge the benefits of true liberty. "I tell her I must have my freedom, net. She does not understand my point of view." Laura has heard this many times. Braggioni scratches the guitar and meditates. "She is an instinctively virtuous woman, pure gold, no doubt of that. If she were not, I should lock her up, and she knows it."

His wife, who works so hard for the good of the factory girls, employs part of her leisure lying on the floor weeping[2] because there are so many women in the world, and only one husband for her, and she never knows where nor when to look for him. He told her: "Unless you can learn to cry when I am not here, I must go away for good." That day he went away and took a room at the Hot? Madrid.

It is this month of separation for the sake of higher principles that has been spoiled not only for Mrs. Braggioni, whose sense of reality is beyond criticism, but for Laura, who feels herself bogged in a nightmare.[3] Tonight Laura envies Mrs. Braggioni, who is alone, and free to weep as much as she pleases about a concrete wrong. Laura has just come from a visit to the prison, and she is waiting for tomorrow with a bitter anxiety as if tomorrow may not come, but time may be caught immovably in this hour,[4] with herself transfixed,[5] Braggioni singing on forever, and Eugenio's body not yet discovered by the guard.

Braggioni says: "Are you going to sleep?" Almost before she can shake her head, he begins telling her about the May-day disturbances

---

1) picket lines: lines posted by a labor organization at a place of work affected by a strike.

2) employs part of her leisure... weeping: 한가할 때면 마루바닥에 엎드려 우는 일이 있었다. employ=occupy; devote.

3) who feels herself bogged in a nightmare: 악몽 속에 빠졌다고 느끼고 있는. bog =sink or get stuck in a soft, wet, spongy ground.

4) but time may be caught immovably in this hour: 그러나 시간은 이 순간에 딱 멈출지도 (모른다는 것치럼).

5) with herself transfixed: 자기는 선 채로 오금을 못쓰고. transfixed=made motionless (with amazement, terror, etc.).

coming on in Morelia, for the Catholics hold a festival in honor of the Blessed Virgin,[1] and the Socialists celebrate their martyrs on that day. "There will be two independent processions, starting from ?t her end of town, and they will march until they meet, and the rest depends . . ." He asks her to oil and load his pistols. Standing up, he unbuckles his ammunition belt, and spreads it laden[2] across her knees. Laura sits with the shells slipping through the cleaning cloth dipped in oil, and he says again he cannot understand why she works so hard for the revolutionary idea unless she loves some man who is in it. "Are you not in love with someone?" "No," says Laura. "And no one is in love with you?" "No." "Then it is your own fault. No woman need go begging. Why, what is the matter with you? The legless beggar woman in the Alameda has a perfectly faithful lover. Did you know that?"

Laura peers down the pistol barrel and says nothing, but a long, slow faintness rises and subsides in her; Braggioni curves his swollen fingers around the throat of the guitar and softly smothers the music out of it, and when she hears him again he seems to have forgotten her, and is speaking in the hypnotic voice[3] he uses when talking in small rooms to a listening, close-gathered crowd. Some day this world, now seemingly so composed and eternal, to the edges of every sea shall be merely a tangle[4] of gaping trenches, of crashing walls and broken bodies. Everything must be torn from its accustomed place where it has rotted for centuries, hurled skyward and distributed, cast down again clean as rain, without separate identity.[5] Nothing shall survive that the stiffened hands of poverty have created for the rich and no one shall be left alive except the elect spirits destined to procreate a new world cleansed of cruelty and injustice, ruled by benevolent anarchy:[6] "Pistols are good, I love them, cannon are even better, but

1) a festival in honor of the Blessed Virgin: 성모마리아를 위한 축제.
2) laden: loaded; burdened.
3) in the hypnotic voice: 최면술에 걸린 것 같은 목소리로.
4) tangle: confused mess.
5) without separate identity: 골고루.
6) no one shall be left alive. . . , ruled by benevolent anarchy: 잔인과 부정도 깨끗이 씻겨지고, 자비심 많은 무정부에 의해서 다스려지는 신세계를 창조하게끔 운영지어진 선택된 사람 이외에는 아무도 살아남지 않을 것이다.

in the end I pin my faith to good dynamite,[1]" he concludes, and strokes the pistol lying in her hands. "Once I dreamed of destroying this city, in case it offered resistance to General Ortiz, but it fell into his hands like an overripe pear."

He is made restless by his own words, rises and stands waiting. Laura holds up the belt to him: "Put that on, and go kill somebody in Morelia, and you will be happier," she says softly. The presence of death in the room makes her bold. "Today, I found Eugenio going into a stupor. He refused to allow me to call the prison doctor. He had taken all the tablets I brought him yesterday. He said he took them because he was bored."

"He is a fool, and his death is his own business," says Braggioni, fastening his belt carefully.

"I told him if he had wait? only a little while longer, you would have got him set free," says Laura. "He said he did not want to wait."

"He is a fool and we are well rid of him," says Braggioni, reaching for his hat.

He goes away. Laura knows his mood has changed, she will not see him any more for a while. He will send word when he needs her to go on errands into strange streets, to speak to the strange faces that will appear, like clay masks with the power of human speech,[2] to mutter their thanks to Braggioni for his help. Now she is free, and she thinks, I must run while there is time. But she does not go.

Braggioni enters his own house where for a month his wife has spent many hours every night weeping and tangling her hair upon her pillow. She is weeping now, and she weeps more at the sight of him, the cause of all her sorrows. He looks about the room. Nothing is changed, the smells are good and familiar, he is well acquainted with the woman who comes toward him with no reproach except grief on her face. He ways to her tenderly: "You are so good, please don't cry any more, you dear good creature." She says, "Are you tired,

---

1) but in the end I pin my faith to good dynamite: 결국 내가 의뢰하는 것은 다이나마이트야.

2) like clay masks with the power of human speech: 인간의 말을 이해할 줄 아는 진흙 인형처럼.

my angel? Sit here and I will wash your feet." She brings a bowl of water, and kneeling, unlaces his shoes, and when from her knees she raises her sad eyes under her blackened lids, he is sorry for everything, and bursts into tears. "Ah, yes, I am hungry, I am tired, let us eat something together," he says, between sobs. His wife leans her head on his arm and says, "Forgive me!" and this time he is refreshed by the solemn, endless rain of her tears.

Laura takes off her serge dress and puts on a white linen nightgown and goes to bed. She turns her head a little to one side, and lying still, reminds herself that it is time to sleep. Numbers tick[1)] in her brain like little clocks, soundless doors close of themselves around her. If you would sleep, you must not remember anything, the children will say tomorrow, good morning, my teacher, the poor prisoners who come every day bringing flowers to their jailor. 1-2-3-4-5-it is monstrous to confuse love with revolution, night with day, life with death — ah, Eugenio!

The tolling of the midnight bell is a signal, but what does it mean? Get up, Laura, and follow me: come out of your sleep, out of your bed, out of this strange house. What are you doing in this house? Without a word, without fear she rose and reached for Eugenio's hand, but he eluded[2)] her with a sharp, sly smile and drifted away. This is not all, you shall see — Murderer, he said, follow me, I will show you a new country, but it is far away and we must hurry. No, said Laura, not unless you take my hand, no; and she clung first to the stair rail, and then to the topmost branch of the Judas tree[3)] that bent down slowly and set her upon the earth, and then to the rocky ledge of a cliff, and then to the jagged wave of a sea that was not water but a desert of crumbling stone. Where are you taking me, she asked in wonder but without fear. To death, and it is a long way off, and we must hurry, said Eugenio. No, said Laura, not unless you take my hand. Then eat these flowers, poor prisoner, said Eugenio in a

---

1) tick=make a tick, as a clock.
2) eluded: slipped away from; escaped by cleverness, quickness.
3) Judas tree: tree that has red, pink, or purplish flowers before the leaves come out.

voice of pity, take and eat: and from the Judas tree he stripped the warm bleeding flowers, and held them to her lips. She saw that his hand was fleshless, a cluster of small white petrified branches,[1] and his eye sockets were without light, but she ate the flowers greedily for they satisfied both hunger and thirst. Murderer! said Eugenio, and Cannibal![2] This is my body and my blood. Laura cried No! and at the sound of her own voice, she awoke trembling, and was afraid to sleep again.

---

1) a cluster of small white petrified branches: 한 송이의 조그만 가지의 화석(化石).
2) Cannibal: person who eats human flesh.

The Snake

by John Steinbeck

John Steinbeck (1902-1968) born at Salinas, California, grew up in a rich but strike-tormented valley where he learned at first hand about the life of the agricultural and factory workers. From 1919 through 1925 he attended Standford University, taking the courses that attracted him without worrying about degree requirements and dropping out now and then to work as a common laborer. Already determined to be a writer, he contributed to the university magazines. After leaving Standford, he worked briefly as a reporter in New York City. Illness caused him to return to California, where he became a caretaker on a mountain estate. His first published book, *Cup of Gold*, said. to be the fourth that he wrote, appeared in 1929. Steinbeck's popularity began with *Tortilla Flat* (1935), rejected by nine publishers before it was accepted by Covici. In 1940 he received the Pulitzer Prize for *Grapes of Wrath*, and in 1962 he was awarded the Nobel Prize for Literature.

Steinbeck has been called a primitivist, and it is true that he tends to glorify rudimentary folk. Yet, as Frederick Ives Carpenter has pointed out, he combines several of the great skeins of American's sense of democracy, and a pragmatic belief in effective action. Though aware of human failure, Steinbeck still creates in his characters a zest in living which is perhaps more essential for survival than an understanding of life.

IT WAS almost dark when young Dr. Phillips swung his sack to his shoulder and left the tide pool. He climbed up over the rocks and squashed along the street in his rubber boots. The street lights were on[1] by the time he arrived at his little commercial laboratory on the cannery[2] street of Monterey. It was a tight little building, standing partly on piers over the bay water and partly on the land. On both sides the big corrugated-iron sardine canneries crowded in on it.

Dr. Phillips climbed the wooden steps and opened the door. The white rats in their cages scampered up and down the wire, and the captive cats in their pens mewed for milk. Dr. Phillips turned on the

1) were on: on=(*adj.*) taking place; in progress. *cf.* Radio is on.

2) cannery: factory where meat, fish, fruit, vegetables, etc., are canned.

glaring light over the dissection table and dumped[1] his clammy[2] sack on the floor. He walked to the glass cages by the window where the rattlesnakes lived, leaned over and looked in.

The snakes were bunched and resting in the corners of the cage, but every head was clear; the dusty eyes seemed to look at nothing, but as the young man leaned over the cage the forked tongues, black on the ends and pink behind, twittered out and waved slowly up and down. Then the snakes recognized the man and pulled in their tongues.

Dr. Phillips threw off his leather coat and built a fire in the tin stove; he set a kettle of water on the stove and dropped a can of beans into the water. Then he stood staring down at the sack on the floor. He was a slight young man with the mild, preoccupied eyes of one who looks through a microscope a great deal. He wore a short blond beard.

The draft[3] ran breathily up the chimney and a glow of warmth came from the stove. The little waves washed quietly about the piles under the building. Arranged on shelves about the room were tier above tier of museum jars containing the mounted marine specimens[4] the laboratory dealt in.

Dr. Phillips opened a side door and went into his bedroom, a book-lined cell containing an army cot, a reading light and an uncomfortable wooden chair. He pulled off his rubber boots and put on a pair of sheepskin slippers. When he went back to the other room the water in the kettle was already beginning to hum.

He lifted his sack to the table under the white light and emptied out two dozen common starfish. These he laid out side by side on the table. His preoccupied eyes turned to the busy rats in the wire cages. Taking grain from a paper sack, he poured it into the feeding troughs. Instantly the rats scrambled down from the wire and fell upon the food. A bottle of milk stood on a glass shelf between a small mounted

---

1) dump: empty out; throw down.
2) clammy: cold and damp.
3) draft: current of air.
4) Arranged on shelves about the room were. . . specimens: 방 주위를 뺑 둘러싼 선반 위로 해산물의 표본을 넣은 표본병이 여러 층으로 진열되어 있었다. tier=row; range; rank.

octopus and a jellyfish. Dr. Phillips lifted down the milk and walked to the cat cage, but before he filled the containers he reached in the cage and gently picked out a big rangy alley tabby.[1] He stroked her for a moment and then dropped her in a small black painted box, closed the lid and bolted it and then turned on a petcock[2] which admitted gas into the killing chamber. While the short soft struggle went on in the black box he filled the saucers with milk. One of the cats arched against his hand and he smiled and petted her neck.

The box was quiet now. He turned off the petcock, for the airtight box would be full of gas.

On the stove the pan of water was bubbling furiously about the can of beans. Dr. Phillips lifted out the can with a big pair of forceps, opened it, and emptied the beans into a glass dish. While he ate he watched the starfish on the table. From between the rays little drops of milky fluid were exuding. He bolted his beans and when they were gone he put the dish in the sink and stepped to the equipment cupboard. From this he took a microscope and a pile of little glass dishes. He filled the dishes one by one with sea water from a tap and arranged them in a line beside the starfish. He took out his watch and laid it on the table under the pouring white light. The waves washed with little sighs against the piles under the floor. He took an eyedropper from a drawer and bent over the starfish.

At that moment there were quick soft steps on the wooden stairs and a strong knocking at the door. A slight grimace of annoyance crossed the young man's face[3] as he went to open. A tall, lean woman stood in the doorway. She was dressed in a severe dark suit-her straight black hair, growing low on a flat forehead, was mussed[4] as though the wind had been blowing it. Her black eyes glittered in the strong light.

She spoke in a soft throaty voice, "May I come in? I want to talk

1) a big rangy alley tabby: 크고 흉측한 암고양이 한 마리. rangy=slender and long-limbed.

2) petcock: a small faucet.

3) A slight grimace of annoyance crossed the young man's face: 약간 상을 찌푸리어 귀찮다는 표정이 이 젊은이의 얼굴을 스쳤다.

4) muss: put into disorder; rumple.

to you."

"I'm very busy just now," he said half-heartedly. "I have to do things at times." But he stood away from the door. The tall woman slipped in.

"I'll be quiet until you can talk to me."

He closed the door and brought the uncomfortable chair from bedroom. "You see," he apologized, "the process is started and I must get to[1] it." So many people wandered in and asked questions. He had little routines of explanations for the commoner processes. He could say them without thinking. "Sit here. In a few minutes I'll be able to listen to you."

The tall woman leaned over the table. With the eyedropper the young man gathered fluid from between the rays of the starfish and squirted it into a bowl of water, and then he drew some milky fluid and squirted it in the same bowl and stirred the water gently with the eyedropper. He began his little patter of explanation.[2]

"When starfish are sexually mature they release sperm and ova[3] when they are exposed at low tide. By choosing mature specimens and taking them out of the water, I give them a condition of low tide. Now I've mixed the sperm and eggs. Now I put some of the mixture in each one of these ten watch glasses. In ten minutes I will kill those in the first glass with menthol, twenty minutes later I will kill the second group and then a new group every twenty minutes. Then I will have arrested the process in stages,[4] and I will mount the series on microscope slides[5] for biologic study." He paused. "Would you like to look at this first group under the microscope?"

"No, thank you."

He turned quickly to her. People always wanted to look throguh the glass. She was not looking at the table at all, but at him. Her

---

1) get to: begin to; to begin by chance.

2) He began his little patter of explanation.: He began to explain, talking rapidly and easily without much thought.

3) ova: ovum~plural. a female germ cell; egg.

4) arrest the process in stages: 이 과정을 각 단계에서 정지시키다.

5) mount the series on microscope slides: 현미경의 슬라이드에 일련의 표본을 올려 놓다. mount=put in proper position or order for use.

black eyes were on him, but they did not seem to see him. He realized why — the irises were as dark as the pupils, there was no color line between the two. Dr. Phillips was piqued[1] at her answer. Although answering questions bored him, a lack of interest in what he was doing irritated him. A desire to arouse her grew in him.

"While I'm waiting the first ten minutes I have something to do. Some people don't like to see it. Maybe you'd better step into that room until I finish."

"No," she said in her soft flat tone. "Do what you wish. I will wait until you can talk to me." Her hands rested side by side on her lap. She was completely at rest. Her eyes were bright but the rest of her was almost in a state of suspended animation.[2] He thought, "Low metabolic rate, almost as low as a frog's, from the looks." The desire to shock her out of her inanition[3] possessed him again.

He brought a little wooden cradle to the table, laid out scalpels and scissors and rigged a big hollow needle to a pressure tube. Then from the killing chamber he brought the limp dead cat and laid it in the cradle and tied its legs to hooks in the sides. He glanced sidewise at the woman. She had not moved. She was still at rest.

The cat grinned up into the light, its pink tongue stuck out between its needle teeth. Dr. Phillips deftly snipped open the skin at the throat; with a scalpel he slit through and found an artery. With flawless technique he put the needle in the vessel[4] and tied it with gut. "Embalming fluid,"[5] he explained. "Later I'll inject yellow mass into the venous system[6] and red mass into the arterial system[7] — for bloodstream dissection — biology classes."

He looked around at her again. Her dark eyes seemed veiled with dust. She looked without expression at the cat's open throat. Not a

1) piqued: offended.
2) was almost in a state of suspended animation: 거의 활동을 정지하고 있는 상태하에 놓여 있었다.
3) inanition: emptiness.
4) vessel; tube carrying blood or other fluid.
5) "Embalming fluid"; 방부 보존액.
6) venous system: 정맥 조직.
7) arterial system: 동맥 조직.

drop of blood had escaped. The incision was clean. Dr. Phillips looked at his watch. "Time for the first group." He shook a few crystals of menthol into the first watch glass.

The woman was making him nervous. The rats climbed about on the wire of their cage again and squeaked softly. The waves under the building beat with little shocks on the piles.

The young man shivered. He put a few lumps of coal in the stove and sat down. "Now," he said. "I haven't anything to do for twenty minutes." He noticed how short her chin was between lower lip and point. She seemed to awaken slowly, to come up out of some deep pool of consciousness. Her head raised and her dark dusty eyes moved about the room and then came back to him.

"I was waiting," she said. Her hands remained side by side on her lap. "You have snakes?"

"Why, yes," he said rather loudly. "I have about two dozen rattlesnakes. I milk out the venom[1] and send it to the anti-venom laboratories."

She continued to look at him but her eyes did not center on him, rather they covered him and seemed to see in a big circle all around him. "Have you a male snake, a male rattlesnake?"

"Well, it just happens I know I have. I came in one morning and found a big snake in — in coition[2] with a smaller one. That's very rare in captivity. You see, I do know I have a male snake."

"Where is he?"

"Why, right in the glass cage by the window there."

Her head swung slowly around but her two quiet hands did not move. She turned back toward him. "May I see?"

He got up and walked to the case by the window. On the sand bottom the knot of rattlesnakes lay entwined,[3] but their heads were clear. The tongues came out and flickered a moment and then waved up and down feeling the air for vibrations. Dr. Phillips nervously turned

1) milk out the venom: 독액을 빼내다.
2) coition: sexual intercourse.
3) the knot of rattlesnakes lay entwined: 방울뱀의 무리가 뒤엉켜 누워 있었다. entwin=twin[twist] together.

his head. The woman was standing beside him. He had not heard her get up from the chair. He had heard only the splash of water among the piles and the scampering of the rats on the wire screen.

She said softly, "Which is the male you spoke of?"

He pointed to a thick, dusty gray snake lying by itself in one corner of the cage. "That one. He's nearly five feet long. He comes from Texas. Our Pacific coast snakes are usually smaller. He's been taking all the rats, too. When I want the others to eat I have to take him out."

The woman stared down at the blunt dry head. The forked tongue slipped out and hung quivering for a long moment. "And you're sure he's a male."

"Rattlesnakes are funny," he said glibly. "Nearly every generalization proves wrong. I don't like to say anything definite about rattlesnakes, but — yes — I can assure you he's a male."

Her eyes did not move from the flat head. "Will you sell him to me?"

"Sell him?" he cried. "Sell him to you?"

"You do sell specimens, don't you?"

"Oh — yes. Of course I do. Of course I do."

"How much? Five dollars? Ten?"

"Oh! Not more than five. But — do you know anything about rattlesnakes? You might be bitten."

She looked at him for a moment. "I don't intend to take him. I want to leave him here, but — I want him to be mine. I want to come here and look at him and feed him and to know he's mine." She opened a little purse and took out a five-dollar bill. "Here! Now he is mine."

Dr. Phillips began to be afraid. "You could come to look at him without owning him."

"I want him to be mine."

"Oh, Lord!" he cried. "I've forgotten the time." He ran to the table. "Three minutes over. It won't matter much." He shook menthol crystals into the second watch glass. And then he was drawn back to the cage where the woman still stared at the snake.

She asked, "What does he eat?"

"I feed them white rats, rats from the cage over there."

"Will you put him in the other cage? I want to feed him."

"But he doesn't need food. He's had a rat already this week. Sometimes they don't eat for three or four months. I had one that didn't eat for over a year."

In her low monotone she asked, "Will you sell me a rat?"

He shrugged his shoulders. "I see. You want to watch how rattlesnakes eat. All right. I'll show you. The rat will cost twenty-five cents. It's better than a bullfight if you look at it one way, and it's simply a snake eating his dinner if you look at it another." His tone had become acid. He hated people who made sport of natural processes. He was not a sportsman but a biologist. He could kill a thousand animals for knowledge, but not an insect for pleasure. He'd been over this in his mind before.

She turned her head slowly toward him and the beginning of a smile formed on her thin lips. "I want to feed my snake," she said. "I'll put him in the other cage." She had opened the top of the cage and dipped her hand in before he knew what she was doing. He leaped forward and pulled her back. The lid banged shut.

"Haven't you any sense," he asked fiercely. "Maybe he wouldn't kill you, but he'd make you damned sick in spite of what I could do for you."

"You put him in the other cage then," she said quietly.

Dr. Phillips was shaken. He found that he was avoiding the dark eyes that didn't seem to look at anything. He felt that it was profoundly wrong to put a rat into the cage, deeply sinful; and he didn't know why. Often he had put rats in the cage when someone or other had wanted to see it, but this desire tonight sickened him. He tried to explain himself out of it.

"It's a good thing to see," he said. "It shows you how a snake can work. It makes you have a respect for a rattlesnake. Then, too, lots of people have dreams about the terror of snakes making the kill. I think because it is a subjective rat. The person is the rat. Once you see it the whole matter is objective. The rat is only a rat and the terror is removed."

He took a long stick equipped with a leather noose[1] from the wall. Opening the trap he dropped the noose over the big snake's head and tightened the thong.[2] A piercing dry rattle filled the room. The thick body writhed and slashed about the handle of the stick as he lifted the snake out and dropped it in the feeding cage. It stood ready to strike for a time, but the buzzing gradually ceased. The snake crawled into a corner, made a big figure eight with its body and lay still.

"You see," the young man explained, "these snakes are quite tame. I've had them a long time. I suppose I could handle them if I wanted to, but everyone who does handle rattlesnakes gets bitten sooner or later. I just don't want to take the chance." He glanced at the woman. He hated to put in the rat. She had moved over in front of the new cage; her black eyes were on the stony head of the snake again.

She said, "Put in a rat."

Reluctantly he went to the rat cage. For some reason he was sorry for the rat, and such a feeling had never come to him before. His eyes went over the mass of swarming white bodies climbing up the screen toward him. "Which one?" he thought. "Which one shall it be?" Suddenly he turned angrily to the woman. "Wouldn't you rather I put in a cat? Then you'd see a real fight. The cat might even win, but if it did it might kill the snake. I'll sell you a cat if you like."

She didn't look at him. "Put in a rat," she said. "I want him to eat."

He opened the rat cage and thrust his hand in. His fingers found a tail and he lifted a plump, red-eyed rat out of the cage. It struggled up to try to bite his fingers and, failing, hung spread out and motionless from its tail. He walked quickly across the room, opened the feeding cage and dropped the rat in on the sand floor. "Now, watch it," he cried.

The woman did not answer him. Her eyes were on the snake where it lay still. Its tongue flicking in and out rapidly, tasted the air of the cage.

---

1) noose: snare; loop with a slip knot that tightens as the string or rope is pulled.
2) thong: a narrow strip of leather.

The rat landed on its feet, turned around and sniffed at its pink naked tail and then unconcernedly trotted across the sand, smelling as it went. The room was silent. Dr. Phillips did not know whether the water sighed among the piles or whether the woman sighed. Out of the corner of his eye he saw her body crouch and stiffen.

The snake moved out smoothly, slowly. The tongue flicked in and out. The motion was so gradual, so smooth that it didn't seem to be motion at all. In the other end of the cage the rat perked up[1] in a sitting position and began to lick down the fine white hair on its chest. The snake moved on, keeping always a deep Scurve in its neck.

The silence beat on the young man. He felt the blood drifting up in his body. He said loudly, "See! He keeps the striking curve ready. Rattlesnakes are cautious, almost cowardly animals. The mechanism is so delicate. The snake's dinner is to be got by an operation as deft as a surgeon's job.[2] He takes no chances with his instruments."[3]

The snake had flowed to the middle of the cage by now. The rat looked up, saw the snake and then unconcernedly went back to licking its chest.

"It's the most beautiful thing in the world," the young man said. His veins were throbbing. "It's the most terrible thing in the world."

The snake was close now. Its head lifted a few inches from the sand. The head weaved slowly back and forth, aiming, getting distance, aiming. Dr. Phillips glanced again at the woman. He turned sick. She was weaving too, not much, just a suggestion.

The rat looked up and saw the snake. It dropped to four feet and back up, and then — the stroke.[4] It was impossible to see, simply a flash. The rat jarred as though under an invisible blow. The snake backed hurriedly into the corner from which it had come, and settled down, its tongue working constantly.

---

1) perk up: raise smartly or briskly.

2) by an operation as deft as a surgeon's job: 외과 의사의 일만큼 교묘한 작업에 의해서. deft=skillful; nimble.

3) He takes no chances with his instruments: 자기 도구에 대해서도 만일을 믿지 않았다. take a chance=to accept the risk of failure or loss.

4) the stroke: the attack of paralysis; apoplexy 졸도.

"Perfect!" Dr. Phillips cried. "Right between the shoulde blades. The fangs must almost have reached the heart."

The rat stood still, breathing like a little white bellows. Suddenly it leaped in the air and landed on its side. Its legs kicked spasmodically for a second and it was dead.

Thc woman relaxed, relaxed sleepily.

"Well," the young man demanded, "it was an emotional bath, wasn't it?"

She turned her misty eyes to him. "Will he eat it now?" she asked.

"Of course he'll eat it. He didn't kill it for a thrill. He killed it because he was hungry."

The corners of the woman's mouth turned up a trifle again. She looked back at the snake. "I want to see him eat it."

Now the snake came out of its comer again. There was no striking curve in its neck, but it approached the rat gingerly, ready to jump back in case it attacked. It nudged the body gently with its blunt nose, and drew away. Satisfied that it was dead, the snake touched the body all over with its chin, from head to tail. It seemed to measure the body and to kiss it. Finally it opened its mouth and unhinged its jaws at the corners.

Dr. Phillips put his will against his head[1] to keep it from turning toward the woman. He thought, "If she's opening her mouth, I'll be sick. I'll be afraid." He succeeded in keeping his eyes away.

The snake fitted its jaws over the rat's head and then with a slow peristaltic pulsing,[2] began to engulf the rat. The jaws gripped and the whole throat crawled up, and the jaws gripped again.

Dr. Phillips turned away and went to his work table. "You've made me miss one of the series," he said bitterly. "The set won't be complete." He put one of the watch glasses under a low-power microscope and looked at it, and then angrily he poured the content of all the dishes into the sink. The waves had fallen so that only a wet whisper came up through the floor. The young man lifted a trapdoor at his feet and

1) put his will against his head: (그 여인 쪽으로 돌아가는) 자기의 머리를 의지로 막았다.

2) with a slow peristaltic pulsing: 느릿한 유동적인 맥박으로(쥐를 삼키기 시작했다).

dropped the starfish down into the black water. He paused at the cat, crucified in the cradle and grinning comically into the light. Its body was puffed with embalming fluid.[1] He shut off the pressure, withdrew the needle and tied the vein.

"Would you like some coffee?" he asked.

"No, thank you. I shall be going pretty soon."

He walked to her where she stood in front of the snake cage. The rat was swallowed, all except an inch of pink tail that stuck out of the snake's mouth like a sardonic tongue. The throat heaved again and the tail disappeared. The jaws snapped back into their sockets, and the big snake crawled heavily to the corner, made a big eight and dropped its head on the sand.

"He's asleep now," the woman said. "I'm going now. But I'll come back and feed my snake every little while. I'll pay for the rats. I want him to have plenty. And sometime — I'll take him away with me." Her eyes came out of their dusty dream for a moment. "Remember, he's mine. Don't take his poison. I want him to have it. Goodnight." She walked swiftly to the door and went out. He heard her footsteps on the stairs, but he could not hear her walk away on the pavement.

Dr. Phillips turned a chair around and sat down in front of the snake cage. He tried to comb out[2] his thought as he looked at the torpid snake. "I've read so much about psychological sex symbols," he thought. "It doesn't seem to explain. Maybe I'm too much alone. Maybe I should kill the snake. If I knew — no, I can't pray to anything."

For weeks he expected her to return. "I will go out and leave her alone here when she comes," he decided. "I won't see the damned thing again."

She never came again. For months he looked for her when he walked about in the town. Several times he ran after some tall woman thinking it might be she. But he never saw her again — ever.

---

1) embalming fluid: 방부제.

2) comb out: search out.

Love

by Jesse Stuart

The son of an illiterate tenant farmer from eastern Kentucky, Jesse Stuart (1907-) had little formal education as a child. When he finally managed to attend high school, and then college, he discovered that he had a talent for writing. He has pursued a successful career as a writer, at the same time serving as a teacher and administrator in southern schools.

In addition to short stories, Stuart has written poetry, novels, an autobiography (*The Thread that Runs So True,* 1958) and a biography of his father (*God's Oddling,* 1960). It was from his father that the author gained his great love of nature and appreciation of individuality. And it was almost certainly from his father that the idea for "Love" came.

YESTERDAY WHEN the bright sun blazed down on the wilted[1] corn my father and I walked around the edge of the new ground to plan a fence. The cows kept coming through the chestnut oaks[2] on the cliff and running over the young corn. They bit off the tips of the corn and trampled down the stubble.[3]

My father walked in the cornbalk.[4] Bob, our Collie,[5] walked in front of my father. We heard a ground squirrel whistle down over the bluff[6] among the dead treetops at the clearing's[7] edge. "Whoop, take him, Bob," said my father. He lifted up a young stalk of corn, with wilted dried roots, where the ground squirrel had dug it up for the sweet grain of corn left on its tender roots. This has been a dry spring and the corn has kept well in the earth where the grain has

---

1) wilted: drooping from heat and lack of water.
2) chestnut oaks: a tree of eastern and central North America with leaves similar to those of a chestnut tree.
3) stubble: here, the short of corn left after the cows had eaten the tender tops.
4) cornbalk: the rows of planted corn.
5) Collie: a breed of dog, related to the sheepdog.
6) bluff: a cliff.
7) clearing: an open space of cleared land in a forest.

sprouted. The ground squirrels love this corn. They dig up rows of it and eat the sweet grains. The young corn stalks are killed and we have to replant the corn.

I can see my father keep sicking[1)] Bob after the ground squirrel. He jumped over the corn rows. He started to run toward the ground squirrel. I, too, started running toward the clearing's edge where Bob was jumping and barking. The dust flew in tiny swirls behind our feet. There was a cloud of dust behind us. "It's a big bull[2)] blacksnake," said my father. "Kill him, Bob! Kill him, Bob!"

Bob was jumping and snapping at the snake so as to make it strike and throw itself off guard. Bob had killed twenty-eight copperheads[3)] this spring. He knows how to kill a snake. He doesn't rush to do it. He takes his time and does the job well. "Let's don't[4)] kill the snake," I said. "A blacksnake is a harmless snake. It kills poison snakes. It kills the copperhead. It catches more mice from the fields than a cat."

I could see the snake didn't want to fight the dog. The snake wanted to get away. Bob wouldn't let it. I wondered why it was crawling toward a heap of black loamy[5)] earth at the bench[6)] of the hill. I wondered why it had come from the chestnut oak sprouts[7)] and the matted greenbriars[8)] on the cliff. I looked as the snake lifted its pretty head in response to one of Bob's jumps. "It's not a bull blacksnake," I said. "It's a she-snake. Look at the white on her throat." "A snake is an enemy to me," my father snapped. "I hate a snake. Kill it, Bob. Go in there and get that snake and quit playing with it!"

Bob obeyed my father. I hated to see him take this snake by the throat. She was so beautifully poised in the sunlight. Bob grabbed the white patch on her throat. He cracked her long body like an ox whip

---

1) sicking: urging (the dog) to attack.
2) bull: male.
3) copperhead: a kind of poisonous snake.
4) Let's don't : Let's not.
5) loamy: adjective form of loam "rich soil".
6) bench: a level, narrow stretch of land (just below the hill).
7) sprout: a shoot of a plant.
8) greenbriar: a kind of bush covered with thorns.

in the wind. He cracked it against the wind only. The blood spurted from her fine-curved throat. Something hit against my legs like pellets.[1) Bob threw the snake down. I looked to see what had struck my legs. It was snake eggs. Bob had slung them from her body. She was going to the sand heap to lay her eggs, where the sun is the setting-hen[2) that warms them and hatches them.

Bob grabbed her body there on the earth where the red blood was running down on the gray-piled loam. Her body was still writhing[3) in pain. She acted like a greenweed[4) held over a new-ground fire. Bob slung[5) her viciously many times. He cracked her limp body against the wind. She was now limber as a shoestring in the wind. Bob threw her riddled[6) body back on the sand. She quivered like a leaf in the lazy wind, then her riddled body lay perfectly still. The blood colored the loamy earth around the snake. "Look at the eggs, won't you?" said my father. We counted thirty-seven eggs. I picked an egg up and held it in my hand.

Only a minute ago there was life in it. It was an immature seed. It would not hatch. Mother sun could not incubate[7) it on the warm earth. The egg I held in my hand was almost the size of a quail's[8) egg. The shell on it was thin and tough and the egg appeared under the surface to be a watery egg. "Well, Bob, I guess you see now why this snake couldn't fight," I said, "It is life. Stronger devour[9) the weaker even among human beings. Dog kills snake. Snake kills birds. Birds kill the butterflies. Man conquers all. Man, too, kills for sport." Bob was panting. He walked ahead of us back to the house. His tongue was out of his mouth. He was tired. He was hot under his shaggy

---

1) pellet: a little ball of mud, paper, food, medicine, etc.; pill.
2) setting-hen: a hen that sits on eggs to keep them warm until they hatch.
3) writhing: twisting.
4) greenweed: a small shrub with yellow flowers; the weed shrivels and twists when thrown on a fire.
5) slung: past tense of sling "throw with force".
6) riddled: filled with holes.
7) incubate: to warm (an egg) as by bodily heat, so that the embryo will develop.
8) quail: a brownish-gray game bird; the eggs are about 1/3 the size of a chicken's eggs.
9) devour: eat hungrily or greedily.

coat of hair. His tongue nearly touched the dry dirt and white flecks of foam dripped from it. We walked toward the house. Neither my father nor I spoke. I still thought about the dead snake. The sun was going down over the chestnut ridge. A lark[1] was singing. It was late for a lark to sing. The red evening clouds floated above the pine trees on our pasture hill. My father stood beside the path. His black hair was moved by the wind. His face was red in the blue wind of day. His eyes looked toward the sinking sun. "And my father hates a snake," I thought. I thought about the agony women know of giving birth. I thought about how they will fight to save their children. Then, I thought of the snake. I thought it was silly for me to think such thoughts.

This morning my father and I got up with the chickens.[2] He says one has to get up with the chickens to do a day's work. We got the posthole digger,[3] ax, spud,[4] measuring pole and the mattock.[5] We started for the clearing's edge. Bob didn't go along.

The dew was on the corn. My father walked behind with the posthole digger across his shoulder. I walked in front. The wind was blowing. It was a good morning wind to breathe and a wind that makes one feel like he can get under the edge of a hill and heave[6] the whole hill upside down.

I walked out the corn row where we had come yesterday afternoon. I looked in front of me. I saw something. I saw it move. It was moving like a huge black rope winds around a windlass.[7] "Steady," I says[8] to my father. "Here is the bull blacksnake." He took one step up beside me and stood. His eyes grew wide apart.[9] "What do you know about

---

1) lark: a bird with a melodious song; larks often live in fields.
2) got up with the chickens: got up very early.
3) posthole digger: a tool for digging holes into which posts are put; a fence will be attached to these posts.
4) spud: a sharp tool used for digging out weeds.
5) mattock: a tool used to break up hard ground.
6) heave: move with great effort.
7) windlass: a machine for pulling or lifting things by means of a rope or chain which is wound around a cylinder or drum and turned by a crank.
8) says: used instead of "said" to give immediacy to a conversational narrative.
9) His eyes grew wide apart: "His eyes grew as big as saucers."가 common phrase 이다.

this," he said. "You have seen the bull blacksnake now," I said. "Take a good look at him! He is lying beside his dead mate. He has come to her. He, perhaps, was on her trail[1] yesterday."

The male snake had trailed her to her doom. He had come in the night, under the roof of stars, as the moon shed[2] rays of light on[3] the quivering[4] clouds of green. He had found his lover dead. He was coiled beside her, and she was dead.

The bull blacksnake lifted his head and followed us as we walked around the dead snake. He would have fought us to his death. He would have fought Bob to his death. "Take a stick," said my father, "and throw him over the hill so Bob won't find him. Did you ever see anything to beat that?[5] I've heard they'd do that. But this is my first time to see it." I took a stick and threw him over the bank into the dewy sprouts on the cliff.

1) on her trail: on the trail of the she-snake. on the trail of. ~을 추적하여.
2) shed: past tense of shed "cast, throw".
3) shed rays of light on: illuminated.
4) quivering: vibrating.
5) (to) beat that: (Colloq.) more astonishing than that.

The Secret Life of Walter Mitty

by James Thurber

After spending his boyhood and university days in Columbus, Ohio, James Thurber (1894-1961) worked as a reporter, serving for a time as a foreign correspondent in France. He was one of the young, talented writers — E.B. White was another — recruited when Harold Ross founded *The New Yorker* in 1925, a period recounted in Thurber's best-selling My *Years with Ross (1959)*.

Thurber subsequently devoted full time to writing and illustrating some two dozen books of stories and essays. He collaborated with Elliott Nugent in writing a play, *The Male Animal,* which ran successfully in New York in 1940. Several of Thurber's stories and sketches were also presented on Broadway in *Three by Thurber* (1955) and *A Thurber Carnival* (1960). A number of his stories, including "The Unicorn in the Garden" and "The Secret Life of Walter Mitty" have been produced as movies.

A representative selection of Thurber's short stories, fables, essays and cartoons is available in *The Thurber Carnival (1945)*. His wide-eyed dogs, predatory women, and timid men have made him one of America's best-loved humorists.

"WE'RE GOING through!" The Commander's voice was like thin ice breaking. He wore his full-dress uniform, with the heavily braided[1] white cap pulled down rakishly[2] over one cold gray eye. "We can't make it, sir. It's spoiling for a hurricane,[3] if you ask me." "I'm not asking you, Lieutenant Berg," said the Commander. "Throw on the power lights! Rev her up[4] to 8500! We're going through!" The pounding of the cylinders increased: ta-pocketa-pocketa-pocketa-*pocketa-pocketa*. The Commander stared at the ice forming on the pilot window. He walked over and twisted[5] a row of complicated dials. "Switch on No. 8 auxiliary!"[6] he shouted. "Switch on No. 8 auxiliary!" repeated

1) heavily braided: decorated with a lot of white braid, indicating high rank.
2) rakishly: as a nautical term, rakish means having a trim, stream-lined appearance; here, there is also the connotation of stylish, smart.
3) It's spoiling for a hurricane: It looks like a hurricane is coming.
4) rev her up: increase the number of revolutions per minute in the engines.
5) twisted: turned.
6) Switch on No. 8 auxiliary!: 8번 보조(엔진)에 스윗치를 넣어라.

Lieutenant Berg. "Full strength in No. 3 turret!"[1] shouted the Commander. "Full strength in No. 3 turret!" The crew, bending to their various tasks in the huge, hurtling[2] eight-engined Navy hydroplane, looked at each other and grinned. "The Old Man'll get us through," they said to one another. "The Old Man ain't afraid of hell!"...

"Not so fast! You're driving too fast!" said Mrs. Mitty. "What are you driving so fast for?"

"Hmm?" said Walter Mitty. He looked at his wife, in the seat beside him, with shocked astonishment. She seemed grossly[3] unfamiliar, like a strange woman who had yelled at him in a crowd. "You were up to fifty-five," she said. "You know I don't like to go more than forty. You were up to fifty-five." Walter Mitty drove on toward Waterbury[4] in silence, the roaring of the SN202 through the worst storm in twenty years of Navy flying fading in the remote, intimate airways of his mind. "You're tensed up[5] again," said Mrs. Mitty. "It's one of your days.[6] I wish you'd let Dr. Renshaw look you over."

Walter Mitty stopped the car in front of the building where his wife went to have her hair done. "Remember to get those overshoes[7] while I'm having my hair done," she said. "I don't need overshoes," said Mitty. She put her mirror back into her bag. "We've been all through that,"[8] she said, getting out of the car. "You're not a young man any longer." He raced the engine[9] a little. "Why don't you wear your gloves? Have you lost your gloves?" Walter Mitty reached in a pocket and brought out the gloves. He put them on, but after she had turned and gone into the building and he had driven on to a red light, he

---

1) Full strength in No. 3 turret!: 3번 터릿에 총력을.
2) hurtling: moving with great speed and power.
3) grossly: inappropriately, obviously wrong.
4) Waterbury: a city in Connecticut.
5) tensed up: tense, nervous.
6) your days: 전성기.
7) overshoes: low rubber boots worn to protect shoes from rain or snow.
8) We've been all through that: 그건 다 끝났다.
9) raced the engine: caused the engine to run fast when the gears were disengaged; pushed down on the gas pedal with the car in neutral gear.

took them off again. "Pick it up, brother!"[1] snapped a cop as the light changed, and Mitty hastily pulled on his gloves and lurched[2] ahead. He drove around the streets aimlessly for a time, and then he drove past the hospital on his way to the parking lot.

. . . "It's the millionaire banker, Wellington McMillan," said the pretty nurse. "Yes?" said Walter Mitty, removing his gloves slowly. "Who has the case?" "Dr. Renshaw and Dr. Benbow, but there are two specialists here, Dr. Remington from New York and Dr. Pritchard-Mitford from London. He flew over." A door opened down a long, cool corridor and Dr. Renshaw came out. He looked distraught[3] and haggard.[4] "Hello, Mitty," he said. "We're having the devil's own time[5] with McMillan, the millionaire banker and close personal friend of Roosevelt.[6] Obstreosis of the ductal tract.[7] Tertiary.[8] Wish you'd take a look at him." "Glad to," said Mitty.

In the operating room there were whispered introductions: "Dr. Remington, Dr. Mitty. Dr. Pritchard-Mitford, Dr. Mitty." "I've read your book on streptothricosis,[9]" said Pritchard-Mitford, shaking hands. "A brilliant performance, sir." "Thank you," said Walter Mitty. "Didn't know you were in the States, Mitty," grumbled Remington. "Coals to Newcastle,[10] bringing Mitford and me up here for a tertiary." "You are very kind," said Mitty. A huge, complicated machine, connected

---

1) Pick it up, brother!: Start your car moving again!; brother is a very causal form of address. (Slang)

2) lurched: moved suddenly and jerkily.

3) distraught: preoccupied with troubles.

4) haggard: tired, worn out.

5) having the devil's own time: having a lot of difficulty.

6) Roosevelt: Franklin D., the U.S. president at the time the story takes place.

7) Obstreosis of the ductal tract: meaning terms which sound impressively medical: Obstruction of the digestive tract. 소화기 장애에서 생각해 낸 말인지? 주인공 walter는 word-play를 잘한다.

8) Tertiary: third.

9) streptothricosis: 이것은 invented word. streptococcus(=a kind of bacteria which cause bad sore throats)에서 꾸며낸 말인지?

10) coals to Newcastle: (to carry) coals to Newcastle: to supply something that is already abundant. 헛수고하다, 쓸데없는 일을 하다. Newcastle=a coal-mining center in England.

to the operating table, with many tubes and wires, began at this moment to go pocketa-pocketa-pocketa. "The new anesthetizer is giving way!" shouted an interne. "There is no one in the East who knows how to fix it!" "Quiet, man!" said Mitty, in a low, cool voice. He sprang to the machine, which was now going pocketa-pocketa-queep-pocketa-queep. He began fingering delicately a row of glistening dials. "Give me a fountain pen!" he snapped. Someone handed him a fountain pen. He pulled a faulty piston out of the machine and inserted the pen in its place. "That will hold for ten minutes," he said. "Get on with the operation. A nurse hurried over and whispered to Renshaw, and Mitty saw the man turn pale. "Coreopsis[1] has set in,[2]" said Renshaw nervously. "If you would take over, Mitty?" Mitty looked at him and at the craven[3] figure of Benbow, who drank, and at the grave, uncertain faces of the two great specialists. "If you wish," he said. They slipped a white gown on him, he adjusted a mask[4] and drew on thin gloves; nurses handed him shining . . .

"Back it up,[5] Mac!! Look out for that Buick!" Walter Mitty jammed on the brakes.[6] "Wrong lane, Mac,[7]" said the parking-lot attendant, looking at Mitty closely. "Gee. Yeh," muttered Mitty. He began cautiously to back out of the lane marked "Exit Only." "Leave her sit there,"[8] said the attendant. "I'll put her away." Mitty got out of the car. "Hey, better leave the key." "Oh," said Mitty, handing the man the ignition key. The attendant vaulted into the car, backed it up with insolent skill, and put it where it belonged.

They're so damn cocky[9], thought Walter Mitty, walking along Main

---

1) coreopsis: a kind of plant with daisy-like yellow or soptted flowers, from the Latin "resembling a bed bug".
2) set in: begin; start; develop.
3) craven: cowardly.
4) mask: a surgical mask, used to cover a doctor's mouth while he is performing an operation.
5) Back it up: Move it backwards.
6) jammed on the brakes: stopped the car suddenly.
7) Mac: an all-purpose name for addressing a man whose name you don't know (Slang).
8) Leave her sit there: Leave it there; Let it sit there.
9) cocky: conceited; very sure of oneself.

Street; they think they know everything. Once he had tried to take his chains[1)] off, outside New Milford,[2)] and he had got them wound around the axles.[3)] A man had had to come out in a wrecking car and unwind them, a young, grinning garageman. Since then Mrs. Mitty always made him drive to a garage to have the chains taken off. The next time, he thought, I'll wear my right arm in a sling[4)]; they won't grin at me then. I'll have my right arm in a sling and they'll see I couldn't possibly take the chains off myself. He kicked at the slush[5)] on the sidewalk. "Overshoes," he said to himself, and he began looking for a shoe store.

When he came out into the street again, with the overshoes in a box under his arm, Walter Mitty began to wonder what the other thing was his wife had told him to get. She had told him, twice before they set out from their house for Waterbury. In a way he hated these weekly trips to town — he was always getting something wrong. Kleenex,[6)] he thought, Squibb's,[7)] razor blades? No. Tooth paste, toothbrush, bicarbonate,[8)] Carborundum,[9)] initiative and referendum?[10)] He gave it up. But she would remember it. "Where's the what's-its-name?" she would ask. "Don't tell me you forgot the what's-its-name." A newsboy went by shouting something about the Waterbury trial.

... "Perhaps this will refresh your memory." The District Attorney[11)] suddenly thrust a heavy automatic[12)] at the quiet figure on the witness

---

1) chains: used to keep tires from sliding on snow.
2) New Milford: a town in Connecticut.
3) axle: the rod which passes through the center of a pair of wheels.
4) sling: a band of materical used to support a broken arm.
5) slush: snow which has built up and begun to melt.
6) Kleenex: paper handkerchiefs.
7) Squibb's: short sticks of wood with cotton at each end used for cleaning the ears.
8) bicarbonate: of soda, used to calm upset stomachs.
9) carborundum: a hard compound of carbon and silicon, used for polishing and grinding.
10) initiative and referendum: a process by which citizens may propose and vote on legislation. 의안제출전.
11) District Attorney: the prosecuting officer of an American judicial court.
12) a heavy automatic: a gun을 말함.

stand. "Have you ever seen this before?" Walter Mitty took the gun and examined it expertly. "This is my Webley-Vickers 50.80,[1]" he said calmly. An excited buzz ran around the courtroom. The Judge rapped for order. "You are a crack shot[2] with any sort of firearms, I believe?" said the District Attorney, insinuatingly.[3] "Objection!" shouted Mitty's attorney. "We have shown that the defendant could not have fired the shot. We have shown that he wore his right arm in a sling on the night of the fourteenth of July." Walter Mitty raised his hand briefly and the bickering[4] attorneys were stilled. "With any known make of gun," he said evenly, "I could have killed Gregory Fitzhurst at three hundred feet *with my left hand*." Pandemonium[5] broke loose in the courtroom. A woman's scream rose above the bedlam and suddenly a lovely, dark-haired girl was in Walter Mitty's arms. The District Attorney struck at her savagely. Without rising from his chair, Mitty let the man have it[6] on the point of the chin. "You miserable cur![7]" . . .

"Puppy biscuit,[8]" said Walter Mitty. He stopped walking and the buildings of Waterbury rose up out of the misty courtroom and surrounded him again. A woman who was passing laughed. "He said 'Puppy biscuit,'" she said to her companion. "That man said 'Puppy biscuit' to himself." Walter Mitty hurried on. He went into an A. & P.,[9] not the first one he came to but a smaller one farther up the street. "I want some biscuit for small, young dogs," he said to the clerk. "Any special brand, sir?" The greatest pistol shot in the world thought a moment. "It says 'Puppies Bark for It' on the box," said Walter Mitty.

---

1) Webley-Vickers 50.80: a fictitious handgun of fantastic size.
2) crack shot: a person who shoots well.
3) insinuatingly: suggesting more than he is saying.
4) bickering: quarreling.
5) Pandemonium: wild and noisy disorder; bedlam.
6) let the man have it: (Slang) hit him.
7) cur: a bad-tempered or worthless dog; here, an insult implying that the man is cowardly and contemptible.
8) Puppy biscuit: biscuit for small, young dogs.
9) A. & P.: The Atlantic and Pacific Tea Company, a large chain of super-markets.

His wife would be through at the hairdresser's in fifteen minutes' Mitty saw in looking at his watch, unless they had trouble drying it; sometimes they had trouble drying it. She didn't like to get to the hotel first, she would want him to be there waiting for her as usual. He found a big leather chair in the lobby, facing a window, and he put the overshoes and the puppy biscuit on the floor beside it. He picked up an old copy of *Liberty*[1] and sank down into the chair. "Can Germany Conquer the World Through the Air?" Walter Mitty looked at the pictures of bombing planes and of ruined streets.

... "The cannonading has got the wind up[2] in young Raleigh, sir," said the sergeant. Captain Mitty looked up at him through tousled[3] hair. "Get him to bed," he said wearily, "with the others. I'll fly alone." "But you can't, sir," said the sergeant anxiously. "It takes two men to handle that bomber and the Archies[4] are pounding hell out of the air. Von Richtman's[5] circus is between here and Saulier.[6]" "Somebody's got to get that ammunition dump," said Mitty. "I'm going over. Spot[7] of brandy?" He poured a drink for the sergeant and one for himself. War thundered and whined around the dugout[8] and battered at the door. There was a rending[9] of wood and splinters flew through the room. "A bit of a near thing," said Captain Mitty carelessly. 'The box barrage[10] is closing in," said the sergeant. "We only live once, Sergeant," said Mitty, with his faint, fleeting smile. "Or do we?" He poured another brandy and tossed it off.[11] "I never

1) *Liberty* : a fictitious popular illustrated magazine.
2) got the wind up: (British; Slang) frightened.
3) tousled: uncombed; disordered.
4) Archie: (Slang) an anti-aircraft gun.
5) Von Richtman: Baron Manfed von Richthofen (1892-1918) known as the "Red Baron," was the most famous German military pilot of World War I; he was credited with shooting down more than 80 enemy planes.
6) Saulier: an imaginary town in France.
7) spot: (British; Colloq.) a small quantity of something.
8) dugout: a rough covered shelter used by soldiers.
9) rending: breaking, splintering.
10) box barrage: a heavy screen of artillery fire, here, in a three-dimensional, rectangular [box-shaped] pattern.
11) tossed it off: drank it in one gulp.

see a man could hold his brandy like you, sir," said the sergeant. "Begging your pardon, sir." Captain Mitty stood up and strapped on his huge Webley-Vickers automatic. "It's forty kilometers through hell, sir," said the sergeant. Mitty finished one last brandy. "After all," he said softly, "what isn't?" The pounding of the cannon increased; there was the rat-tat-tatting of machine guns, and from somewhere came the menacing pocketa-pocketa-pocketa of the new flame-throwers. Walter Mitty walked to the door of the dugout humming "Auprès de Ma Blonde.[1]" He turned and waved to the sergeant. "Cheerio!"[2] he said. . . .

Something struck his shoulder. "I've been looking all over this hotel for you," said Mrs. Mitty. "Why do you have to hide in this old chair? How did you expect me to find you?" "Things close in," said Walter Mitty vaguely. "What?" Mrs. Mitty said. "Did you get the what's-its-name? The puppy biscuit? What's in that box?" "Overshoes," said Mitty. "Couldn't you have put them on in the store?" 'I was thinking," said Walter Mitty. "Does it ever occur to you that I am sometimes thinking?" She looked at him. "I'm going to take your temperature when I get you home," she said.

They went out through the revolving doors that made a faintly derisive[3] whistling sound when you pushed them. It was two blocks to the parking lot. At the drugstore on the corner she said, "Wait here for me. I forgot something. I won't be a minute." She was more than a minute. Walter Mitty lighted a cigarette. It began to rain, rain with sleet[4] in it. He stood up against the wall of the drugstore, smoking. . . . He put his shoulders back and his heels together. "To hell with the handkerchief," said Waker Mitty scornfully. He took one last drag on his cigarette and snapped it away. Then, with that faint, fleeting smile playing about his lips, he faced the firing squad[5]; erect and

---

1) Auprès de Ma Blonde: a jaunty French popular song from World War I; "Next to My Blonde"라는 뜻.
2) Cheerio!: (British; Colloq.) good-by.
3) derisive: mocking; scoffing.
4) sleet: falling snow or hail mixed with rain.
5) firing squad: a group of men charged with executing someone by gun fire.

motionless, proud and disdainful,[1] Walter Mitty the Undefeated, inscrutable[2] to the last.

1) disdainful: contemptuous.
2) inscrutable: mysterious; unknowable.

A Red-Lettet[1] Day

by Elizabeth Taylor

Elizabeth Taylor (1912-) was born in Reading, Berkeshire, England. She began to write stories as a young child and always wanted to be a novelist. Elizabeth Taylor's work belongs to that fine English tradition of "novels of sensibility". Her prose is one of the most beautiful and exact instruments of precision in use today. She writes with meticulous care and craftmanship.

THE HEDGEROW was beaded with silver. In the English November fog, the leaves dripped[2] with a deadly intensity, as if each falling drop were a drop of acid.

Through the mist, cabs came suddenly face to face with one another, passing and repassing between station and school. Backing into the hedges — twigs, withered berries striking the windows — drivers leaned out to exchange remarks incomprehensible to their passengers, who felt oddly at their mercy. Town parents, especially, shrank from this malevolent landscape — the wastes of rotting cabbages, flint cottages with rakish privies,[3] rubbish heaps, gray napkins drooping on clotheslines,[4] soil like plum cake. Even turning in at the rather superior school gates, they were dismayed by the mossy stone and the smell of fungus. Then, as the building itself came into view, they could see Matron standing at the top of the steps, fantastically white, shaming Nature, her hands laid affectionately upon the shoulders of such boys as could not resist her. The weather was put in its place.[5] The day

---

1) red-letter: memorable; especially happy.

2) drip: fall or let fall in drops.

3) flint cottages with rakish privies: 멋진 화장실이 달린 돌집. privy=a small outhouse as a toilet.

4) gray napkins drooping on clotheslines: 빨랫줄에 초라하게 걸려 있는 재빛깔의 손수건.

5) The weather was put in its place.: 날씨는 제 날씨였다.

would take its course. She had an air of professional bonhomie,[1] as if she shared in the gaiety of the occasion. But, each term, Visiting Day to her was like Christmas Day to a clergyman, a great climax of work and preparation.

Tory was one of the last to get a cab. Having no man to exert authority for her, she must merely take her turn and stand on the slimy pavement waiting for a car to come back to the station empty. She stamped her feet, feeling the damp creeping through her shoes. When she left home, she had thought herself suitably dressed; even for such an early hour, her hat was surely plain enough? One after another, she had tried on everyone she owned, and had come out, in the end, leaving hats all over the bed, so that it resembled a new grave with its mound of wreathed flowers. But the other mothers had hats of undreamed-of austerity,[2] and the most sensible of Tory's shoes could not withstand the insidious damp.

One other woman was on her own,[3] Tory eyed her with distaste. Her sons (for surely there were more than one; she looked as if she had what is often called a teeming womb,[4] like a woman symbolizing maternity in a pageant),[5] her many sons would never feel the lack of a father (as Tory's one boy was bound to), for she was large enough to be both father and mother to them. Yes, Tory thought, she would have them out on the lawn and bowl at them by the hour,[6] would coach them in mathematics, oil their bats, dub[7] their boots, tan[8] their backsides. Tory was working herself up into a hatred of this woman,[9]

---

1) bonhomie: good nature; pleasant ways.
2) hats of undreamed-of austerity: 꿈에도 생각지 못한 위엄을 갖춘 모자.
3) (was) on her own: on her own account, responsibility, resources, etc. 여기서는 혼자서 있었다라는 뜻.
4) a teeming womb: 다산(多産) 자궁. teem=full of abound; swarm.
5) like a woman symbolizing maternity in a pageant: 연극에서 모성을 상징하는 여인처럼.
6) by the hour: 시간제로.
7) dub: polish.
8) tan: (Colloq.) thrash.
9) was working herself up Into a hatred of this woman: 이 여인에 대한 증오심이 자꾸만 치솟고 있었다.

who seemed to be all that she herself was not,[1] with only one love affair in her life, or, rather, one mating. She has probably eaten her husband now that her child-bearing days[2] are over, Tory thought. He would never have dared to ask for a divorce, as mine did. The woman still carried her "mother's bag"[3] — the vast thing that, full of diapers, bibs, bottles of orange juice, accompanies babies out to tea.

Tory wondered what was in it now. Sensible things — a Bradshaw,[4] ration books, a bag of biscuits, large, clean handkerchiefs, a tablet of soap, and aspirins?

A jolly manner. ("I love young people — I feed on them," Tory thought spitefully.) The furs on the woman's shoulders made her even larger; they clasped paws across her great, authoritative back, like hands across the ocean. Tory lifted her muff to hide her smile.

Nervous dread made her feel fretful and vicious. In *her* life, all was frail, precarious — emotions fleeting, relationships fragmentary. Her life with her husband had suddenly loosened and dissolved; her love for her son was painful, shadowed by guilt — the guilt of having nothing solid to offer, of having grown up and forgotten, of adventuring still, away from her child, of not being able to resist those emotional adventures, the tenuous grasping after life.[5] He was threatened by the very look of her, attracting those delicious secret glances, glimpses, and whispers, by the challenge she always felt, and the excitement — not deeply sexual, for she was merely flirtatious. But I am not, she thought, watching Mrs. Hay-Hardy (whose name she was soon to learn but did not yet know) rearranging her furs on her shoulders, I am not a great feather bed of oblivion. Between Edward and me there is no premise of love, none at all — nothing taken for granted, as between most sons and mothers, but all tentative and agonized.[6]

---

1) seemed to be all that she herself was not: 자기와는 생판 다른 여자인 것 같았다.
2) child-bearing days: 출산기.
3) mother's bag: 기저귀 가방.
4) a Bradshaw: 브래드쇼 여행 안내서.
5) the tenuous grasping after life: 인생을 파악하려는 가냘픈 노력. tenuous=thin; slender; having slight importance.
6) but all tentative and agonized: 다만 모두가 실험적이고 고통스러웠다. entative= experimental.

We are indeed amateurs, both of us; no tradition behind us, no gift for the job. All we achieve is too hard come by. We try too piteously to please one another, and if we do, feel frightened by the miracle of it. I do indeed love him above all others. Above all others, but not exclusively. . . .

Here a taxi swerved against the station curb and palpitated as she stepped forward quickly, triumphantly, before Mrs. Hay-Hardy could do so, and settled herself in the back seat.

"Could we share?" Mrs. Hay-Hardy asked, her voice confident, melodious, and one foot definitely on the running board.[1] Tory smiled and moved over much farther than was necessary, as if such a teeming womb could scarcely be accommodated on the seat beside her.

Shifting her furs on her shoulders, settling herself, Mrs. Hay-Hardy glanced out through the filming windows, undaunted by the weather, which, she said, would clear, would lift. Oh, she was confident that it would lift by midday!

"One has to get up so early it seems midday now," Tory complained.

But Mrs. Hay-Hardy explained that she had not risen until six, so, naturally, it still seemed only eleven to her, as it was.

She will share the fare, down to the last penny, Tory thought. There will be a loud and forthright women's argument. She will count out coppers and make a fuss.

This did happen. At the top of the steps, Matron still waited, with the three Hay-Hardy boys grouped about her, and Edward, who blushed and whitened alternately with terrible excitement,[2] a little to one side. Yes, he had grown, Tory thought, and his shorts were high above his roughened knees. He looked more than eleven, but his complexion was peachy and downy still, like a younger child's, and his long lashes threw shadows across his eyes. As an only son, he had not the same claim to Matron's attention as the Hay-Hardys, and she had chosen them to encircle. Sensing this, perhaps, Edward stood apart.

---

1) running board: a metal piece along the side of some automobiles, near the ground.

2) blushed and whitened alternately with terrible excitement; 흥분 때문에 얼굴이 붉으락푸르락했다.

To meet this wonderful customer, this profitable womb, the headmaster's wife herself came into the hall. Her husband had sent her, instructing her with deft cynicism[1] from behind his detective novel. He himself, of course, was one of those gods who rarely descend, except, like Zeus, in a very private capacity.[2]

This is the moment I marked off on the calendar, Edward thought. Here it is. Every night, he and the other boys had thrown one of their pebbles out of the window to mark a day gone. The little stones had dropped back onto the gravel under the window, quite lost, untraceable — the days of their lives.

As smooth as minnows were Mrs. Lancaster's phrases of welcome; she had soothed so many mothers, mothered[3] so many boys. Her words swam all one way, in unison, but her heart never moved. Matron, on the other hand, was always nervous; the results of her work were so much on the surface, so easily checked. The rest of the staff could hide their inefficiency or shift their responsibility. She could not. If Mrs. Hay-Hardy cried, as she did today, "Dear boy, your teeth!" to her first-born,[4] it was Matron's work she criticized, and Matron flushed. And Mrs. Lancaster flushed for Matron, and Derrick Hay-Hardy flushed for his mother.

"Perhaps I am not a born[5] mother," Tory thought, going down the steps with Edward. They would walk back to the town and have lunch at the Crown, she said to him. Edward pressed her arm as a taxi, bulging with Hay-Hardys,[6] went away down the drive.

"Do you mean you wanted to go with them?" Tory asked. They will get there long before us, she thought. They will have eaten everything.

"No."

"Don't you like them?"

---

1) instructing her with deft cynicism. . . : (탐정 소설을 읽고 있다가) 능란한 냉소적인 언사로 부인을 타이르면서.
2) except in avery private capacity: 극히 개인적인 입장(자격)에서가 아니고는.
3) mother: (*v.*) be mother of; act as mother to.
4) first-born: oldest child.
5) born: by birth, by nature.
6) bulging with Hay-Hardys: 해이하디 일가를 가득히 태운.

"No."

"But why?"

"They don't like me."

Unbearable news for any mother, for surely all the world loves one's child, one's only child. Doubt set in,[1] a little, nagging toothache of doubt. You *are* happy? she wanted to ask. "I've looked forward so much to this," she said instead. "So much."

He stared ahead. All around the gateposts, drops of moisture fell from one leaf to another, and the stone griffins[2] hunched up in misery.[3]

"But I imagined it being a different day," Tory added. "Quite different."

"It will be nice to get something different to eat," Edward said.

They walked down the road toward the Crown in silence, as if they could not make any progress[4] until they had reached that point.

"You *are* warm enough at night?" Tory asked when at last they were sitting in the hotel dining room.

"Yes," he said absently, and then, bringing himself back to the earlier, distant politeness,[5] added, "Stifling hot."

"Stifling? But surely you have plenty of fresh air?" She could feel her questions sliding off him.

"*I* do," he said reassuringly. "My bed's just under the window. Perishing. I have to keep my head under the bedclothes, or I get earache."

I am asking for all this, she thought. When the waiter brought her pink gin, she drank it quickly, conscious that Mrs. Hay-Hardy, across the hotel dining room, was pouring out a nice glass of water for herself, was so full of jokes that Tory felt she had perhaps brought a collection of them[6] along with her in her shopping bag. Laughter ran around and around the Hay-Hardy's table, above the glasses of water. Edward

---

1) Doubt set in: 의심이 들었다.

2) griffin: (Ok. myth) creature with the head and wings of an eagle, and the body of a lion.

3) were hunched up in misery: 비참하게 구부리고 있었다.

4) as if they could not make any progress: as if they could not continue to talk any more.

5) bring himself back to the earlier politeness: 전과 같은 공손한 태도로 돌아가서.

6) a collection of them: a collection of jokes.

turned once, and she glimpsed the faintest quiver under one eye,[1) and an answering quiver on the middle Hay-Hardy's face.[2)]

She felt exasperated.[3)] Cold had settled in her; her mouth — her heart, too — felt stiff.

"What would you like to do after lunch?" she asked.

"We could look round the shops," Edward said, nibbling away at his bread, as if to keep hunger at arm's length.[4)]

The shops were in the market square. At the draper's, the hats were steadily coming around into fashion again. "1 could astonish everyone with one of these," Tory thought, setting her own hat right by her reflection in the window. Bales of cotton apron print rose on both sides; a wax-faced boy[5)] wore a stiff suit, its price ticket[6)] dangling from his yellow, broken fingers, his painted blue eyes turned mildly upon the street. Edward gave him a look of contempt and went to the shop door. Breathing on the glass, peering in through a little space among suspended bibs and jabots and parlormaids' caps, he watched the cages flying overhead between cashier and counter.

The Hay-Hardys streamed by, heading for the open country.

Most minutely, Tory and Edward examined the windows of the draper's shop, the bicycle shop, the family grocer's. There was nothing to say. They were just reading the postcards in the news agent's window when Edward's best friend greeted them. His father, a clergyman, snatched off his hat and clapped it to his chest at the sight of Tory. When she turned back to the postcards, she could see how unsuitable they were — jokes about bloomers,[7)] about twins; a great seaside world of fat men in striped bathing suits; enormous women trotted down

1) the faintest quiver under one eye: Edward의 한쪽 눈이 움직이는 기색.
2) an answering quiver on the middle Hay-Hardy's face: 해이하디의 가운데 아들의 얼굴에서 대꾸하는 기색(을 힐끔 보았다).
3) felt exasperated: felt annoyed extremely; felt irritated.
4) as if to keep hunger at arm's length: as if to keep hunger from being too familiar.
5) a wax-faced boy: 밀초 얼굴을 한 소년 마네킹.
6) its price ticket: 가격표.
7) bloomers: a loose trousers, gathered at the knee, worn by women and girls for physical training.

to the sea's edge while crabs humorously nipped their behinds;[1] farcical situations arose over bathing machines; and little boys had trouble with their water. She blushed.

The afternoon seemed to give a little sigh, stirred itself, and shook down a spattering of rain over the pavements. Beyond the market square, the countryside, which had absorbed the Hay-Hardys lowered[2] at them.

"Is there anything you want?" Tory asked desperately, coveting[3] the warm interiors of the shops.

"I could do with a new puncture outfit[4] for my bike," Edward said.

They went back to the bicycle shop. My God, it's only three o'clock, Tory thought in despair as she glanced secretly under her glove at her watch.

The Museum Room at the Guildhall was not gay, but at least there were Roman remains, a few instruments of torture, and half of a mammoth's[5] jawbone. Tory sat down on a seat among all the broken terra cotta[6] and took out a cigarette.

"No smoking, please," the attendant said, coming out from behind a case of stuffed deer.

"Oh, please!" Tory begged. She sat primly on the chair, her feet together, and when she looked up at him, her violet eyes flashed with tears. Edward wandered away.

The attendant struck a match for her, and his hand, curving around it, trembled.

"It's the insurance," he apologized. "I'll have this later, if I may," he said when she offered him a cigarette, and he put it very carefully in his breast pocket, as if it were a lock of her hair.

---

1) behinds: (Colloq.) buttocks.

2) lower: look dark and threatening.

3) covet: desire eagerly.

4) a puncture outfit: 펑크 수리 기구.

5) mammoth: a very large, extinct kind of elephant with a hairy skin and long curved tusks.

6) terra cotta: a kind of hard, brownish-red earthenware, used for vases, statuettes, etc.

"Do you have to stay here all day long with these dull little broken jugs and things?" she asked, looking about.

He forgave her at once for belittling his life's work, only pointing out his pride, the fine mosaic[1] on the wall.

"But floors should be lying down," she said naively, without innocence.

Edward came tiptoeing back.

"You see that quite delightful floor hanging up there?" she said to him. "This gentleman will tell you all about it. . . . My son adores Greek mythology," she explained to the attendant.

"Your son!" he repeated, affecting gallant disbelief, his glance stripping ten or fifteen years from her'[2] Then, "This happens to be a Byzantine mosaic," he said, and looked reproachfully at it for not being what it could not be. Edward listened grudgingly. His mother had forced him into similar situations at other times — in the armory of the Tower of London and, once, at Kew. It was as if she kindled in men a flicker of interest and admiration that her son must keep fanned, for she would not.[3] Boredom drew her away again, yet her charm must still hold sway. So now Edward listened crossly to the story of the Byzantine mosaic as, last holidays, he had minutely observed the chasing[4] on Henry VIII's breastplate, and in utter exasperation, the holidays before, had watched curlews through field glasses ("Edward is so very keen on birds") for the whole of a hot day while Tory dozed elegantly in the heather.[5]

Ordinary days perhaps are better, Edward thought. Sinking down through him were the lees of despair,[6] which must at all costs be hidden from his mother. He glanced up at every clock they passed,

---

1) mosaic: small pieces of stone, glass, wood, etc. of different colors inlaid to form a picture or design.

2) his glance stripping ten or fifteen years from her: 그녀의 나이를 10년이나 15년쯤 감해 보는 눈치.

3) for she wonld not: 자기는 그렇게 하기 싫어서.

4) chasing: engraving. 조각.

5) heather: a low, evergreen shrub with stalks of small, rosy-pink, bellshaped flowers, covering many heaths of Scotland and North England.

6) Sinking down through him were the lees of despair: 절망의 찌꺼기가 그의 몸 안에서 가라앉고 있었다. lees=dregs; sediment, as from wine.

and wondered about his friends. Alone with his mother, he felt unsafe, wounded and wounding, and, oppressed by responsibility he saw himself in relation to the outside world. Thoughts of the future and even — as they stood in the church porch to shelter from another little gust of rain — of death seemed to brush[1] against him, alight on him, and they disturbed him, as they would not do if he were at school, anonymous and safe.

Tory sat down on a seat and read a notice about missionaries, chafing her hands inside her muff, while all her bracelets jingled softly.

Flapping, black, in his cassock, a clergyman came hurrying through the graveyard, between the dripping umbrella trees.[2] Edward stepped guiltily off the porch, as if he had been trespassing.

"Good afternoon," the vicar said.

"Good afternoon," Tory replied. She looked up from blowing the fur of her muff into divisions and her smile broke warmly, beautifully, over the dark afternoon.

Then "The weather — " they both began ruefully, broke off, and hesitated, then laughed at one another.

It was wonderful; now they would soon be saying goodbye. It was over. The day they had longed for was almost over — the polite little tea among the chintz[3] and the wheel back chairs of the Copper Kettle, Tory frosty and imperious with the waitresses,[4] and, once, Edward beginning, "Father. . . ," at which she looked up sharply before she could gather together the careful indifference she always assumed at this name. Edward faltered, "He sent me a parcel." "How nice!" said Tory, laying ice all over his heart. She called the waitress. Her cup was cracked. She could not drink tea from riveted china, however prettily painted. The waitress went sulkily away. All around them sat other small boys with their parents. Tory's bracelets tinkled as she clasped her hands tightly together and leaned forward. "And how is

1) brush: touch lightly in passing.
2) betweeu the dripping umbrella trees: 물망울이 떨어지는 우산 모양의 나무 사이로.
3) chintz: a cotton cloth printed in patterns of various colors and often glazed.
4) Tory frosty and imperious with the waitresses: 토리가 웨이트레스에게 쌀쌀하고 오만하게 굴었던 일.

your father's wife?" she asked brightly, indifferently.

They took a taxi back to the school. Sullenly, the day withdrew; as they turned in at the gates, they could see lights in the ground-floor windows. She thought of going back in the train, of a lonely evening. She would take a drink up to her bedroom and sip it while she did her hair, the gas fire roaring in its white ribs, Edward's photograph beside her bed.

The Hay-Hardys were unloading at the foot of the school steps; flushed from their country walk and all their laughter, they seemed to swarm and shout.

Edward got out of the taxi and stood looking up at Tory, his new puncture outfit clasped tightly in his hand. Uncertainly, awaiting a cue[1)] from her, he tried to begin his goodbye.

Warm, musky-scented, softly rustling with the sound of her bracelets, the touch of her fur, she leaned and kissed him. "So lovely, darling!" she murmured. She had no cue to give him. Mrs. Hay-Hardy had gone into the school to have a word with Matron, so Tory must find her own way of saying farewell.

They smiled gaily, as if they were greeting one another.

"See you soon," she said.

"Yes, see you soon."

"Goodbye, then, darling."

"Goodbye," said Edward.

She slammed the door and, as the taxi moved off, leaned toward the window and waved. He stood there uncertainly, waving back, radiant with relief. Then, as she disappeared around the curve of the drive, he ran quickly up the steps to find his friends, and safety.

---

1) cue: hint or suggestion as to what to do or when to act.

The Orphaned Swimming Pool

by John Updike

John Updike (1932-) was born in a small town in western Pennsylvania, where his father taught school, having previously been a telephone cable-splicer (cf. "a telephone lineman" among the orphaned swimming pool's assorted users). After graduating from Harvard, John Updike spent a year at Oxford and then joined *The New York* as a staff writer, following in the steps of Thurber and White. Indeed he has cited Thurbers as one of his first "literary idols." He left the magazine in 1957 to devote all his time to writing serious fiction.

One of the most successful contemporary American writers, Updike is a perfectionist, a master of both technique and style. His short stories, humorous poems, and essays appears regularly and he has published a number of novels, among them *Rabbit, Run* (1960), perhaps his best work, and *The Centaur* (1963), which won the National Book Award for fiction. His short stories have been collected in several volumes, among them *Pigeon Fathers* (1962) and *Museums and Women* (1972), from which "The Orphaned Swimming Pool" is taken.

MARRIAGES, LIKE chemical unions, release upon dissolution[1] packets of the energy locked up in their bonding.[2] There is the piano no one wants, the cocker spaniel[3] no one can take care of. Shelves of books suddenly stand revealed as burdensomely dated and unlikely to be reread; indeed, it is difficult to remember who read them in the first place. And what of those old skis in the attic? Or the doll house waiting to be repaired in the basement? The piano goes out of tune, the dog goes mad.[4] The summer that the Turners got their divorce, their swimming pool had neither a master nor a mistress, though the sun beat down day after day, and a state of drought[5] was declared in

1) upon dissolution: when (marriage) dissolve. 이혼할 때.
2) bonding: A chemical bond is the force which holds atoms together in a molecule.
3) cocker spaniel: a breed of dog. Cockers are popular pets because of their good disposition and relatively small size.
4) mad: insane.
5) drought: a long period without any rain.

Connecticut.[1)]

It was a young pool, only two years old, of the fragile type fashioned by laying a plastic liner within a carefully carved hole in the ground. The Turners' side yard looked infernal[2)] while it was being done; one bulldozer sank into the mud and had to be pulled free by another. But by midsummer the new grass was sprouting, the encircling flagstone s[3)] were in place, the blue plastic tinted the water a heavenly blue, and it had to be admitted that the Turners had scored again.[4)] They were always a little in advance of their friends. He was a tall, hairy-backed man with long arms, and a nose flattened by football,[5)] and a sullen look of too much blood; she was a fine-boned blonde with dry blue eyes and lips usually held parted and crinkled as if about to ask a worrisome, or whimsical,[6)] question. They never seemed happier, nor their marriage healthier, than those two summers. They grew brown and supple and smooth with swimming. Ted would begin his day with a swim, before dressing to catch the train,[7)] and Linda would hold court all day amid crowds of wet matrons[8)] and children, and Ted would return from work to find a poolside cocktail party in progress, and the couple would end their day at midnight, when their friends had finally left, by swimming nude, before bed. What ecstasy! In darkness the water felt mild as milk and buoyant as helium[9)] and the swimmers became giants, gliding from side to side in a single languorous[10)] stroke.

1) Connecticut: one of the New England States. It's southern border is just north of New York City.
2) infernal: hellish. 지옥과 같은.
3) flagstone: a flat, fine-grained stone which is split into slabs and used for paving. It is expensive and is considered quite elegant.
4) the Turners had scored again: 터너가(家)는 다시 성공을 거두었다(득점했다).
5) football: It is not uncommon for an American man to have been injured playing high school or college football.
6) whimsical: fanciful; playful.
7) catch the train: Ted was a commuter, taking the train to New York each day to go to the office.
8) matron: a married woman.
9) buoyant as helium: 헬륨처럼 부양성이 있는.
10) languorous: sensuously lazy, without effort.

The next May, the pool was filled as usual, and the usual after-school gangs of mothers and children gathered, but Linda, unlike her, stayed indoors. She could be heard within the house, moving from room to room, but she no longer emerged, as in the other summers, with a cheerful tray of ice and brace of bottles,[1] and Triscuits[2] and lemonade for the children. Their friends felt less comfortable about appearing, towels in hand, at the Turners' on weekends. Though Linda had lost some weight and looked elegant, and Ted was cumbersomely jovial,[3] they gave off the faint, sleepless, awkward-making aroma of a couple in trouble.[4] Then, the day after school was out, Linda fled with the children to her parents in Ohio.[5] Ted stayed nights in the city, and the pool was deserted. Though the pump that ran the water through the filter continued to mutter in the lilacs, the cerulean[6] pool grew cloudy. The bodies of dead horseflies and wasps dotted the still surface. A speckled plastic ball drifted into a corner beside the diving board and stayed there. The grass between the flagstones grew lank. On the glasstopped poolside table, a spray can of Off![7] had lost its pressure and a gin-and-tonic glass[8] held a sere[9] mint leaf. The pool looked desolate and haunted, like a stagnant jungle spring; it looked poisonous and ashamed. The postman, stuffing overdue notices and pornography solicitations into the mailbox, averted his eyes from the side yard politely.

Some June weekends, Ted sneaked[10] out from the city. Families driving to church glimpsed him dolefully[11] sprinkling chemical substances

---

1) brace of bottles: a pair of two bottles of liquor such as Scoth and gin. brace = a pair of two like things.
2) Triscuits: a brand of salty wheat cracker.
3) jovial: good-humored and merry.
4) they gave off the faint, . . . aroma of a couple in trouble: 문제(를 일으키고 있는) 부부가 뿜는 … 희미한 냄새를 풍겼다.
5) Ohio: a Midwestern state, about 500 miles from Connecticut.
6) cerulean: sky blue.
7) Off!: a brand of insect-repellent spray.
8) gin-and-tonic glass: a tall glass, used for serving a popular summer drink made with gin and quinine water.
9) sere: (Poetic) withered; dry.
10) sneak: move in a stealthy, sly way.
11) dolefully: sadly; without enthusiasm.

into the pool. He looked pale and thin. He instructed Roscoe Chace, his neighbor on the left, how to switch on the pump and change the filter, and how much chlorine and Algitrol[1] should be added weekly. He explained he would not be able to make it out[2] every weekend — as if the distance that for years he had traveled twice each day, gliding in and out of New York, had become an impossibly steep climb back into the past. Linda, he confided vaguely, had left her parents in Akron[3] and was visiting her sister in Minneapolis. As the shock of the Turners' joint disappearance wore off,[4] their pool seemed less haunted and forbidding. The Murtaugh children — the Murtaughs, a rowdy, numerous family, were the Turners' right-hand neighbors — began to use it, without supervision. So Linda's old friends, with their children, began to show up,[5] "to keep the Murtaughs from drowning each other." For if anything were to happen to a Murtaugh, the poor Turners (the adjective had become automatic) would be sued for everything,[6] right when they could least afford it.[7] It became, then, a kind of duty, a test of loyalty, to use the pool.

July was the hottest in twenty-seven years. People brought their own lawn furniture[8] over in station wagons and set it up. Teenage offspring and Swiss *au-pair*[9] girls were established as lifeguards. A nylon rope with flotation corks, meant to divide the wading end from the diving end of the pool, was found coiled in the garage and reinstalled. Agnes Kleefield contributed an old refrigerator, which was wired to an outlet above Ted's basement workbench[10] and used to store ice, quinine water,

---

1) chlorine and Algitrol: chemical substances used to keep the pool clean.
2) make it out: come out from the city to his home.
3) Akron: an industrial city in northern Ohio.
4) wear off: become less.
5) show up: appear; arrive.
6) sued for everything: be required by a court of law to pay a large sum of money in compensation for dangers.
7) right when they could least afford it: 그럴 이유가 전혀 없었던 바로 그때.
8) lawn furniture: folding chairs with aluminum frames.
9) *au-pair*: a girl from overseas who does light homework and/or looks after young children in exchange for room and board.
10) workbench: a sturdy table. Many suburban man have a workbench and tools for doing odd jobs.

and soft drinks.[1] An honor system[2] shoebox containing change appeared beside it; a little lost-and-found[3] — an array of forgotten sunglasses, flippers, towels, lotions, paperbacks, shirts, even underwear — materialized on the Turners' side steps. When people, that July, said, "Meet you at the pool," they did not mean the public pool past the shopping center, or the country-club pool beside the first tee.[4] They meant the Turners'. Restrictions on admission were difficult to enforce tactfully. A visiting Methodist bishop, two Taiwanese economists, an entire girls' softball team from Darien,[5] an eminent Canadian poet, the archery champion of Hartford,[6] the six members of a black rock group called the Good Intentions, an ex-mistress of Aly Khan, the lavender-haired[7] mother-in-law of a Nixon adviser not quite of Cabinet rank, an infant of six weeks, a man who was killed the next day on the Merritt Parkway,[8] a Filipino who could stay on the pool bottom for eighty seconds, two Texans who kept cigars in their mouths and hats on their heads, three telephone linemen,[9] four expatriate Czechs, a student Maoist from Wesleyan,[10] and the postman all swam, as guests, in the Turners' pool, though not all at once. After the daytime crowd ebbed,[11] and the shoebox was put back in the refrigerator, and the last *au-pair* girl took the last goosefleshed,[12] wrinkled child shivering home to supper, there was a tide of evening activity, trysts.[13] (Mrs. Kleefield and the Nicholson boy, most noto-

---

1) soft drink: non-alcoholic beverages.
2) honor system: a system of trust where each person stakes his good name on the fulfilment of his promise; here, to pay for what he ate or drink.
3) lost-and-found: 유실물 취급소.
4) first tee: the beginning of the golf course.
5) Darien: a wealthy, fashionable town in Connecticut.
6) Hartford: the capital of Connecticut; known primarily for the many insurance companies located there.
7) lavender-haired: a hair color, a very pale tint of bluish purple.
8) Merritt Parkway: a busy highway in Connecticut.
9) linemen: men who work outdoors installing or repairing telephone lines.
10) Wesleyan: a university in western Connecticut.
11) ebbed: retreated.
12) goosefleshed: skin momentarily covered by small bumps as a result of a cold. 소름이 끼친.
13) tryst: a secret, romantic meeting.

ously) and what some called, overdramatically, orgies,[1] True, late splashes and excited guffaws[2] did often keep Mrs. Chace awake, and the Murtaugh children spent hours at their attic window with binoculars. And there was the evidence of the lost underwear.

One Saturday early in August, the morning arrivals[3] found an unknown car with New York plates[4] parked in the garage. But cars of all sorts were so common — the parking tangle[5] frequently extended into the road — that nothing much was thought of it, even when someone noticed that the bedroom windows upstairs were open. And nothing came of it, except that around suppertime, in the lull before the evening crowds began to arrive in force, Ted and an unknown woman, of the same physical type as Linda but brunette, swiftly exited from the kitchen door, got into the car, and drove back to New York. The few lingering babysitters and beaux[6] thus unwittingly glimpsed the root of the divorce. The two lovers had been trapped inside the house all day; Ted was fearful of the legal consequences[7] of their being seen by anyone who might write and tell Linda. The settlement was at a ticklish[8] stage; nothing less than terror of Linda's lawyers would have led Ted to suppress his indignation at seeing, from behind the window screen, his private pool turned public carnival. For long thereafter, though in the end he did not marry the woman, he remembered that day when they lived together like fugitives in a cave, feeding on love and ice water, tiptoeing barefoot to the depleted cupboards, which they, arriving late last night, had hoped to stock in the morning, not foreseeing the onslaught of interlopers[9] that would

1) orgies: wild, drunken revels.
2) guffaw: a loud, sudden laugh. 너털 웃음.
3) arrivals: persons that arrive.
4) plates: license plates.
5) tangle: a tangled condition. 혼잡.
6) beaux: (F.) the plural of beau "a young man who is courting a girl"; here, it refers to the babysitters' boyfriends.
7) legal consequences: Evidently the divorce was to be on the grounds of incompatibility, rather than adultery; if Linda could prove the latter, she might either refuse Ted the divorce or demand higher alimony payment.
8) ticklish: delicate, easily upset.
9) interlopers: someone who comes without being invited.

pin them in. Her hair, he remembered, had tickled his shoulders as she crouched behind him at the window, and through the angry pounding of his own blood he had felt her slim body breathless with the attempt not to giggle.

August drew in, with cloudy days. Children grew bored with swimming. Roscoe Chace went on vacation to Italy; the pump broke down, and no one repaired it. Dead dragonflies accumulated on the surface of the pool. Small deluded toads hopped in and swam around hopelessly. Linda at last returned. From Minneapolis she had gone on to Idaho[1] for six weeks, to be divorced. She and the children had burnt faces from riding and hiking; her lips looked drier and more quizzical than ever, still seeking to frame that troubling question. She stood at the window, in the house that already seemed to lack its furniture, at the same side window where the lovers had crouched, and gazed at the deserted pool. The grass around it was green from splashing, save where a longlying towel had smothered a rectangle and left it brown. Aluminum furniture she didn't recognize lay strewn and broken. She counted a dozen bottles beneath the glass-topped table. The nylon divider bad parted, and its two halves floated independently. The blue plastic beneath the colorless water tried to make a cheerful, otherworldy statement, but Linda saw that the pool in truth had no bottom, it held bottomless loss, it was one huge blue tear. Thank God no one had drowned in it. Except her. She saw that she could never live here again. In September the place was sold to a family with toddling infants, who for safety's sake have not only drained the pool but have sealed it over with iron pipes and a heavy mesh, and put warning signs around, as around a chained dog.

1) Idabo: 이혼법은 주에 따라 다르다. 6주일 거주하면 그 주의 법률에 따라 이혼할 수 있다. Linda는 쉽게 이혼할 수 있는 Idaho주에 간 것이다.

Why I Live at the P.O.

by Eudora Welty

A native of Jackson, Mississippi, Eudora Welty (1909-) still makes her home in the town in which she was born. Also she remained close to home by attending the Mississippi State College for Women, she left the state to study at the University of Wisconsin and Columbia, and she worked at various writing and publicity jobs before she began to write seriously about the small-town Mississippi life so familiar to her. Her novels and short stories have won many awards.

Characteristic of Miss Welty's work is the accurate reproduction of colloquial speech for comic effort and the creation of characters whose personalities are a grotesque and at times symbolic combination of the ordinary and the eccentric.

I WAS getting along fine with Mama, Papa-Daddy and Uncle Rondo until my sister Stella-Rondo just separated from her husband and came back home again. Mr. Whitaker! Of course I went with Mr. Whitaker first, when he first appeared here in China Grove, taking "Pose Yourself" photos,[1] and Stella-Rondo broke us up. Told him I was one-sided. Bigger on one-sided[2] than the other, which is a deliberate, calculated falsehood: I'm the same. Stella-Rondo is exactly twelve months to the day younger than I am and for that reason she's spoiled.

She's always had anything in the world she wanted and then she'd throw it away. Papa-Daddy gave her this gorgeous Add-a-Pearl necklace[3] when she was eight years old and she threw it away playing baseball when she was nine, with only two pearls.

So as soon as she got married and moved away from home the first thing she did was separate! From Mr. Whitaker! This photographer with the popeyes she said she trusted. Came home from one of those towns up in Illinois and to our complete surprise brought this child

---

1) taking "Pose Yourself" photos: 인물사진을 찍다.

2) one-sided: uneven; unequal.

3) Add-a-Pearl necklace: 해마다 한 개씩 진주를 보태기로 되어 있는 목걸이.

of two.

Mama said she like to made her drop dead for a second.[1] "Here you had this marvelous blonde child and never so much as wrote your mother a word about it,[2]" says Mama. "I'm thoroughly ashamed of you." But of course she wasn't.

Stella-Rondo just calmly takes off this *hat*, I wish you could see it. She says, "Why, Mama, Shirley-T.'s adopted, I can prove it."

"How?" says Mama, but all I says was, "H'm!" There I was over the hot stove, trying to stretch two chickens over five people and a completely unexpected child into the bargain, without one moment's notice.

"What do you mean 'H'm!'?" says Stella-Rondo, and Mama says, "I heard that, Sister."

I said that oh, I didn't mean a thing, only that whoever Shirley-T. was, she was the spit-image of Papa-Daddy[3] if he'd cut off his beard, which of course he'd never do in the world. Papa-Daddy's Mama's papa and sulks.[4]

Stella-Rondo got furious! She said, "Sister, I don't need to tell you you got a lot of nerve and always did have and I'll thank you to make no future reference to my adopted child[5] whatsoever."

"Very well," I said. "Very well, very well. Of course I noticed at once she looks like Mr. Whitaker's side too. That frown. She looks like a cross[6] between Mr. Whitaker and Papa-Daddy."

"Well, all I can say is she isn't."

"She looks exactly like Shirley Temple to me," says Mama, but Shirley-T. just ran away from her.

So the first thing Stella-Rondo did at the table was turn Papa-Daddy

---

1) she like to made her drop dead for a second: 잠시나마 쓰러져 죽어버렸으면 하다.
2) (you) never so much as wrote your mother a word about it: 어미한테 한마디 말도 써 보내지 않았다.
3) was the spit-image of Papa-Daddy: 할아버지와 꼭 닮았다. spit=perfect likeness; counterpart. *Ex.* He is the spit(and image) of his father. Papa-Daddy=Grandfather.
4) Papa-Daddy's Mama's papa and sulks: 할아버지는 엄마의 아빠였고 참 샐쭉 할아버지였다. sulk=the ill humor shown by sulking.
5) make no future reference to my adopted child: 앞으로 저의 양녀에 대해서는 뭐라고 간섭하지 않는다.
6) cross: a mixing of breeds, races, or the like; also, the product of such intermixture.

against me.[1)]

"Papa-Daddy," she says. He was trying to cut up his meat. "Papa-Daddy!" I was taken completely by surprise. Papa-Daddy is about a million years old and's got this long-long beard. "Papa-Daddy, Sister says she fails to understand why you don't cut off your beard."

So Papa Daddy l-a-y-s down his knife and fork! He's real rich. Mama says he is, he says he isn't. So he says, "Have I heard correctly? You don't understand why I don't cut off my beard?"

"Why," I says, "Papa-Daddy, of course I understand, I did not say any such of a thing, the idea!"

He says, "Hussy![2)]"

I says, "Papa-Daddy, you know I wouldn't any more want you to cut off your beard than the man in the moon. It was the farthest thing from my mind![3)] Stella-Rondo sat there and made that up[4)] while she was eating breast of chicken."

But he says, "So the postmistress[5)] fails to understand why I don't cut off my beard. Which job I got you through my influence with the government.[6)] 'Bird's nest'—is that what you call it?"

Not that it isn't the next to smallest P.O.[7)] in the entire state of Mississippi.

I says, "Oh, Papa-Daddy," I says, "I didn't say any such of a thing, I never dreamed it was a bird's nest, I have always been grateful though this is the next to smallest P.O. in the state of Mississippi, and I do not enjoy being referred to as a hussy by my own grandfather."

But Stella-Rondo says, "Yes, you did say it too. Anybody in the world could of heard you,[8)] that had ears.[9)]"

---

1) was turn Papa-Daddy against me: 할아버지를 나의 적으로 만드는 것이었다.
2) Hussy: a bad-mannered or pert girl; a worthless woman.
3) It was the farthest thing from my mind: 꿈에도 생각하지 않았던 것이다.
4) made that up: 꾸며냈다.
5) postmistress: women in charge of a post office. *cf.* postmaster.
6) Which job I got you through my influence with the government.: 내가 정부에 영향력이 있어 그 자리를 구해 주었다.
7) Not that it isn't the next to smallest P.O.: 두 번째로 작은 우체국인 것은 사실이다.
8) could of heard you: could have heard you.
9) that had ears: anybody that had ears.

"Stop right there," says Mama, looking at *me*.

So I pulled my napkin straight back through the napkin ring and left the table.

As soon as I was out of the room Mama says, "Call her back, or she'll starve to death," but Papa-Daddy says, "This is the beard I started growing on the Coast when I was fifteen years old." He would of gone[1] on till nightfall if Shirley-T. hadn't lost the Milky Way[2] she ate in Cairo.

So Papa-Daddy says, "I am going out and lie in the hammock, and you can all sit here and remember my words: I'll never cut off my beard as long as I live, even one inch, and I don't appreciate it in you at all." Passed right by me in the hall and went straight out and got in the hammock.

It would be a holiday. It wasn't five minutes before Uncle Rondo suddenly appeared in the hall in one of Stella-Rondo's flesh-colored kimonos,[3] all cut on the bias,[4] like something Mr. Whitaker probably thought was gorgeous.

"Uncle Rondo!" I says. "I didn't know who that was! Where are you going?"

"Sister," he says, "get out of my way, I'm poisoned."

"If you're poisoned stay away from Papa-Daddy," I says. "Keep out of the hammock. Papa-Daddy will certainly beat you on the head if you come within forty miles of him. He thinks I deliberately said he ought to cut off his beard after he got me the P.O., and I've told him and told him and told him, and he acts like he just don't hear me. Papa-Daddy must of gone stone deaf."[5]

"He picked a fine day to do it then,"[6] says Uncle Rondo, and before you could say "Jack Robinson"[7] flew out in the yard.

---

1) would of gone: would have gone.
2) the Milky Way: 과자(초콜릿) 이름.
3) kimono: a woman's loose dressing gown.
4) all cut on the bias: all cut diagonally across the weave. 천을 비스듬히 잘라 재단한.
5) must of gone stone deaf: 귀머거리가 되었음에 틀림없다. stone deaf=totally deaf.
6) He picked a fine day to do it then.: 오늘 같이 좋은 날에 화낼 필요는 없다.
7) before you could say "Jack Robinson": 눈 깜짝할 사이에.

What he'd really done, he'd drunk another bottle of that prescription. He does it every single Fourth of July as sure as shooting,[1] and it's horribly expensive. Then he falls over in the hammock and snores. So he insisted on zigzagging right on out to the hammock, looking like a half-wit.[2]

Papa-Daddy woke up with this horrible yell and right there without moving an inch[3] he tried to turn Uncle Rondo against me. I heard every word he said. Oh, he told Uncle Rondo I didn't learn to read till I was eight years old and he didn't see how in the world I ever got the mail put up at the P.O., much less read it all, and he said if Uncle Rondo could only fathom[4] the lengths he had gone to[5] to get me that job! And he said on the other hand he thought Stella-Rondo had a brilliant mind and deserved credit for getting out of town. All the time he was just lying there swinging as pretty as you please and looping out[6] his beard, and poor Uncle Rondo was *pleading* with him to slow down the hammock, it was making him as dizzy as a witch to watch it. But that's what Papa-Daddy likes about a hammock. So Uncle Rondo was too dizzy to get turned against me for the time being. He's Mama's only brother and is a good case of a one-track[7] mind. Ask anybody. A certified pharmacist.

Just then I heard Stella-Rondo raising the upstairs window. While she was married she got this peculiar idea that it's cooler with the windows shut and locked. So she has to raise the window before she can make a soul hear her outdoors.[8]

So she raises the window and says, "*Oh!*" You would have thought she was mortally wounded.

Uncle Rondo and Papa-Daddy didn't even look up, but kept right

---

1) as sure as shooting: as sure as a gun.
2) half-wit: a feeble-minded person; a stupid, foolish person.
3) right there without moving an inch: 바로 그 자리에서.
4) fathom: understand fully.
5) the lengths he had gone to: 그가 간 길이. 즉 그가 한 굉장한 수고라는 뜻.
6) looping out: make [form] a loop of.
7) one-track: (Colloq.) understanding or doing only one thing at a time.
8) before she can make a soul hear her outdoors: 바깥에 있는 누구에게 말을 하기 전에.

on with what they were doing. I had to laugh.

I flew up the stairs and threw the door open! I says, "What in the wide world's the matter, Stella-Rondo? You mortally wounded?"

"No," she says, "I am not mortally wounded but I wish you would do me the favor of looking out that window there and telling me what you see."

So I shade my eyes and look out the window.

"I see the front yard," I says.

"Don't you see any human beings?" she says.

"I see Uncle Rondo trying to run Papa-Daddy out of the hammock," I says. "Nothing more. Naturally, it's so suffocating-hot in the house, with all the windows shut and locked, everybody who cares to stay in their right mind will have to go out and get in the hammock before the Fourth of July is over."

"Don't you notice anything different about Uncle Rondo?" asks Stella-Rondo.

"Why, no, except he's got on some terrible-looking flesh-colored contraption[1)] I wouldn't be found dead in,[2)] is all I can see," I says.

"Never mind, you won't be found dead in it, because it happens to be part of my trousseau,[3)] and Mr. Whitaker took several dozen photographs of me in it," says Stella-Rondo. "What on earth could Uncle Rondo *mean* by wearing part of my trousseau out in the broad open daylight without saying so much as 'Kiss my foot,' *knowing* I only got home this morning after my separation and hung my negligee up on the bathroom door, just as nervous as I could be?"

"I'm sure I don't know, and what do you expect me to do about it?" I says. "Jump out the window?"

"No, I expect nothing of the kind. I simply declare that Uncle Rondo looks like a fool in it, that's all," she says. "It makes me sick to my stomach."

"Well, he looks as good as he can," I says. "As good as anybody

---

1) contraption: (Colloq.) contrivance; device, gadget. 새로 고안해 낸 옷(물건).
2) I wouldn't be found dead in: 죽었으면 죽었지, 나 같으면 입지 않을.
3) trousseau: a bride's outfit of clothes, linen, etc.

in reason[1] could." I stood up for[2] Uncle Rondo, please remember. And I said to Stella-Rondo, "I think I would do well not to criticize so freely if I were you and came home with a two-year-old child I had never said a word about, and no explanation whatever about my separation."

"I asked you the instant I entered this house not to refer one more time to my adopted child, and you gave me your word of honor you would not,[3]" was all Stella-Rondo would say, and started pulling out every one of her eyebrows with some cheap Kress tweezers.

So I merely slammed the door behind me and went down and made some green-tomato pickle. Somebody had to do it. Of course Mama had turned both the neggers[4] loose[5]; she always said no earthly power could hold one anyway on the Fourth of July, so she wouldn't even try. It turned out that Jaypan fell in the lake and came within a very narrow limit of drowning.[6]

So Mama trots in. Lifts up the lid and says, "H'm! Not very good for your Uncle Rondo in his precarious condition,[7] I must say. Or poor little adopted Shirley-T. Shame on you!"

That made me tired. I says, "Well, Stella-Rondo had better thank her lucky stars it was her instead of me came trotting in with that very peculiar-looking child. Now if it had been me that trotted in from Illinois and brought a peculiar-looking child of two, I shudder to think of the reception I'd of got,[8] much less controlled the diet of an entire family."[9]

---

1) anybody in reason: 보통 사람.
2) stood up for: take the part of; defend; support.
3) you gave me your word of honor you would not: you promised not to(refer to my adopted child).
4) neggers: negro.
5) turn ~ loose: let ~ loose; to give freedom to do something; to allow (someone) to do what he wants.
6) came within a very narrow limit of drowning: 하마터면 물에 빠져 죽을 뻔했다.
7) in his precarious condition: in his dangerous, uncertain, risky condition. 여기서는 '술 취해 있는 상태에서는'의 뜻.
8) I shudder to think of the reception I'd of got: 내가 받았을 대우를 생각만 해도 끔찍하다.
9) much less controlled the diet of an entire family: 하물며 온 식구의 식사마저 지배하고 말다니.

"But you must remember, Sister, that you were never married to Mr. Whitaker in the first place and didn't go up to Illinois to live," says Mama, shaking a spoon in my face. "If you had I would of been just as overjoyed to see you and your little adopted girl as I was to see Stella-Rondo, when you wound up[1] with your separation and came on back home."

"You would not," I says.

"Don't contradict me, I would," says Mama.

But I said she couldn't convince me though she talked till she was blue in the face. Then I said, "Besides, you know as well as I do that that child is not adopted."

"She most certainly is adopted," says Mama, stiff as a poker.

I says, "Why, Mama, Stella-Rondo had her just as sure as anything in this world, and just too stuck up to admit it."[2]

"Why, Sister," said Mama. "Here I thought we were going to have a pleasant Fourth of July, and you start right out not believing a word your own baby sister tells you!"

"Just like Cousin Annie Flo. Went to her grave denying the facts of life," I remind Mama.

"I told you if you ever mentioned Annie Flo's name I'd slap your face," says Mama, and slaps my face.

"All right, you wait and see," I says.

"I," says Mama, "*I* prefer to take my children's word for anything when it's humanly possible." You ought to see Mama, she weighs two hundred pounds and has real tiny feet.

Just then something perfectly horrible occurred to me.

"Mama," I says, "can that child talk?" I simply had to whisper! "Mama, I wonder if that child can be — you know — in any way? Do you realize," I says, "that she hasn't spoken one single, solitary word to a human being up to this minute? This is the way she looks," I says, and I looked like this.

Well, Mama and I just stood there and stared at each other. It was

1) wound up: end; settle; conclude.
2) just too stuck up to admit it: 너무 건방져서 그런 말을 하지 않을 뿐이다. stuck up=acting as if other people are not as good as you are; conceited; snobbish.

horrible!

"I remember well that Joe Whitaker frequently drank like a fish," says Mama. "I believed to my soul he drank *chemicals*.[1]" And without another word she marches to the foot of the stairs and calls Stella-Rondo.

"Stella-Rondo? O-o-o-o-o! Stella-Rondo!"

"What?" says Stella-Rondo from upstairs. Not even the grace to get up off the bed.

"Can that child of yours talk?" asks Mama.

Stella-Rondo says, "Can she what?"

"Talk! Talk!" says Mama. "Burdyburdyburdyburdy!"

So Stella-Rondo yells back, "Who says she can't talk?"

"Sister says so," says Mama.

"You didn't have to tell me, I know whose word of honor don't mean a thing[2] in this house," says Stella-Rondo.

And in a minute the loudest Yankee[3] voice I ever heard in my life yells out, "OE'm Pop-OE the Sailor-r-r-r Ma-a-an!" and then somebody jumps up and down in the upstairs hall. In another second the house would of fallen down.

"Not only talks, she can tap-dance!" calls Stella-Rondo. "Which is more than some people I won't name can do."[4]

"Why, the little precious darling thing!" Mama says, so surprised. "Just as smart as she can be!" Starts talking baby talk right there.[5] Then she turns on me. "Sister, you ought to be thoroughly ashamed! Run upstairs this instant and apologize to Stella-Rondo and Shirley-T."

"Apologize for what?" I says. "I merely wondered if the child was normal, that's all. Now that she's proved she is, why, I have nothing further to say."

But Mama just turned on her heel and flew out, furious. She ran right upstairs and hugged the baby. She believed it was adopted. Stella-Rondo hadn't done a thing but turn her against me[6] from upstairs

---

1) *chemicals*: alcohol을 말함.
2) whose word of honor don't mean a thing: '약속을 지키지 않는다'라는 뜻.
3) Yankee: native of New England or the Northern Stated; Northerner.
4) Which is more than … can do.: She can do it better than anybody.
5) Starts talking baby talk right there: Baby starts to talk right there.
6) hadn't done a thing but turn her against me: turn against. 거역(반항)하다.

while I stood there helpless over the hot stove. So that made Mama, Papa-Daddy and the baby all on Stella-Rondo's side.

Next, Uncle Rondo.

I must say that Uncle Rondo has been marvelous to me at various times in the past and I was completely unprepared to be made to jump out of my skin,[1] the way it turned out.[2] Once Stella-Rondo did something perfectly horrible to him — broke a chain letter[3] from Flanders Field — and he took the radio back he had given her and gave it to me. Stella-Rondo was furious! For six months we all had to call her Stella instead of Stella-Rondo, or she wouldn't answer. I always thought Uncle Rondo had all the brains of the entire family. Another time he sent me to Mammoth Cave,[4] with all expenses paid.

But this would be the day he was drinking that prescription, the Fourth of July.

So at supper Stella-Rondo speaks up and says she thinks Uncle Rondo ought to try to eat a little something. So finally Uncle Rondo said he would try a little cold biscuits and ketchup, but that was all. So *she* brought it to him.

"Do you think it wise to disport[5] with ketchup in Stella-Rondo's flesh-colored kimono?" I says. Trying to be considerate! If Stella-Rondo couldn't watch out[6] for her trousseau, somebody had to.

"Any objections?" asks Uncle Rondo, just about to pour out all the ketchup.

"Don't mind what she says, Uncle Rondo," says Stella-Rondo. "Sister has been devoting this solid afternoon to sneering out my bedroom window at the way you look."

"What's that?" says Unde Rondo. Uncle Rondo has got the most terrible temper in the world. Anything is liable to make him tear the house down if it comes at the wrong time.[7]

---

1) jump out of my skin: to be badly frightened; be very much surprised.
2) the way it turned out: the way as it became [resulted].
3) chain letter: a letter designed to pass from one to another of a series of recipients.
4) Mammoth Cave: Kentucky주에 있는 국립공원. 거대한 종유굴로 유명함.
5) disport: amuse(oneself); sport; play.
6) watch out: be careful; be on guard.
7) if it comes at the wrong time: 잘못하다가는.

So Stella-Rondo says, "Sister says, 'Uncle Rondo certainly does look like a fool in that pink kimono!' "

Do you remember who it was really said that?

Unde Rondo spills out all the ketchup and jumps out of his chair and tears off the kimono and throws it down on the dirty floor and puts his foot on it. It had to be sent all the way[1] to Jackson to the cleaners and re-pleated.

"So that's your opinion of your Uncle Rondo, is it?" he says. "I look like a fool, do I? Well, that's the last straw. A whole day in this house with nothing to do, and then to hear you come out with a remark like that behind my back!"

"I didn't say any such of a thing, Uncle Rondo," I says, "and I'm not saying who did, either. Why, I think you look all right. Just try to take care of yourself and not talk and eat at the same time," I says. "I think you better go lie down."

"Lie down my foot," says Uncle Rondo. I ought to of known by that he was fixing to do something perfectly horrible.

So he didn't do anything that night in the precarious state he was in[2]—just played Casino[3] with Mama and Stella-Rondo and Shirley-T. and gave Shirley-T. a nickel with a head on both sides. It tickled[4] her nearly to death, and she called him "Papa." But at 6:30 A.M. the next morning, he threw a whole five-cent package of some unsold one-inch firecrackers from the store as hard as he could into my bedroom and they every one went off.[5] Not one bad one in the string.[6] Anybody else,[7] there'd be one that wouldn't go off.

Well, I'm just terribly susceptible to noise of any kind, the doctor has always told me I was the most sensitive person he had ever seen in his whole life, and I was simply prostrated. I couldn't eat! People tell me they heard it as far as the cemetery, and old Aunt Jep Patterson,

1) all the way: from start to finish; during the whole distance or time.
2) in the precarious state he was in: 술에 취한 상태에서.
3) Casino: cassino; a card game.
4) tickle: excite pleasantly; amuse.
5) went off: fired; exploded.
6) Not one bad one in the string.: 그 줄엔 불발탄이 된 것이 하나도 없었다.
7) Anybody else: If anybody else threw it.

that had been holding her own so good,[1] thought it was Judgment Day and she was going to meet her whole family. It's usually so quiet here.

And I'll tell you it didn't take me any longer than a minute to make up my mind what to do. There I was with the whole entire house on Stella-Rondo's side and turned against me. If I have anything at all I have pride.

So I just decided I'd go straight down to the P.O. There's plenty of room there in the back, I says to myself.

Well! I made no bones[2] about letting the family catch on to[3] what I was up to.[4] I didn't try to conceal it.

The first thing they knew, I marched in where they were all playing Old Maid and pulled the electric oscillating fan out by the plug, and everything got real hot. Next I snatched the pillow I'd done the needlepoint on[5] right off the davenport from behind Papa-Daddy. He went "Ugh!" I beat Stella-Rondo up[6] the stairs and finally found my charm bracelet in her bureau drawer under a picture of Nelson Eddy.

"So that's the way the land lies," says Uncle Rondo. There he was, piecing[7] on the ham. "Well, Sister, I'll be glad to donate my army cot if you got any place to set it up, providing[8] you'll leave right this minute and let me get some peace." Uncle Rondo was in France.

"Thank you kindly for the cot and 'peace' is hardly the word I would select if I had to resort to firecrackers at 6:30 A.M. in a young girl's bedroom," I says back to him.[9] "And as to where I intend to go, you seem to forget my position as postmistress of China Grove, Mississippi," I says. "I've always got the P.O."

---

1) that had been holding her own so good: 지금까지 그처럼 쟁쟁하였다.
2) make no bones: to have no doubts; not to worry about right or wrong; not to be against.
3) catch on to: to understand; learn about.
4) what I was up to: what I was doing [about to do; plotting]
5) do the needlepoint on: embroider.
6) beat up: attack; thrash.
7) piecing: 햄을 맞붙이고 있었다.
8) providing: on the condition that.
9) says back to him: 그에게 쏘아붙이다.

Well, that made them all sit up and take notice.

I went out front and started digging up some four-o'clocks[1] to plant around the P.O.

"Ah-ah-ah!" says Mama, raising the window. "Those happen to be my four-o'clocks. Everything planted in that star is mine. I've never known you to make anything grow in your life."

"Very well," I says. "But I take the fern. Even you, Mama, can't stand there and deny that I'm the one watered that fern. And I happen to know where I can send in a box top and get a packet of one thousand mixed seeds, no two the same kind, free."

"Oh, where?" Mama wants to know.

But I says, "Too late. You tend[2] to your house, and I'll 'tend to mine. You hear things like that all the time if you know how to listen to the radio. Perfectly marvelous offers. Get anything you want free."

So I hope to tell you I marched in and got that radio, and they could of all bit a nail in two,[3] especially Stella-Rondo, that it used to belong to, and she well knew she couldn't get it back, I'd sue for it like a shot.[4] And I very politely took the sewing-machine motor I helped pay the most on to give Mama for Christmas back in 1929, and a good big calendar, with the first-aid remedies on it.[5] The thermometer and the Hawaiian ukulele[6] certainly were rightfully mine, and I stood on the step-ladder and got all my watermelon-rind[7] preserves[8] and every fruit and vegetable I'd put up, every jar. Then I began to pull the tacks out of the bluebird wall vases on the archway to the dining room.

"Who told you you could have those, Miss Priss?" says Mama, fanning as hard as she could.

---

1) four-o'clocks: the common garden species, with fragrant yellow, fed, or white flowers opening late in the afternoon.
2) 'tend: attend; pay attention to; give care and thought.
3) bit a nail in two: 손톱을 깨물며 이를 갈았다.
4) I'd sue for it like a shot: 당장에 고소했을 것이다. sue=take action in law.
5) with the first-aid remedies on it: 응급치료 방법이 쓰여 있는.
6) ukulele: a small guitar with four strings.
7) rind: the firm outer covering of fruits.
8) preserves: fruit cooked with suger and sealed from the air.

"I bought 'em and I'll keep track of[1] 'em," I says. "I'll tack 'em up one on each side the post-office window, and you can see 'em when you come to ask me for your mail, if you're so dead to see 'em."

"Not I! I'll never darken the door[2] to that post office again if I live to be a hundred," Mama says. "Ungrateful child! After all the money we spent on you at the Normal.[3]"

"Me either," says Stella-Rondo. "You can just let my mail lie there and *rot*, for all I care.[4] I'll never come and relieve[5] you of a single, solitary piece."

"I should worry," I says. "And who you think's going to sit down and write you all those big fat letters and postcards, by the way? Mr. Whitaker? Just because he was the only man ever dropped down in China Grove and you got him — unfairly — is he going to sit down and write you a lengthy correspondence after you come home giving no rhyme nor reason whatsoever for your separation and no explanation for the presence of that child? I may not have your brilliant mind, but I fail to see it."

So Mama says, "Sister, I've told you a thousand times that Stella-Rondo simply got homesick, and this child is far too big to be hers," and she says, "Now, why don't you all just sit down and play Casino?"

Then Shirley-T. sticks out her tongue at me in this perfectly horrible way. She has no more manners than the man in the moon. I told her she was going to cross her eyes[6] like that some day and they'd stick.

"It's too late to stop me now," I says. "You should have tried that yesterday. I'm going to the P.O. and the only way you can possibly

---

1) keep track of: keep within one's sight, knowledge or attention. 간직하다.
2) darken the door: to appear, as in a doorway; enter someone's home or establishment.
3) the Normal: the Normal School; school where people are trained to be teachers.
4) for all I care: for all=to the extent that; used like a negative with care and know. Ex. For all I care, you can throw it away.(=I don't care if you throw it away.).
5) relieve: set free.
6) to cross her eyes: to be cross-eyed.

see me is to visit me there."

So Papa-Daddy says, "You'll never catch me setting foot in that post office, even if I should take a notion into my head to write a letter some place." He says, "I won't have you reachin' out of that little old window with a pair of shears and cuttin' off any beard of mine. I'm too smart for you!"

"We all are," says Stella-Rondo.

But I said, "If you're so smart, where's Mr. Whitaker?"

So then Uncle Rondo says, "I'll thank you from now on to stop reading all the orders I get on postcards and telling everybody in China Grove what you think is the matter with them," but I says, "I draw my own conclusions and will continue in the future to draw them." I says, "If people want to write their inmost secrets on penny postcards, there's nothing in the wide world you can do about it, Uncle Rondo."

"And if you think we'll ever *write* another postcard you're sadly mistaken," says Mama.

"Cutting off your nose to spite your face then," I says. "But if you're all determined to have no more to do with the U.S. mail, think of this: What will Stella-Rondo do now, if she wants to tell Mr. Whitaker to come after her?"

"Wah!" says Stella-Rondo. I knew she'd cry. She had a conniption fit[1] right there in the kitchen.

"It will be interesting to see how long she holds out,[2]" I says. "And now — I am leaving."

"Good-bye," says Uncle Rondo.

"Oh, I declare," says Mama, "to think that a family of mine should quarrel on the Fourth of July, or the day after, over Stella-Rondo leaving old Mr. Whitaker and having the sweetest little adopted child! It looks like we'd all be glad!"

"Wah!" says Stella-Rondo, and has a fresh conniption fit.

"*He* left *her* — you mark my words," I says. "That's Mr. Whitaker. I know Mr. Whitaker. After all, I knew him first. I said from the beginning he'd up and leave her. I foretold every single thing that's

---

1) conniption fit: a fit of anger, hysteria, etc.; tantrum.

2) hold out: continue; last; extend; keep resisting.

happened."

"Where did he go?" asks Mama.

"Probably to the North Pole, if he knows what's good for him," I says.

But Stella-Rondo just bawled and wouldn't say another word. She flew to her room and slammed the door.

"Now look what you've gone and done, Sister," says Mama. "You go apologize."

"I haven't got time, I'm leaving," I says.

"Well, what are you waiting around for?" asks Uncle Rondo.

So I just picked up the kitchen clock and marched off, without saying "Kiss my foot" or anything, and never did tell Stella-Rondo good-bye.

There was a girl going along on a little wagon right in front.

"Girl," I says, "come help me haul these things down the hill, I'm going to live in the post office."

Took her nine trips in her express wagon. Uncle Rondo came out on the porch and threw her a nickel.

And that's the last I've laid eyes on any of my family or my family laid eyes on me for five solid days and nights. Stella-Rondo may be telling the most horrible tales in the world about Mr. Whitaker, but I haven't heard them. As I tell everybody, I draw my own conclusions.

But oh, I like it here. It's ideal, as I've been saying. You see, I've got everything cater-cornered,[1] the way I like it. Hear the radio? All the war news. Radio, sewing machine, book ends, ironing board and that great big piano lamp — peace, that's what I like. Butter-bean vines planted all along the front where the strings are.

Of course, there's not much mail. My family are naturally the main people in China Grove, and if they prefer to vanish from the face of the earth, for all the mail they get or the mail they write, why, I'm not going to open my mouth. Some of the folks here in town are taking up for[2] me and some turned against[3] me. I know which is which. There are always people who will quit buying stamps just

1) cater-cornered: diagonally.
2) taking up for: to come to the defense of; to support or fight for.
3) turned against: oppose.

to get on the right side of Papa-Daddy.

But here I am, and here I'll stay. I want the world to know I'm happy.

And if Stella-Rondo should come to me this minute, on bended knees,[1] and *attempt* to explain the incidents of her life with Mr. Whitaker, I'd simply put my fingers in both my ears and refuse to listen.

1) on bended knees: 무릎을 꿇고.

The Use of Force

by William Carlos Williams

The son of immigrants — his father was English, his mother Puerto Rican — Williams (1883-1963) was born in Rutherford, New Jersey. He attended preparatory schools in New York and Switzerland, graduated from the University of Pennsyhlvania Medical School, and studied pediatrics in Leipzig, Germany.

For 40 years, Williams practiced medicine in Rutherford, specializing in the care of infants and children. At the same time, he was one of the most prolific twentieth-century American authors, publishing his first volume of poems at the age of 23. In all he has written 600 poems, 52 short stories, four novels, an opera libretto, history, essays, biography and an autobiography, *Autobiography of William Carlos Williams* (1951).

In his poetry, as in "The Use of Force," Williams writes of familiar objects and events — a daisy, a wheelbarrow, a funeral — them as the basis for philosophical speculation. His work is included in all the standard anthologies of modern American poetry.

THEY WERE new patients to me, all I had was the name, Olson.[1] Please come down as soon as you can, my daughter is very sick.

When I arrived I was met by the mother, a big startled looking woman, very clean and apologetic who merely said, Is this the doctor? and let me in. In the back, she added. You must excuse us, doctor, we have her in the kitchen where it is warm. It is very damp here sometimes.

The child was fully dressed and sitting on her father's lap near the kitchen table. He tried to get up, but I motioned for him not to bother, took off my overcoat and started to look things over. I could see that they were all very nervous, eyeing me up and down[2] distrustfully. As often, in such cases, they weren't telling me more than they had to, it was up to me[3] to tell them; that's why they were spending three dollars on me.

---

1) Olson: a common family name of Scandinavian origin.

2) eyeing me up and down; looking st me from head to toe.

3) it was up to me: it was my responsibility.

The child was fairly eating me up[1] with her cold, steady eyes, and no expression to her face whatever. She did not move and seemed, inwardly, quiet; an unusually attractive little thing, and as strong as a heifer[2] in appearance. But her face was flushed,[3] she was breathing rapidly, and I realized that she had a high fever. She had magnificent blonde hair, in profusion.[4] One of those picture children often reproduced in advertising leaflets and the photogravure sections[5] of the Sunday papers.

She's had a fever for three days, began the father and we don't know what it comes from. My wife has given her things, you know, like people do, but it don't do no good.[6] And there's been a lot of sickness around. So we tho't[7] you'd better look her over[8] and tell us what is the matter.

As doctors often do I took a trial shot[9] at it as a point of departure. Has she had a sore throat?

Both parents answered me together, No . . . No, she says her throat don't hurt her.

Does your throat hurt you? added the mother to the child. But the little girl's expression didn't change nor did she move her eyes from my face.

Have you looked?

I tried to, said the mother, but I couldn't see.

As it happens we had been having a number of cases of diphtheria[10]

---

1) fairly eating me up: was looking at me very intently; here fairly means "almost" (rural colloquialism).

2) heifer: a young cow.

3) flushed: red; here, because of a fever.

4) in profusion.: in abundance, abundantly.

5) photogravure sections: a special section of the weeked newspaper filled with colored pictures reproduced by the photogravure process in which a picture is reproduced on a metal plate from a photographic negative; the final printing is done from the plate.

6) it don't do no good: it hasn't done any good.

7) tho't: thought.

8) look her over: give her a medical examination.

9) took a trial shot: made a first attempt; here, an attempt to diagnose the illness.

10) diphtheria: a serious infections disease of the throat.

in the school to which this child went during that month and we were all, quite apparently, thinking of that, though no one had as yet spoken of the thing.

Well, I said, suppose we take a look at the throat first. I smiled in my best professional manner and asking for the child's first name I said, come on, Mathilda, open your mouth and let's take a look at your throat.

Nothing doing.

Aw, come on, I coaxed,[1)] just open your mouth wide and let me take a look. Look, I said opening both hands wide, I haven't anything in my hands. Just open up and let me see.

Such a nice man,[2)] put in the mother. Look how kind he is to you. Come on, do what he tells you to. He won't hurt you.

At that I ground my teeth in disgust. If only they wouldn't use the word "hurt" I might be able to get somewhere. But I did not allow myself to be hurried or disturbed but speaking quietly and slowly I approached the child again.

As I moved my chair a little nearer suddenly with one catlike movement both her hands clawed[3)] instinctively for my eyes and she almost reached them too. In fact she knocked my glasses flying and they fell, though unbroken, several feet away from me on the kitchen floor.

Both the mother and father almost turned themselves inside out[4)] in embarrassment and apology. You bad girl, said the mother, taking her and shaking her by one arm. Look what you've done. The nice man . . .

For heaven's sake, I broke in.[5)] Don't call me a nice man to her. I'm here to look at her throat on the chance that she might have diphtheria and possibly die of it. But that's nothing to her. Look here,

---

1) coaxed: asked gently, encouragingly.
2) Such a nice man: a formula used by mothers to reassure their children about kind strangers.
3) clawed: used her fingers to attack, as an animal uses its claws.
4) almost turned themselves inside out: This use of exaggeration for emphasis is typical of American speech.
5) broke in: interrupted.

I said to the child, we're going to look at your throat. You're old enough to understand what I'm saying. Will you open it now by yourself or shall we have to open it for you?

Not a move. Even her expression hadn't changed. Her breaths however were coming faster and faster. Then the battle began. I had to do it. I had to have a throat culture[1] for her own protection. But first I told the parents that it was entirely up to them. I explained the danger but said that I would not insist on a throat examination so long as they would take the responsibility.

If you don't do what the doctor says you'll have to go to the hospital, the mother admonished[2] her severely.

Oh yeah?[3] I had to smile to myself. After all, I had already fallen in love with the savage brat,[4] the parents were contemptible to me. In the ensuing[5] struggle they grew more and more abject,[6] crushed, exhausted while she surely rose to magnificent heights of insane fury of effort bred[7] of her terror of me.

The father tried his best, and he was a big man but the fact that she was his daughter, his shame at her behavior and his dread[8] of hurting her made him release her just at the critical times when I had almost achieved success, till I wanted to kill him. But his dread also that she might have diphtheria made him tell me to go on, go on though he himself was almost fainting, while the mother moved back and forth behind us raising and lowering her hands in an agony of apprehension.

Put her in front of you on your lap, I ordered, and hold both her wrists.

But as soon as he did the child let out[9] a scream. Don't, you're

---

1) culture: a sample of(throat) tissue to be tested for infection in a laboratory.
2) admonished: warned.
3) Oh yeah?: Oh yes?; an expression of skepticism.
4) brat: a contemptuous word for child.
5) ensuing: following.
6) abject: deserving contempt because behaving in a cowardly or self-abasing manner.
7) bred: breed의 과거분사. 여기서는 be the cause of의 뜻.
8) dread: great fear.
9) let out: uttered.

hurting me. Let go of my hands.[1] Let them go[2] I tell you. Then she shrieked[3] terrifyingly, hysterically. Stop it! Stop it! You're killing me!

Do you think she can stand it, doctor! said the mother.

You get out, said the husband to his wife. Do you want her to die of diphtheria?

Come on now,[4] hold her, I said.

Then I grasped the child's head with my left hand and tried to get the wooden tongue depressor[5] between her teeth. She fought, with clenched[6] teeth, desperately! But now I also had grown furious — at a child. I tried to hold myself down[7] but I couldn't. I know how to expose a throat for inspection. And I did my best. When finally I got the wooden spatula[8] behind the last teeth and just the point of it into the mouth cavity, she opened up for an instant but before I could see anything she came down again and gripping the wooden blade between her molars[9] she reduced it to splinters[10] before I could get it out again.

Aren't you ashamed, the mother yelled at her. Aren't you ashamed to act like that in front of the doctor?

Get me a smooth-handled spoon of some sort, I told the mother. We're going through with this. The child's mouth was already bleeding. Her tongue was cut and she was screaming in wild hysterical shrieks. Perhaps I should have desisted[11] and come back in an hour or more.

---

1) Let go of my hands: Stop holding my hands.; Don't hold my hands.
2) Let them go: Pay no attention to them (my hands). Let go=neglect.
3) shrieked: screamed.
4) Come on (now): (Informal) Please do it! — Used in begging=someone to do something.
5) tongue depressor: a thin, flat piece of wood used by a doctor to hold down a patient's tongue in order to examine his throat.
6) clenched: held together tightly.
7) hold myself down: control myself.
8) spatula: a tool with a wide, flat, flexible blade; here, it refers to the tongue depressor.
9) molars: the back teeth.
10) splinter: a small, sharp fragment (of wood, glass or metal).
11) desisted: stopped.

No doubt it would have been better. But I have seen at least two children lying dead in bed of neglect in such cases, and feeling that I must get a diagnosis now or never I went at it again.[1] But the worst of it was that I too had got beyond reason. I could have torn the child apart in my own fury and enjoyed it. It was a pleasure to attack hcr. My face was burning with it.

The damned little brat must be protected against her own idiocy, one says to one's self at such times. Others must be protected against her. It is a social necessity. And all these things are true. But a blind fury, a feeling of adult shame, bred of a longing for muscular release[2] are the operatives.[3] One goes on to the end.

In a final unreasoning assault I overpowered the child's neck and jaws. I forced the heavy silver spoon back of her teeth and down her throat till she gagged.[4] And there it was — both tonsils[5] covered with membrane.[6] She had fought valiantly to keep me from knowing her secret. She had been hiding that sore throat for three days at least and lying to her parents in order to escape just such an outcome as this.

Now truly she was furious. She had been on the defensive before but now she attacked. Tried to get off her father's lap and fly at[7] me while tears of defeat blinded her eyes.

1) never I went at it again: I never started to fight with it again; I never attacked it again.
2) bred of a longing for muscular release: 근육의 해방을 갈망한 데서 온.
3) operatives: the immediate, compelling motives.
4) gagged: choked.
5) tonsils: the two small oval masses of lymphoid tissue in the back of the throat.
6) membrane: soft, thin tissue; here, a sign of disease.
7) fly at: attack.

양병택

문학박사
한국영어영문학회 회장 역임
경희대학교 영문학과 교수 역임

The 20th Century
English American Short Stories

WITH ESSAYS IN CRITICISM

20세기 영미단편-주석과 비평

1판 1쇄 찍음 • 1986년 2월 10일
1판 10쇄 펴냄 • 2004년 2월 20일
2판 3쇄 펴냄 • 2017년 2월 20일

편 주 자 · 양 병 택
발 행 인 · 정 현 걸
발 행 · 신 아 사
인 쇄 · 예지인쇄
출판등록 · 1956년 1월 5일 (제9-52호)
주 소 · 서울특별시 은평구 통일로 59길 4(2F)
전 화 · 02)382-6411 • 팩스 02)382-6401
홈페이지 · www.shinasa.co.kr
E-MAIL · shinasa@daum.net

ISBN 978-89-8396-729-9(93840)

정가 *14,000* **원**